AFFEERCE
Volume I – The Vision
4.1.5

It is a position not to be controverted that the earth, in its natural, uncultivated state was, and ever would have continued to be, the common property of the human race. In that state every man would have been born to property. He would have been a joint life proprietor with rest in the property of the soil, and in all its natural productions, vegetable and animal...Every proprietor, therefore, of cultivated lands, owes to the community a ground-rent (for I know of no better term to express the idea) for the land which he holds; and it is from this ground-rent that the fund proposed in this plan is to issue. – Thomas Paine

Jeff Graubart

DEDICATION

To the World

ACKNOWLEDGMENTS

I thank the following individuals and organizations for helping in some way, big or small, in helping to shape the vision and the plan. Inclusion in this list does not imply endorsement of AFFEERCE or any of the ideas presented. All errors are my responsibility, alone.

Nate Blair, Kevin Carson, Mike Curtis, Ed Dodson, Fred Foldvary, Lawrence Hartman, Henry George School of Chicago, Todd Kemnitz, Lorraine Lee, Peter Loudon, Helen Marsh, Edward Miller, Will Schnack, Jami Steinberg

Table of Contents

Introduction 1

    The Law of Rent...2

Chapter 1 – What is AFFEERCE? 9

    A Summary 9

    The Acronym 12

    The Assumptions...14

    A Brief Survey of the Tax Burden..16

    The Fundamental Relations..18

    The VIP 19

Chapter 2 – Collection of the Ground Rents..24

    Introduction 24

    Land Speculation 24

    Location Value..26

        Objective Value 26

        Subjective Value 26

        Georgist Theory of Value...26

        Profits and Location Value..27

    Problems with Land Assessment...27

        Objective Scoring 27

        Corruption 28

        Other Biases 28

        Comparable Sales 29

        Location Monopoly 29

        Leverage and the High Location Value Land Tax 30

        Moral Hazard and Assessor Criteria 32

        The Land Value Tax is an Oxymoron...32

    Rental of the Commons...33

        How Can We Solve the Problems of Land Assessment...33

        Self-assessment...33

        The Synthesis of Objectivism and Subjectivism 34

The Basis for Common Ownership of the Land 34

U.S. Land Use 35

Trebling 36

  Beware the Treblers? 36

  Online Trebling System 36

  How does Trebling Work 37

  Zero Sum 39

  What if the Ground Rent isn't Paid? 39

  Trebling Law 39

  Monopoly of Location Value 40

  How Trebling Determines a Fair Ground Rent 40

  Treble Equilibrium 41

  How Ground Rent Is Paid 43

  Trebling and Bank Loans (Trebler Mortgages) 43

Reasonable Use of the Land 45

Objective Depreciated Value (ODV) 45

Covenants 45

  Jurisdictional Covenants 46

  Purchased Covenants 46

  Covenant Patterns 47

Ground Rent and Industry 48

  Hostile Takeover 48

  Oil and Minerals 50

  Agriculture-Cropland and Repairing Damage from the Farm Subsidies...................................52

  Rangeland and Timberland 53

  Trebling the Spectrum 53

  Office Buildings and Prime Retail 54

  How do Ground Rents Compare with Today's Taxes 56

  Standard Office and Retail 57

  How Do Vacancies Affect Ground Rent? 58

  Ball-park Total Corporate Distribution Package Contribution 59

The Initial Ground Rents...59

Apartments and Residences 61

    Downtown Apartment Tower 61

    Standard 4-Story Apartment 61

    The Effects of Depreciation 62

    Real Wages and their Effect on the Apartment Market 63

    Residences 65

Severability of Land 66

Roads 67

A Word to the Wise Land Speculator 68

Trebler Wars 69

    Anatomy of a Trebler War 70

The Online Land System 71

    Early History 71

    General Functionality 71

Chapter 3 – Distribution of the Ground Rents 73

Natural Laws 73

Intellectual Property: Monopoly vs. Distribution 73

    Today..73

    Profit from Location Value and Innovation 74

    Copyrights (Copyshares) and Patents 75

    Tranches and Distribution 77

The Problem with Local Distribution 78

Each of Us and All of Us 80

The Solution – A Synthesis of Objectivism and Subjectivism 82

Personal Distribution Bias 83

Local Land Capture 84

A Controlled Distribution 86

The Withering Away of the Allocations 88

Chapter 4 – Reproductive Freedom and Control 89

Introduction 89

The Means of Reproduction 90

    Reproduction in Pre-Modern Times 90

    Reproduction in Modern Times...91

The Postmodern Era 92

Women's Rights...95

The Baby Tax as the Best Investment Ever 96

How Feminists Define Reproductive Rights 97

On the Natural Right to Bear Children 98

Rage and the Apocryphal Racist Narrative 99

The Tragedy of the Commons 101

   Freedom to Breed Is Intolerable 102

   Conscience Is Self-Eliminating 103

   Mutual Coercion Mutually Agreed Upon 103

   Recognition of Necessity 104

   A Georgist Perspective 104

   A Gentle Response..105

The Fundamental Relations of Reproductive Control...105

Procreative Law Should not be Complex 106

Sterilization and Wrongful Life 107

Contraceptives..108

Abortion 109

Transgenic Babies 110

Surrogacy..110

In Vitro Gestation 111

Social Imbalance 111

Summary 111

Chapter 5 – The Consumption and Other Taxes...113

Introduction...113

Baby Tax 114

Excise Taxes 114

Pigovian Taxes 115

2% Discretionary Tax 115

Stopping Choke 116

Totals..117

Social Constructivism and Taxes 117

Elements of Social Constructivism...117

Avoiding Taxes 118

Chapter 6 - The Balance of the RCs and the Treasury 121

Philosophy..121

The Distribution Package...122

Basic Flow...122

Interest on the Distribution Package and Fertility...123

The Rent Multiplier 123

Trebling is Inevitable 123

Meltdown and Choke...124

The Withering Away of the Allocations 126

The 10% Assumption..127

Future-Baby Accounts 127

Cropland Imbalance 128

Immigration and the Treasury 128

Citizenship Tax...129

Chapter 7 – Summary of Part I – Funding Freedom through the Collection and Distribution of Ground Rents...131

Collection Theory 131

Distribution Theory 132

Balance Theory 133

Final Thoughts 133

Chapter 8 – The Natural Rights of Mankind 136

Philosophy..136

More on the Right to Property in an AFFEERCE Society 136

The Right to Life and Insurrection 136

Childbirth and Natural Rights 137

The Gun Control Debate 137

The Smoking Debate 138

When Natural Rights are in Conflict 139

Chapter 9 – Government, Law and Justice 141

Introduction 141

Cellular Federation 142

Constitutional Rights 143

Elements of a Bill 144

    Prohibition...144

    Extent 145

    Punishment 145

The AFFEERCE Principle of Judicial Review 145

The Three Classes of Law 145

    Class I bills: 146

    Class II bills: 146

    Class III Bills: 147

Direct Democracy 149

The Right to Leave 149

The Cellular Democracy 152

    Definitions 152

    National Cell Populations 154

    The Government Distribution 155

    Enterprise Districts and Distribution...158

    Distribution Disbursement 159

The Cellular Aristocracy 160

    Introduction..160

    Obtaining Aristocracy 161

    Aristocracy Hosts Government 162

    Chancelleries 163

Community Dynamics..164

Civil Rights 165

Penitentiaries 166

Isolation Centers 168

How AFFEERCE Eliminates Crime..169

Penalties 170

Judiciary and Public Defense 172

    The Judiciary and Rogue States 173

Regulation 174

    Bureau of Standards 175

Functions and Features of the VSG 177

VSGs at Lower Levels of Dominion 178

Functions and Features of the VOS 178

Deregulation 179

The Right to a Safe Workplace 179

Labor Unions 180

Denial of Service 181

Contracts with the Public – A Legal VOS 181

Accuracy of Information 182

Chapter 10 – Economic Principles 183

Introduction 183

The Wealth of the Nation 184

Subjective, Objective, and AFFEERCE Theories of Value 184

How Does AFFEERCE Contribute to National Wealth? 186

Investment 186

Innovation 186

Skills 187

Enterprise 187

Competition 187

The Family Division of Labor 187

The Family Economy of Scale 188

Profit and Location Value 189

Competition, Collusion, and Monopoly 190

Citizen Investors 191

Scrip 193

Trickle-down and Bubble-up Economics 194

Trickle-Down 194

Bubble-Up 194

Strangling the Economy 195

The Detroit Auto Bailout - Too Big to Fail 195

Minimum Wage 196

Trust 198

City Passes 198

Corporations and Why They Pay No Tax 198

Capital Expenditures and Purchase Paths 199

Gold and Barter 199

Foreign Exchange and Implications 200

Foreign Investment and the Spread of AFFEERCE 201

Failure to Pay a Debt 202

Inheritance 202

The Redistribution of Wealth at Death 202

Banks 203

The Concentration of Capital 205

The Amazing List 207

Chapter 11 – Universal Distribution 210

Class Warfare 211

Benefits of Universal Distribution 211

Tranches 212

Non-transferability of Distributions 212

Rebates 213

Rogue States and Distributions 213

The Food Distribution - $220 213

The Housing Distribution - $370 216

Leasing 219

The Housing Distribution and Home Ownership 220

The Cash Distribution - $35 222

The Education Distribution - $50 223

Chancelleries 224

Teachers 224

Schools 225

The University 226

Which Level of the Dominion Pays for Education? 226

Online Education 226

Trade Schools 227

Tutors and Home Instruction 227

Textbooks, Papers, and other Assigned reading...228

Grades...228

The 2% + 2% Achievement Annuity...228

The 2% School Achievement Annuity...230

Achievement Annuity Distribution in the Early Days of AFFEERCE...230

The Testing/Certification Distribution - $2...230

Non-Universal/Disability Distribution - $97...231

The Medical Distribution - $120...232

The AFFEERCE Medical Plan...234

Malpractice Liability...236

Intellectual Property...236

Medical School...236

Diagnosis and Prognosis...237

Sickness Away from Home...237

Effects of Self-Insurance and the Medical Rebate...238

Test Results and the VIP...238

Radical Medical Deregulation...238

Uncovered Medical Procedures...240

Mental Health...240

Reproduction and Gestation...240

Hypochondria...241

Nursing Home, Long Term, and Hospice Care...242

The Social Worker Distribution - $10...243

Fire Protection Distribution - $5...244

Law Enforcement and Prosecution Distribution - $30...246

Judiciary and Public Defense Distribution - $9...246

Transportation and Sanitation - $35...247

Intellectual Property - $92...250

National Defense - $75...250

Capital Expenses, Depreciation, and Ground Rent - $20...252

National Infrastructure, VIP and Online Land System - $10...252

Monthly Distribution Total...253

Chapter 12 –Families, Collectives, and Mutual Organizations...255

Physical Family Requirements 255

Family Law 256

Age of Majority 257

Child Abuse 257

Roles 259

Final Thoughts 260

Chapter 13 – Enlightenment 261

Free Will and Moral Responsibility 261

AFFEERCE and Enlightenment 261

The Future of AFFEERCE Enlightenment 261

In Conclusion 262

Appendix I - The Fundamental Relations 264

Appendix II – Anatomy of AFFEERCE Mercantilism 271

Footnotes 272

Index 275

Introduction

Most solutions for a better world require widespread dissemination of an ideology, the victory of a political party at the polls, or the seizure of power by some class or social group. My solution calls for none of this.

My vision begins as a seed planted in the old. It grows and is nurtured by the positive things this world has to offer, at the same time gaining strength from resolving contradictions that rip us apart. The embryo becomes stronger as the old world dies, until finally, a new world is born and the old one passes into history.

The seed is a business plan; a profitable business whose shareholders benefit by bringing this new world into being. By tapping in to natural laws of political economy, we create an embryo that will grow to overwhelm and peacefully overtake the old order, achieving personal success in the process. That is not the subject of this volume, but of *AFFEERCE Volume II – The Plan.* The plan describes a business that becomes an incorporated municipality, ultimately buying up most of the land in a single U.S. state, and turning it over to the commons for a hefty profit.

The outcome of that plan is the subject of this book, *AFFEERCE Volume I – The Vision.* The vision comes first, because no plan is possible without a goal. The plan takes almost 60 years to complete and many of us will not live to see the outcome. During that time, the vision will undergo many changes, so it might seem foolish to put things so definitively in Volume I. But it is actually foolish not to. The vision is an integrated solution. An integrated solution is like a fine-tuned machine. All the parts are designed to work together. Granted, we might find a better solution for one of the parts, but the important question is whether the machine will still work. If so, the part can be replaced. If not, it is back to the drawing board. After all, if our integrated solution will break with a better part, it is worthwhile to ask why. Perhaps replacing 2 or 3 parts as a group will allow our solution to work with the best parts. That is why detail is so necessary. We must always have a working machine. Mathematicians call this "logical consistency." Although we might spend the next 60 years replacing parts, as long as we maintain logical consistency, the solution can only improve.

I don't want to belabor the point, but many of today's popular ideologies are fixated on one part to the exclusion of all the others. "From each according to their ability, to each according to their need" might sound good, but logic and years of experience have shown it destroys productivity. The slogan "If everybody pursued their own rational self-interest, we would have an ideal society" is equally worthless both in terms of failing to understand human nature and in failing to see what a horrid world would result if everybody did indeed pursue their own financial self-interest.

I invite you to try and improve on the Volume I model for a future society, as well as the Volume II business plan to bring it about. Try and keep your criticism germane to the volume at hand. A number of people have commented after reading Volume I, "They'll never let that happen." But how it happens is the subject of Volume II. In Volume I, you must ask, "Do all the parts work well together?," "Can I improve one or more of those parts, so they still work well together?" and "Is this a society that **I** would really enjoy living in?" In reference to the last question, I'm not interested in whether you think somebody else would dislike this future vision, just you. Let them speak for themselves.

As for Volume II, I often get the criticism that "This is not a society I would care to promote." But a world we can all support is the subject of Volume I. Volume II is a business plan to bring about a society that you probably will wish to promote. Yes, the plan involves land speculation, subsistence labor and other less onerous things proven effective by the Law of Rent, but nothing illegal or subversive. The new world is as an embryo in the old, and it must use the tools provided by the old world to nurture itself. The caterpillar does not resemble the butterfly. This is not hypocrisy, but the path to lasting change.

The Law of Rent

Much of what you read in both volumes has its origins in the law of rent. Most classical economists from Adam Smith and David Ricardo to Henry George saw this law as the bedrock of political economy. As formulated by David Ricardo, the law of rent states:

> The rent of a land site is equal to the economic advantage obtained by using the site in its most productive use, relative to the advantage obtained by using marginal (i.e., the best rent-free) land for the same purpose, given the same inputs of labor and capital.[FTN.6]

If you are not an economist, this might be confusing. In my experience, however, the best way to understand the enormous implications of the law of rent is not with Ricardo's definition, but with a simple, common-sense example. Let us go to San Francisco.

In San Francisco the minimum wage has been raised to $15. This must seem like the Promised Land for those making $7.25 an hour working at a fast food job in small town America. But, before those small town burger flippers pack up the truck and head west, they should consider this. The average rent for a studio apartment in San Francisco is $2,000/month, although a studio can be had in the rough Tenderloin district for $1,500. If they're willing to live 45 minutes to an hour away by rapid transit, a studio for $750 a month might be found – with a little luck. That's still twice the cost of the $375 per month garden apartment they would have left behind, just two blocks from work in a very safe neighborhood.

The law of rent claims that rent is the great equalizer. All other things being equal save rent and wages, the difference, wages minus rent, must also be equal. If wages minus rent are called real wages, then real wages for the same job are fairly standard everywhere in the country. More generally, given two cities A and B, all other things being equal, $\text{Wages}_A - \text{Rent}_A = \text{Wages}_B - \text{Rent}_B$.

For the convenience of living two blocks away from the fast food restaurant in a safe neighborhood in the heart of San Francisco, one must pay $2,000/month. That is $1,625 more than rent on the same size studio in small town America. Compare nominal wages. At 160 work-hours per month, $1,160 is earned in the small town, while $2,400 is earned in San Francisco. However, looking at real wages, wages minus rent, flipping burgers in a small town pays $785/month, while the same job in San Francisco pays a mere $400/month. Why the difference? San Francisco has a diversity of retail and culture, great entertainment, nightlife, proximity to airports and seaports. Although a homeless person might beg to differ, those are wages too. In this case, wages equal to $385/month.

Think of it this way. Suppose you could move to San Francisco and find nearby inexpensive rent that boosted your real wages above the rest of the country. You would likely make the move. And so too, would many others. With all those people pouring into town, inexpensive rents would quickly disappear. As sure as the sun rises in the morning, rents would rise until people stopped coming. No matter what you call it; equilibrium, the law of supply and demand, or Mr. Market, the effect is the same; real wages are always equal to those same wages at the margin of production (a mythical place where land is free).

Henry George, in his seminal work from 1879, *Progress and Poverty*, took the law of rent to its logical conclusion. It isn't just wages that are equalized by rent. In the city we can take advantage of economies of scale and divisions of labor that lead to specialization, a diversity of suppliers, and great efficiency in production. The entrepreneur moves from the countryside to the city to take advantage of these efficiencies. But the more entrepreneurs that move to the city, the higher the rents go, and lo and behold, all those efficiencies are lost to rent.

There are also wages in kind, like the $385/month San Francisco amenities in the example above. Every bridge, theater, park, opera house, public transit system, bike path, sidewalk café, museum, sport's team, or cultural center, draws people and thereby increases rent.

Like San Francisco, the increase in rents from all these factors exceeds the increase in wages. This pushes the poor out of their homes in a process of gentrification. Since before the industrial revolution, humanity has dreamed of nicer homes, nicer cities, cleaner streets, more conveniences, and all the benefits of technology. How sadly ironic that many poor people are demanding that their old decrepit homes and apartments be left standing, as the only alternative to living under viaducts.

At the beginning of this marvelous era it was natural to expect, and it was expected, that labor-saving inventions would lighten the toil and improve the condition of the laborer; that the enormous increase in the power of producing wealth would make real poverty a thing of the past – Henry George.

George wrote those words over 100 years ago. Today, envisioning a technological future, we are predisposed to the same assumptions. Certainly in an era of robots that do our household chores, drive our cars, transport goods without human intervention, and work the assembly lines day and night, there can be no more poverty.

But these labor-saving devices are made from our natural resources. They consume our natural resources to operate. They require a small part of our limited space on Earth to operate. The closer these robots work together, the more efficiently they produce, so we give them our most valuable land in the center of cities. The more they produce for us, the more space we give them, the more natural resources we feed them. Our appetite for what they give us is insatiable.

Like theaters, good paying jobs, and sidewalk cafes, automation drives up the value of land.

As productive power increases, rent tends to increase even more – constantly forcing down wages. – Henry George

Unlike opera houses and museums, automation replaces many low-skill jobs with a few high-paying ones. Not only are rents so much higher, but even less people can afford them. And do not be deceived that the answer lies in education. If everyone were to obtain the skills needed to program and manage automation, then these jobs, too, would be reduced to subsistence wages.

Industry, skill, frugality, and intelligence can help the individual only so far as they are superior to the general level. Just as in a race, speed benefits a runner only if it exceeds that of the competitors. If one person works harder, or with superior skill or intelligence than ordinary people, that person will get ahead. But if the average is brought up to this higher point, the extra effort will bring only average wages. To get ahead, one must work harder still. – Henry George

By now you might have gathered that AFFEERCE is a form of Georgism. It is heavily influenced by the writings of Henry George on political economy; but particularly on the question of land.

We might ask ourselves, what is it that gives land value? Is it the work done on the land, the improvements to the land that gives it value? Surprisingly, the answer is no. If one were to build a skyscraper in the badlands of Wyoming, it would be an albatross. Not even worth the cost to heat it. It might have cost $80 million to build, and yet it would be worse than worthless. As for the land around it, that might gain in value as a place for tourists to come and gawk and buy refreshments as they stare at the monstrosity.

The value of land is a function of community. It is the community that builds the roads needed to go from place to place. It is the community that brings electric and water and cable to one's home. It is the community that lays the sidewalks for the sidewalk cafes, and protects life and property with police, fire, and paramedics. All of these bring industry that provide jobs and make the land more valuable still. And through this concert of community, industry, and residents, great cities are built.

We have seen that high wages and conveniences raise rent. Automation is more insidious, at least to the replaced worker. It not only raises rent, but kills jobs as well. Yet, there is something more devastating than automation. It not only raises rent and kills jobs but, unlike automation which creates goods useful to society, has no redeeming social value whatsoever.

It is land speculation. The land speculator buys land in a growing community, and withholds it from use to force the community to grow around the land, making the land that much more valuable. Land speculation is like a vampire sucking the lifeblood of the community, contributing nothing to the community but higher rents, less jobs, and less available goods.

The remedy for all this is so simple, one cannot blame the early followers of Henry George from assuming that once the truth was known, it could not help but be adopted.

What man has produced belongs to the individual producer; what God has created belongs equally to all men ... therefore abolish all taxation save on the value of land – Henry George

Each of us is entitled to the fruits of our own labor. That which God or Nature provides, belongs to each of us and all of us. The land and all of the Earth's natural wealth is our common property. What are the fruits of our labor, if not the product of our labors on this natural wealth? Both trivial and profound: we labor on material things. Denied access to these ingredients of our productivity, is to be denied the fruits of our own labor. Such labors demand exclusive use of a parcel of land. But natural law demands that rents paid for those exclusive rights "go to the community." Yet, what is community? That important question will be answered later.

We have seen that good wages, conveniences and automation drive up rents. But distribute those rents to each of us equally and for the first time in recorded history, all of us become the beneficiaries of rising wages, all of us become the beneficiary of gentrification, and opera houses, sidewalk cafes, and beautiful streets. More importantly for the future, as the world becomes more automated, all of us become the beneficiary of automation.

But I get ahead of myself. For it was not the distribution of the ground rents that initially attracted George and his followers, but their collection. When a fair rent is charged for a piece of land, that land must be used as productively as possible. Ideally, if the rent is just right, every parcel of land will be occupied by its most efficient user. Combined, the collection and distribution of ground rents are the building blocks of utopia.

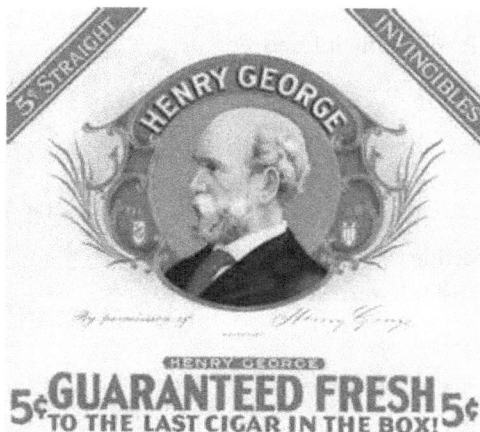

You might wonder why you are reading this promising idea for the first time, now. Why isn't everyone talking about Henry George and his solution if the answer is so simple?

Once upon a time, you would have. His book *Progress and Poverty* was the best-selling economics book of all time; more than Marx's *Das Kapital* and even more than Ayn Rand's *Atlas Shrugged*. At the time, *Progress and Poverty* outsold every book but the Bible. George took on Tammany Hall and almost became mayor of New York. He was praised by the great minds of the day and even had a cigar named after him. Unfortunately, rising political stars tend to compromise on principles. His "single tax on land value," popular as it was, was a far cry from common ownership of the land, as presented in *Progress and Poverty*. As we will see later, a tax on land value tends to consume its own tax base. But even holding to the orthodox view of common land ownership, collecting ground rents, miraculous as that might be, does not a political economy make. There are so many questions raised on assessment, distribution, democracy and government, freedom and security, population and productivity, that those whose economic interests were at odds with Georgism, waited out the hoopla and won.

AFFEERCE is a variety of Georgism. It has elements of geo-libertarianism and geo-mutualism, the geo prefix conveniently standing for both George and Earth. The AFFEERCE acronym, now more historic than accurate, will be explained shortly.

I spent much of my life considering what constituted a just society, and more importantly, how to obtain one. I believed there were important ideas coming from both the socialist left and the objectivist right. Though these two philosophies seemed to be at odds on most everything, I felt there was a fundamental truth that lay at the root of both. When I discovered Henry George, that fundamental truth acquired a real basis. The final pieces of AFFEERCE fell into place.

I came to Georgism through the back door and saw things many Georgists failed to see. Those insights are found in the early chapters on collection and distribution theory. *Volume I – The Vision*, in its entirety describes a Georgist polity that captures the essence of the left (security) and the essence of the right (freedom). Uncompromising in its defense of natural rights, AFFEERCE shows a higher vision of society that all men and women of good faith can aspire to, beyond the false dichotomy of left and right.

AFFEERCE is a world where each of us creates our own reality. It is a world of entrepreneurs, and the true flourishing of free enterprise. It is a world of collectives; from each according to their ability, to each according to their need. It is a world of adventure; dominions, aristocracy, allegiance swapping, and the conquest of land; all peaceful. It is a world of direct democracy, citizen control of budgets, and a government whose sole purpose is to protect our natural rights,. It is a world of education where unlimited time can be spent seeking a job or seeking the truth, and many wise teachers will be there to show us the way. It is a world where each of us, alone or together with others of like mind, is free to seek out our unique dreams without fear of hunger or homelessness. All of this is part of a logically consistent and simple Georgist framework.

Henry George was once the biggest thing since sliced bread, and now he is almost forgotten. The Georgists have been saying for over a century that if only people knew what George had to say, they would certainly jump on the bandwagon. With an endorsement from some of the greatest minds of the time, it seemed inevitable. It never happened.

Beyond George's error with the "single tax," it was and is in the economic interests of those who live off land and other rents to erase Henry George from our collective memory. And that is what happened.

In *Volume II – The Plan*, I show what few Georgists have figured out: Georgism contains the seeds of its own creation. Like any good self-defense technique, we can use the enemy's strength to our advantage. The law of rent can be harnessed to bring about a Georgist society. We understand land speculation. We understand how wages, convenience, and progress all make land more valuable, and increase rents. With that knowledge alone, the world is ours for the taking.

I hope that *Volume I – The Vision* and *Volume II – The Plan*, inspire you, give you hope in a world with so little, and motivate you to change your life to achieve these goals. Enjoy! But first, here are some quotes from great minds on

Henry George. I've taken them from the Cooperative Individualism website and Adam Monroe's wonderful statement introducing the Georgist Party of America. [FTN.3, FTN.4] It shows that once upon a time, over 100 years ago, the greatest minds on Earth understood how we could save the world. Perhaps it was WWI or the Great Depression, or perhaps it was the flaw of a single tax solution, that extinguished this candle that once burned so brightly. *AFFEERCE Volume I – The Vision* and *Volume II – The Plan* bring these ideas back in a thoroughly modern way.

I need to say a few words about format. In chapters 2 through 10, Parts I and II, much of the text is optional. Sections will either begin with a summary, enclosed in a shadow box or Required Reading in a similar shadow box that directly follows the section name. Either the entire section is required reading or the pertinent points can be found in the shadow box. The casual reader can skip from shadow box to shadow box, provided the section is not required reading. If the reader is skeptical, or the points are unclear, the full text of the section can be studied.

I find it very difficult to disagree with the principles of Henry George. ...I believe in the taxation of land values only. – Louis D. Brandeis

The earth belongs to the people. I believe in the gospel of the Single Tax. – Samuel Clemens

Henry George was one of the real prophets of the world; one of the seers of the world. ...His was a wonderful mind; he saw a question from every side. ...When we learn that the value of land belongs to all of us, then we will be free men -- no need to legislate to keep men and women from working themselves to death; no need to legislate against the white slave traffic. ...The "single tax" is so simple, so fundamental and so easy to carry into effect that I have no doubt that it will be about the last land reform the world will ever get. People in this world are not often logical. – Clarence Darrow

Henry George is one of the great names among the world's social philosophers. It would require less than the fingers of the two hands to enumerate those who, from Plato down, rank with him. ... No man, no graduate of a higher educational institution has a right to regard himself as educated in social thought unless he has some firsthand acquaintance with the theoretical contribution of this great American thinker. – John Dewey

I have already read Henry George's great book and really learnt a great deal from it. Yesterday evening I read with admiration -- the address about Moses. Men like Henry George are rare, unfortunately. One cannot imagine a more beautiful combination of intellectual keenness, artistic form, and fervent love of justice. Every line is written as if for our generation. The spreading of these works is a really deserving cause, for our generation especially has many and important things to learn from Henry George. – Albert Einstein

We ought to tax all idle land the way Henry George said -- tax it heavily, so that its owners would have to make it productive. – Henry Ford

There's a sense in which all taxes are antagonistic to free enterprise -- and yet we need taxes. ....So the question is, which are the least bad taxes? In my opinion the least bad tax is the property tax on the unimproved value of land, the Henry George argument of many, many years ago. – Milton Friedman

I believe in the Single Tax. I count it a great privilege to have been a friend of Henry George and to have been one of those who helped to make him understood in New York and elsewhere... – Samuel Gompers

If I were now to rewrite the book (Brave New World), I would offer a third alternative ... the possibility of sanity ... Economics would be decentralist and Henry Georgian, - Aldous Huxley

Who reads shall find in Henry George's philosophy a rare beauty and power of inspiration, and a splendid faith in the essential nobility of human nature. – Helen Keller

...one of the most cogent and audacious thinkers, ...George's book was a revelation not only for the workers, but also for the intellectuals. Only Darwin, in the natural sciences, left an impression comparable to that of George in the social sciences. ...His devotion can be compared to the love of Nazarene, expressed in the language of our times. – Jose Marti

I went one night quite casually into a hall in London, and I heard a man deliver a speech which changed the whole current of my life. That man was an American -- Henry George... Well, Henry George put me on to the economic tack, and the tack of political science. Very shortly afterwards I read Karl Marx, and I read all the early political sciences of that time; but It was the American, Henry George, who started me. Therefore, as that happened at the beginning of my life, I have thought it fitting that now at the end of my life... I might come and give here In America back a little of that shove that Henry George gave to me. – George Bernard Shaw

People do not argue with the teachings of [Henry] George, they simply do not know it. And it is impossible to do otherwise with his teaching, for he who becomes acquainted with it cannot but agree. ...Solving the land question means the solving of all social questions. ...Possession of land by people who do not use it is immoral -- just like the possession of slaves. – Leo Tolstoy

All this country needs is a new and sincere body of thought in politics, coherently, distinctly and boldly uttered by men who are sure of their ground. The power of men like Henry George seems to me to mean that; and why should not men who have sane purposes avail themselves of this thirst and enthusiasm for better, higher, more hopeful purpose in politics than either of the present, moribund parties can give? – Woodrow Wilson

Henry George showed us ... the only organic solution of the land problem... – Frank Lloyd Wright

The teaching of Henry George will be the basis of our program of reform. ...The (land tax) as the only means of supporting the government is an infinitely just, reasonable and equitably distributed tax, and on it we will found our new system. The centuries of heavy and irregular taxation for the benefit of the Manchus have shown China the injustice of any other system of taxation. – Sun Yat-Sen

Chapter 1 – What is AFFEERCE?

A Summary

AFFEERCE is pronounced as though it would mean "not fierce." Picture an army of warriors chanting the words, "a – fierce, a – fierce, a – fierce…" Then consider they are chanting a synonym for gentleness. Such contradictory imagery is appropriate for the study of our plan and vision, where logic will be used to resolve contradictions in unexpected ways.

Gentleness is how the United States will transition to AFFEERCE. At least, I expect no civil war or blood in the streets. Land speculators might put up some resistance, but they will be overwhelmed by the vast majority of voters; citizens who demand true free enterprise, with collection and distributions of the ground rents, bounty paid for exclusive use of Mother Earth.

While the implementation in these volumes is specifically geared to the United States, it can easily be extended to other countries and regions. The goals are universal, and although national states are anticipated in the near term, ultimately the collection and distribution of ground rents will be on an international scale, atop a web of diverse cultures and political systems.

AFFEERCE is an implementation of Georgism that favors industries owned by mutual groups of coworkers with a distribution philosophy that favors economies of scale, division of labor, and the availability of inexpensive credit. Unlike hard-core mutualism, the AFFEERCE currency is backed by land value, and in that context the free market will determine interest rates and profits. AFFEERCE is a minarchy, promoting the minimum government/state needed to protect our natural rights. The actual AFFEERCE government framework is a cellular democracy, where direct democracy and intimate representation, together, promote the highest level of freedom and democracy. It is called a framework, because within a remote cell, there is the freedom for the consensus of like-minded pioneers to create myriad non-standard social, business, economic, and political structures. This is called panarchy. These embryos of new structures will grow and fade. They might leave behind the legacy of a new idea, or one might even replace AFFEERCE as the dominant polity.

AFFEERCE is an attempt to logically integrate the best ideas from many domains of political and economic thought. In addition to the collection and distribution of the ground rents, cellular and direct democracy, panarchy and soft-mutualism, AFFEERCE borrows from monetary theory, feminist theory, natural rights and justice, and even aristocracy.

AFFEERCE eliminates the worst elements of risk with a safety net through which none can fall, providing everyone the opportunity to rise as high as their ability can take them. This claim will not be based on idle promises or even theoretical "proofs", but an on the reality of an actual working economy, an embryonic nation that will serve as a laboratory and proving ground for the ideas expressed within this volume. We plan to grow this embryo to fill one of the fifty states of the union. The developed embryo will be blessed with so much wealth from executing the business plan proposed in *Volume II*, simple applications of the law of rent, that the host-state will be the envy of the other forty-nine. In the end, the embryo will share its prosperity with the rest of the nation in exchange for passage of constitutional amendments that will not only obliterate hunger and homelessness, but free enterprise from the stranglehold of government.

This embryo, the subject of the next volume, will have a lifespan of almost 60 years. As it changes from a caterpillar into a butterfly, the great economic benefits from the collection and distribution of ground rents and the extreme competitive benefits of a landlord-working class, will propel it beyond the rest of the nation. Rather than proselytizing, our job will be to contain the demands of U.S. citizens, desperate for this new age, until such time as the machinery is in place for a smooth transition. For this reason, our second priority, after building our own infrastructure, is the health and success of the U.S. economy and polity.

Many readers will not live to see the dream of this vision realized in their lifetime, but we can live to see the embryo form, develop, and begin to grow. Although forming that embryo within the borders of the United States is the subject of *Volume II – The Plan,* the vision described in this volume cannot be appreciated without the knowledge that there is a roadmap to take us from here to there.

The day that all the United States comes under the machinery of AFFEERCE is called the capitulation. Ironically, it is likely that the citizens of the embryonic nation will be the ones capitulating, and not the citizens of the other 49 states who will hunger for what we have to offer.

Many things in the vision are likely to change over the course of 60 years. So why have a vision? It cannot be overly emphasized that without a vision, we would be lost. One would never tell a ship's captain to set no course, since the course is likely to change anyway. Without a course, there could be no course correction. Without a vision, there could be no vision correction. It is precisely the specific nature of the vision that allows it to be modified. Those who prefer a general description early on, will sink in a quagmire of their own making.

So when you read exact rules, numbers even with decimal points, and very specific ways of doing things, and think, "Oh, he's trying to dictate the way things will be. He is a control freak," you are missing the point completely. The dictator controls with ambiguity and lack of information. Instead, I am presenting a logically consistent political economy, to the extent such a creature is possible. By including many details, logical consistency can be tested with each proposed change or set of changes. Some of these logically consistent details are more fundamental than others.

Most fundamental of all, is the collection and distribution of the ground rents; the beneficence of Mother Earth. These are public distributions for government, infrastructure, police and fire protection, a judiciary, transportation and sanitation, education, and a national defense. These are personal distributions for food, housing, and medical care.

The government, a cellular democracy, shall be organized as the perfect combination of representative and direct democracy. When additional revenue is needed, beyond the ground rent distribution, only a super-plurality of the dominion shall make that call. Indeed, the direct democracy is required whenever a decision is needed on a question of natural rights. The right to surrender a natural right is itself a natural right.

Where fantasy meets reality, opulent government buildings will be built that are not supported by rent distributions, but rather, by a new aristocracy, in exchange for social privilege.

The old saw that every lost job is a new opportunity has more credibility in an AFFEERCE economy. Government employees who lose their jobs to the new efficiency should feel no distress. Loss of a job opens up a world of opportunity. Universal distribution provides every citizen with nutritious meals, warm and safe shelter, quality medical care and unlimited free education. We will see later why personal distributions must be greater than public ones; how this is a natural law of ground rent distribution.

Personal distributions are often greeted with skepticism, the "no free lunch" syndrome, but there is simply no piper to pay. There will be no penalty for working, for saving, or for taking advantage of the economies of scale. All existing taxes will be abolished and the ground rent that replaces them will save most everyone, rich and poor alike, a considerable sum.

Freedom, like it has never been seen before, will abound throughout the nation; both free enterprise and social freedoms. Even the freedom to form a repressive sub-culture. The natural rights of mankind shall triumph over all. As physical or repetitive labor is replaced by technology, we shall become a nation of entrepreneurs, artists, scientists, innovators, caregivers, adventurers, growers, athletes, to name but a few of the possibilities. Regardless of whether our endeavors produce monetary gain, all will share in the bounty of the Earth.

Gravitating to those who share our visions, we will build large families, communities, and cities. We can embrace the themes of our lives, building castles, dungeons, arenas, academies, communes, seminaries, principalities, kibbutzim, futuristic cities, green cities, borrowing themes from the popular culture, such as Star Wars, The Hobbit, or Harry Potter, with all the pomp, ritual and falderal we desire. Unlike today, communities can be designed around religion, creed, sexuality, or even ethnicity. There is no political correctness, just freedom.

It violates our common sense to suppose all this can come without a price. But what price does the bird, the fish, and the lion pay? The bounty of the Earth supports every other species with ease, why not humans? The answer lies with the balance of nature. Man is his own predator. When the demands of populations exceed the supply of productivity, wars are fought to restore the balance. Coercive force is applied, whether just or unjust, to prevent the poor from seizing resources. Nature enters the act when disease ravages overcrowded populations. The essence of government throughout recorded history is in maintaining a balance of nature that also maintains the power of the privileged.

Years ago I decided that two things were fundamentally true. One was that all taxes, particularly the income tax, were criminal, in that they destroyed productivity. The second was that no child should ever be denied access to nutrition, warm and safe shelter, medical care and an education, because their parents were poor; in other words, a level playing field was a right. It seemed that the world was divided into three camps; those who believed that taxes were the problem, those who believed that poverty was the problem, and the majority who believed that some sort of compromise was needed between the two. At the time I heard no voices who said the evils of both taxation and poverty were crippling our world, and both must be abolished without compromise.

I mulled over the problem for some time until I arrived at a solution. This solution solved the problems of both poverty and taxation. It was a baby tax that supplied the present value of a lifetime of distributions for food, shelter, medical care, and education, as well as police and fire protection, transportation, sanitation, local government, and national defense. It was like Social Security for the child from day one, with premiums paid by the parents before the child could be born. Carrying the analysis further, I discovered that almost every problem that plagues society today could be solved by the elimination of poverty and taxation.

Except for that damn baby tax. How could it be enforced? Some felt this was a worse tyranny than the tyranny of poverty and taxation; a medicine worse than the disease. I was accused of being a Malthusian on a good day and a Nazi on a bad one. Still, with all the problems in the world, it seemed that if utopia could be purchased for the price of a baby tax, it was a worthwhile discussion to have. So the RC in AFFEE**RC**E began life as "Reproductive Control."

As mentioned in the Introduction, my discovery of Henry George and his notion that that which we produce with our own labor belongs to us alone, and that which God or Nature provides, belongs to each of us and all of us, led to my further enlightenment. If all land and natural resources were in the commons, then renting exclusive use of location to the highest bidder, would pay for the nutritious meals, warm and safe shelter, medical care and education, as well as the police and fire protection, streets and sanitation, local government and national defense. And to further the myth that this was destiny, "Rental of the Commons" is also abbreviated RC.

My first thought was that universal distribution would be funded half by the baby tax and half by ground rents. Then, as I learned more about location value, the ratio shifted in favor of ground rents, with 90% funded by the ground rents and only 10% funded by the baby tax. The more I realized just how much wealth could be attributed to location value, something unknown to many Georgists (although well-known to some), the more I wanted to chuck the baby tax altogether. But as you will read in Chapter 3, a phenomenon known as "the tragedy of the commons" can result if all funding for universal distribution comes only from rental of the commons.

It occurred to me that balancing the two RC's as a source of funding for universal distribution, was very similar in effect to the balance of nature itself. Even if the baby tax is tiny, and never increased unless the fertility rate is well in excess of 2.1, there is an elegance in balancing these two that provides a formula for everlasting prosperity. These tools are examined in detail in Chapter 6, where we will see how a fertility rate under 2, as it is today in much of the Western democracies, would likely lead to a baby credit instead of a tax. You will learn in Chapter 3, that the "baby tax" comes as a liberator. It is small enough to be within every family's reach and large enough to prevent the abuse of women, children, and the Earth. A balanced RC can assure prosperity until the end of mankind's dominion.

Our new balance of nature allows humans to live as freely as the other species, by funding universal distribution. In its full form, it includes both the collection and distribution of rents. It does not deny human nature. Competition, loyalty, and even wars are embraced by the new natural order. But these wars, called trebler wars and described in Chapter 2, will not be violent. The loser will end up with more wealth than the winner and the plunder will add to the bounty of the Earth.

There are few parts of this vision that are unique. But, never before have they been assembled in one place and integrated into a single solution. Distinguished contributors include Thomas Paine and Henry George. But in terms of collection of the rents, none is more important than Dr. Sun Yat-Sen. Distribution theory borrows much from those who advocate for a basic income, as well as George's ideas of distribution of wealth. The distributions and availability of credit promote the mutualism of Proudhon. The panarchy is reminiscent of de Puydt. In *Volume II – The Plan*, the ideas of Jane Jacobs are critical to success, as well as generally known corollaries of David Ricardo's law of rent. Still, it is in the integration that new and valuable ideas emerge.

I want to clear up a confusion early on. Many will refer to ground rent as a land value tax or LVT. I will avoid that terminology. When you pay a tax, you get nothing in return. Furthermore, a land value tax implies that a tax is being paid on land one owns. Yet the land is owned by the commons. When you pay ground rent you are simply purchasing location value. This purchased value is a tool to enhance your business, your convenience and your status. Taxes are not voluntary. As you will see in Chapter 2, the amount you pay for this valuable resource is completely up to you.

The Acronym

As an acronym, AFFEERCE is broken down as follows:

AF – **A**lternative **F**amily	FE – **F**ree **E**nterprise	E – Universal **E**ntitlement
RC – Balance of the **RC**s (**R**eproductive **C**ontrol and **R**ental of the **C**ommons)		E – **E**nlightenment

Each of these AFFEERCE foundations will be covered in a separate chapter.

Alternative **F**amily does not mean one has to run off and join a commune or have a 5-way sexual relationship. It does mean complete freedom to self-organize into families, including the traditional 1 man + 1 woman + children. Or one can choose to live alone. The problem for single people and couples, regardless of their sexual orientation, is that larger families will try and entice them in. Because each person comes with a basic income, not only do Children=Wealth, but People=Wealth. Each person's value as a human being is much easier to recognize when they bring money to the table. This may sound cynical, but it is human nature. To be enticed into a larger family, increases everyone's wealth, due to the economies of scale.

Family sexuality is a different dimension altogether. In some families, all members will be chaste, while other families will be collections of couples or other sexual arrangements, and still others will be amorphous and pansexual. Everyone is free to choose a family whose sexual ideas match their own.

The evolution of panarchy within AFFEERCE has extended the "right of family to its own social order," beyond alternative family boundaries. These much larger mutual organizations include collectives, tribes, worker syndicates, kibbutzim, and new forms limited only by the imagination. The requirements for family coercion are a private entrance and common eating area, while a larger organization that wishes to violate rights in the same manner requires the approval of a 5/6 plurality of its dominion and financial exit rights as well. Beyond that, families and mutual organizations are, for the most part, interchangeable.

Free Enterprise means laissez-faire. It means government keeps its hands off business. It means no minimum wage and no inflation. It means no corporate income tax of any kind. It means the marketplace will determine if monopolies should form and the effectiveness of collusion.

Honesty, above all else, will be valued in business and law. Merchants, employers, police, prosecutors, and even lawyers will be legally accountable for dishonest practices.

Voluntary standards groups with 50% industry representation will set service and product standards. Deviations from these standards must be fully disclosed. However, businesses will seek full disclosure because it limits or eliminates liability.

Free enterprise also means no civil rights protection and no right to a job. Those are scary propositions today, but in an AFFEERCE economy they are of no consequence at all.

The shackles of intellectual property will be lifted, with free downloading of copyrighted materials, and the free sharing of patented materials and processes. Yet artists and innovators will be generously compensated, and patents and copyrights will exceed the lifetime of the creator.

Freedom goes beyond enterprise. It means consumers and workers, can picket, boycott, strike, leaflet, and organize against any business, using a weapon that is forbidden by law today: the right to deny service to polluters, bigots, or any other person or group creating an unwholesome environment in violation of community standards.

Universal **Entitlement** – The U in Universal is not highlighted because it doesn't fit into the acronym, but still is critical to the definition. As for the 'E' in Entitlement, it is no longer relevant: 'Universal Entitlement' has been renamed 'Universal Distribution'. But, alas, I am stuck with the AFFEERCE acronym.

The bounty of the earth, initially within the nation, is divided equally between all citizens. This gift of nature is called universal distribution. Universal distribution is not based on need. A billionaire receives the same distribution for food and housing as a pauper. Every person in a family of 50 receives the same dollar amount for food and housing as someone living alone.

Universal distribution is both a personal and public distribution. The distribution supports an allocated guaranteed basic income of food and shelter along with necessary public services such as government, education, medical care, police and fire protection, streets and sanitation services, and a national defense. Even though it is not usually distributed in its entirety to each of us personally, it is most assuredly ours. No matter how the voters in our community decide to reallocate funds for public services, when we move from town to town, our distributions for public services will follow.

Rental of the **C**ommons – Land, airwaves, minerals, timber, fresh water, fresh air, and wild fish and game should belong equally to all of us. At one time or another, all land was seized by coercive force. Ground rents provide each of us (we are the true landlords, after all), with payment for exclusive use of the land. Through free market forces, rents adjust according to the land's desirability, natural wealth, and potential productivity. In so doing it makes all land equally worthless. A home on one acre of the Hamptons in New York would cost about the same as a similar home on one acre of Wyoming's badlands. The equalizer is in the rental cost of the land.

Depending on public policy, ground rents will pay from 90% to 100% of the cost for universal distribution.

Reproductive **C**ontrol – At this stage of human cultural evolution, the value of something purchased is more recognized than value given for nothing. By paying a small portion of the child's future distributions before birth, there is consideration in the contract to supply the child with the basic necessities for the rest of their life. This is but one small reason for the "baby tax" that will be shown to protect the rights of the child, the rights of women in general, the rights of society as a collective, and consideration of the Earth's burden. The "baby tax" pays up to 10% of universal distribution if the fertility rate is well above 2.1.

If the fertility rate is below 2.0 certain generated funds can be used for a birth credit.

To facilitate reproductive control, all contraception will be free without copay and available everywhere. Contraceptive medical procedures will be free, as will their reversal. There will be free abortion on demand in the first trimester, although the incidence of abortion is expected to dramatically decrease with better methods of contraception, such as vasectomies for men with a remote controlled on/off switch.

If it is hard to fathom paying for the privilege of having a child, think of it like Social Security. You pay all your working years, and at the age of 66, you become entitled to Social Security for the rest of your life. In an AFFEERCE economy, while you can't pay into the system before birth, your family can. They save and scrimp, and muster their resources. Because of the distributions, it is less difficult than it seems. All employment income is discretionary. Not only is the tax a great investment for a lifetime of nutritious meals, warm and safe shelter, quality medical care and unlimited free education, but I suspect it will favorably change our entire perspective on value and what is truly important in life.

Enlightenment – In a free society, all religions, spiritualties, beliefs or lack thereof, are welcome. The AFFEERCE enlightenment is a reliance on the truths in nature. You will be in greatest harmony with an AFFEERCE society if you recognize that natural wealth belongs to everyone.

The direction in thought since the original Enlightenment has been toward increased objectivism. Many have worked hard to purge subjectivity from our science, our business, and our laws. It seems we have become biological machines. Some scientists go so far as to say, we are indeed machines. It is said the universe has no purpose, life is a random accident and free will does not exist [FTN1.02]. Dishonesty in business and law is commonplace. Everything is about how well you "play the game." These questions are explored in far more detail in *Volume III – The Philosophy*. In this volume, enlightenment is the realization of the human benefits of the common ownership of natural wealth.

The Assumptions

It is essential to use a consistent set of data, even though conditions will change dramatically over the 60 year time period of the plan. Because the most recent land survey in the United States took place in 2002, that is the year in which calculations will be based. A population of 288 million is assumed, living and working on 60 million acres of residential and commercial property. Interestingly, land values in 2002 were not too different than they are today in 2016, post-crash.

The baby tax is assumed to be $10,000. We will have 60 years to debate the feasibility of that number. The issues raised in Chapter 3, are a prerequisite to this debate.

The parameters of the solution are likely to undergo radical change, as well. Yet, without numbers, the book would be too abstract and unable to demonstrate the viability of AFFEERCE. Some of the distribution numbers might seem low, but as the book progresses you will see that these numbers are not only viable, but can lead to abundance in large families. The bulk of the funding for universal distribution comes from the ground rents. Because citizens born before the AFFEERCE capitulation (initially, all of us) have paid no baby tax a 2% consumption tax, that declines to zero with the passage of time, is used to make up the discrepancy. In the assumptions, the consumption tax also funds a 2% discretionary tax, and a 2% + 2% academic/school achievement annuity, all of which will be described later. Thus, a total consumption tax of 8% is used in the examples. Such a tax is not mandatory and might be absent when AFFEERCE comes to fruition.

Assumed Monthly Distributions in U.S. Dollars	
Food	220
Housing	370
Cash	35
Education	50
Testing	2
Medical	120
Non Universal (disability, age, incarceration)	97
Social Worker	10
Fire Protection	5
Law Enforcement	30
Judiciary and Public Defense	9
Transportation and sanitation	35
Infrastructure and VIP	10
Government	20
Building Capital/Depreciation/Rents	20
Intellectual Property Royalties	92
National Defense	75
TOTAL MONTHLY DISTRIBUTION	**1,200**

These numbers are discussed in detail in *Chapter 11 – Universal Distribution*. This is how the bounty of the Earth will be allocated for each of us. Those who object to such specificity in categories that are bound to change over 60 years are failing to grasp the importance of detail in measuring the effects of change on a logically consistent system.

Notice that many of these distributions are not paid to the individual, but to those providing services for a group of individuals. AFFEERCE theory holds that the value of the individual in the community is enhanced when social services are paid in this manner. Of the $30 law enforcement distribution, the $25 tranche for local law enforcement would increase by $25 per month when a person moves into the district and decrease by $25 when a person moves out. If a person moves to the remote wilderness, that $25 would go directly to the individual (to buy a shotgun, perhaps). Those who provide public services have a strong motivation to keep their constituents happy.

It is not envisioned that the allocated distributions will grow. Instead, it is assumed the AFFEERCE Enlightenment will allow additional productivity, as reflected in the rental value of land, to be distributed as cash, in the form of a citizens' dividend to adults only. The theory of distribution is discussed in chapters 2, 3, 5 and 7.

AFFEERCE Georgism allows us to solve many problems in political economy, previously unsolvable. The creative reader should be on the lookout for better solutions than the ones I present. Logical consistency is the principle test.

A Brief Survey of the Tax Burden

Ground rents are not a tax, but anybody who needs or desires location value for their home or business, will end up paying for "location, location, location" as the saying goes. While ground rents provide the bulk of universal distribution, there is also an initial 8% consumption tax on goods not purchased with the distributions. What kind of burden is this for the average taxpayer, for the wealthy, and for the poor? Has the tyranny of taxation merely changed its guise?

The results are surprising. Not only will most people come out ahead, but they will come out considerably ahead. There will be no more federal income tax, Social Security tax, Medicare tax, state income tax, or local income tax. For the average person, the ground rents will be not too different than their property tax today. And that is before they make use of the housing distribution!

Suppose you earn $150,000 with a stay-at-home spouse and two kids. Today you would pay about $33,000 in federal tax, $8000 in Social Security tax, $2000 in Medicare tax, and assume $6,000 in state income tax. [FTN1.01] You also own a home and pay $6,000 in property tax. And you pay $10,000 a year for family coverage under your insurance plan at work.

In an AFFEERCE economy, there is no income tax, and all financial instruments and savings grow tax free. The table below shows the scenario where almost everything earned gets spent. Conservatively, the ground rents will be figured at twice the property tax.

Today		AFFEERCE	
$33,000	Federal Tax[FTN1.01]	$10,400	8% consumption tax on $130,000 spending
8,000	Social Security	(17,760)	Housing distribution for 4
2,000	Medicare	(10,560)	Food distribution for 4
6,000	State Income Tax	(1,680)	Sundry cash distribution for 4
6,000	Property Tax	12,000	Ground rent
10,000	Medical Insurance Premium		
------------		------------	
$65,000	Total Net Tax	($7,600)	Total Net benefit

Wow! A middle class family of 4 saves 100% of their tax and related expenses, and gets a benefit credit of $7,600. This number conservatively assumes no savings, as there is no consumption tax on money saved. In actuality, this family will benefit even more, since today there is already an average sales tax of 8%. Because quality medical care is free, there is no longer a need for the $10,000 medical insurance, although some might wish to supplement their policy to cover private hospital rooms, private nurses, renowned specialists, and high-price experimental procedures. In an

AFFEERCE economy, unlimited education for the two kids will also be free. Furthermore, this already reasonable consumption tax will drop yearly, as new children are born with a baby-tax and older adults, without one, pass away.

Next, look at an AFFEERCE tax comparison for a well-to-do single person earning that same $150,000 a year. Assume she lives in a luxury apartment and medical insurance is provided free at work. The ground rent in high-rise condos will tend to be less than property taxes today, because of the efficient use of land. Assume the ground rent will equal the property tax.

Today		AFFEERCE	
$38,000	Federal Tax[FTN1.01]	$10,400	8% CT on $130,000 spending
8,000	Social Security	(4,440)	Housing distribution for 1
2,000	Medicare	(2,640)	Food distribution for 1
6,000	State Income Tax	(420)	Sundry cash distribution for 1
6,000	Property Tax	6,000	Ground rent
-------------		--------------	
$65,000	Total Net Tax	$8,900	Total Net Tax

Even a single person earning $150,000 a year living in a luxury apartment saves at least $56,100 a year in taxes, over 70%, and much more with savings. You expect a slight disadvantage for the single person, since, in AFFEERCE, Children=Wealth and People=Wealth.

At the low end of the income spectrum, consider a family of four earning $35,000 a year. After earned income credits there is no federal tax and no state tax. Assume this family rents a 3 bedroom apartment for $1,200 a month, both today, and in an AFFEERCE economy. Assume that property taxes paid by the landlord today, will equal ground rent paid by the landlord in an AFFEERCE economy, so the apartment rent will remain unchanged. Significantly, there will be no consumption tax on spending the distributions.

Today		AFFEERCE	
$0	Federal Tax[FTN1.01]	$2,400	8% CT on $30,000 spending
2,000	Social Security	(17,600)	Housing distribution for 4
400	Medicare	(10,560)	Food distribution for 4
0	State Income Tax	(1,680)	Sundry cash distribution for 4
-------------		--------------	
$2,400	Total Net Tax	($27,440)	Total Net Benefit

The low income family of 4 benefits by over $29,800 [$2,400 – (-$27,440)]. And that does not even take into account the following: Today, they could not afford healthcare in states without Medicaid, or higher education for the kids. In an AFFEERCE economy, both are free! The low income family is no longer poor. In fact, poverty, hunger and homelessness cease to exist in an AFFEERCE economy. As you will see later, they are not even possible.

If poor and middle class families make out like bandits, it must be the rich who get soaked. Consider a wealthy person with a family of four and an income of 3.5 million dollars a year; 2 million in income and 1.5 million in capital gains. Assume today an 18% capital gains rate and a 39% income tax rate. As a worst-case assumption, the family will spend every dime of that 2 million, and use the capital gains to pay the consumption tax and ground rents. The critical tax factor revolves around land holdings. Suppose this family has a 4-bedroom apartment in a Manhattan high rise, and a 5-bedroom 4-acre home in the Hamptons. How badly will this wealthy family fare under AFFEERCE?

Today		AFFEERCE	
$780,000	Federal Tax[FTN1.01]	$160,000	8% CT on $2 million spending
$360,000	Capital Gains Tax		
8,000	Social Security	(17,760)	Housing distribution for 4
29,000	Medicare	(10,560)	Food distribution for 4
80,000	State Income Tax	(1,680)	Sundry cash distribution for 4
24,000	Property Tax-Manhattan	24,000	Ground rent (GR) Manhattan Condo
25,000	Property Tax-Hamptons, N.Y.	800,000	GR Hamptons @$200,000 per acre
10,000	Medical Insurance Premium	2,000	Private room/exotic procedure med. ins.
170,000	8.5% Sales tax		
--------------		--------------	
$1,486,000	Total Net Tax	$956,000	Total Net Tax

Even the multi-millionaire saves money on taxes, unless they own huge landed estates. However, the biggest enticement for AFFEERCE among the uber-rich will not be the savings of a few hundred thousand on personal taxes, but the massive benefits to their corporations.

> Corporations pay no income tax! They also pay no consumption tax on capital expenditures.

Every person and family, from the $30,000 family to the $4 million dollar family is a corporation, and earns their money in a tax-free corporate account. It is only when money is taken out to buy a house, a car, a vacation, clothing, furniture, or anything not covered by the distributions that the consumption tax kicks in. So unless this wealthy family really does spend all of those 2 million dollars, their tax bill will be considerably less.

Wealthy business owners have other reasons to love AFFEERCE. Free markets allow profits to be maximized, none of which are taxed until they are moved into personal spending accounts or paid out as employee perks.

How can all this be provided without somebody paying more in taxes? The poor, the middle class and the rich all are better off. The wealth of the nation is equal to its productivity and AFFEERCE rapidly increases productivity in over 40 ways. These are listed at the end of *Chapter 10 – Economic Principles*. By way of example, I include four such productivity enhancers below.

1) Many businesses will form to serve the needs of the formerly poor.
2) Large families by their very organization, add considerably to the productivity of the nation.
3) Free market benefits, especially the elimination of the minimum wage, and corporate income tax, will cause national productivity to explode.
4) We will no longer be supporting a bloated government bureaucracy.

Only productivity enhancer #4, the elimination of the bloated government bureaucracy, including a 70% reduction in military spending (without a reduction in security), plus increases for basic income, are used when estimating feasibility. The other three productivity enhancers in this list, and many more described later, support the vision, but are not relied upon to prove the workability of AFFEERCE.

The Fundamental Relations

The fundamental relations are fascinating, but incomplete. They date to a much earlier version of AFFEERCE, but are no less true, today. Missing are relations for collection and distribution theory, panarchy, cellular aristocracy, and legal classification. Lack of completeness, however, does not diminish the importance of the early relations. Appendix I lists the original set and a new set for cellular democracy.

Many of the relations take the form of natural laws. That is, they are eternal truths of political economy. Fundamental relation (1) is still as poignant today as it was in 2011 when it was first written:

(1) Prevents Social Collapse – Without the basic income of universal distribution, free markets show no mercy. Massive dislocations can occur as unproductive companies are punished. Workers bargain in desperation. Conditions lead to theft, sabotage and revolution. However, the distributions allow the free market to function without causing harm.

The VIP

Technology allows government to abuse power in new and frightening ways. We cannot, nor should we stop the advance of technology. The solution is to limit the powers of government so abuse has no benefit to them. AFFEERCE makes it financially painful to incarcerate, removes the power of legislatures to raise revenue, is structured with a cellular democracy and has a well-paid fully independent judiciary

The technology that makes these limits on government so essential is the VIP, a biometric identity for each citizen. Real-time biometric identification did not even exist a few years ago. As of this writing, we are still shy of a full implementation. The time element is essential to assuage fears. The business plan in *Volume-II* gives us 60 years to gain trust, and address privacy and security concerns as they occur.

Biometric identity is critical to the future society. Without it, AFFEERCE would be very difficult, if not impossible, to implement. The initials VIP stand for Voice, Iris, and Palm. Using the patterns of your voice, the vessels in your eye, and the lines on your palm, a unique signature is created. While the three together might be considered redundant, it can guarantee theft-proof identity to 100% accuracy. Actual VIP readers might employ other biometrics, such as fingerprints and facial recognition, or work in conjunction with mobile devices. VIP is used generically throughout this book, regardless of which biometrics are ultimately employed.

Security experts recommend a 1 to 4 digit PIN in addition to the biometric identity. This will dissuade anyone from an elaborate and frankly horrific attempt to steal someone's identity. Three sequential attempts with an incorrect PIN will force the person to go to the nearest VIP office and re-verify in person.

Universal implementation of VIP creates a new freedom, the right to travel without a wallet. There are no more dollar bills or coins in your pocket. The only currency is a virtual currency. Access to bank accounts, credit cards, library books, online voting, and much more, is done in the blink of an eye: literally. Using the VIP, keys to the house and automobile can also be eliminated; a paperless, card-less, cashless, key-less, wallet-less society. Beyond a short PIN, there will be no more passwords to memorize.

The only contact with the virtual currency will be through the VIP reader. These VIP dollars (VIP$) will exist only in the computers of the AFFEERCE Treasury (although it will be a sound debt-free currency backed by land value). Every transaction is the movement of VIP$ from one account to another. Every transaction is safe, secure, and recorded in multiple places around the nation. The term VIP might be used in many different ways, as noun, adjective, and even verb, to refer to the apparatus that reads biometric information, to personal identity, to the VIP network, to the money, and even to contracts signed with VIP identities.

The requirements of AFFEERCE will drive the universal availability of VIP readers. Consider a mobile workforce and the right to travel freely. Most people will use the housing distribution for ground rent, apartment rent, mortgage, and utilities. But some romantics will hit the highway, searching for that ever elusive opportunity. The VIP versatility in the use of food and housing distributions to procure tiny rooms along the byways with continental brunch the next morning, is a boon to the young, the restless, the mobile, and freedom, itself.

But without the VIP, this way of life for kings of the road could never be. Without real-time identification, forgeries, theft, imaginary companions, double-dipping for both travel and home, and other mischief is virtually impossible to prevent. These petty offenses would likewise be difficult to pursue by the authorities for all but the most egregious offenders.

The VIP eliminates any possibility of corruption in universal distribution. If there are rebates to be had for skipping meals or sleeping under the stars, it is the VIP that insures rebated VIP$ make it to the correct account.

Beyond the distributions, the VIP enforced earmarking of funds allows for new kinds of contracts and safety in investment, including the signing of contracts online. The citizen investors (discussed later) use earmarking to make available significant capital to small enterprises. The VIP eliminates identity theft and makes hitchhiking and jitney cabs safe for both driver and rider. It is essential to the family, allowing designated shoppers to spend the combined food distribution for all family members, or pay the rent or mortgage with the combined housing distribution.

Where identity does not involve the transfer of a large amount of funds, or the potential users are already security restricted, a simple wave of the palm is sufficient to establish identity for room entry, entrance to a dining room, airport security, guests only entrance to entertainment areas and so forth.

Even foreign workers and tourists will find it convenient to acquire a VIP account for visits. It will be a joy to visit a country where the nightmare of losing your wallet or passport is gone forever.

The freedom to travel the country comfortably without a nickel to your name, to have a workforce more mobile than any that has ever existed in history, to travel without keys, wallet or any physical identification, to not be a target for thieves, to have instant access to your own money and the distributions wherever you roam, to sign contracts, transfer funds, vote, shop for family, go quickly through security checkpoints, and much more, is a great enhancer of life. Still, even with the constitutional protections of a reigned in government, it will be feared by some. For them, Big Brother is watching. The government knows where you slept and where you had your last meal.

Yes comrade, you thought this vas utopia. Ha-ha, ha, ha, ha!

Sounds scary, but look at the facts.

1. The AFFEERCE cellular democracy couldn't care less. Recent revelations of U.S. government spying on citizens on a massive scale, is a legitimate reason for being skeptical of this claim. But what these revelations really demonstrate is the futility of any such effort. No matter how powerful computers become, many eyes will be needed to interpret the data. In a free society, there will always be a Chelsea Manning or Edward Snowden who risk everything and stand up to potential tyrants. An AFFEERCE government will have no motivation to even try.

2. In an AFFEERCE economy, the VIP is a practical requirement, but not a legal one. One can forego distributions and conduct all transactions in gold or alternative currencies. Of course, the freedoms sacrificed and vulnerability to thieves is a high price to pay for paranoia.

3. Even today, every time you use a credit card or ATM, your location is known. If you pay property taxes or vote or have a library card, the government knows where you live. Use a registered cell-phone and the government can pin-point your location exactly. If you are on the lam (or abducted), real-time access to credit card, ATM and cell phone use is already a reality.

4. Freedoms of speech, assembly, and religion are constitutionally-enshrined natural rights. A government official who uses VIP information to arrest or otherwise harass a law abiding citizen is in violation of the law and can be imprisoned.

5. Government officials have no incentive to imprison anyone, since they receive their pay after funds are drawn for certain penitentiary expenses. They cannot raise revenue through the governing council, and laws that involve a conflict in rights must be passed by a super plurality of the electorate.

VIP design will likely be a joint project of large corporations, national and international standards' bodies, and the Affeercianado Guild (See *Volume II – The Plan*). Clearly, it is impossible to predict the timing and extent of technological developments exactly. I assume the specification will include public and private encryption schemes, GPS, central identity databases, local identity storage, and the ability to associate programmable applications with accounts.

On a less technical level, a grocery store VIP purchase might go like this. When the total appears, confirm by entering the PIN and looking into the camera. Your iris alone might be sufficient for transactions below $200 at retail. Behind the scenes, the retail VIP application will download the food distribution account(s) associated with your identity. The app will debit the account or accounts for qualified food purchases. If you are the designated family shopper, distribution accounts of all family members will be debited equally, unless otherwise specified. If the distribution has been exhausted, or if there are non-qualified items, the app will download access to your personal spending account . If the personal spending account is exhausted, the app will access and move funds from your personal corporate account to your personal spending account. In the process, any consumption taxes in effect will be moved from your personal corporate account to the Treasury. If the personal corporate account is empty, the app will check for a default credit account. If credit is available, money will be moved from there to the personal spending account with an additional consumption tax debit. Other options will allow for more hands-on control. Complex, but transparent. All you need to do is say OK and blink.

For people with disabilities who cannot take advantage of one or more of voice, iris, and palm identification, special efforts will be made to implement a custom biometric identity, using the capabilities of existing readers. It could be a foot, or fingers positioned in a certain way; these in conjunction with a certain noise, or even an artificial sound. A longer PIN could compensate for reduced biometrics.

The VIP system will be designed to employ extensive redundancy. Identity determination will be available from multiple sites around the country, all protected by natural and military security, and several levels of backup power. Block chain technology, currently used with Bitcoin, allows for transaction data to be stored redundantly on many different servers with little or no possibility of tampering. Thumb drives or mobile devices can hold your personal encrypted identity, biometrics, local cash, and access lists for devices you control. In the event of a catastrophe, thumb drive and battery backup gives you offline biometric access to your home, car, locked rooms and safes. VIP cash stored locally maintains its own transaction history until it is deposited in an online account.

New versions of the software will be run in parallel with the previous version to insure the integrity of all transactions. Transactions that involve specific companies, banks, and VIP readers are also stored redundantly at the institution or within the reader.

Although only citizens receive distributions, foreign visitors are encouraged to register their identity, deposit funds in a bank, and take advantage of wallet-free travel. Very likely, it will become the standard mode of travel, with VIP identity established at the international terminals.

Without the revolutionary VIP, AFFEERCE would not be possible. Distributions would likely be swallowed by a bureaucratic sea, corruption and red tape. Without AFFEERCE, the VIP would be problematic. Dispersing biometric identity among competing corporations would require an added layer of authentication and added costs. Even with a regulated monopoly controlling biometric identity, fees would be enormous, not to mention citizens' distrust that can only be countered by a trusted government over many years. With credit card processing much cheaper, and no distributions, merchants today have no reason to install VIP readers.

Part I – Funding Freedom Through The Collection and Distribution of the Rents

LVT

Birth Tax

George
Rental of the Commons

Hardin
Tragedy of the Commons

The Balance of the RCs

AFFEERCE
Proclaim Freedom
Everywhere

The equal right of all men to the use of land is as clear as their equal right to breathe the air--it is a right proclaimed by the fact of their existence. For we cannot suppose that some men have a right to be in this world, and others no right. -- Henry George

It is a position not to be controverted that the earth, in its natural, uncultivated state was, and ever would have continued to be, the common property of the human race. In that state every man would have been born to property. He would have been a joint life proprietor with rest in the property of the soil, and in all its natural productions, vegetable and animal…Every proprietor, therefore, of cultivated lands, owes to the community a ground-rent (for I know of no better term to express the idea) for the land which he holds; and it is from this ground-rent that the fund proposed in this plan is to issue. – Thomas Paine

…to equalise the financial resources of Society. Our first aim is to be the solution of the land problem. … The government makes two regulations: first, that it will collect taxes according to the declared value (by the landowners) of the land; second, that it can also buy the land at the same price. – Sun Yat-Sen

Chapter 2 – Collection of the Ground Rents

To facilitate rapid reading in Chapters 2 through 10, each section will be denoted by either Required Reading which indicates the short section should be read in its entirety, or a summary, beneath the section name, which is also enclosed in a shadow box and allows the satisfied reader to skip over the discussion.

Location value is defined as the annual value of the location to an individual or business. It is bracketed on the low side by the annual interest and taxes paid for the land, and on the high side by the annual profits made from the land. **Land value** is the total value of the land to that same individual or business. It is approximately equal to the location value divided by the interest rate. **Land price** is the price paid for the land. **Imputed rent** is roughly defined as (land value minus land price) multiplied by the interest rate. **Land value tax** is a tax on privately owned land assumedly based on its location value. **Ground rent** is the rent collected for exclusive use of commonly owned land.

Introduction

Required Reading

Today, land is not very exciting, particularly when compared with stocks or derivatives. It is doubtful that anyone is glued to their computer all day playing the land market. Land just sort of sits there. Or so it seems. Yet from the agrarian revolution to the present day there have been innumerable wars. These were not fought for shares of a corporation, or options on those shares. In every single battle, men fought and died for land.

We have already discussed an interesting property of land that seems to justify these strong emotions. All unilateral wage increases, innovations, conveniences, efficiencies, and improvements increase the value of land. This leads to rent increases that counter many benefits of progress.

Henry George advocated that the rent be collected by and returned to the community. By these rents, he was referring only to the ground rents, the rent on the location value of the land. This has little to do with building rents, such as monthly rent paid to the landlord of an apartment. Nor is this a tax on those apartments; unlike a property tax, ground rent does not tax improvements on the land.

Location value is created by nature or the community. Even the contribution by nature is a function of the community. Therefore, all of the collected rent should be returned to the community.

There is an intimate relationship between collection of the ground rents and their distribution. This relationship revolves around at least three questions: What is location value? What is community? How does distribution of the rent affect location value? The third question highlights a feedback mechanism that could generate unpredictable chaos in the mathematical sense, and instability followed by severe dislocations in a real economy. It therefore behooves us to have a solid theory of collection and distribution and not limit our theory to Georgist platitudes, compelling as they might be.

Land Speculation

Land speculation has no social benefit. It leads to a loss of productivity and lower wages. Collection of a ground rent nips land speculation in the bud.

There is, however, one Georgist platitude that accurately describes an economic truth today and is likely independent of rent distribution. It is the tale of the land speculator whose profits derive exclusively from the productivity of others. Knowledge of where such productive gains occur next is of little or no social benefit. George's disdain for the speculator can be seen in the following quotation from *Progress and Poverty* which according to Robert Heilbroner in *The Worldly Philosophers* represents the crux of George's economic philosophy[FTN2.28].

Take now... some hard-headed business man, who has no theories, but knows how to make money. Say to him: "Here is a little village; in ten years it will be a great city-in ten years the railroad will have taken the place of the stage coach, the electric light of the candle; it will abound with all the machinery and improvements that so enormously multiply the effective power of labor. Will in ten years, interest be any higher?" He will tell you, "No!" "Will the wages of the common labor be any higher...?" He will tell you, "No the wages of common labor will not be any higher..." "What, then, will be higher?" "Rent, the value of land. Go, get yourself a piece of ground, and hold possession." And if, under such circumstances, you take his advice, you need do nothing more. You may sit down and smoke your pipe; you may lie around...; you may go up in a balloon or down a hole in the ground; and without doing one stroke of work, without adding one iota of wealth to the community, in ten years you will be rich! In the new city you may have a luxurious mansion, but among its public buildings will be an almshouse.

It is hard to argue that the land speculator is anything more than a parasite. Unlike the capitalist or worker who perform real services, the land speculator contributes nothing. Land speculation is said to extend the margin. In simpler words, good land is kept idle, pushing people onto inferior land, which nowadays tends to be land farther from the city center. This leads to a loss of productivity and urban sprawl. It also tends to lower wages. To understand why, consider the law of rent discussed earlier. Mathematically, given two cities A and B, all other things being equal, $\text{Wages}_A - \text{Rent}_A = \text{Wages}_B - \text{Rent}_B$. We can consider A to be the city center, and B to be the furthest reaches of the burbs. Assume that the ground rents at B are insignificant, and the cost to rent an apartment is minimal. The wages at B are reduced by the cost of the commute, the extra gas needed to shop, the higher prices from increased shipping distance, the increased wait time for police, fire, and medical emergencies, and the distance from hospitals, shops, restaurants, theaters, museums, and civilization in general. It is fair to say that in absence of a new city center, the wages at B will decrease as the distance from A increases. When the rent at B can go no lower, $\text{Wages}_B = \text{Wages}_A - \text{Rent}_A$, real wages drop at A and B, as B gets farther from A. This might seem counter-intuitive, but it can be no other way. If real wages at A were temporarily higher, people would move from B to A, driving up rents at A, until the real wages in the center of the city were equal to the real wages at the margin.

Land speculation lowers both productivity and wages, without providing any benefit in return. It is most common in a growing metropolis where taxes on unimproved land are low. The first and easiest hurdle for an adequate ground rent is one that nips land speculation in the bud. Making holding land without putting it to use, expensive, will stop speculation. However, as we will see in a later example, even this simple bar is not so trivial to achieve.

The final line of George's quote, "In the new city you may have a luxurious mansion, but among its public buildings will be an almshouse" can be attributed to the loss of productivity and wages due to land speculation. But it could also could be speculating on a future, where taxes on productivity – most notoriously the income tax – are replaced with proceeds from the ground rents.

Location Value

Objective Value

> **Land is objectively worthless and the price tends toward zero when only objective criterion is used. Land value is created by the community.**

This is a corollary of David Ricardo's law of rent from 1809:

> *...the rent of a land site is equal to the economic advantage obtained by using the site in its most productive use, relative to the advantage obtained by using marginal (i.e., the best rent-free) land for the same purpose, given the same inputs of labor and capital*[FTN2.20].

In other words, Ricardo's economic advantage minus the ground rent equals zero. Think of it this way. If all location value is captured by the community, the location has no value left. The land would have no price beyond a nominal one. We will see below that attempts to return only part of the location value to the community and maintain a price or rental value are fraught with serious problems as well.

Under the labor theory of value, an objective theory, land also has no value. No labor went into creating it. It does not need to be rehabbed every so often. It does not depreciate.

Regardless of which objective theory of value is used, the objective value of land tends to zero.

Subjective Value

> **The subjective value of land is arbitrarily high, potentially of infinite value. Many have killed and died for land.**

Ironically, under the subjective theory of value, land can be priceless, worth billions. Throughout history most wars were fought over land; so many have died for land. So many have killed for land.

> *The land is sacred. These words are at the core of your being. The land is our mother, the rivers our blood. Take our land away and we die. That is, the Indian in us dies.* — Mary Brave Bird

> *He who has known how to love the land has loved eternity.* — Stefan Zeromski

> *We are seeking to incite the nation to rise up to liberate its land and to jihad for the sake of God.* — Osama Bin Laden

> *Since the land is the parent, let the citizens take care of her more carefully than children do their mother.* — Plato

Georgist Theory of Value

> **Henry George's objective theory of value, holds that the objective value of a commodity is its price in an active market. However, this fails to account for land value.**

Georgists synthesize the objective and subjective theories of value. They hold that the objective value of a commodity is the price realized in an active market. Active market implies frequent trading by unaffiliated participants with competing interests on price.

It is likely that Henry George saw the parallels between his theory of value and the objective laws of thermodynamics and statistical mechanics that were big in his time. These objective laws emerged from the random motion of particles, just as objective value emerges from the random actions of a market.

While George's theory of value works well for commodities, it fails for land that has neither objective value nor a sufficiently active market. Unfortunately, George and many of his followers failed to see this.

Profits and Location Value

> **Location value is violently discontinuous. The main source of location value is profit from location. Most business profit is profit from location. To maximize profits in general, the most efficient user should occupy every property. Wages too, are a function of location. Collecting 100% of location value as rent would eliminate profits and cut into wages.**

The biggest roadblock to an adequate theory of land value is a failure to understand that true location value is violently discontinuous. The location value of one acre could be several million dollars annually, while an immediate neighboring property might be free land. Such an extreme variance might be due to a large noisy factory that generates millions in profit from its key location, but causes the neighboring land to be uninhabitable due to the noise, and not favorable to industry because it is off the road and rail tracks.

The main source of location value is profit from location. Take any business, put it in the heart of the Wyoming badlands and recalculate the profit. The difference is the profit from location value. Strictly speaking, we measure profit from location value by comparison with the same business on the nearest land where rent is free or nominal, but using the badlands emphasizes just how important location value is as a primary source of business profit.

Location value is not only the primary source of business profit, but a source of wages as well. We saw earlier that higher rents require higher wages. We need to be aware that returning 100% of the rent to the community could be as devastating to the business as moving it to the badlands.

The goal of a free economy is to maximize total profit. This occurs if the most efficient user occupies every property. But this will not occur if 100% of the location value is returned to the community.

Problems with Land Assessment

Land assessment is not the best way to generate ground rents. Because so many Georgists favor an assessor based LVT implementation, it is instructive to examine the serious problems with this approach.

Objective Scoring

> **How can an assessor determine land value? Any objective score can be positive, negative or neutral depending on business, culture, or individual preference. Land value can only be determined in a market.**

Location value is determined by location value profit of the most efficient user of that land. How can a land assessor determine location value? Is objectively scoring various features of the land viable?

Valuing land with objective scores for different location features is necessarily biased. Any given feature can be a positive, negative, or neutral depending on the business, culture or individual preferences. A nearby community center has no draw for most businesses, but if the town has no more need for residences, the land will go idle because of the higher rents. Idle land has a further dampening effect on growth. At the other extreme, airport noise is a negative for residences but business might make super profits due to proximity to transportation and lower rents. Both idle land and super-profits from location value, lead to a loss of revenue for the people.

Different businesses will price the same location with a different value based on need for raw materials, kind and size of labor force, nature of the customer base, and need for resources both natural and manmade. Individuals in search of a home will likewise use myriad subjective criteria in determining the perfect location.

The flaws of objective scoring, make it clear that location value cannot be measured outside of a market. In this respect, location value is very much like art; subjectively valued in absence of an active market.

Corruption

Required Reading

The difficulty of assessing value may not explain completely the observed inconsistency in current property tax assessments. Recent studies call the property tax assessment system "certainly among the most corrupt of urban functions."[FTN2.34] One commentator explained that "the actual work of valuing property is done by 'street level bureaucrats' over whom there is generally little effective supervision" and that assessing "is both discretionary and subjective, combining constant temptation with minimal likelihood of exposure. [FTN2.35, FTN2.36]

Other Biases

Required Reading

Mason Gaffney points out several land assessment biases. First, there is the wealth and power of landowners, and the selective responsiveness of courts to lawyers that only wealthy litigants can afford. [FTN2.37]

Gaffney also points out a time bias. The infrequency of assessment favors appreciating land. [FTN2.37]

The invisibility of minerals and the bias of whether or not to include visible minerals in the assessment of location value has no objective solution.

Perhaps one of the biggest biases against raising land values is the interdependence of land values. The assessor who raises one land value must raise several adjoining ones. This leads to a group of protestors all at once who can organize politically. Gaffney cites some well-known cases of this. [FTN2.37]

Problems with land assessment are not new:

> In a 1796 United States Supreme Court opinion, Justice William Paterson noted that leaving the valuation process up to assessors would cause numerous bureaucratic complexities, as well as non-uniform assessments due to imperfect policies and their interpretations[FTN2.21].

Certainly, there are many who believe that it is impossible to fairly assess valuation. I share this view with Libertarian Murray Rothbard[FTN2.21].

Comparable Sales

Required Reading

The most common response to the impossibility of assessing using subjective criteria or objective scoring, is that only objective comparable sales of unimproved land should be used in land assessment. This suffers from several serious defects, and some fatal ones as well. The serious defects are:

1. Sales of unimproved land are few and far between in precisely those areas where land is most valuable.
2. Even neighboring properties can have radically different location values due to the immediate environment.
3. Location value changes with time and each sale. Over time, use of land in the neighborhood can undergo radical changes. Every vacant lot that is sold and gets built usually increases the location value of neighboring land, but by how much?
4. Location value is significantly affected by changes outside the neighborhood, such as the opening or closing of a factory, or mall, or general economic conditions. Neighboring land that sold for $400,000/acre before the only employer in town shut their doors is no longer relevant to objective assessment.
5. Since we are looking at sales prices, it is always the location value of the less efficient seller and not the location value of the more efficient buyer. These can be orders of magnitude apart.
6. Sales price includes the location value of the improvements which is actually location value of the land that is often ignored by an assessor. For instance, a motel at the intersection of two interstates. If the assessor plans for a motel at that intersection by setting the location value sufficiently high, freedom is sacrificed in the name of planning.

Other defects with land assessment, discussed below, are more serious, or even fatal.

Location Monopoly

Required Reading

If all land in an area is owned by the same developer, with no sales by the developer as the land is improved, then there is no way to use comparable sales as a way to increase the assessed land tax. Tenant rents on improvements could reach the stratosphere and there would be no way to increase ground rents without taxing those improvements.

By selling select plots at very low prices, the developer generates comps that significantly lower assessed land tax.

Prior to a land value tax, land speculation tends to push the margin out. A land value tax based on comps will push the margin in. Speculation will be confined to a ring around the developed area, isolating it from comparable sales. Monopoly and collusion within the speculative ring will keep the land value tax low. Interestingly, the speculative ring is one strategy of the embryonic viral community to gain economic advantage, as discussed in *Volume II – The Plan*. Despite its utility in helping to spread Georgism, it is contrary to equitable rent collection.

Leverage and the High Location Value Land Tax

It is demonstrated that the higher the percent of location value taxed, the lower the land price, leading to land taxes that can be greater than the price of the land itself. A collusion between buyer and seller to reduce the nominal price of the unimproved land in the total transaction becomes inevitable. Not only does such a land tax fail to curb land speculation, but it delivers no revenue!

Is a fair tax for unimproved land the price of the land multiplied by the interest rate? Not really. That assertion has two assumptions that are today only approximately true today, and absolutely false when the tax is a high percentage of location value.

We define location value strictly as the annual amount a holder of land rights is willing to pay for those rights. Land has no objective value, but we can nonetheless define land value strictly as location value divided by the interest rate. Thus if a land rights owner is willing to pay $10,000 annually for a parcel of land and if the interest rate is 5%, then the land value for that parcel is $200,000 ($10,000 / .05).

Notice that this definition says nothing about either land price or a land tax. But there are certain relationships that are axiomatic. For one:

LAND_TAX + INTEREST_RATE x LAND_PRICE = LOCATION_VALUE (Eq. 1)

Since location value is what the land rights owner is willing to pay annually, and the land tax + interest on land price is what they will, in fact, pay, they will tend to be equal in a free market. That is, if the LVT (land value tax) is 70% location value, then interest on the land price will tend to be 30% location value in a perfect market.

When land is privately owned, LVT is a function of the interest rate and a government policy (e.g. 70% location value, 90% location value, 30% location value, etc.).

LAND_TAX = PERCENT_LOCATION x LOCATION_VALUE (Eq. 2)

Combining Equations 1 and 2,

INTEREST_RATE x LAND_PRICE =
          LOCATION_VALUE – PERCENT_LOCATION x LOCATION_VALUE (Eq. 3)

Dividing by interest rate and simplifying

LAND_PRICE = (LOCATION_VALUE/INTEREST_RATE) x (1 – PERCENT_LOCATION) (Eq. 4)

Using the definition of land value we get an alternate form of Equation 4.

LAND_PRICE = LAND_VALUE x (1 – PERCENT_LOCATION) (Eq. 5)

Regardless of the interest rate, if the policy calls for a land tax of 50% location value, the purchase price is 50% the land value. A rent of 90% location value produces a land price that is 10% of land value.

Assume the policy of the government is to eliminate land speculation. This means that land price must appreciate at a rate that is less than or equal to the cost of land which is simply the location value. We know that location value increases with the growth rate (population density and progress). If the speculator can make more money from land appreciation than is paid out in interest, speculation is profitable. So:

GROWTH_RATE x (1 – PERCENT_LOCATION) < INTEREST_RATE will stop speculation.

Thus, if the GROWTH_RATE is 10% and the INTEREST_RATE is 5%, then the PERCENT_LOCATION must exceed 50% to prevent speculation. However, it is not uncommon in hot areas for land prices to double in a years' time. And interest rates in recent history are far less than 5%.

With a GROWTH_RATE of 30% (land doubles ever 2.5 years) and an INTEREST_RATE of 3%, a tax of 90% location value is required to stop speculation.

In general, most advocates of an LVT believe the tax should be 80% of location value or higher.

Because location value is subjective, or objective only for a specific business or culture, and based on un-measurables such as progress and efficient density, land tax needs to be defined in terms of land price. Rearranging equation 4,

LOCATION_VALUE = LAND_PRICE x INTEREST_RATE/(1 – PERCENT_LOCATION) (Eq. 6)

And substituting into Equation 2,

LAND_TAX = PERCENT_LOCATION x LAND_PRICE x INTEREST_RATE/(1 – PERCENT_LOCATION) (Eq. 7)

Let PERCENT_LOCATION = .90, LAND_PRICE=$10,000, INT=.05 then
RENT = $4,500, LOCATION_VALUE = $5,000, LAND_VALUE = $100,000

The beauty of these equations belies the fatal problems that emerge when taken together with George's most important natural law: people will attempt to satisfy their desires with the least exertion. As the equations demonstrate, the common mental image of land tax as perhaps 5% of land price is utterly false. Instead, LVT is infinitesimally close to land price at 100% location value, and 90% of land price at 90% location value.

The buyer not only pays the land price to the seller, but pays almost the same land price every year thereafter to the people. It is clearly in the interest of the buyer to pay as little as possible for the land. In fact, the buyer will pay a premium to the seller in exchange for a lower LVT going forward.

A market is made when the interests of buyer and seller are opposite. In the case of land sales with an LVT, the interests of buyer and seller are the same: land must represent the smallest possible fraction of the total transaction. This then is not a market, but a collusion.

If unimproved land is the total transaction then buyer and seller must make sure that that is not the case. If the land has a location value to the buyer of $5,000, he will gladly pay $6,000 to the seller for a finger-painting done by the seller's child in kindergarten, and in a separate transaction, $1 for the land. While such collusive agreements are not enforceable in courts, they are enforceable by custom and in the rare event the seller reneges on the land deal, after selling the finger-painting, or the buyer reneges on the painting after buying the land, they are enforced by organized crime.

The extreme leverage gained from LVT equaling a high percentage of location value allows the owner of a very large development to sell a plot of land for $1 with no counter-transaction at all. This would provide a comparable sale that would cause LVT on the development to plummet, creating vast profits from location value, and ironically, making land speculation quite profitable.

In fact, we can guess that the amount of land speculation that is made profitable from the leverage of high percentages of location value is equal to the speculation made unprofitable by the same high percentages. In other words, we reach the shocking conclusion that a land value tax has absolutely no effect on land speculation!

Furthermore, by collusive agreements and speculative frenzy, land prices will be pushed to zero universally. Rents follow suit. We state the second shocking conclusion that a land value tax delivers no revenue!

These conclusions are unfair to the extent that peer pressure and regulation prevent collusive transactions below some point, perhaps 50% location value. This is consistent with the positive effects of LVT today in some communities. However, both the profitability and temptation for collusion increase exponentially with LVT above 50% location value.

I define the Ostrom-Hardin tipping point as that point in a continuum where personal benefit so exceeds benefit to the commons that all social sanctions against the behavior disappear. (A further discussion of Elinor Ostrom, Garret Hardin, and the tragedy of the commons is found in Chapter 4.) The percent of location value taxed is such a continuum. Once we pass the Ostrom-Hardin tipping point, the tragedy of the commons takes hold, collusion becomes universal, and the above conclusions become absolute.

Moral Hazard and Assessor Criteria

Required Reading

There is a problematic moral hazard associated with a land value tax. As shown above, the tax naturally eats its own tax base. To preserve the base, dishonest and corrupt behavior is essential. The form of that dishonest and corrupt behavior is determined by the criteria employed by the assessor; objective, subjective, or a combination.

If a land assessor uses only objective criteria in determining land value, over time, all land prices and rents approach as a limit the objective value of land, which is $0, as individuals are encouraged to engage in immoral behavior. If the only tax is the land value tax, feudalism is the preferable outcome to barbarism or extinction. Feudalism would result because all government services would cease and protection services would be privately owned and offered in exchange for fealty.

On the other hand, if a land assessor uses only subjective criteria in determining land value, all assessed valuation approaches as a limit the subjective value of land which is arbitrarily large (subsistence for all "non-connected" exclusive users). Assessors are encouraged to engage in immoral behavior. Totalitarianism, barbarism, or extinction are the possible outcomes.

If a land assessor uses both objective and subjective criteria, the extremes will be avoided, however, society will be corrupt and immoral. Services will be underfunded and the land tax will be too high for those without sufficient clout.

The Land Value Tax is an Oxymoron

Required Reading

The land value tax is a contradiction in and of itself. Land has no objective value. In a Georgist society there is no market for land! The payments that normally go to a bank as interest, go to the community instead. The land purchase price is zero, nominal, or equal to a small down payment. It is arbitrary and capricious in its relationship to land value.

- **Axiom: If rent is based on 100% of location value, then all land is free.**

- Corollary: As soon as land develops a price, it is undervalued
- Corollary: If a buyer pays a price for land which causes an upward reassessment then they are paying for the land twice.

Land cannot effectively be owned by an individual and taxed on its location value! **Land must be rented from the commons.** Although there are some land value tax implementations that use the principles I develop in the next section, and which might be useful in negotiations for capitulation, they are little more than a disguised rental of land in the commons, and present a possible moral hazard through obfuscation. I will not speak of a land value tax again.

Rental of the Commons

How Can We Solve the Problems of Land Assessment

Required Reading

- How can we end land speculation?
- How can the most efficient producer have the best land?
- How can we have all land be free and collect an equitable location value?
- How can we eliminate mendacity in land transactions?
- How can we completely eliminate objective criteria, subjective criteria, and the assessor bureaucracy?
- How can we have fully funded government services, a safety net through which none can fall, and enthusiasm in the paying of ground rents?

Consider the words of Dr. Sun Yat Sen, a Georgist and father of modern China.

How indeed can the price of the land be determined? I would advocate that the landowner himself should fix the price. The landowner reports the value of his land to the government and the government levies a land tax accordingly...

The government makes two regulations: first, that it will collect taxes according to the declared value of the land; second, that it can also buy back the land at the same price...

According to my plan, if the landowner makes a low assessment, he will be afraid lest the government buy back his land at that value and make him lose his property; if he makes too high an assessment, he will be afraid of the government taxes according to this value.

...he will certainly not want to report the value of his land too high or too low; he will strike a mean and report the true market price to the government FTN2.26

Self-assessment

> **With self-assessment and land seizure, people will always pay what the land is worth to them. For the most efficient user, this is, by definition, the true ground rent. AFFEERCE self-assessment differs from Sun Yat-Sen's in that all land is owned by the commons and individuals and business, not government, can seize the land.**

There are major differences between Sun's system and AFFEERCE self-assessment.

1. Sun talks of the landowner, but in collection theory, all land is part of the commons.

2. Sun gives the government the right to set taxes and/or seize land. In collection theory, these are rights of individuals and business, not governments.

3. Sun's land valuations are static or annual at best. Collection theory requires a continuous market of land value without jeopardizing exclusive use or the ground rent revenue stream to the people.

In a self-assessed system, the renter decides on the amount of rent they will pay. If the rent is too low, they risk having their land seized by someone who will pay a much higher rent.

The Synthesis of Objectivism and Subjectivism

A philosophy called the synthesis of objectivism and subjectivism is behind the motivation and implementation of the collection and distribution of rents.

We have seen the failure of land assessment using objective criteria, subjective criteria, or a compromise between the two. Self-assessment is something totally new, a market approach that eliminates all of the problems seen in the last section. I consider it to be part of a grand synthesis. For those readers interested in philosophy, here are some important points about the synthesis of objectivism and subjectivism.

- Basis for self-assessment in collection theory
- Basis for the proper distribution of rents in distribution theory
- George's theory of value is part of the synthesis, works for commodities, but has no relevance to land
- A superset of the synthesis of individualism and collectivism
- Extends beyond politics and economics to all disciplines including the sciences and philosophy
- Firmly rooted in the idea that truth is found in Nature
- I believe it will replace postmodernism in the next epoch

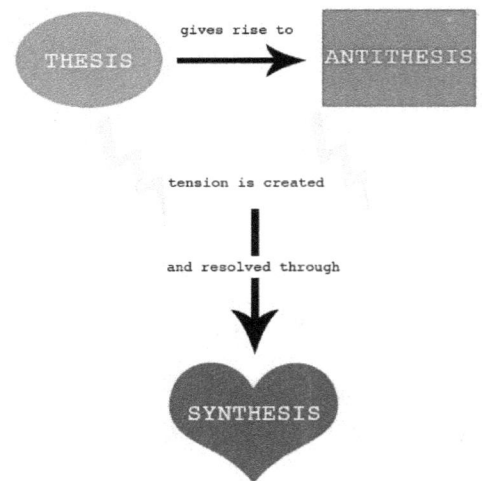

THESIS — gives rise to → ANTITHESIS

tension is created

and resolved through

SYNTHESIS

The Basis for Common Ownership of the Land

Every piece of land, now owned, was initially acquired through violence. Land is a gift of nature that is the joint property of all living creatures. Exclusive use of a parcel of land requires payment of rent to the people.

Once upon a time, the land belonged to all inhabitants of Earth, including the nomadic peoples. When humanity became agrarian, the notions of land ownership, private property, and territory, developed. It was reasonable to assert "This field, in which I have planted wheat, no longer belongs to the collective. It belongs to me."

Because all land was stolen initially, there is no moral impediment to stealing it again. War never displaced the rightful owner of the land, because there are no rightful owners. Some claim using the land productively created ownership rights. But, what if the land could be used even more productively by others?

Land, a gift of nature, is the joint property of all living creatures. This is not a naïve view contradicting economic efficiency. The principle does not mean we should all share collectively in the administration of a property. Unfettered use of land by a single owner is required for free enterprise to prosper. But this right to exclusive use, protected by the state, is won by paying rent to the real owners; the inhabitants of Earth. That rent is based on the land's current potential, as derived from the surrounding community and nature, and as determined by the free market. Although the land is the joint property of all living creatures, humans, by virtue of their ability to reason and treat other species with respect, in harmony with the balance of nature, have special rights to the land.

U.S. Land Use

In 2002, 60 million acres or 2.6% of U.S. land was residential or commercial. This is the primary source of ground rent.

While the idea of a nation might be artificial, elimination of national borders is not possible until all human inhabitants share equally in the Earth's bounty within their nation. Therefore, following text is specifically geared to the United States and its vast land reserves.

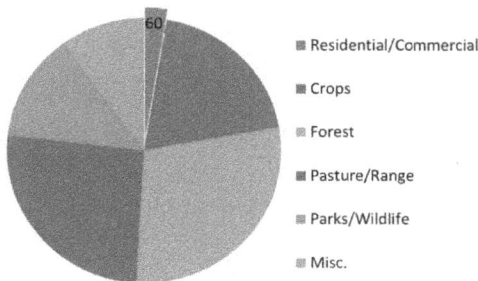

The United States has 2.3 billion acres of land, yet only 60 million acres is residential or commercial. In 2002, major uses were forest land, 651 million acres (28.8 percent); grassland pasture and range land, 587 million acres (25.9 percent); cropland, 442 million acres (19.5 percent); special uses (primarily parks and wildlife areas), 297 million acres (13.1 percent); miscellaneous other uses, 228 million acres (10.1 percent); and residential/commercial land, 60 million acres (2.6 percent).[FTN2.01]

Today, land ownership is shrouded in secrecy. This legacy of the Earth's inhabitants has been hijacked by governments, hoarded by speculators, and restricted by zoning and other regulations. The United States is likely among the worst offenders; 228 million acres for miscellaneous other uses indeed!

How many of those 442 million acres of cropland are being used efficiently? Some acres can produce annual profits of thousands per acre on specialty crops[FTN2.29], but average Midwestern grains bring in from $56 to $246 per acre[FTN2.30], and Great Plains wheat, only $29 to $37 per acre[FTN2.31]. On the other hand, a factory might produce a million dollars or more on that same acre. For many people it would be worth far more than $246/acre to live on that land, as opposed to a crowded apartment building. Allowing market forces to work would nibble away at our least productive farmland causing food prices to rise.

The least productive 15% of farmland is equal to all the urban land in the United States; all the cities and all the suburbs combined. So putting that land to more productive use would make it seem as though the size of the country doubled. Currently, the government of the United States makes certain this does not happen by using tax dollars to subsidize unproductive farms. AFFEERCE provides an easy way to restore the free market to agriculture, using the ground rent and food distribution as tools. This solution, discussed later in this chapter, is painless for both the consumer and the farmer.

There are 228 million acres for miscellaneous other uses. About 58 million is under treaty to Native Americans [FTN2.02], who would have the option of joining the Georgist economy of AFFEERCE, even as they maintain their tribal government. Some of the remaining acres are badlands, but no doubt much of it is perfectly good land for residence and commerce, government owned, sitting idle, going to waste. They say that our frontier days are over, but the numbers tell a different story. Our best frontier days lie ahead!

Chapter 2 – Collection of the Ground Rents

How does ground rent translate into freedom and a new frontier? How does it increase productivity dramatically? How can it pay for nutritious meals, warm and safe shelter, quality medical care and unlimited free education for all? The answer lies in trebling.

Trebling

Beware the Treblers?

Required Reading

The treblers are not alien creatures, although they might be feared. A trebler is a person who seeks profit and productivity and they seek to earn it on YOUR land! By trebling the current ground rent you pay and paying you 150% for improvements, the land becomes theirs. Hasta la vista, baby!

What kind of world is it where anybody with enough money can seize your land? Actually, not all that different from today where it is foolish not to sell land for the right price. The differences are:

1. You have already been compensated for the land. You are just a renter from the commons with exclusive rights to the land.
2. The compensation for your improvements will be considerably greater than depreciated value.
3. As long as you are willing to match the trebled rent, the land rights remain yours.
4. The land seizure or rent increase on your part will measurably decrease the rental expenses of every person in the nation and allow for population growth.
5. You will receive a full refund of the one year of rents paid in advance or provided as compensation for the land.

With all these benefits….To paraphrase an old Henny Youngman joke, "Take my land…Please!"

The trebler might be an entrepreneur who uses trebling to enhance or acquire an existing enterprise, or to develop new enterprises around trebling opportunities. Some will treble to satisfy the ancient bloodlust of land conquest. Whether this will disappear with the AFFEERCE enlightenment is anybody's guess. Dominion trebling in the panarchy and competition of the cellular aristocracy will also change the geography of city states and other regions. The need of many animal species for territory is well-documented, and that base instinct is certainly present in mankind as well. Unlike wars of the past, satisfaction of this need through trebling will lead to unimaginable wealth for the nation, without violence.

Online Trebling System

The online trebling system has detailed information and maps of every property in the country. It is used to initiate a treble or an auction and record property improvements. The database allows sophisticated search.

Trebling is done through an online system integrated with the VIP (biometric currency and related systems) and freely available to all. The smallest and most common unit of land in the database will be a square yard; at property boundaries, the unit will be less than two square yards. There are 4,840 square yards in an acre, resulting in slightly more than 12 trillion units of land in the United States. These plots of land are associated with attributes.

Units can be individually owned, and contiguous units are called a property. If each unit contributed equally to the ground rent, the revenue required for universal distribution, about $4.2 trillion would come to .44 per unit per year, or almost 4 cents a month per square yard. With only 2.6% of the land currently sporting homes and industry (excluding farmland), the average rent must be about $12 per square yard, or $1/sq. yard/month. This is equal to $59,000/acre/year. Yet this is only an average. Actual rents will range two orders of magnitude (100 times) or more, higher or lower.

The entrepreneur uses the online system to search for parcels with specific attributes, such as the following sample searches.

1. Lowest ground rent property in Chicago.
2. Queens, New York where depreciated improvements are greater than $10,000 and less than $20,000.
3. Unclaimed lands within 100 miles of Denver.
4. Cropland with soil feldspar > 50% in Kansas
5. Pennsylvania forest with at least 80% 20 year old timber.
6. Properties with abandoned buildings in Cincinnati.

How could the database contain such detailed information? If it were compiled by a government bureaucracy, the system would be expensive, inaccurate and for the most part, useless. Instead, the land rights owner has an economic incentive to record improvements: maximum compensation if the land is trebled. The VIP aids in automating this process when expenditures are associated with properties. Personal, family, or donated labor can be imputed according to an objective value system.

Failure to maintain accurate and updated information places the objective value of the property at the mercy of an appraisal which is generally lower. For instance, the cost of adding a garage is far greater than the appraised increase. For those who keep records, the objective value of the property is the greater of depreciated recorded value or appraisal. The online system acts as a personal accounting system and profit engine for properties, publicly available to the nation. When selling a property (presumably an event more common than trebling) prospective buyers will expect to see a complete description and history of the property online. Such public and accurate accounting greatly increases the liquidity of property which further increases the productivity of the nation.

How does Trebling Work

> **In conjunction with the online land system and VIP, the trebler places 3x, one year of the current rent, in escrow and purchases an appraisal of the improvements, escrowing the greater of 150% of the appraised or recorded objective depreciated value. The current land rights owner can match or accept the treble.**

How does a trebler seize land? While the procedure will be fine-tuned in the 60 years prior to capitulation, here is a good working version.

1. A trebling is initiated through the online land system.
2. The online land system interfaces with the VIP to escrow 3 or more times the annual effective ground rent on the property. (Effective rent = rent x current multiplier – *discussed below*).
3. Regardless of record keeping, the trebler purchases an appraisal through the land system from a random pool of local appraisers.
4. When the appraisal comes back, the land system interfaces with the VIP to escrow 150% of the greater of the appraised value and depreciated value from the property owner's records + property severance costs. (This huge premium serves to adequately discourage trebling of recently improved and well-maintained properties).

5. If the discrepancy between the land rights owner's records and the appraisal is greater than 30%, the trebler can demand a docket in Chancery Court, surrendering the universal $35 deductible. (The judge will reverse this if fraud or mischief is discovered on the part of land rights owner).

6. The online land system informs the property owner of the trebling. They are notified whenever they use the VIP for transactions and must respond that they have read the notification. They then have 3 days to respond.

7. The property owner has three options.

    A. Accept the 150% package and agree to vacate in one months' time.

    B. Respond to the trebling by raising their ground rent to match the trebled value. While the trebler could have initially more than trebled the rent to decrease the likelihood of this response, now they are forced to re-treble, if they wish to pursue the property. A re-treble does not require a new appraisal.

    C. Respond to the treble in chancery court if the appraisal does not accurately reflect the objective value of the improvements, if the treble will create a hardship not covered in the standard schedule of land severance costs, or if this is an illegal partial property treble. The property owner will surrender the universal $35 deductible. The judge will reverse this, if this is an illegal partial property treble.

8. When the trebling has closed, the escrowed ground rent goes to the Treasury, where the multiplier for the entire nation is adjusted downward. Ground rent is paid a year in advance, so the original property owner's rent advance is refunded.

Anatomy of a Treble

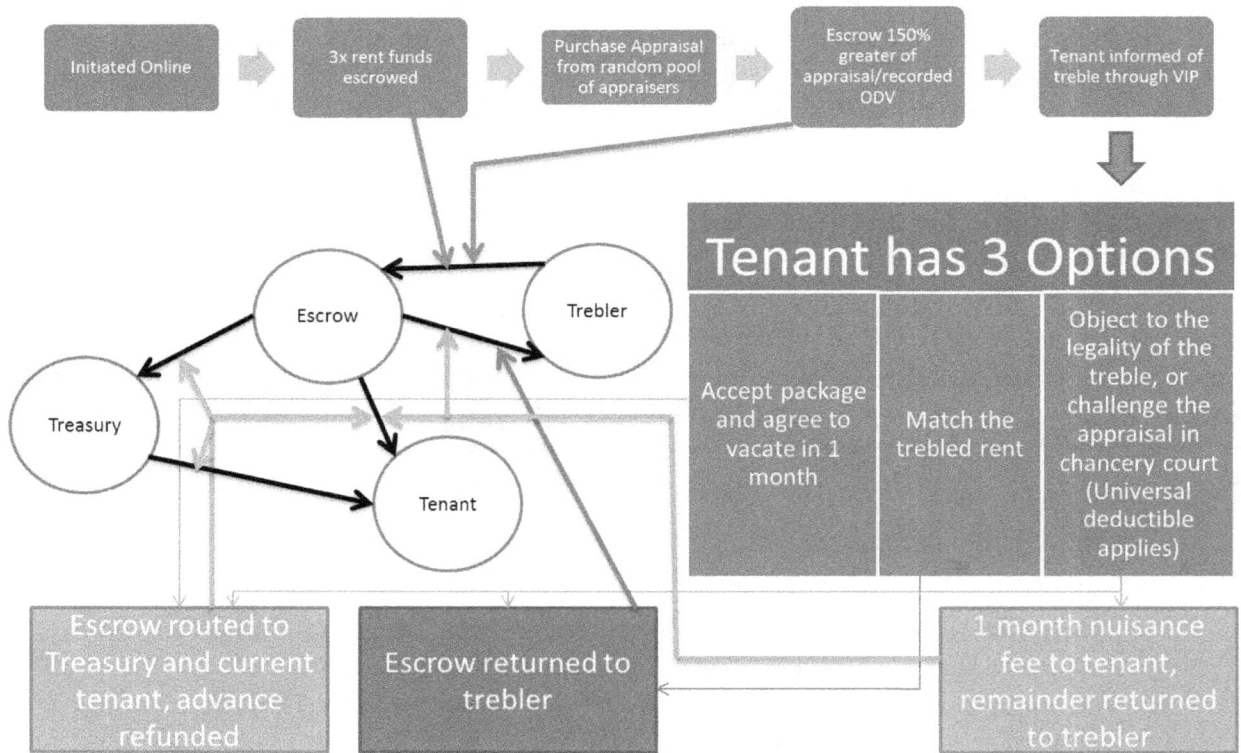

Zero Sum

> **Limited to a 10% drop annually, whenever ground rents are raised anywhere, non-frozen rents are lowered everywhere else. Once established, the ground rent for any property will drop on a regular basis, ultimately down to the minimum $12 per year. Only the land rights owner can raise their own rent or freeze it.**

Zero-sum is often used in the negative to describe ownership of limited resources. But here it is used to describe the relationship between the collection of ground rents and their distribution. In particular, the size of the distribution package is fixed for each person. Given zero population growth, the total fixed distribution does not change.

Zero-sum is a misnomer for the actual balancing procedure performed by the Treasury. But simplistically, whenever the ground rents in one area increase, they must decrease everywhere else, so that the total ground rent is constant. To handle this, there is a fractional multiplier that decreases with every increase in rent. For those who do not freeze their ground rent, the rent owed is the self-assessed rent times the multiplier. Later, when we examine the relatively simple calculus of productivity, population, ground rents and the multiplier, you will discover that the controlling parameter is a multiplier that decreases at a constant rate. This is tasked to the Treasury.

In a sense, the ground rent is voluntary. If you allow your rent to fade away over time, the government will not come after you. More significantly, they will not protect "your land" from those who do.

Because the ground rent is constantly and uniformly decreasing, there is a single value maintained at the United States Treasury Department called the rent multiplier. The multiplier begins at 1 and decreases until it hits .01, at which time all rents are divided by 100, and the multiplier is renormalized to 1. If one's rent was $5000 per year at the start of such a period, it would be $50 at the end without intervention. At a constant rent rate of fall of 10% annually, this complete cycle of the multiplier would take about 25 years.

What if the Ground Rent isn't Paid?

Required Reading

The ground rent is automatically charged against the housing distributions for family members. In most cases, the distributions will be sufficient. For those who must come up with additional funds each month, failure to pay will cause a lien against improvements. Improvements, to the extent they are encumbered, are only payable by the trebler at 100%, instead of 150% for unencumbered improvements. Furthermore, any freeze on the rents will be removed. As the rent drops and more of the improvements are available at 100% objective depreciated value (ODV), the probability of trebling increases, as well as the probability that the land rights owner can catch up.

Trebling Law

> **Trebling law has never existed, so all precedents in chancery court will either be fresh or resolved during the 60 embryonic years. These will likely have to do with partial property trebles, time to vacate, and severance costs, if any. Other issues relate to personal property and proprietary signage.**

The property owner has the right to remove any personal property, but why bother moving refrigerators and other appliances when the trebler will pay 150% of their depreciated value. The original property owner not only saves on moving costs, but the trebler is paying the original owner for brand new appliances at their new location. However, the property owner must indicate in advance, in the online land system, moveable property to be treated as a land improvement. Appliances designated as part of the property are also subject to liens.

Trademarks and proprietary signage are not considered intellectual property and must be removed as provided for in existing statutes. The tear down/transplant cost of a working factory can be prohibitive. This is at the discretion of the property owner, who can leave the factory intact for a substantial 50% profit. The current land rights owner is cautioned that removing critical components from machines can render their objective value worthless. If the machines contained intellectual property of the original land rights owner, the original land rights owner will continue to receive intellectual property distribution payments for the same product produced on those machines by the new owner. This is true of intellectual property, in general, and has nothing to do with trebling per se. The intellectual property distribution is discussed in *Chapter 3 – Intellectual Property Distribution*.

If all parties agree, chancery court can be conducted in a video conference on the online land system to expedite matters. Should the trebler change his mind or lose the case in chancery court, one month of the escrowed trebled ground rent would be given to the original property owner as a nuisance fee.

Mortgages and liens are paid off first from proceeds. If the mortgage is more than 50% under water, the bank loses.

Monopoly of Location Value

Required Reading

It is impossible to stop monopoly of location value. If we could measure fine enough, for any given business, there is one and only one property where business profits will be maximized. In some cases, it is not a question of an insignificant differential between properties but one where unique resources are critical to operations.

Trebling and land seizure give the monopoly to the most efficient user of the land. This is opposed to assessment of land value which either keeps the property idle or gives the monopoly to cronies.

How Trebling Determines a Fair Ground Rent

Required Reading

Our major goals with self-assessment are:

1. Eliminate land speculation
2. Encourage development
3. Eliminate corruption, mendacity, and bureaucracy
4. Provide plenty of free land (nominal rent)
5. Provide sufficient revenue for universal distribution
6. Keep the economy on an even keel
7. Maximize business profits by allowing the most efficient user access to the land

With self-assessment, none of these goals are at cross-purposes. There is no other system that maximizes any one of them better, let alone all of them.

It is fundamental to trebling that if one pays a ground rent of 34% net profits from location value of the most efficient business on that property, then no trebler can profit from the land in the first year. Less efficient businesses who have attachments to the property must pay the same rent. This rent has nothing to do with the profits of the less efficient business. Rent is only a function of the most efficient business.

However, 34% net profits from location value of the most efficient business on the land does not assure treble safety. Because rent falls by a constant, assumed now to be 10%, every year, the trebler might forego profits in the first few years, if the land is sufficiently profitable in subsequent years.

As we have seen, it is a problem of impossible complexity to determine the location value of the most efficient business on a property. If a neighborhood has no grocery store, somebody is going to get trebled, although zoning covenants can be purchased (discussed below). Once land has been captured for a grocery store, a second grocery store is not as efficient, allowing residents to let their ground rents fall, although the very presence of the first grocery store might counter this by increasing location value for residents. We don't know and we don't care. The market liberates us from these concerns. There are no land assessors and being trebled is free money.

When location value of the most efficient business is unclear, the greatest benefit to both the individual and society is to allow ground rents to fall without fear and either match or accept the treble when it comes. The individual benefits by living without fear of the trebler, paying the minimum ground rent possible over time, and/or collecting a 50% premium on ODV. Society benefits by having access to the best land available to the most efficient businesses.

Because ground rents are paid a year in advance (discussed below), taking the optimal path requires sufficient liquid funds to match the treble, if that is the intention. Freezing rents at a higher level to avoid the trebler altogether will likely be a more costly option.

Ironically, high ground rents will have no influence on an order of magnitude trebler. If the trebler is going to replace a three-flat with an office tower and raise the rent by a factor of 30 over a fair rent for a three-flat at that location, then even if the three-flat owners were paying a rent 10 times higher than the fair rent, it would have absolutely no effect on the trebler's bottom line.

The best way to thwart the office tower trebler is to improve the property. Material and labor must be paid at 150% ODV. After paying 150% for the well-kept building, the trebler needs to demolish it. This will have a significant effect on the bottom line of treblers. All things being equal, the trebler will set their sights on run-down property.

It is very likely that if a homeowner keeps their home in perfect shape, they will ultimately pay only a nominal ground rent. While Georgists often claim that improvements on a property have no effect on that property's land assessment, a doubtful claim with land assessors, only with self-assessment/land-seizure can improvements actually lead to lower rents or even nominal rent.

Treble Equilibrium

People will attempt to satisfy their desires with the least amount of exertion. Most will allow ground rents to fall until they are trebled. The trebler will decide based on factors such as profit from location, improvement depreciation, the rate of fall of the rent multiplier, and the risk free rate of return. At a certain point, the rent becomes so low that the probability of a treble is 100%. This is called the treble point. With a 10% rate of fall of the rent multiplier, once trebled, ground rents return to their pre-trebled value in just over 11 years.

For recently improved and well-maintained property, particularly property where the land rights owner has frozen the ground rent, normal transfers might predominate over trebling. However, a natural law, proposed by Henry George suggests that trebling will be quite common: People will attempt to satisfy their desires with the least amount of exertion.

This means people will attempt to pay the smallest possible ground rent, especially since this is both in their own best interest as well as in the best interest of the collective.

The phrase "net rents" refers to rents received from tenants (after business expenses), or other profits from location value. It is very different than the term "ground rents" which is the money paid to the people for exclusive use of the land. However, the ground rent is likely a function of the net rent for the most efficient business. And net rent is often used as a synonym for location value, as in "The ground rent is 30% location value" or equivalently, "The ground rent is 30% net rent." Where there is any ambiguity, the generic "rent" will be qualified with "net" or "ground", or rarely some other qualifier.

As the ground rents on business properties fall below 30% net rent, they will be trebled to 90% net rent (location value). Notice that this still produces a profit of 10% on location value, even if the same business is maintained. Nevertheless, with the interest on 1 year's advance ground rent and 150% ODV, this likely will be a loss. The rate of fall of the rent multiplier determines whether or not this treble will occur. The technically false, but useful, meme of zero-sum means that twice the trebled ground rent (new ground rent is 3 times the old rent, minus the old rent, equals twice the old rent) is used to reduce everyone's ground rent (including the trebler's).

The Treasury is tasked with the job of keeping the rent rate of fall, constant, and at a level where the average existing business is trebled at 30% location value to 90% location value, capturing, on average about 69% of location value. The desired rent rate of fall is a function of the treble point and the interest rate. **The treble point is defined as a ground rent at the lowest percentage of the net rent that either produces a profit exceeding the risk free rate of return in every year, or produces a total rate of return by the 12th year that is 12x higher than the risk free rate of return.** Assume for now that the desired rate of fall is 10%. That means 5% of all ground rents must be trebled annually. (This is not renters but rents and can be better understood in table 2.6 below.) The tiers will not develop perfectly evenly and in some years less than 5% of rents will be trebled and in others, more than 5%. We will examine this more closely in *Chapter 6 – Balance of the RCs and the Treasury.*

After many years, renters will be distributed evenly between 30% and 90% location value with an uncounted group residing on free land and outliers below 30% and above 90%.

If 5% of the total ground rents, paying 30% of location value, are trebled, then 15% of the total rents will be paying 90% of location value. In the table below, renters are divided into 11 tiers representing the 11 year journey from ground rents of 90% location value to ground rents of 30% location value.

Percent of location value	Percent of total rents
90%	15%
81	14%
72	13%
66	12%
59	11%
53	10%
48	9%
43	8%
39	7%
35	6%
31	5%
Table 2.6 - Distribution of rents at 30% treble point	

From this table we compute that trebling results in an average ground rent of 69% location value as determined by the most efficient user of the location. This leaves 31% of location value for business profit. Notice that the 69% is independent of the rate of fall. Regardless of the number of years it takes to drop from 90% to 30%, the average rent is always 69% of location value, for those properties where trebling occurs at 30% location value on average.

How Ground Rent Is Paid

> **Ground rent is paid a year in advance at acquisition, and then month to month thereafter. Provided there are no past due ground rents, the one year advance will be refunded when the property is relinquished.**

Ground rent is paid a year in advance at purchase, auction or trebling seizure. At capitulation, landowners will be compensated with credit for a year's advance rent. The rent is then paid month to month thereafter, so there is always one full year of rent in reserve.

The one year advance payment protects the people from default. Failure to pay ground rent in a timely manner will cause a lien to be placed on property improvements and any self-assessed rent freeze to be lifted. The size of the lien might be equal to the rent owed plus 4%. The lien is subtracted from ODV and can be trebled at 100%.

Suppose the objective depreciated value of improvements is $90,000. Typically, the trebler would compensate the owner at 150%, or $135,000. However, if there was a $40,000 lien, the trebler would pay the lien at 100%, or $40,000. The remaining $50,000 of unencumbered improvements would be paid to the land rights owner at 150%, or $75,000. With the lien, the trebler pays a total of $115,000, saving $20,000. The former land rights owner collects under $80,000 as opposed to $135,000, with the people collecting $40,000 plus 4% interest.

The falling ground rent of property under lien not only entices treblers, but gives the property owner a chance to remove liens by catching up on rent payments. If the lien covered all rents in arrears, and interest, the former land rights owner would receive 100% refund of their one year advance payment of rent, assuming they vacate in one month's time.

If land is leased to build a project that fails, the best way to receive a maximum refund of advance payment is to relinquish all claims to the land, triggering an online land auction. In rent auctions, the winner pays the second highest bid. The difference is the amount of rent the most efficient user of the land can justly retain. This bid amount, up to the rent currently being paid, is the rent that can be refunded from the full 12 month advance. Because of subscriptions to land auction alerts, auctions can begin without notice and last up to 24 hours.

Most citizens will live in diverse urban or suburban communities and won't pay a penny of their own money for ground rent. They will never be trebled, go to chancery court, or worry about losing their property. By choosing not to live in an extremely hot area one cannot afford, rapidly developing rural areas, eschewing a large estate, and not involving oneself in the competitions of exotic cultures, the entire brouhaha is avoided. One simply profits from the bounty.

Trebling and Bank Loans (Trebler Mortgages)

> **A trebler mortgage covers the one year advance payment of rent, while a standard mortgage does not. As the ground rent drops each year, refunds from the advance payment are used to repay principle. Because the rent rate of fall tends to fall much faster than changes increasing business or location risk, defaults for businesses with an initial viable plan, will be unlikely, although bank risk increases when ODV exceeds 3 time location value. Worksheet examples later in the text assume a 23 year trebler mortgage.**

It is expected that a typical home mortgage in an AFFEERCE economy will not cover the 1 year advance payment of ground rents. These will be carried over from property to property and are inexpensive compared to the home. It is expected that mortgages on improvements will be 3% down, 3% principle, and 3% interest which translates to a mortgage length of about 23 years.

A trebler mortgage might require 20% down, 3% principle, and 3% interest. It will cover the 1 year advance payment of rent. Until such time as the ground rent becomes safe and efficient, a trebler will always take advantage of the 10% rent rate of fall. Each month, the monthly advance payment will be exactly 10% too large. Instead of being refunded to the trebler, it is used to pay off the principle. This allows the bank or citizen investor (See *Chapter 6 - Economic Principles*) to safely issue a mortgage even when improvement value is as much as three times location value. Keep in mind that the improvement is under water to start with at 150% ODV. However, in the case where location value is greater than or equal to improvement value, the bank receives principle payments equal to 33% of the loan in the first year (20% down + 3% principle + 10% rent refund). If such a business is viable at trebled rents, the bank will have received in the first year the entire premium to ODV, and have a loan outstanding to a business that is even more viable at rents that are 10% lower, and dropping. That is a dream loan.

A loan where improvement value is three time location value is riskier. But how much so? Consider a motel where net rent from location value is $666,667 and the current ODV is $2 million. Suppose the current owner pays a ground rent of 33.33% location value or $222,223/year. The trebler would need a package of $3 million for 150% ODV of the building and 100% of the location value, $666,667 for the trebled rent or $3,666,667. Consider the risk taken by the bank or citizen investor.

The trebler pays a down payment of 20% or $733,333. In the unlikely event there is a new treble while the loan is still being repaid, the entire 1 year advance ground rent payment, and the new trebler's 150% ODV first go to repay the loan, so the creditor is fully protected. Below is the amortization table for this trebler mortgage, compounded yearly.

3% trebler mortgage where ODV = 3 x LV, Rent freeze in Year 9

Year	Principle at Start	Rent	P&I Payment	Interest (3%)	Principle from falling rents	Principle from P&I	100% ODV	1 year advance	Bank Default Risk
1	$2,933,334	$666,667	$176,000	$88,000	$66,667	$88,000	$2,000,000	$600,000	$333,333
2	$2,778,667	$600,000	$176,000	$83,360	$60,000	$92,640	$1,940,000	$540,000	$298,667
3	$2,626,027	$540,000	$176,000	$78,781	$54,000	$97,219	$1,881,800	$486,000	$258,227
4	$2,474,808	$486,000	$176,000	$74,244	$48,600	$101,756	$1,825,346	$437,400	$212,061
5	$2,324,452	$437,400	$176,000	$69,734	$43,740	$106,266	$1,770,586	$393,660	$160,206
6	$2,174,445	$393,660	$176,000	$65,233	$39,366	$110,767	$1,717,468	$354,294	$102,683
7	$2,024,313	$354,294	$176,000	$60,729	$35,429	$115,271	$1,665,944	$318,865	$39,504
8	$1,873,613	$318,865	$176,000	$56,208	$31,886	$119,792	$1,615,966	$286,978	($29,331)
9	$1,721,935	$286,978	$176,000	$51,658	$28,698	$124,342	$1,567,487	$286,978	($132,530)
10	$1,568,895	$286,978	$176,000	$47,067	$0	$128,933	$1,520,462	$286,978	($238,546)
11	$1,439,962	$286,978	$176,000	$43,199	$0	$132,801	$1,474,848	$286,978	($321,865)
12	$1,307,160	$286,978	$176,000	$39,215	$0	$136,785	$1,430,603	$215,212	($338,654)
13	$1,170,375	$286,978	$176,000	$35,111	$0	$140,889	$1,387,685	$286,978	($504,288)
14	$1,029,486	$286,978	$176,000	$30,885	$0	$145,115	$1,346,054	$286,978	($603,546)
15	$884,371	$286,978	$176,000	$26,531	$0	$149,469	$1,305,673	$286,978	($708,280)
16	$734,902	$286,978	$176,000	$22,047	$0	$153,953	$1,266,502	$286,978	($818,579)
17	$580,949	$286,978	$176,000	$17,428	$0	$158,572	$1,228,507	$286,978	($934,536)
18	$422,378	$286,978	$176,000	$12,671	$0	$163,329	$1,191,652	$286,978	($1,056,253)
19	$259,049	$286,978	$176,000	$7,771	$0	$168,229	$1,155,903	$286,978	($1,183,832)
20	$90,820	$286,978	$176,000	$2,725	$0	$173,275	$1,121,225	$286,978	($1,317,383)

The bank's default risk is eliminated by Year 7. The numbers assume no improvements are made to the property, that the property depreciates at a rate of 3%, and the maximum the bank can get for the property is 100% ODV. While a maximum risk of $333,333 in the first year seems high, keep in mind that if the bank felt that the business was viable after paying 150% ODV, certainly the business would be viable paying only the bank's default risk premium of $333,333 or 117% ODV, and that is if default occurs in the first month. The loan becomes more viable with every passing month.

If this example was analyzed in the "business takeover worksheet," discussed later, it would show that the treble was viable provided additional loans of $163,000, $101,223, and $44,260 were made at the start of the first three years. A positive profitability ratio of 6.12 in year 12 indicates medium viability. A profitability ratio of 12 or more is optimal.

Worksheet examples below will assume a 20/3/3 trebler mortgage unless stated otherwise.

Reasonable Use of the Land

Required Reading

Trebling cannot be used to divide another's property. The land seized must be contiguous, straight-edged for non-borders, and include at least one border of the property seized. Plot size can be restricted to customary sizes. If the seized land includes a boundary wall or fence, the judge can require rebuilding the boundary wall or fence.

If a treble does not change the dominion of the land, cellular zoning ordinances and other restrictions of the district must be followed. A dominion treble places the land under the new dominion's zoning, if any, however, purchased covenants cannot be broken. (See *Chapter 9 – Government, Law, and Justice*)

Objective Depreciated Value (ODV)

Required Reading

The objective depreciated value of improvements is based on the total investment of time and capital in building and improving structures on the land and features of the land, after application of standard depreciation tables. Imputed labor cost must be set to the regional average for the job. Nor can actual labor costs be applied at more than twice the regional average.

It is the responsibility of the property owner to enter all improvements into the property profile in the online land system, either automatically through the VIP (use of virtual cash for material purchase), or manually. Failure to enter improvements will result in an appraised valuation which is generally less than the cost of improvements.

The value does not include unattached personal property unless explicitly stated in the property profile as remaining with the land, in which case, it too is subject to depreciation. Likewise, attached property that will be removed on a treble must be explicitly excluded in the property profile.

Although the objective depreciated value of a property cannot fall below zero, certain property features subtract from positive value. These include, dumps, abandoned mining equipment, un-reforested timber cuts, non-code septic systems, and any non-coded systems deemed hazardous to children under age 14. Any structure, past its age of standard depreciation, with numerous code violations, despite cosmetic improvements and the availability of utilities, is apt to have an objective depreciated value of zero.

Covenants

A covenant is a usage restriction or requirement for land.

Jurisdictional Covenants

> **A district of the cellular democracy, by ratification of a majority of its citizens, can place a jurisdictional covenant on the land. These usage restrictions are limited to a tiny percentage of the dominion. Restricting trebler usage drives ground rents to a minimum reducing the cost of public goods.**

Land placed under jurisdictional covenant by a level of federation cannot exceed a set percentage of the dominion, based on level. Levels 2, 3, and 4 can each place up to 3% of their dominion under jurisdictional covenant. Levels 5, 6, and 7 can each place up to 2% of their dominion under jurisdictional covenant. Covenants are used for parks, zoos, schools, government buildings and palaces, chancelleries, sporting areas, wetlands, and historical landmarks, among others. Roads, with their driver and utility easements, are not counted in the maximum under jurisdictional covenant.

Jurisdictional covenants significantly lower the land value due to their usage restrictions. The more specific the covenant is, the lower the treble-safe ground rent. Jurisdictional covenants allow a governing district to pay low rent on public lands.

A jurisdictional covenant does not prevent trebling, although it restricts trebler usage. A dominion treble can explicitly break a jurisdictional covenant, since it will move the borderland under covenant into a different dominion. A dominion treble can implicitly break a jurisdictional covenant by reducing the size of the dominion causing existing land area under jurisdictional covenant to exceed the allotted 2% or 3%. A jurisdictional covenant can also be broken by a 2/3 plurality of a higher level of federation.

Parks, beaches and other attractions placed under jurisdictional covenant before capitulation will be assigned an initial ground rent of $12 per acre, if possible. The ability to do so will be determined by a qualitative assessment of the 60 million residential/commercial acres we have to work with. If those 60 million acres include beaches and parks, the rent will be higher. Whatever the initial rent, multiplier dynamics will likely drop the rent of jurisdictional covenants to the minimum $12 per acre over time.

A jurisdictional covenant on unclaimed land is invalid. Land is unclaimed if nobody will pay the minimum ground rent. For instance, Yellowstone Park has 2,219,823 acres. The minimum rent for the land is over $26 million. Within the park are various towns and tourist areas. It is possible that remote portions of the park will be unclaimed although Yellowstone will be a frequent recipient of the discretionary tax, and has many concessions.

Purchased Covenants

> **Covenants in excess of those allotted jurisdictions must be purchased. These insurance policies are used for zoning, and require large payouts from those who break the covenant to covenant members.**

These covenants generally apply to a large portion, if not 100% of the land within a dominion, and will be used for zoning. They are likely to be positive covenants such as "only single family homes" or negative covenants such as "no factories." Purchased covenants can be vetoed by 2/3 of the population within the lowest level of federation enclosing the covenant. The cost of a covenant might be 1 cent for every ten dollars of coverage, should the covenant be broken. The 1 cent premium is added to ground rent owed by each member of the covenant. Should any current or future land rights owner break the covenant, they must pay the full amount of coverage ($10 per penny of premium), in addition to their ground rent.

The full amount of coverage does not go to the Treasury, but is distributed among remaining members of the covenant as compensation. Coverage falls with the rent rate of fall multiplier.

If a property owner chooses to leave a covenant they no longer pay the premium, or are entitled to the distributions, however, they and future land rights owners on the property remain bound to the covenant and must pay the coverage as a ground rent surcharge if they break the covenant. The base amount of coverage is fixed on the day the land rights owner leaves the covenant and falls with the rent rate of fall multiplier. The relationship of the property to the covenant will be completely severed after 25 years, or until the covenant is no longer extant, whichever is less.

A dominion treble has no effect on a purchased covenant except that a new set of voters has veto power over the terms of the covenant. Multiple covenants can be combined into a single covenant as long as they each cover the exact same set of properties. Otherwise, covenants must be purchased separately.

A land rights owner who violates the covenant has one month from a verdict in chancery court to 1) rectify the violation, possibly including the payment of damages, 2) pay the coverage as a ground rent surcharge

Covenant Patterns

> **A covenant pattern is a small plot of land completely surrounded by a single property. As long as this plot remains completely surrounded by that property, an arbitrarily strict covenant can be established on the plot, and the land rights owner can allow the ground rent on that plot to drop so that it is easily sold or trebled.**

It is illegal to treble land completely surrounded by a single property that isn't your own. The exception is covenant patterns established by the land rights owner.

The covenant can have any degree of specificity, such as restricting trebling to a Walgreen's drugstore, or any drugstore, or any store selling over the counter medications, or a McDonalds, or any fast-food restaurant, or any restaurant open only for breakfast and lunch, or a luxury home meeting one of three architectural patterns. This is a free society, so the covenant could have provisions that some would find offensive.

Ball parks can use covenant patterns for their concessions. Public parks can use covenant patterns to allow vendors to open a carousel, petting zoo, food stand, or bike rental. Airports can use covenant patterns for restaurants and other vendors. Theme parks or themed communities can use covenant patterns to keep all homes and vendors in theme.

The owner of the surrounding land can expel a covenant pattern holder in chancery court. However, the land rights owner must pay the covenant pattern holder 150% of all improvements permitted by the covenant. Improvements not permitted by the covenant will not be compensated.

The covenant pattern is the building block of the planned community or private city. Wealthy entrepreneurs can use covenant patterns to create their dreams. Private counties (owned by very wealthy counts) can use nested covenant patterns to position future cities along the transportation infrastructure of the county.

A community can expand its borders with a dominion treble. Afterward, covenant patterns aid in re-architecting conquered lands while shifting the ground rent burden to loyal subjects.

Ground Rent and Industry

Hostile Takeover

When a factory or business is trebled for similar use by the trebler, this is called a hostile takeover. 150% ODV compensation and the intellectual property distribution make it worthwhile for the original owner to keep the machinery intact. A worksheet is available to aid the trebler in determining whether a hostile takeover is wise. In the absence of unpaid labor and intellectual property royalties, EBITDA, or net rents, is used for location value. The worksheet has no relevance when trebling for a completely different use.

The more uniquely suited a corporate campus is to one particular firm, the lower the ground rent. If the campus cannot be used as a regular office building, it is rarely cost effective to pay 150% ODV to demolish it. Individual firms, however, can be the subject of a hostile takeover. As a defense, these firms can leave machines, tools, and appliances, non-functional; leaving them with an ODV of zero. It is a new dilemma for corporations in a world where intellectual property value increases with sharing (See, *Chapter 3 – Intellectual Property Distribution*). Leaving the factory intact is an open invitation to competitors. Demolishing the factory reduces compensation. Yet, in trebler war, generally, cooperation is advantageous to both parties.

Hostile takeovers might occur because the current owner is paying insufficient ground rent or is underutilizing the property and therefore computing an insufficient location value. Of course, the pursuing trebler might have made a serious mistake by failing to understand the target company or the costs involved.

In the latter case, the bank or citizen investor will be more than happy to return the property to the original land rights owner provided the loan is paid in full. Although the original owner received 150% ODV for the business, if default occurs in the first month, the cost to the original owner to get the improvements back will only be 117% ODV if the trebler put 20% down and paid 3% interest. Unfortunately, for the original owner, the ground rent will be the trebled rent with only 1 month's drop. If 33% ODV profit is insufficient to support the new rent profitably, and the bank is unwilling to deal, the property will go to auction.

In auctions, improvements are bundled with the land, increasing the ground rent bid. Instead of 33% ODV, the original owner has 150% ODV and a year's worth of refunded rent to match the new higher ground rent, giving the original owner a significant advantage at auction. The rent realized at auction is the second highest bid. That is what the winner will pay. It is in the interest of treblers, who quickly realize that the takeover was a failure, and their creditors, to keep the property in top shape for auction.

There is no safe ground rent, because an "order of magnitude" trebler who has a qualitatively more efficient use for the land will treble it no matter what the self-assessed rent. However, there is a safe rent to prevent a hostile takeover. This leads to two different strategies for setting ground rent; setting a rent safe from hostile takeover, or allowing rent to fall freely and matching trebles from corporate raiders. Factors such as urban density contribute to the decision on strategy. Because of the myriad uses with high density, there is no safe rent unless the current use happens to be the most efficient one. The best strategy is to allow the rent to fall freely and match or accept trebles as they come. Closer to the margin, as land becomes cheaper relative to improvements, only a corporate raider whose goal is to seize the business will treble. There is an abundance of free land and no reason for anyone to pay 150% for improvements.

There are two endpoints that describe a ground rent in terms of its safety from hostile takeover, and its efficiency. The low point, called the treble point, is the most efficient, but completely unsafe. It is the point where anyone with knowledge of the objective location value from the perspective of the current business will treble. It is free money with little or no risk. At the high end is a safe rent that is inefficient. Between the two is a rent that maximizes both safety and efficiency.

In Table 2.6, we saw that trebled ground rents over the course of 11+ years return to their original value if the rent rate of fall is 10%. For the purpose of this book, I will define a minimum absolutely safe rent as the lowest rent where the trebler would earn less than or equal to the risk-free rate of return at the end of the 11 year period. A safe and efficient rent is defined as the rent that returns to the trebler less than the business/location risk rate of return at the end of the 11 year period. The treble point is the rent that produces a profit in every year greater than the risk free rate of return, or more arbitrarily produces profits 12 times the risk free rate of return at the end of the 11 year period after repaying the loan. I will use the following worksheet, available on the website, for calculations.

Location value is the net rents from location. For this motel it is net utilities, linen, maid service, management, breakfast bar, etc. Also called EBITDA it is $20/room/night. ODV is the objective depreciated value of the motel itself, not the land.

Percent Location Value is the percent of the location value that will be paid as ground rent. The calculated rent will always be seen under the blue line as Pre-treble Rent and also in Year 12 of the table.

150% ODV is what a trebler must pay the current owner of the motel.

Annual Depreciation is the depreciation the trebler must charge against 150% ODV at the depreciation rate specified directly above the blue line.

The loan amount is 80% of the Cost to Treble.

Business Takeover Worksheet (50 room motel)		
Location Value	$350,000	Use net rents from location value before interest,taxes,depreciation
ODV	$1,200,000	Rent Rate of Fall	10%
Percent Location Value	38%	Business Interest Rate	3%
Depreciation Rate	3%	Risk Free Rate of Return	2%

150% ODV	$1,800,000	Pre-Treble Rent	$133,000	
Annual Depreciation	$45,000	Cost to treble	$2,199,000	
Loan Amount	$1,759,200	Risk Free Return on 20% Down	$8,796	
Annual Interest	$52,776	Average %LV if treble point	86.29%	

Numbers do not reflect business/location/vacancy risk

Year	Rent	Profit/Loss	Cumulative Profit/Loss	Risk Free Profit
1	$399,000	($146,776)	($146,776)	$8,796
2	$359,100	($111,279)	($258,055)	$17,768
3	$323,190	($78,708)	($336,763)	$26,919
4	$290,871	($48,750)	($385,513)	$36,254
5	$261,784	($21,125)	($406,638)	$45,775
6	$235,606	$4,419	($402,219)	$55,486
7	$212,045	$28,112	($374,106)	$65,392
8	$190,840	$50,160	($323,946)	$75,496
9	$171,756	$70,749	($253,197)	$85,802
10	$154,581	$90,047	($163,149)	$96,314
11	$139,123	$108,207	($54,943)	$107,036
12	$133,000	$117,576	$62,633	$117,973
			Profitability ratio in year 12	0.53

The table shows the progression of a trebled rent over 11 years. In equilibrium, actual rents will be evenly distributed throughout the continuum.

The Treasury controlled rent rate of fall as new location value is created.

The Business Interest Rate is used to compute the Annual Interest from the Loan Amount, as well as interest on any losses (not seen here) reflected in the table.

Risk Free Rate of Return is the interest rate the trebler would get if instead of trebling they invested the 20% down payment in risk free bonds.

Cost to treble is the cost of 1 year trebled rent plus 150% ODV. In this case $399,000 plus $1,800,000. The trebled rent can also be seen in Year 1 of the table.

The Average %Location Value if treble point does a calculation on the 11 years of the table and computes the average rent received by the people as a percent of locaiton value. Keep in mind that higher trebled rents constitute a greater percentage of the total.

At the start of the 12th year cuculative profit is compared to the cumulative risk free rate of return. A number between 0 and 1 is a safe and efficient rent. A negative number is absolutely safe, but not efficient. A number 12 or greater indicates a treble will be highly profitable and will occur.

The comments referencing the profitability ratio of .53 at the bottom of the worksheet are too conservative when there is business or location risk. Profitability ratios as high as 4 times the risk free rate of return are safe and efficient given enough location and business risk. However, a profitability ratio of 12 is an instant treble even for the riskiest of businesses that a bank or citizen investors would consider.

This worksheet is for a 50 room motel that fills all rooms with an average charge of $70/night. EBITDA (**E**arnings **B**efore **I**nterest [on the Loan Amount], **T**axes [or in this case ground rent], **D**epreciation [of the motel], **A**mortization [principal payments on the loan]) is about $20/night/room or $350,000 per year. This is after all salaries are paid, so the profit is due solely to location value. Because the value of the building is over twice as high as the value of the land, safe and efficient ground rents will be under 40% . In this case, paying a ground rent of 38% location value ($133,000/year) is quite safe because it would return a profit to the trebler after

Business Takeover Worksheet (Motel)		
Location Value	$700,000	Use net rents from location value before interest,taxes,depreciation
ODV	$1,200,000	Rent Rate of Fall	10%
Percent Location Value	38%	Business Interest Rate	3%
Depreciation Rate	3%	Risk Free Rate of Return	2%

150% ODV	$1,800,000	Pre-Treble Rent	$266,000	
Annual Depreciation	$54,000	Cost to treble	$2,598,000	
Loan Amount	$2,078,400	Risk Free Return on 20% Down	$10,392	
Annual Interest	$62,352	Average %LV if treble point	86.29%	

Numbers do not reflect business/location/vacancy risk

Year	Rent	Profit/Loss	Cumulative Profit/Loss	Risk Free Profit
1	$798,000	($214,352)	($214,352)	$10,392
2	$718,200	($140,983)	($355,335)	$20,992
3	$646,380	($73,392)	($428,727)	$31,804
4	$581,742	($10,956)	($439,682)	$42,832
5	$523,568	$46,890	($392,793)	$54,080
6	$471,211	$100,653	($292,139)	$65,554
7	$424,090	$150,794	($141,346)	$77,257
8	$381,681	$197,727	$56,381	$89,194
9	$343,513	$240,135	$296,516	$101,370
10	$309,162	$274,486	$571,003	$113,790
11	$278,245	$305,403	$876,405	$126,457
12	$266,000	$317,648	$1,194,053	$139,378
			Profitability ratio in year 12	8.57

interest, ground rent, and depreciation, which is about half (.53) as large as what the trebler would get if they put the 20% down payment in risk free bonds over the same time period. Repayment of the loan is not shown in the table. Neither are refunds of advance paid ground rents that will likely be demanded by creditors as payment on principle.

Suppose that the trebler realized that market conditions would support a room charge of $90/night and thereby increase profits to $40/night.

The location value has doubled to $700,000 and the trebler will receive almost 9 times the risk-free rate of return at the start of the 12th year.

It is likely this treble will happen, even though the ground rent has doubled along with the location value. That is because the location value is a greater percentage of ODV. (Compare with the annotated worksheet above.) This profitability ratio of 8.57 is only slightly below 12, considered the treble point. That is, the point where a treble is certain.

If the current motel owner realizes the true value, they will raise the ground rent to stop a treble, (unless they want the $1.8 million to retire with.)

Business Takeover Worksheet (Motel)

Location Value	$700,000	Use net rents from location value before interest,taxes,depreciation	
ODV	$1,200,000	Rent Rate of Fall	10%
Percent Location Value	45%	Business Interest Rate	3%
Depreciation Rate	3%	Risk Free Rate of Return	2%

150% ODV	$1,800,000	Pre-Treble Rent	$315,000
Annual Depreciation	$54,000	Cost to treble	$2,745,000
Loan Amount	$2,196,000	Risk Free Return on 20% Down	$10,980
Annual Interest	$65,880	Average %LV if treble point	102.18%

Numbers do not reflect business/location/vacancy risk

Year	Rent	Profit/Loss	Cumulative Profit/Loss	Risk Free Profit
1	$945,000	($364,880)	($364,880)	$10,980
2	$850,500	($281,326)	($646,206)	$22,180
3	$765,450	($204,716)	($850,923)	$33,603
4	$688,905	($134,313)	($985,235)	$45,255
5	$620,015	($69,452)	($1,054,687)	$57,140
6	$558,013	($9,534)	($1,064,220)	$69,263
7	$502,212	$45,982	($1,018,239)	$81,628
8	$451,991	$97,582	($920,657)	$94,241
9	$406,792	$145,709	($774,948)	$107,106
10	$366,112	$190,759	($584,189)	$120,228
11	$329,501	$233,093	($351,095)	$133,612
12	$315,000	$254,587	($96,508)	$147,265
		Profitability ratio in year 12	(0.66)	

This example is a bit of overkill, but by raising the rent to 45% location value, or $315,000, the current motel owner insures the trebler will not break even by Year 12. Notice that a trebler would experience a loss in the first six years in excess of the profit in the next six. The trebler would be paying an average rent over the 12 year span of 102.18% location value.

The lands rights owner should keep in mind that land value is usually rising, and a treble-safe ground rent one day will tend to become unsafe the next. Increasing density and diversity also increases the likelihood that an "order of magnitude" trebler will treble for an altogether different and more efficient use, regardless of the rent.

Oil and Minerals

> **Because of low ODV, the treble safe rent for natural resources is quite high. A typical long-lived mine will have a treble-safe rent of 51% location value with average rents near 100% location value due to mining innovation and improper self-assessment. A trebling system automatically leads to the highest possible rent for depleting the Earth's resources.**

Natural resource companies such as oil fields and mines will generally have a much higher treble-safe rent than 34% of net profits. Without an innovation that makes the mining more efficient, all profits will be from location value. Extraction must be non-stop over three shifts or the mine will be trebled. Maximum efficiency is essential.

The problem is that the ODV is very low, perhaps even zero, if the mining equipment is all portable. Suppose the mine has 50 years' worth of ore and returns EBITDA of $10,000,000 annually with only $100,000 of improvements that stay with the land. We see that even paying a ground rent of 40% the $10 million location value, a trebler would make over 45 times the risk-free rate of return at the start of year 12. Despite big losses in the first 3 years, this mine, with 50 years' worth of ore, will be trebled instantly. Even though this property has a ground rent that is too low, the average location value returned to the people from the trebling of a 40% ground rent is 90.83%.

Business Takeover Worksheet (Mine)

Location Value	$10,000,000	Use net rents from location value before interest,taxes,depreciation	
ODV	$100,000	Rent Rate of Fall	10%
Percent Location Value	40%	Business Interest Rate	3%
Depreciation Rate	3%	Risk Free Rate of Return	2%

150% ODV	$150,000	Pre-Treble Rent	$4,000,000
Annual Depreciation	$4,500	Cost to treble	$12,150,000
Loan Amount	$9,720,000	Risk Free Return on 20% Down	$48,600
Annual Interest	$291,600	Average %LV if treble point	90.83%

Numbers do not reflect business/location/vacancy risk

Year	Rent	Profit/Loss	Cumulative Profit/Loss	Risk Free Profit
1	$12,000,000	($2,296,100)	($2,296,100)	$48,600
2	$10,800,000	($1,164,983)	($3,461,083)	$98,172
3	$9,720,000	($119,932)	($3,581,015)	$148,735
4	$8,748,000	$848,470	($2,732,546)	$200,310
5	$7,873,200	$1,748,724	($983,822)	$252,916
6	$7,085,880	$2,588,505	$1,604,683	$306,575
7	$6,377,292	$3,326,608	$4,931,291	$361,306
8	$5,739,563	$3,964,337	$8,895,628	$417,132
9	$5,165,607	$4,538,293	$13,433,922	$474,075
10	$4,649,046	$5,054,854	$18,488,776	$532,156
11	$4,184,141	$5,519,759	$24,008,535	$591,400
12	$4,000,000	$5,703,900	$29,712,435	$651,828
		Profitability ratio in year 12		45.58

What is the treble point for this mine and how much location value does that return to the people?

Without showing the worksheet, the treble point is 48%. That is, any time the rent is less than $4.8 million, the mine will be trebled for 12 times the risk-free rate of return at the start of Year 12. This returns an average location value back to the people of 108.99% location value! Of course, the smart mine operator will freeze the rent at this next level before it returns to the treble point and is trebled again.

Business Takeover Worksheet (Mine)

Location Value	$10,000,000	Use net rents from location value before interest,taxes,depreciation	
ODV	$100,000	Rent Rate of Fall	10%
Percent Location Value	52%	Business Interest Rate	3%
Depreciation Rate	3%	Risk Free Rate of Return	2%

150% ODV	$150,000	Pre-Treble Rent	$5,150,000
Annual Depreciation	$4,500	Cost to treble	$15,600,000
Loan Amount	$12,480,000	Risk Free Return on 20% Down	$62,400
Annual Interest	$374,400	Average %LV if treble point	116.94%

Numbers do not reflect business/location/vacancy risk

Year	Rent	Profit/Loss	Cumulative Profit/Loss	Risk Free Profit
1	$15,450,000	($5,828,900)	($5,828,900)	$62,400
2	$13,905,000	($4,458,767)	($10,287,667)	$126,048
3	$12,514,500	($3,202,030)	($13,489,697)	$190,969
4	$11,263,050	($2,046,641)	($15,536,338)	$257,188
5	$10,136,745	($981,735)	($16,518,073)	$324,732
6	$9,123,071	$2,487	($16,515,586)	$393,627
7	$8,210,763	$914,869	($15,600,717)	$463,899
8	$7,389,687	$1,763,391	($13,837,325)	$535,577
9	$6,650,718	$2,555,262	($11,282,064)	$608,689
10	$5,985,647	$3,296,992	($7,985,072)	$683,263
11	$5,387,082	$3,994,466	($3,990,606)	$759,328
12	$5,150,000	$4,351,382	$360,776	$836,914
		Profitability ratio in year 12		0.43

If 48% is the treble point, what is a safe ground rent for the mine that will not be trebled?

That number turns out to be 51.5%. By paying a ground rent of $5,150,000, the mine will not be trebled. The annual profit at this rent can be seen in the 2nd column of the 12th year in the table. It is $4,352,420 after interest, rent, and depreciation.

Notice that if this mine were trebled the average location value returned to the people over the 11 year journey back to 51.5% would be 116.94%.

Ground rent of 90.83% location value or more returned to the people for mines with many more than 12 years of life reflects the moral principle that nature's gifts belong to all of us.

How will the oil companies react to a safe ground rent of 51.5% net profits? These rents will be less than the taxes oil companies currently pay! In the previous 25 years, they paid $2.2 trillion in taxes and made only .7 trillion in profits. Much of that $2.2 trillion went to foreign governments[FTN2.03]. Consider, too, that oil companies had to pay for the land they drill on. Sometimes this takes the form of a government grant for exclusive oil rights in exchange for a non-competitive payment[FTN10.23]. With land rented from the commons, undeveloped land is free and the safe rent following discovery is less than what is currently paid to foreign governments. Over the 25 years, $3 trillion in profits, excluding the massive savings from free land, would require a 51.5% rent of $1.54 trillion. The effect of land rental would be to bring oil production home, saving the companies over $.6 trillion in taxes over 25 years, increase U.S. energy independence, and move revenues from foreign taxes to U.S. ground rents. The oil barons should be pleased, provided they can avoid trebler wars.

The estimated value of all minerals mined and processed (including coal) in the United States in 2005 totaled $500.3 billion.[FTN2.04] Excluding existing taxes, profits are near $200 billion. If half of the mineral land is able to find a safe rent of 51% LV and the other half is trebled with an average rent of 108% LV, that $200 billion will generate $160 billion in rents or over 3% of the total distribution package, roughly twice that of oil.

The total rental contribution from oil and minerals is about 5% - 7% of the distribution package (funds required for basic income and public services) depending on the amount of trebling.

Lands for mining are frequently acquired through mineral leases. If a land rights owner leases mineral rights, that lease is only as good as the joint effort of the land rights owner and mining company to fend off treblers. A land rights owner that sits on significant mineral deposits or other valuable natural resources without the means to exploit those resources will most certainly be trebled.

Agriculture-Cropland and Repairing Damage from the Farm Subsidies

> **Current agricultural subsidies and cropland protectionism will make AFFEERCE cropland vulnerable to non-agricultural treblers. A temporary protective ground rent surcharge will be applied to converted cropland. By routing the trebled ground rents plus surcharge into an increase in the food distribution, excess profits will flow to farmers owing to the decreased supply of cropland. Much of these profits can be used to raise ground rent, allowing the surcharge to be dropped. This continues until the surcharge is zero and the free market is restored in agriculture.**

The initial ground rent on an acre of cropland is set at $36. This amounts to over 120 free acres per farmer or farm family member based on the housing distribution. Even with cropland rent expected to increase dramatically, the housing distribution gives the family farm, commune or kibbutz a competitive edge over the large corporate farm. Initially, $16.3 billion or a mere .5% of the total distribution package is paid by cropland. Without protection, at $36, most cropland near communities would be trebled. For developers, farm land is gold, compared with an average rural residential rent of $30,000 per acre (see, *Initial Rent*, below). How can the farmer and food supply be protected, and the free market respected?

Today, farming is supported by government subsidies that will disappear under AFFEERCE. There is a way the ground rent can be used as a tool to prevent catastrophe, and restore the free market. An initial rent surcharge of $20,000 for cropland conversion is on par with an average rural residential rent of $30,000 per acre. Trebling proceeds as normal, but with $20,000 in escrow, conversion occurs when the transaction is completed. The new rent is $20,108 or $20,000 plus whatever the trebled outcome. A land rights owner can convert their own cropland to residential by adding $20,000 to the one year advance payment in escrow and subsequent payments at the higher ground rent.

Converting non-cropland to cropland, does not affect the ground rent directly, but forces the trebler to pay the surcharge. The land rights owner can then allow the rent to naturally fall to much lower levels. As long as the surcharge exists, vegetable gardens encircling a property's periphery, protect against trebling, allow savings on the rent, and bring in cash through direct sales to consumers, increasing land productivity.

The goal is to eliminate the surcharge. In the Treasury administered program, additional ground rent from converted cropland is divided between reducing the multiplier and increasing the food distribution. Currently, for every dollar spent on food, only 5% goes to the farmer[FTN2.32]. Using Midwestern grain (about $230 profit/$700 revenue per acre), about $30 of the $220 per month per person food distribution ($95 billion of the $700 billion) is farm revenue. The following 9 steps eliminate the surcharge. They are not sequential, but concurrent and incremental, possibly over several years.

Since the Treasury is tasked with keeping the rate of fall of the multiplier at a constant 10%, we will assume that all trebles outside the conversion go to other accounts that will be discussed in the chapter on balance of the RCs.

1. 60 million acres of cropland converted with average ground rent of $21,000. Rent increases by $1.26 trillion.
2. $430 billion reduces the multiplier by 10%, lowering average rural rent to $27,000.
3. $830 billion raises the food distribution to $450 per person.
4. Competition cuts into manufacturer, retailer margins. Most of $830 billion goes to the farmer due to decrease in cropland supply with increased consumer demand giving a 9-fold increase in revenue and 20-fold increase in profits or better.
5. To protect super-profits from growing frenzy, farmers increase ground rent by 50% of profits, $415 billion.
6. Average rent increases $415 billion/382 million acres = $1,086 per acre. Total around $1,200 per acre.
7. Average cropland conversion now generates rent of **$23,600**.
8. In the following year, rent increases of $415 billion plus $15 from other sources reduces multiplier by 10%, lowering average rural ground rent to **$24,300**.
9. In one year's time the difference between rural residential and trebled farmland has gone from $6,000 to $900. In about 3 additional months, it will go negative, and the process will halt or reverse.
10. When the process halts or reverses (rent in step 7 exceeds rent in step 8), the surcharge is dropped by $1000, and the process continues until the surcharge is eliminated.

Rangeland was excluded from the analysis for simplification. An increased food distribution would also increase rangeland ground rent. Rangeland might or might not share the same surcharge with cropland.

When the surcharge is eliminated, the most productive cropland will remain, farmers will earn a good profit that can be invested in expanding productivity, and the free market will be restored in agriculture.

Rangeland and Timberland

> **These lands sport initial ground rent of $12 per acre and contribute less than 1% to the distribution package.**

Trebling in active lumber areas could raise rents to $108/acre or more. Planting of grass on rangeland might qualify the acreage for the cropland surcharge. Re-forestation of timberland might invoke a special surcharge subsequently conditioned on good timber management. Planting grass seed or trees are improvements paid at 150% on a treble. A billion acres of range and timberland funds only $12-$36 billion toward the distribution package (.5 to 1%), although the rent on rangeland should grow considerably with the Treasury program of raising the food distribution to free agricultural markets.

Trebling the Spectrum

> **Trebling for radio spectrum within geographical boundaries will easily supply 1% of the distribution package.**

In an AFFEERCE economy, physical locations will not be the only resources owned in common by the people. The limited radio spectrum will also be owned in common. It is in high demand by mobile carriers, radio stations, and other enterprises requiring exclusive use of a frequency. Since 1994 the FCC has conducted 87 spectrum auctions, raising over $60 billion for the treasury. Collusion is generally accepted in these auctions which become negotiations between bidders. A number of social policies take precedence over maximizing profit[FTN2.33]. Standard AM and FM radio frequencies were grandfathered before the auctions began.

Subjecting frequencies to trebling should produce far more revenue than the auctions. Each frequency is represented by a map of the United States. Frequencies would be apportioned to the 7 levels of the cellular democracy, alternating between dominions to prevent interference. Social goals or propaganda associated with the frequency could be passed by a 2/3 or 5/6 plurality of the dominion. (See, *Chapter 9 – Government, Law, and Justice*).

Wireless companies might pay up to 50% of spectrum profit to protect their spectrum from treblers. Like natural resource extraction, trebling of frequencies will generate ground rents not much below 100% of profits. The percentage is a function of supply and demand, but clearly the winners will be those who use the spectrum most efficiently. Spectrum taxes could easily supply 1% ($40 billion) of the distribution package.

Office Buildings and Prime Retail

> Luxury and prime retail on the ground floor of smaller office buildings have treble-safe ground rents of 51% location value with average ground rents near 100% location value. As the attached office buildings become more efficient and as the retail becomes less exclusive, ground rents for prime retail/office can drop as low as 23% location value with average rents of 52% location value. It is a fundamental law of AFFEERCE trebling that well-maintained improvements and increased efficiency will lower the ground rents on a property.

Business Takeover Worksheet (Uniqlo Building - Stand alone)

Location Value	$12,967,500	Use net rents from location value before interest,taxes,depreciation	
ODV	$1,200,000	Rent Rate of Fall	10%
Percent Location Value	51%	Business Interest Rate	3%
Depreciation Rate	3%	Risk Free Rate of Return	2%

150% ODV	$1,800,000	Pre-Treble Rent	$6,613,425
Annual Depreciation	$54,000	Cost to treble	$21,640,275
Loan Amount	$17,312,220	Risk Free Return on 20% Down	$86,561
Annual Interest	$519,367	Average %LV if treble point	115.81%

Numbers do not reflect business/location/vacancy risk

Year	Rent	Profit/Loss	Cumulative Profit/Loss	Risk Free Profit
1	$19,840,275	($7,446,142)	($7,446,142)	$86,561
2	$17,856,248	($5,685,498)	($13,131,640)	$174,853
3	$16,070,623	($4,070,439)	($17,202,078)	$264,912
4	$14,463,560	($2,585,489)	($19,787,568)	$356,771
5	$13,017,204	($1,216,698)	($21,004,266)	$450,467
6	$11,715,484	$48,521	($20,955,745)	$546,038
7	$10,543,936	$1,221,525	($19,734,219)	$643,520
8	$9,489,542	$2,312,565	($17,421,654)	$742,951
9	$8,540,588	$3,330,896	($14,090,758)	$844,371
10	$7,686,529	$4,284,882	($9,805,877)	$947,820
11	$6,917,876	$5,182,081	($4,623,796)	$1,053,337
12	$6,613,425	$5,641,995	$1,018,199	$1,160,965
		Profitability ratio in year 12	0.88	

Japan's fast-fashion Uniqlo chain paid $2,000 a square foot per year to establish its U.S. flagship on Fifth Avenue in New York. The 15-year lease, reported to be a New York City record, is valued at more than $300 million.[FTN2.06]

The Uniqlo ground floor lease runs $13 million a year for 6,500 square feet of retail space. For

simplicity, pretend this is a single story 6,500 square foot building; a 100' x 65' structure; the kind with an ODV under $1.2 million. A trebler need pay at most $1.8 million (150% objective depreciated value). With typical costs of only $5/square foot, net rents are $1,995/sq. ft./year.

The land rights owner would pay $6,613,425 per year or 51% of the $12,967,500 location value to be safe from treblers. This would correspond to a ground rent of $44 million/acre. Without a doubt, the highest location value in the United State.

But in reality, Uniqlo is not a single story standalone building but a high-ceilinged ground floor with a 2nd and 3rd floor built around the periphery, underneath an office tower. With all those offices above the store, will the total ground rent for the location be higher or lower? It might surprise you that the more efficient the building, the lower the ground rent, even though total profits for the landlord (we the people) are higher.

For the sake of example, assume (incorrectly) that there are 17 office floors above the Uniqlo retail. Assume the same building size of 100' x 65'.

Uniqlo retail	$1,995 sq. ft.	$12,967,500 per year
Office 2nd-18th floor	$20 sq. ft. (net rent $15 sq. ft.)	$1,657,500 per year

Business Takeover Worksheet (Uniqlo Building w/Office Tower)

Location Value	$14,625,000	Use net rents from location value before interest,taxes,depreciation	
ODV	$20,358,000	Rent Rate of Fall	10%
Percent Location Value	45%	Business Interest Rate	3%
Depreciation Rate	3%	Risk Free Rate of Return	2%

150% ODV	$30,537,000	Pre-Treble Rent	$6,581,250
Annual Depreciation	$916,110	Cost to treble	$50,280,750
Loan Amount	$40,224,600	Risk Free Return on 20% Down	$201,123
Annual Interest	$1,206,738	Average %LV if treble point	102.18%

Numbers do not reflect business/location/vacancy risk

Year	Rent	Profit/Loss	Cumulative Profit/Loss	Risk Free Profit
1	$19,743,750	($7,241,598)	($7,241,598)	$201,123
2	$17,769,375	($5,484,471)	($12,726,069)	$406,268
3	$15,992,438	($3,872,068)	($16,598,137)	$615,517
4	$14,393,194	($2,388,986)	($18,987,122)	$828,950
5	$12,953,874	($1,021,336)	($20,008,458)	$1,046,652
6	$11,658,487	$243,411	($19,765,047)	$1,268,708
7	$10,492,638	$1,416,562	($18,348,485)	$1,495,205
8	$9,443,374	$2,508,323	($15,840,162)	$1,726,232
9	$8,499,037	$3,527,910	($12,312,252)	$1,961,880
10	$7,649,133	$4,483,651	($7,828,600)	$2,202,241
11	$6,884,220	$5,383,074	($2,445,526)	$2,447,409
12	$6,581,250	$5,847,536	$3,402,010	$2,697,480

Profitability ratio in year 12   1.26

Construction cost is calculated at $174/ sq. ft. or $20.4 million[FTN2.08]. Notice that the location value jumps to $14,625,000 and the ODV jumps to $20,358,000 – assuming it is a brand new building.

Ground rent for Uniqlo plus the office tower is only 45% of the location value, rather than the 51% location value rent for a stand-alone Uniqlo. Not only relatively, but the rent is lower in absolute terms as well. $6,613,425 for the hypothetical stand-alone Uniqlo and $6,610,500 for the Uniqlo with office tower.

A more realistic look at prime retail shows that ground rents will be lower still.

On Michigan Avenue in Chicago, average yearly net rent for a retail outlet is $125/sq. ft.[FTN2.06] This is typical for prime real estate. An annual lease on 6,500 sq. ft. of Michigan Avenue retail space is $812,500. The $125/ sq. ft. is an average including vertical malls and retail on higher floors of office buildings.[FTN2.06] Magnificent Mile storefronts in Chicago go for more than $500/ sq. ft., 25% of the most expensive 5th avenue prices. [FTN2.06]

Office buildings above prime retail charge a much lower net rent; about $15/ sq. ft.[FTN2.07] Here is a hypothetical 30 story prime office tower on a quarter of an acre, about 11,000 sq. ft.

1st floor retail	$300 sq. ft.	$3.3 million per year
2nd floor retail	$100 sq. ft.	$1.1 million per year
3rd-30th floor	$20 sq. ft. (net rent $15 sq. ft.)	$4.6 million net rent per year

Construction cost is calculated at $174/ sq. ft. or $57 million[FTN2.08]. We subtract an additional $500,000 from net rents for building management and additional insurance expense, leaving net rent of $8.5 million.

Far more typical of the real world, outside of natural resource extraction and extreme luxury, the prime retail office tower has a treble safe ground rent of 23% location value or $1,955,000/Year.

That is a ground rent of well over $7 million per acre, paying for over 550 distributions. Not shown, the treble point on this property is 14%, giving an average ground rent for prime 30 story office towers of 31%.

We have seen that motels, mines, and super luxury have treble points well above the 30% average. It is reassuring to see that efficiency, even in prime areas, has a much lower treble point.

These values are based on net rents today. Will they differ in an AFFEERCE economy? Elimination of the corporate income tax will increase demand for office space. However, the ground rent will make vacancies more costly. That will keep net rents stable, or even declining. Loyal tenants will be rewarded.

Business Takeover Worksheet (Prime 30 story office tower)

Location Value	$8,500,000	Use net rents from location value before interest,taxes,depreciation	
ODV	$57,000,000	Rent Rate of Fall	10%
Percent Location Value	23%	Business Interest Rate	3%
Depreciation Rate	3%	Risk Free Rate of Return	2%

150% ODV	$85,500,000	Pre-Treble Rent	$1,955,000
Annual Depreciation	$2,565,000	Cost to treble	$91,365,000
Loan Amount	$73,092,000	Risk Free Return on 20% Down	$365,460
Annual Interest	$2,192,760	Average %LV if treble point	52.23%

Numbers do not reflect business/location/vacancy risk

Year	Rent	Profit/Loss	Cumulative Profit/Loss	Risk Free Profit
1	$5,865,000	($2,122,760)	($2,122,760)	$365,460
2	$5,278,500	($1,599,943)	($3,722,703)	$738,229
3	$4,750,650	($1,120,091)	($4,842,794)	$1,118,454
4	$4,275,585	($678,629)	($5,521,423)	$1,506,283
5	$3,848,027	($271,429)	($5,792,852)	$1,901,869
6	$3,463,224	$105,231	($5,687,621)	$2,305,366
7	$3,116,901	$454,710	($5,232,911)	$2,716,933
8	$2,805,211	$780,041	($4,452,870)	$3,136,732
9	$2,524,690	$1,083,964	($3,368,906)	$3,564,927
10	$2,272,221	$1,368,952	($1,999,955)	$4,001,685
11	$2,044,999	$1,637,242	($362,712)	$4,447,179
12	$1,955,000	$1,776,359	$1,413,646	$4,901,582
			Profitability ratio in year 12	0.29

Inefficiency is punished. Suppose a $2 million mansion, sits on 1/4 acre with a ground rent of $300,900, surrounded by 30 story office buildings. If there is demand for another office tower, the location value is $8,500,000 as seen above.

Business Takeover Worksheet (Mansion on Office Tower land)

Location Value	$8,500,000	Use net rents from location value before interest,taxes,depreciation	
ODV	$2,000,000	Rent Rate of Fall	10%
Percent Location Value	4%	Business Interest Rate	3%
Depreciation Rate	3%	Risk Free Rate of Return	2%

150% ODV	$3,000,000	Pre-Treble Rent	$300,900
Annual Depreciation	$90,000	Cost to treble	$3,902,700
Loan Amount	$3,122,160	Risk Free Return on 20% Down	$15,611
Annual Interest	$93,665	Average %LV if treble point	8.04%

Numbers do not reflect business/location/vacancy risk

Year	Rent	Profit/Loss	Cumulative Profit/Loss	Risk Free Profit
1	$902,700	$7,413,635	$7,413,635	$15,611
2	$812,430	$7,503,905	$14,917,540	$31,534
3	$731,187	$7,585,148	$22,502,689	$47,775
4	$658,068	$7,658,267	$30,160,956	$64,342
5	$592,261	$7,724,074	$37,885,029	$81,239
6	$533,035	$7,783,300	$45,668,329	$98,475
7	$479,732	$7,836,603	$53,504,933	$116,055
8	$431,759	$7,884,577	$61,389,509	$133,987
9	$388,583	$7,927,752	$69,317,262	$152,278
10	$349,724	$7,966,611	$77,283,872	$170,934
11	$314,752	$8,001,583	$85,285,455	$189,963
12	$300,900	$8,015,435	$93,300,891	$209,373
			Profitability ratio in year 12	445.62

In order to get the ground rent down to $300,900, a Percent Location Value of 3.54% (shown as 4%) is used. Right from Year 1, profitability of the treble compared to a risk free return on the down payment is over 400 times greater!

This property could not even exist unless some covenant just expired. The moment it did, the treblers would be waiting.

How do Ground Rents Compare with Today's Taxes

Required Reading

How does a treble-safe ground rent for office towers compare with taxes today? Today, a 35% federal corporate income tax rate + an average 5% state corporate income tax rate[FTN2.13] results in a 40% total tax. This is after taking out property tax, which might be half the rent or more. Clearly paying a treble-safe ground rent provides the building owner with significant savings versus taxes today.

Standard Office and Retail

> With standard office and retail in small cities everywhere, a 30 story office tower is an albatross that will not be trebled even for no rent at all. However, a 3-story retail/office is treble-safe at only 16% location value. After 15 years of depreciation, that same retail/office is only treble safe at 35%. In this section we see that the most efficient use of the land is rarely the tallest building possible. Failure to maintain a property is an invitation to treblers. Nobody can "just sit back and collect the rent" for long. With trebling/land seizure, the existence of neighborhood blight is virtually impossible!

Business Takeover Worksheet (Office tower in small town)

Location Value	$3,707,000	Use net rents from location value before interest,taxes,depreciation	
ODV	$57,000,000	Rent Rate of Fall	10%
Percent Location Value	0%	Business Interest Rate	3%
Depreciation Rate	3%	Risk Free Rate of Return	2%

150% ODV	$85,500,000	Pre-Treble Rent	$0
Annual Depreciation	$2,565,000	Cost to treble	$85,500,000
Loan Amount	$68,400,000	Risk Free Return on 20% Down	$342,000
Annual Interest	$2,052,000	Average %LV if treble point	0.00%

Numbers do not reflect business/location/vacancy risk

Year	Rent	Profit/Loss	Cumulative Profit/Loss	Risk Free Profit
1	$0	($910,000)	($910,000)	$342,000
2	$0	($937,300)	($1,847,300)	$690,840
3	$0	($965,419)	($2,812,719)	$1,046,657
4	$0	($994,382)	($3,807,101)	$1,409,590
5	$0	($1,024,213)	($4,831,314)	$1,779,782
6	$0	($1,054,939)	($5,886,253)	$2,157,377
7	$0	($1,086,588)	($6,972,841)	$2,542,525
8	$0	($1,119,185)	($8,092,026)	$2,935,375
9	$0	($1,152,761)	($9,244,787)	$3,336,083
10	$0	($1,187,344)	($10,432,130)	$3,744,805
11	$0	($1,222,964)	($11,655,094)	$4,161,701
12	$0	($1,259,653)	($12,914,747)	$4,586,935
			Profitability ratio in year 12	(2.82)

A net rent of $10/sq. ft. for new construction non-prime office and $32/sq. ft. for new construction non-prime ground floor retail is fairly standard in cities large and small. Higher sq. ft. construction costs for smaller buildings are equalized by lower labor costs in smaller cities, so $174/sq. ft. can be used as a standard generally[FTN2.08], although construction costs should be less in an AFFEERCE economy. Here is the same 30 story office tower constructed in a small city.

1st floor retail	$32 sq. ft.	$.352 million per year
2nd floor retail	$25 sq. ft.	$.275 million per year
3rd-30th floor	$15 sq. ft. (net rent $10 sq. ft.)	$3.08 million net rent per year

Business Takeover Worksheet (3-story retail/office in small town)

Location Value	$713,000	Use net rents from location value before interest,taxes,depreciation	
ODV	$5,742,000	Rent Rate of Fall	10%
Percent Location Value	16%	Business Interest Rate	3%
Depreciation Rate	3%	Risk Free Rate of Return	2%

150% ODV	$8,613,000	Pre-Treble Rent	$114,080
Annual Depreciation	$258,390	Cost to treble	$8,955,240
Loan Amount	$7,164,192	Risk Free Return on 20% Down	$35,821
Annual Interest	$214,926	Average %LV if treble point	36.33%

Numbers do not reflect business/location/vacancy risk

Year	Rent	Profit/Loss	Cumulative Profit/Loss	Risk Free Profit
1	$342,240	($102,556)	($102,556)	$35,821
2	$308,016	($71,408)	($173,964)	$72,358
3	$277,214	($42,749)	($216,713)	$109,626
4	$249,493	($16,310)	($233,023)	$147,640
5	$224,544	$8,150	($224,874)	$186,414
6	$202,089	$30,849	($194,025)	$225,963
7	$181,880	$51,983	($142,042)	$266,303
8	$163,692	$71,731	($70,311)	$307,450
9	$147,323	$90,252	$19,941	$349,420
10	$132,591	$107,093	$127,034	$392,230
11	$119,332	$120,353	$247,387	$435,895
12	$114,080	$125,604	$372,991	$480,434
			Profitability ratio in year 12	0.78

The total net rent is $3.707 million. The building however, still costs $57 million for construction.

This building is a money loser that will never turn a profit. Of course, ground rents cannot go negative, but this one would certainly go to zero. "Take my land…Please!"

The net rents are insufficient to justify the building cost, particularly at 150%.

The most efficient use of land in a small community is not an office tower. Consider a 3 story building instead. The net rents as a percent of cost are much greater because of the higher net rents on the first and second floors.

1st floor retail	$32 sq. ft.	$.352 million per year
2nd floor retail	$25 sq. ft.	$.251 million per year
3rd floor office	$15 sq. ft. (net rent $10 sq. ft.)	$.110 million net rent per year

The net rent is now $713,000. The cost of the building is $5.742 million.

The 3-story retail office is far more suitable in a small city than a 30-story office tower. This building shows a ground rent of 16% location value or $114,080 and a profit of $125,604. The treble point on this 3-story building is 9%.

While the office floor is an objective loser, the 3rd floor of offices might enhance the retail net rents in a small town and thus increase the location value.

A trebling environment is a marketplace that puts the best business in the best location.

One of the expenses that negatively affects trebler net rent is the depreciation rate. If depreciation funds are not reinvested in the building, the ODV will drop. Consider the 3-story retail/office above after 15 years with a depreciation rate of 3%. The land rights owners decide to milk the building and not reinvest the depreciation. They decide to freeze the ground rent at $114,080."

In 15 years, the ODV goes from $5,742,000 to $2,624,000 since the owners haven't been keeping up the building. However, 150% ODV at $3,936,000 is actually less than the original construction loan. The net rents, however, have stayed the same. With no rent increases over 15 years, tenants are reluctant to leave even if the number of maintenance issues are growing.

Business Takeover Worksheet (Depr. 3-story retail/office in small town)

Location Value	$713,000	Use net rents from location value before interest,taxes,depreciation	
ODV	$2,624,000	Rent Rate of Fall	10%
Percent Location Value	16%	Business Interest Rate	3%
Depreciation Rate	3%	Risk Free Rate of Return	2%

150% ODV	$3,936,000	Pre-Treble Rent	$114,080
Annual Depreciation	$118,080	Cost to treble	$4,278,240
Loan Amount	$3,422,592	Risk Free Return on 20% Down	$17,113
Annual Interest	$102,678	Average %LV if treble point	36.33%

Numbers do not reflect business/location/vacancy risk

Year	Rent	Profit/Loss	Cumulative Profit/Loss	Risk Free Profit
1	$342,240	$150,002	$150,002	$17,113
2	$308,016	$184,226	$334,228	$34,568
3	$277,214	$215,028	$549,256	$52,373
4	$249,493	$242,749	$792,006	$70,533
5	$224,544	$267,699	$1,059,704	$89,057
6	$202,089	$290,153	$1,349,857	$107,951
7	$181,880	$310,362	$1,660,219	$127,223
8	$163,692	$328,550	$1,988,769	$146,880
9	$147,323	$344,919	$2,333,688	$166,931
10	$132,591	$359,651	$2,693,339	$187,382
11	$119,332	$372,911	$3,066,250	$208,243
12	$114,080	$378,162	$3,444,412	$229,521
			Profitability ratio in year 12	15.01

The profit over the risk free rate of return is over 8 times in Year 1 and grows to 15 times in Year 12. Treblers would not have waited 15 years to treble this gem.

As a general rule, failure to reinvest depreciation funds in the building will cause a treble. Financially, it is still more advantageous to milk the building, keeping the depreciation, rather than investing it. But the property will quickly be lost to a more conscientious owner who enjoys running the building, and keeping it in top shape. The tragedy today where people are penalized with higher property taxes for improving their home, and rewarded with lower taxes for allowing their neighborhood to become run-down, will finally end.

The examples point out how increased development on a given property lowers ground rents on that property, and how overbuilding and a supply glut lower ground rents to zero.

How Do Vacancies Affect Ground Rent?

Vacancies do not allow the ground rent to fall! While a regional supply glut will drive down ground rents, a supply glut in one building will do no such thing. Trebling deplores inefficiency and will drive down net rents to achieve 100% occupancy.

It should be apparent by now that the net rent of the most efficient use is equal to the location value. Vacancies across a region will lower ground rents everywhere, but vacancies in a single building will do no such thing. To some, that might seem as unintuitive as maintenance problems causing the rent to rise, as they do, or renovations lowering the rent, which they also do. After all, wouldn't the trebler have the same problems filling the space? Not if space is what is sought.

Suppose the CEO of a new business is looking for a corporate headquarters exactly specified by this 20% vacancy. She trebles $1,858,400 to $5,575,200. There is no profit from the net rents. But six vacant floors of the building become the new corporate headquarters! Although it takes slightly more than 12 years to have a cumulative profit, the business that supports this corporate headquarters free of charge, turns a profit in Year 7.

Business Takeover Worksheet (Prime office tower w/20% vacancy)

Location Value	$8,080,000	Use net rents from location value before interest,taxes,depreciation	
ODV	$57,000,000	Rent Rate of Fall	10%
Percent Location Value	23%	Business Interest Rate	3%
Depreciation Rate	3%	Risk Free Rate of Return	2%

150% ODV	$85,500,000	Pre-Treble Rent		$1,858,400
Annual Depreciation	$2,565,000	Cost to treble		$91,075,200
Loan Amount	$72,860,160	Risk Free Return on 20% Down		$364,301
Annual Interest	$2,185,805	Average %LV if treble point		52.23%

Numbers do not reflect business/location/vacancy risk

Year	Rent	Profit/Loss	Cumulative Profit/Loss	Risk Free Profit
1	$5,575,200	($2,246,005)	($2,246,005)	$364,301
2	$5,017,680	($1,755,865)	($4,001,870)	$735,888
3	$4,515,912	($1,306,773)	($5,308,643)	$1,114,906
4	$4,064,321	($894,385)	($6,203,028)	$1,501,505
5	$3,657,889	($514,784)	($6,717,812)	$1,895,836
6	$3,292,100	($164,439)	($6,882,251)	$2,298,054
7	$2,962,890	$159,838	($6,722,413)	$2,708,315
8	$2,666,601	$460,922	($6,261,491)	$3,126,782
9	$2,399,941	$741,410	($5,520,081)	$3,553,619
10	$2,159,947	$1,003,646	($4,516,435)	$3,988,992
11	$1,943,952	$1,249,750	($3,266,685)	$4,433,073
12	$1,858,400	$1,372,795	($1,893,891)	$4,886,035
		Profitability ratio in year 12		(0.39)

Ball-park Total Corporate Distribution Package Contribution

Required Reading

The following is an estimate of the commercial contribution to the distribution package. The total of all reported corporate profits in 2013 was $2.2 trillion[FTN2.10]. This is after certain taxes and fees that do not apply in an AFFEERCE economy, particularly property tax. Nor does it include income of partnerships such as lawyers, and accountants. Conservatively guessing partnership income to be 10% of the 8 trillion in personal income[FTN2.14], at .8 trillion, will bring total commercial profits to at least 3 trillion. For the most part, those are location value profits. At the predicted 69% net rents, this translates into a commercial ground rent contribution of about $2 trillion.

The Initial Ground Rents

Commercial and residential ground rents will be initialized to $100,000/acre and $60,000/acre respectively. This fully funds the needed distribution package. As individuals and businesses raise their rent for protection, pure zero sum is used to lower non-frozen rents. This occurs prior to capitulation. It is financially unwise to assess one's property too high or too low. Floating residential rents are expected to drop to $47,500/acre at capitulation.

Table 2.7	Proposed Initial Ground Rent		
Timberland & Rangeland	$12 per acre	1 billion acres	$.012 trillion
Cropland	$36 per acre	442 million acres	$.016 trillion
Oil and Mining	$40,000 per acre		$ .25 trillion
Other/w spectrum		800 million acres	$ .25 trillion
Residential	$60,000 per acre	58 million acres	$3.48 trillion
Commercial	$100,000 per acre	1.9 million acres	$ .19 trillion
TOTAL		**~ 2.3 billion acres**	**$4.2 trillion**

How will the initial ground rents be established prior to capitulation? Very simply! The same automated technique that powers the day to day operation of rents will power the startup. We begin by initializing ground rents to the values in Table 2.7.

The distribution package in 2002 population and dollars is $4.2 trillion. The $190 billion from commercial property is far less than the predicted $2 trillion estimated above, leaving plenty of room for trebling and self-assessed increases, allowing the free market to adjust rates prior to capitulation. For high-rise apartments and condominiums, $60,000 per acre is likely 90% lower than current property taxes, and easy prey for treblers. Older buildings are even more vulnerable. Trebling and the actual payment of ground rents will not begin until capitulation, but individuals and businesses will have many months beforehand to set a safe and efficient rent. Expect considerable action and decreases to floating rents before the first ground rent is even paid. The 10% annual rent rate of fall cap is not used during this adjustment period when floating rents can fall as much as 50% or more. Except for the unlikely event of default on residential or commercial property, rent adjustment is truly zero-sum during the adjustment period.

At capitulation, the AFFEERCE Treasury provides landowners with an entire year advance payment on the ground rent, as compensation for the land. Henry George believed there should be no compensation at all, that it was tantamount to compensating thieves for returning stolen property, but our attitudes today are different.

It might seem that claiming a high ground-rent could be quite profitable. However, an advance of $1 million dollars is better than an advance of $45,000 only if the land is trebled or sold, in which case the original owner would receive the rebate. But, of course, the higher the rent, the less likely the land will be trebled or sold. And the current owner must make rent payments at the rate established (with a 10% drop per year) until the land is sold. Even if the claim is surrendered, the people are assured this rent for one years' time. The original owner will receive a refund only of the rent realized at auction. This problem is known as the dilemma of Sun Yat-Sen, who proposed a self-assessed ground rent for China in the early 20th century that unfortunately never was implemented. However, weaker variants led to explosive productivity in Taiwan, Hong Kong, and Singapore[FTN2.26]. **There is no benefit from assessing anything but a fair rent to one's land.** A ground rent too high or too low can be financially devastating!

As we saw above, funding the distribution package is a zero sum game during this period. For instance, the prime real estate/office land rights owner discussed earlier, with a safe and efficient ground rent of $1.95 million is assigned an initial rent of $25,000 for a quarter acre. That land rights owner will certainly change the rent in the online system to its proper value before capitulation, to gain a $1.95 million advance credit versus a $25,000 one. Sun Yat-Sen's dilemma will encourage everyone to seek their optimal rent. When ground rent is increased, all commercial and residential property rents, except those frozen by the land rights owner, automatically decrease by an equal portion of the increased valuation. These are called floating properties. In this case, with 60 million acres of residential or commercial, and rent raised from $25,000 to $1.95 million, the extra $1.945 million lowers the per-acre rent of a floating $40,000 rent by about 2 cents.

2 million identical events anywhere in the nation will drop the $40,000 ground rent of a floating residential property to a minimum $12 per acre. More realistically a minimum rise of the rent of all commercial real estate from .19 trillion to $1 trillion will lower floating residential rents from $60,000/acre to $47,500/acre. The process demonstrates how a falling multiplier will give most land rights owners the opportunity to lock in a safe and efficient ground rent.

Apartments and Residences

To understand ground rents for apartment buildings and single family homes, we will need to deal with facts about an AFFEERCE economy that are not obviously related to the collection of rent. First, consider a downtown apartment tower.

Downtown Apartment Tower

> **Low worksheet ground rents for downtown luxury apartments seems to violate the law of rent.**

In newer downtown apartments, absent property taxes, net rent exceeds $24 per square foot[FTN2.15]. An 11,000 sq. ft. 30 story tower, fully occupied would produce net revenue of 11,000 x 30 x $24 = $7.9 million.

At only 20% location value, these new apartment buildings have ground rents of $1.58 million per 11,000/sq. ft., or about $6 million/acre. If there are 10, 1000 sq. ft. apartments per floor, or 300 apartments total, about $438/month of each units net rent would go for the ground rent. The $370/month housing distribution per person means that a single person in a luxury apartment only pays $58/month of their own money for ground rent.

Business Takeover Worksheet (30 story downtown apartment)

Location Value	$7,900,000	Use net rents from location value before interest,taxes,depreciation	
ODV	$57,000,000	Rent Rate of Fall	10%
Percent Location Value	20%	Business Interest Rate	3%
Depreciation Rate	3%	Risk Free Rate of Return	2%

150% ODV	$85,500,000	Pre-Treble Rent	$1,580,000
Annual Depreciation	$2,565,000	Cost to treble	$90,240,000
Loan Amount	$72,192,000	Risk Free Return on 20% Down	$360,960
Annual Interest	$2,165,760	Average %LV if treble point	45.41%

Numbers do not reflect business/location/vacancy risk

Year	Rent	Profit/Loss	Cumulative Profit/Loss	Risk Free Profit
1	$4,740,000	($1,570,760)	($1,570,760)	$360,960
2	$4,266,000	($1,143,883)	($2,714,643)	$729,139
3	$3,839,400	($751,599)	($3,466,242)	$1,104,682
4	$3,455,460	($390,207)	($3,856,449)	$1,487,736
5	$3,109,914	($56,367)	($3,912,817)	$1,878,450
6	$2,798,923	$252,933	($3,659,884)	$2,276,979
7	$2,519,030	$540,413	($3,119,471)	$2,683,479
8	$2,267,127	$808,529	($2,310,942)	$3,098,109
9	$2,040,415	$1,059,497	($1,251,445)	$3,521,031
10	$1,836,373	$1,295,324	$43,878	$3,952,411
11	$1,652,736	$1,516,504	$1,560,383	$4,392,420
12	$1,580,000	$1,589,240	$3,149,623	$4,841,228
			Profitability ratio in year 12	0.65

Since they are residential, these luxury apartments are only assigned an initial ground rent of $60,000/acre. Rents will be increased 100 times before trebling even begins. But even that is too low.

Keep in mind that these apartments are brand new, in the heart of downtown. Yet the worksheet shows it only takes a ground rent of 20% location value to fend off treblers. Single people paying only $58/month of their own funds for ground rent on a 1000 sq. ft. luxury apartment is a violation of the law of rent. What fast food worker would not want to buy a luxury condo? The problem is more acute if we look at apartment rents away from the heart of downtown.

Standard 4-Story Apartment

> **The worksheet predicts ground rents of 0% location value will be common for new apartments away from downtown. This seems to violate the law of rent. What assumptions are incorrect?**

In new 4-story apartments, net rent is about $14/sq. ft. However, the cost to build the apartment is the same whether it is downtown, or 10 miles out. The difference is that downtown apartments can rent (have net rents) for $10 more per square foot.

Using similar parameters to the downtown apartment, assume this apartment building is on 11,000 square feet, with ten 1,000 sq. ft. units per floor.

The ground rent for new apartments away from downtown is zero, zip, nada, as they say. These apartments will simply never be trebled no matter how low the ground rent.

Owning an apartment building is not a high margin activity. Most owners are underwater until the mortgage is paid off. Nobody would treble when apartment buildings are readily available for anybody willing to take on this risk.

Nor is a ground rent of zero necessarily a bad thing, especially for ordinary people who can watch with glee as their ground rent drops by 10% a year until it is the minimum, with no danger of being trebled.

However, there are two fundamental reasons why these numbers do not accurately reflect the market.

The Effects of Depreciation

> **Depreciation significantly raises ground rent. The 4-story apartment with 50% depreciation, requires a ground rent of 22% location value for treble safety. Significantly depreciated apartment buildings are the rule, not the exception. At 80% depreciation, a ground rent of 35% location value is needed for treble safety. Improvements must at least equal the rate of depreciation to prevent the ground rent of the improved property from rising due to depreciation. Depreciation restores trebling to the standard apartment market. It forces owners to maintain their properties.**

We have already alluded to this, but in the case where building cost is so many times greater than location value, the effects are startling. We examine the same 4-story apartment building that is 50% depreciated. There are two points worthy of note.

1. Apartment owners, underwater until the mortgage is paid off, typically do not reinvest depreciation cash back into the building, unless necessary, and use it as a false profit.
2. Tenant rents are more a function of location and apartment size than depreciation, and will be only slightly lower in a depreciated apartment. This is a corollary of the law of rent.

These points show that 50% depreciated apartments are common, and that the rental income is not seriously affected. In this example, we assume 50% depreciation and a net rent of $13/sq. ft. rather than the $14/sq. ft. in the new apartment.

If the owner continued to pay a ground rent of $0, the treblers would come in droves long before the apartment depreciated by 50%. This is free money. Although the worksheet is not shown, a 22% ground rent of $125,840 is needed to stop the trebler.

To protect 50% depreciated apartment buildings, ground rents would have to increase 8 times from the initial rent of $60,000/acre. And 50% depreciated 4-story apartment buildings are as common as mud.

In fact, 50% depreciated buildings are not rat traps. At a 3% rate of depreciation, it would take

Business Takeover Worksheet (4-story apartment 50% depr.)

Location Value	$572,000	Use net rents from location value before interest,taxes,depreciation	
ODV	$3,828,000	Rent Rate of Fall	10%
Percent Location Value	0%	Business Interest Rate	3%
Depreciation Rate	3%	Risk Free Rate of Return	2%

150% ODV	$5,742,000	Pre-Treble Rent	$0
Annual Depreciation	$172,260	Cost to treble	$5,742,000
Loan Amount	$4,593,600	Risk Free Return on 20% Down	$22,968
Annual Interest	$137,808	Average %LV if treble point	0.00%

Numbers do not reflect business/location/vacancy risk

Year	Rent	Profit/Loss	Cumulative Profit/Loss	Risk Free Profit
1	$0	$261,932	$261,932	$22,968
2	$0	$261,932	$523,864	$46,395
3	$0	$261,932	$785,796	$70,291
4	$0	$261,932	$1,047,728	$94,665
5	$0	$261,932	$1,309,660	$119,526
6	$0	$261,932	$1,571,592	$144,885
7	$0	$261,932	$1,833,524	$170,751
8	$0	$261,932	$2,095,456	$197,134
9	$0	$261,932	$2,357,388	$224,044
10	$0	$261,932	$2,619,320	$251,493
11	$0	$261,932	$2,881,252	$279,491
12	$0	$261,932	$3,143,184	$308,049

Profitability ratio in year 12   10.20

24 years of not reinvesting depreciation cash in the building to get a 50% depreciation. As I write this in 2016, some buildings built in 1992 have already reached this point, and only the best kept buildings from 1982 have yet to reach this point. Of course, inflation has obfuscated all of this. If we use the ridiculous IRS depreciation rules, no building from before 1989 has any value left at all; 100% depreciation unless it is sold in which case the land value strangely materializes as new building value.

Consider a moderately well-kept 4-story apartment building from the early 1960s with an 80% depreciation and only $9 sq. ft. net rent.

In this case, a 34.2% location value ground rent of $135,432 would be needed to fend off the trebler.

Business Takeover Worksheet (4-story apartment 80% depr.)

Location Value	$396,000	Use net rents from location value before interest,taxes,depredation	
ODV	$1,531,200	Rent Rate of Fall	10%
Percent Location Value	35%	Business Interest Rate	3%
Depreciation Rate	3%	Risk Free Rate of Return	2%

150% ODV	$2,296,800	Pre-Treble Rent	$138,600
Annual Depreciation	$68,904	Cost to treble	$2,712,600
Loan Amount	$2,170,080	Risk Free Return on 20% Down	$10,850
Annual Interest	$65,102	Average %LV if treble point	79.48%

Numbers do not reflect business/location/vacancy risk

Year	Rent	Profit/Loss	Cumulative Profit/Loss	Risk Free Profit
1	$415,800	($153,806)	($153,806)	$10,850
2	$374,220	($116,841)	($270,647)	$21,918
3	$336,798	($82,924)	($353,571)	$33,207
4	$303,118	($51,732)	($405,303)	$44,721
5	$272,806	($22,972)	($428,274)	$56,466
6	$245,526	$3,620	($424,655)	$68,446
7	$220,973	$28,281	($396,374)	$80,665
8	$198,876	$51,227	($345,147)	$93,129
9	$178,988	$72,651	($272,497)	$105,842
10	$161,089	$92,729	($179,767)	$118,809
11	$144,980	$111,620	($68,147)	$132,035
12	$138,600	$121,349	$53,202	$145,527
		Profitability ratio in year 12		0.37

The building owner will also consider this quite fair. They make a profit of $126,790 plus $64,874 assuming the mortgage has been paid off plus whatever salary they receive for management and maintenance that is not included in net rents.

From this point forward, if they reinvest the depreciation cash, rather than taking it as false profit, depreciation will remain at 80% and ground rent will never increase. Property improvement increases the location value of surrounding land without raising the ground rent of the improved property, so net rents might rise above $9 sq. ft. leading to even greater profit.

Buildings such as this will attract those whose sole source of housing money is the housing distribution.

What would the rent be for a couple renting a 500 sq. ft. 1 bedroom apartment? Net rents of $9/sq. ft. equate to $375/month in net rents for this apartment. Management, maintenance, heat, and water add an extra $150/month for a total rent of $525/month. Remember that net rents are EBITDA; interest, depreciation and ground rents are paid from net rents. With a monthly housing distribution for two of $740, this leaves $215/month for electric, cooking gas, cable, phone, and internet.

We see that depreciation restores trebling to the standard apartment market. It forces owners to maintain their properties. But there is another factor, far more powerful that will bring dynamism independent of depreciation: real wages!

Real Wages and their Effect on the Apartment Market

Elimination of taxes in conjunction with the distributions will create a significant increase in real wages. Lower nominal wages will decrease costs across the board, further increasing real wages. Increased national wealth of 3 to 4 times can be thought of as a multiplier on apartment size, all other things being equal. This allows us to fit a family of 4 into a 400 sq. ft. apartment, since the multiplier will expand the size to 1,200 to 1,600 sq. ft. The ground rent on the 4-story apartment increases from 0% to 26% location value using real wages. Using both real wages and 50% depreciation, the ground rent increases to 38% location value, with average ground rents at 86% location value.

1. The elimination of income taxes, Social Security, and Medicare deductions will prevent about 34%, $17,000, from being deducted from the average salary ($50,000/yr.).
2. The average family of 4 will receive food, housing, and cash distributions of $30,000/yr. This represents a salary increase of 60% if there was one breadwinner earning $50,000.
3. Medical premiums at work of $6,000 for a family of 4 are eliminated.

Suppose the average worker's salary was cut from $50,000 to $30,000. This is equivalent for the company of cutting wages in half because of added company savings in Social Security, Medicare and Healthcare.

The old take-home pay was $50,000 - $17,000 - $6,000 = $27,000. The new take-home pay is $30,000 and that is doubled to $60,000 from the food, housing, and cash distributions.

We see that the average real wage more than doubles. But that is only half the story. Because nominal wages have been cut in half, the price of goods and services will tend to follow due to competition.

It is clear that from these three factors alone, that the wealth of the nation will increase by a factor of 3 to 4. (There are actually over 40 AFFEERCE factors listed at the end of *Chapter 10-Economic Principles* whose total effect on productivity and wealth is so great there is no way to even calculate by how much.)

In computing the effect on apartment rents, I will account for all of this added wealth in the most discretionary component of apartment affordability, apartment size. I will use all of today's numbers with tiny apartments that we assume will be 3 to 4 times larger depending on the effect of real wages.

I will thus have a family of 4 living for free in a 400 sq. ft. apartment, using today's costs under the assumption that the effect of an increase in real wages will be to make the actual size greater than 1000 sq. ft.

Business Takeover Worksheet (4-story apartment - using real wages)

Location Value	$1,320,000	Use net rents from location value before interest,taxes,depreciation	
ODV	$7,656,000	Rent Rate of Fall	10%
Percent Location Value	26%	Business Interest Rate	3%
Depreciation Rate	3%	Risk Free Rate of Return	2%

150% ODV	$11,484,000	Pre-Treble Rent	$343,200
Annual Depreciation	$344,520	Cost to treble	$12,513,600
Loan Amount	$10,010,880	Risk Free Return on 20% Down	$50,054
Annual Interest	$300,326	Average %LV if treble point	59.04%

Numbers do not reflect business/location/vacancy risk

Year	Rent	Profit/Loss	Cumulative Profit/Loss	Risk Free Profit
1	$1,029,600	($354,446)	($354,446)	$50,054
2	$926,640	($262,120)	($616,566)	$101,110
3	$833,976	($177,319)	($793,886)	$153,186
4	$750,578	($99,241)	($893,127)	$206,305
5	$675,521	($27,161)	($920,288)	$260,485
6	$607,969	$39,576	($880,711)	$315,749
7	$547,172	$101,561	($779,151)	$372,119
8	$492,454	$159,325	($619,826)	$429,615
9	$443,209	$213,350	($406,476)	$488,262
10	$398,888	$264,071	($142,405)	$548,082
11	$358,999	$311,882	$169,477	$609,098
12	$343,200	$331,954	$501,431	$671,334
			Profitability ratio in year 12	0.75

Business Takeover Worksheet (4-story apt. -real wages, 50% depr.)

Location Value	$1,232,000	Use net rents from location value before interest,taxes,depreciation	
ODV	$3,828,000	Rent Rate of Fall	10%
Percent Location Value	38%	Business Interest Rate	3%
Depreciation Rate	3%	Risk Free Rate of Return	2%

150% ODV	$5,742,000	Pre-Treble Rent	$468,160
Annual Depreciation	$172,260	Cost to treble	$7,146,480
Loan Amount	$5,717,184	Risk Free Return on 20% Down	$28,586
Annual Interest	$171,516	Average %LV if treble point	86.29%

Eliminating depreciation, we return to a brand new 4 story apartment that was taking in $14 sq. ft. in net rent. The net rent for a 400 sq. ft. apartment is $467. Assuming all utilities are paid, the gross rent adds $233, bringing the total to $700. However, our family of 4 receives $1,480 a month in housing distribution, so the net rent can be comfortably raised to $30/sq. ft. or $1,000 in net rents per month. Add $233 gross which includes all utilities and that still leaves the family $247 for cable, phone, and internet. Plugging our new numbers into an undepreciated 4-story apartment, gives a very different result.

A brand new 4-story apartment, after changes to real wages brought by AFFEERCE will require a $343,200 or 26% of location value ground rent to ward off treblers. We can't say what this will be per acre, since the size multiple is the unknown factor, but certainly we can increase the size of our living quarters by 3 to 4 times all within much less than 1% of the nation's land.

This is a brand new building for free renters. What happens when we factor in both real wages and depreciation? If there is 50% depreciation, the ground rent must increase to 38% location value or $468,160 to ward off treblers.

It is clear that the trebler apartment market will be very lively indeed.

Residences

> Location value for homeowners has absolutely no relationship to business location value. With $370/month of housing distribution per family member, low ground rents from the business takeover worksheet will not stop trebling. Only 150% ODV will stop trebling. Homeowners should allow their rents to drop to the minimum, use all extra funds to maintain their property, and match or accept trebles when they come. With the housing distribution, 95% of all homeowners will pay none of their own funds for ground rent.

Home rental price is not the driving factor in determining ground rent for residences, unless depreciation is significant. The owner of a small $150,000 new home would be extremely lucky to get $1,200 in net rents per month. Gross rents would be much higher due to the difficulty of maintaining and managing a single-family home.

Business Takeover Worksheet ($150,000 single family home)

Location Value	$14,400	Use net rents from location value before interest,taxes,depreciation
ODV	$150,000	Rent Rate of Fall	10%
Percent Location Value	5%	Business Interest Rate	3%
Depreciation Rate	3%	Risk Free Rate of Return	2%

150% ODV	$225,000	Pre-Treble Rent	$720
Annual Depreciation	$6,750	Cost to treble	$227,160
Loan Amount	$181,728	Risk Free Return on 20% Down	$909
Annual Interest	$5,452	Average %LV if treble point	11.35%

Numbers do not reflect business/location/vacancy risk

Year	Rent	Profit/Loss	Cumulative Profit/Loss	Risk Free Profit
1	$2,160	$38	$38	$909
2	$1,944	$254	$292	$1,835
3	$1,750	$449	$741	$2,781
4	$1,575	$624	$1,364	$3,745
5	$1,417	$781	$2,145	$4,729
6	$1,275	$923	$3,068	$5,732
7	$1,148	$1,050	$4,118	$6,755
8	$1,033	$1,165	$5,283	$7,799
9	$930	$1,268	$6,552	$8,863
10	$837	$1,361	$7,913	$9,949
11	$753	$1,445	$9,358	$11,057
12	$720	$1,478	$10,836	$12,187
		Profitability ratio in year 12		0.89

Renting a home also accelerates depreciation and tends to lower neighboring land values as it increases the rented properties ground rents.

Notice that a 5% location value ground rent of $720, would not stop trebling, even though it is supposed to. That is because a ground rent of $2,160/year or $180/month is irrelevant for a house that is loved when all members of the household receive $370/month in housing distribution.

150% ODV is what stops treblers from trebling a house, not ground rent. But that same rule does not apply to the surrounding land.

Subjective valuation is the primary criterion in the decision to treble, or more likely, purchase the house. Location value is a function of the desirability of the neighborhood for residents and the competing desirability of the neighborhood to industry.

Ground rents for houses can be allowed to drop to $12, provided the house is kept in top shape. Houses that are allowed to deteriorate will be trebled regardless of a ground rent anywhere in the standard residential range. It is only the 150% ODV that stops home trebles, not the ground rent. Homeowners should allow their rents to drop to the minimum, use all extra funds to maintain their property, and match or accept trebles when they come.

That said, **this is not true for yards that are large enough to be plots in and of themselves**. If one does not pay dearly for this land, it will be trebled away with little or no compensation to the land rights owner, leaving the house with a much smaller yard.

Likely due to patriotism, guilt, and the belief that there is no free lunch, many home owners will freeze their ground rent the moment it is assigned. Consider a beautiful home on a quarter acre owned by a family with a grandparent, two working parents, and four children. Property taxes on the home were $14,000 year. Then the capitulation to AFFEERCE happens and the family gets a $30,000 windfall in saved income taxes. And with $1,540 for food every month, none of their own money needs to be budgeted for food. Then the bad news: the property tax of $14,000 has been replaced by an initial ground rent of $15,000. However, since there are 7 people living in the house, the housing distribution is an annual $31,080. So rather than pay $15,000, they will receive $16,080 for mortgage, utilities, and renovations. Then the big question. "So what do you want to do, freeze the rent at $15,000, or allow it to drop?" For many people, to do anything but freeze, will be to tempt the gods of their newfound wealth. In fact, by the time they hit the button to freeze it, it will already have dropped by several hundred dollars.

This is good, because it will allow rural residential ground rents and other homes that should be on free land, to drop all the quicker. The lower rural residential rents, the easier it will be to remove the surcharge from cropland. As homeowner ground rents drop toward zero, they would be wise to replace them with purchased covenants. Each $1,000 added to the ground rents of everyone in the covenant generates $1 million in surcharge for a trebler or any land rights owner who breaks the covenant by using the land for another purpose not allowed by the covenant. If the covenant is broken, the surcharge is divided equally among the covenant members.

How affordable are the expected homeowner ground rents in the early years of AFFEERCE?

Suppose grandma is the last family member living in a mortgage-free home on a 30 x 100 Chicago lot. Her ground rent will be $40,000 per acre x 3000 sq. ft. /43,560 sq. ft. per acre = $2755. This is no burden whatsoever, as the rent is automatically deducted from her $4440 housing distribution leaving $1685 for utilities and repairs. Gone are today's property taxes which likely exceeded $2755 even with senior discounts. Even at the highest possible rent of $60,000/acre grandma would be completely covered by the housing distribution, with cash to spare.

The reduction in ground rent from commercial and multi-unit residences tells only part of the story. With potential savings of millions in federal income tax, the wealthy will use the ground rent to protect their landed estates, even before the first trebler war has begun. After all, there is no prohibition against, and very little capital expenditure required to treble a neighbor's land and increase the size of your estate. For that matter, farmers can treble cropland for cropland without paying the $20,000 surcharge. Cowboys can do the same for rangeland. It might seem odd for a peaceful and free nation to encourage such conflict where the richest person or corporation always wins. But to the victor goes "worthless" land; to the vanquished, a 50% premium on their structures; to the citizens, the bounty of the Earth.

Severability of Land

Large properties deemed commercial or residential can be severed, with non-critical holdings surrendered. These properties are immediately put up for auction where the original land rights owner can hope to attain them at a lower rent. If the original land rights owner loses at auction, they are compensated with the lesser of the self-assessed advance payment or the rent realized.

Although ground rent causes no hardship for apartment dwellers, condo owners and those living on standard city or suburban lots, owners of large tracts of land classified as residential/commercial who cannot afford the residential floating rate at capitulation should sever the property. The land rights owner retains the home and desired yard and surrenders claims to the remainder. To prevent unusable space, dimensions of severed land must meet minimum specifications. If needed, an easement to access roads and utilities is added to the surrendered property. This will all be doable through the online land system.

The one-year advance payment of the ground rent for surrendered property is refunded to the original land rights owner to the extent of rent realized at auction. The original land rights owner can participate in the auction in hopes of retaining the land at a lower rent. If the rent heading into capitulation is $45,000 per acre, the original land rights owner might bid $10,000 per acre in hopes of retaining the land at an affordable price. However, there is always the risk of being outbid; a risk far greater than being trebled. Should the original land rights owner win at $10,000 per acre, the one-year advance payment of the rent is not refunded. $35,000 is owed the people, and the remaining $10,000 is the new advance payment. If another bidder wins at auction, they must supply the 12 months advance payment upfront. Keep in mind that the rent realized at auction is the second highest bid. The original land rights owner receives a refund of ground rent paid in advance up to the bid amount. This is true whether the advance was initial compensation, inherited, or paid by the land buyer, the trebler, or the winner at auction.

Roads

Roads, public or private, come with an easement for travel and utilities. The primary source of income for the road is the universal auto and truck pass. A trebler must maintain the travel and utility easements or face a drop in ODV, by law. Private roads are a good compliment to location monopolies on the roadside.

Trebling a road in violation of easements requires that alternative roads be provided for all residences and businesses, and the re-routing of all underground or above ground utilities. However, the easement is lifted if the road is surrounded on two length sides and one width side by the same property. A road is made private when it is trebled and the easements respected.

When a road is trebled, all easements for access and egress must be respected. Failure to do so will lower ODV. Additional access and egress can be sold, but once granted, the easement becomes permanent, and cannot be lifted unless the land rights owner of property that surrounds two length sides and one width side of the access or egress (the other width side connects with the private road) removes the easement.

Business Takeover Worksheet (10 miles of 4 lane highway)

Location Value	$936,000	Use net rents from location value before interest,taxes,depreciation	
ODV	$10,000,000	Rent Rate of Fall	10%
Percent Location Value	4%	Business Interest Rate	3%
Depreciation Rate	3%	Risk Free Rate of Return	2%

150% ODV	$15,000,000	Pre-Treble Rent	$37,440
Annual Depreciation	$450,000	Cost to treble	$15,112,320
Loan Amount	$12,089,856	Risk Free Return on 20% Down	$60,449
Annual Interest	$362,696	Average %LV if treble point	9.08%

Numbers do not reflect business/location/vacancy risk

Year	Rent	Profit/Loss	Cumulative Profit/Loss	Risk Free Profit
1	$112,320	$10,984	$10,984	$60,449
2	$101,088	$22,216	$33,201	$122,108
3	$90,979	$32,325	$65,526	$184,999
4	$81,881	$41,423	$106,949	$249,148
5	$73,693	$49,611	$156,560	$314,580
6	$66,324	$56,980	$213,540	$381,321
7	$59,691	$63,613	$277,153	$449,397
8	$53,722	$69,582	$346,735	$518,834
9	$48,350	$74,954	$421,690	$589,660
10	$43,515	$79,789	$501,479	$661,903
11	$39,164	$84,141	$585,620	$735,590
12	$37,440	$85,864	$671,484	$810,751
		Profitability ratio in year 12		0.83

The primary source of income for a road is the universal auto pass. (See, *Chapter 11 – Transportation and Sanitation Distribution*) Other sources can include additional metered parking, parking permits, selling access and egress, community assessment, gasoline excise taxes, billboards, on-road advertising, and tolls. Using the road surface or ceiling to generate electricity for the grid might be an innovative way to pay the ground rent and maintenance on a road. On roads with sidewalks, the sidewalk and parkway are included as part of the road area. Private roads have access to most of the same funds as public roads, except excise taxes. A private road can be financed with community assessment, provided the road is collectively owned by the community, such as in a gated community. Competition will tend to end metered parking, permits, and tolls, except in areas of extremely high demand.

If a ten mile stretch of a 4-lane highway, cost $1 million/mile, is privately owned and has an average of 1000 cars in the stretch at any one time, the monthly revenue from the auto pass would be the same as if all 1000 cars were permanently parked on the road. The auto pass is explained later, but basically it would provide the roads owner with 1000 x $75 = $75,000. If advertising revenue is $3,000 a month, the annual net rent is $936,000 and the ground rent on this segment should be $37,440 to prevent trebling. All road repairs are taken from the $300,000 depreciation cash each year. Profit is only $85,864. Low margin road trebling only makes sense as part of a larger plan to create a location monopoly.

It makes sense for large trucks to pay $500/month for a pass. They take up much more space, create more of a safety hazard, and do more damage to the surface. Most of that $500 would be returned to the trucker in terms of lower prices at truck stops, lower price nightly electric, water, and sanitary hookups, more truck parking, more roads open to trucks, and moving-truck-friendly apartment buildings. If the highway example above considered truck revenue, the location value, and ground rent percent of location value would both be higher.

Bridges might receive 3 x the auto pass revenue of normal roads, and will have a much lower ground rent in as much as the land underneath is often a raging river. Revenue will tend to be eaten up by much tougher maintenance standards.

Trebling does not change the easement, but building an alternate highway can. The alternate highway will increase neighborhood safety, and decrease travel time and wear and tear on the automobile.

Alternate highways can be surrounded by private property where businesses owned by the land rights owner have an effective monopoly. Effective monopolies are also good candidates for cellular enterprises (See, *Cellular Democracy*). The primary source of revenue is the auto pass, so the goal is to make the highway, and the businesses along the way, as inviting as possible. Trebling the original road after the alternate highway is constructed, allows the highway entrepreneur to bust the original road into sections that enter and exit the highway. This is generally welcomed by the community for safety and efficiency reasons. Although there is no obligation, it might make good business sense to let space along the highway to popular businesses from the original route.

A Word to the Wise Land Speculator

> **To maximize return on residential or commercial land speculatively held prior to capitulation, the land speculator should surrender the land and recoup the second highest bid at auction.**

Those who speculate in timberland, rangeland, badlands, or even cropland will not be materially harmed by the conversion to trebling. The small ground rent is on par or less expensive than pre-capitulation property taxes. Still, there is little advantage to speculating where land is otherwise free, unless one falls in love with a particular property for a future homestead.

Those who speculate in the 60 million acres designated residential/commercial will be severely hurt, with an annual ground rent for unimproved non-downtown land as high as $45,000 per acre. With no land improvements, the only compensation will be a rebate of the 12 months of advance payment. The wise course of action will be to surrender the claim at capitulation so the land can be immediately auctioned. If the rent realized at auction (the 2nd highest bid) is $25,000 on average, that is what the speculator is refunded from the advance payment of rent. If the speculator originally paid $20,000 per acre, they will make a profit. Such profits will be common for speculators who surrender the claim at once. Otherwise, they must pay $45,000/acre/year (dropping 10% per year) that serves them no benefit.

Trebler Wars

Throughout history, the wealthy have bankrupted nations and killed untold millions in a bloodlust for land. With the nuclear age, this epoch will soon come to an end – one way or another.

Yet those wars played a critical role in the evolution of mankind. Limited resources meant some would die by famine and disease, in peace, or on the field of battle in war. But wars, unlike pestilence, have always been associated with glory, new ideas, technological innovation and revolution. Debating this value judgment is moot. Today, ideas are spread around the world at the speed of light, military innovation has bumped up against the nuclear ceiling, and seizing territory is illegal. The epoch of war must end, but there is nothing to replace it with; so we rightly fear annihilation.

Trebling is the game that replaces war. Refugees, if they exist will be welcomed everywhere. Limited resources are allocated without harm, bloodlust satisfied without victims. Instead of bankrupting a nation, wealth is created; instead of injury, medical care; instead of destruction, an end to homelessness; instead of razing fields, the bounty of the Earth will be for all. These are the trebler wars.

The battles will be heated. In the end, the winner gets the land; objectively worthless. The loser is rewarded with 150% of property improvements. The people of planet Earth reap the plunder.

The scope of trebler wars will be as diverse as the numerous interests of a free people. Trebler wars can be fought businessperson to businessperson, or with all the falderal of feudalism. Although entrepreneurs will more typically buy and sell properties, trebling becomes a new form of hostile takeover. With competing suitors for a business, trebling is almost certain. Neighborhood land disputes, too, might be solved with a treble.

Yet I imagine the largest source of trebling, the one that will bring unimaginable prosperity to humanity will be the age-old desire to promote one's own culture over another. While the collection and distribution of rents will ultimately be international in scope, the same will not likely be true for governments and cultures. From this point forward, cultural evolution becomes divorced from destruction. In the cellular democracy, dominion trebling plays a vital role in reshaping successful communities, cities, counties, regions and states, and obliterating failure. It will be used to grow a successful embryo in the panarchy (See, *Chapter 9 – Cellular Democracy*). It can be used to liberate land from backward thinking dominions. Feuds between the medieval imitators, religions, political economies, and lifestyles will come to dominate the trebling scene. Likely, they will be confined to cheap land in rural dominions, led by knights, lords, and an occasional baron. (See, *Chapter 9 – Cellular Aristocracy*). The role of the aristocracy in capturing land creates a mirror image of the past in the future. Not only is the victor the one who gives the most to the people, but the prize for victory is to give even more. The free market and the nature of ground rents prevent any second-rate dominion from becoming too large. Only efficient producers will have the funds to support their conquests.

In addition to dominion trebling, some of the terms introduced in the chapter on cellular democracy related to trebler wars will be switching allegiance, encircle and capture, chancellery trebling, mitosis, and distribution.

Due to the win-win nature of a trebler war, it is unlikely to escalate to violence. Nevertheless, emotions, dedication and loyalty will run high. The national defense distribution, even in a peaceful world, is needed to prevent things from getting out of hand.

Anatomy of a Trebler War

Two wealthy, rival families battle over a large hunting and fishing estate, exposing many of trebling's misconceptions along with the benefits of trebler war.

The Montbush and Fitzwilliam families have been feuding for over a century. Their great-great grandparents competed in the railroads; their great grandparents competed in oil, and their grandparents in automobiles. With the advent of AFFEERCE and the elimination of the corporate income tax in all of their various ventures, both families find themselves hundreds of million dollars wealthier.

The Montbush family owned a 2,000 acre prime hunting and fishing estate in Northern Wisconsin that was the envy of the Fitzwilliam family. Being rural land, the ground rent at capitulation was set to $12 an acre, and the none-too-bright Montbush's never raised it, thinking they had a bargain. To support the estate, they will pay ground rent of only $24,000 a year at $12 per acre. Although public service announcements prior to capitulation warned people of this danger, the Montbush's weren't going to pay a penny more in tax than "required."

Imagine the shock on the face of Jed Montbush when at 12:01 AM on capitulation day, the Fitzwilliam family trebles by a factor of 1000. "I thought trebling meant three," said Jed. The minimum trebling is a factor of 3, but there is no upper limit. Dismayed, but not defeated, the Montbush family matches the treble. The moment they do, the Fitzwilliam family re-trebles, this time by the minimum factor of 3. Ground rent is paid a year in advance, and the Montbush family finds themselves without the liquidity to match this new treble, so the land becomes property of the Fitzwilliam family, who are paying 3000 times the initial rent or $72 million a year for the hunting and fishing estate.

The Montbush family received a refund of the $12 an acre advance payment, in this case a "gift" from the one-time compensation, and 150% on the hunting lodge and a small area they reforested; very paltry remuneration. Comically or tragically, depending on one's point of view, since the Montbush family was willing to pay ground rent 1000 times higher and knew the Fitzwilliam's would be trebling, they should have raised it before capitulation. Then, when the Fitzwilliam family trebled away the land, the Montbush family would receive $12,000 an acre from the advance payment. Not bad for land they paid 15 cents an acre on back in 1919. Poor Jed Montbush, instead, fell victim to the dilemma of Sun Yat-Sen.

In any case, realizing they cheated themselves out of all that money, they direct their anger at the Fitzwilliam family and vow revenge. After rearranging some assets, the Montbush family trebles for the estate using a standard 3x treble. This raises the ground rent to $216 million, almost as much as the corporate income tax the family used to pay. The Fitzwilliam family is defeated. They cannot match the treble without rearranging assets, so they cannot match the advance payment before the chancery court date. Nor can they re-treble at a later date because $648 million a year is simply out of the question.

But the Fitzwilliam family knows the Montbush family members are cheapskates. Rather than fixing the ground rent at $216 million, they will let the rent drop naturally, continuously seeing a reduction in their taxes. In two decades, the Montbush family is paying only $42 million rent on their 2000 acre hunting and fishing estate. The Fitzwilliam family moves in for the kill, trebling the rent up to $300 million. The Montbush family cannot match without rearranging assets. Nor can they re-treble at a later date for $900 million. In this instance, they are remunerated with the remaining advance payment which has dropped to $42 million along the way. The Fitzwilliam family is the final victor. They freeze the rent at $300 million or perhaps let it drop at a million a year for a few decades.

It turns out that the Fitzwilliam family, as a result of their recent treble, have succeeded in becoming the highest aristocratic family in a dominion that stretches from Chicago north through the upper Midwest, replacing the old grand duke who was the U.S. ambassador to France. The now Grand Duchess Barbara Fitzwilliam, Ambassador to France, having ousted the old grand duke, will move the family to the embassy in Paris. (See, *Cellular Aristocracy*).

As for plunder, this particular skirmish between the Montbush and Fitzwilliam families funds the distributions of 25,000 citizens.

The Online Land System

Early History

> **Early work on the land system is now beginning and must be ready to handle the first auction in the embryonic nation. Revenue will come from advertising to those seeking free real estate and accounting services.**

An ever improving and exciting online land system, introduced earlier in this chapter, is critical for promotion of AFFEERCE and the increase of ground rent revenue.

As you read this, the work on the online land system has already begun. Before the first lands are purchased (See, *Volume II – The Plan*), U.S. citizens must have access to an online trebling tool. Far more important than trebling in the early days, are the auctions. The online land system begins as a land auction tool.

The first system and database design comes out of the AFFEERCE Benefit Corporation. In the beginning, all system revenue will come from advertising.

Advertising revenue is used to reward those entering data into the land system database for all U.S. properties outside of AFFEERCE territory. This lengthy task could take years, and capitulation is dependent on virtual completion. Landowners are encouraged to verify their own borders when reviewing or modifying the initial rent, entering attributes or registering improvements on the property. These have U.S. tax benefits and real estate sales benefits even before capitulation. The land system must be able to issue reports for the IRS, prepare a sales brochure, and interface with known accounting systems. The more free services the early land system can perform for the land rights owner, the greater likelihood the land rights owner will enter important data themselves.

General Functionality

Required Reading

The land system displays a map of the United States divided by properties. One can zoom in or out on any area. When a property is selected, the following will likely be displayed:

1. Ground rent and the rent history, including the rent on partial property plots, surcharges and restrictions
2. Dates of and values of any certified appraisals of improvements
3. Objective depreciated value and access to land improvements (labor and material)
4. The owner history with VIP identities, including whether ownership was acquired through auction/surrendered claim, purchase, trebling or inheritance/gift and the price paid
5. History of boundary seizures or expansions
6. Mortgage information including current principle under mortgage
7. Covenants including covenant patterns; dates, amounts and comments if available
8. Birds eye views of the property with dates
9. Pre-AFFEERCE property tax information, if available

10. Price if exclusive use rights for sale
11. Property size and survey if needed
12. Declared land use and sub-type (i.e. residential --- single family home)
13. Current property status if unclaimed/claimed, and in auction/sale/treble process
14. Easements and utility service
15. The seven levels of dominion and orphan status
16. A large collection of property attributes regarding soil, flora, fauna, timber, etc. that can be accessed

The land system will have many features. Among them:

1. Search for a property based on events or arbitrary combinations of database fields
2. Register alerts on innumerable criteria such as any time a claim matching certain parameters is surrendered, any time an auction meeting certain conditions is scheduled, etc.
3. Update property attributes
4. Enter improvements including cost of labor and materials
5. Associate an improvement with a depreciation schedule
6. Allow social networking including exchange of photos and documents
7. Sign contracts with VIP identities
8. Initiate a treble, dominion treble, or chancellery treble including escrow of required funds
9. Purchase an appraisal from a random pool of appraisers
10. Request a date in chancery court
11. Attend chancery court online
12. Increase the ground rent of owned property, revocable up to one week
13. Interface with land counselor to verify extraordinary increases or surrendered property
14. Switch ground rent between fixed and float
15. Buy and sell land rights including offers and closing
16. Bid on land rights at auction
17. Pay the treble option on 5/6 votes to suppress natural rights (See *Government, Law and Justice*)

Chapter 3 – Distribution of the Ground Rents

Natural Laws

Required Reading

Once the ground rents have been collected through self-assessment and trebling, they must be distributed to the landlords. We are the landlords! Unfortunately, such platitudes say very little about the practical distribution of the collected rents. Henry George laid out some natural laws that provide guidance, but don't exactly lay out a roadmap. For those unfamiliar with George, distribution refers to distribution of the wealth, as in the distribution of the rents, and not in the distribution of product which he considered part of the production process.

- Human law is utterly powerless directly to alter distribution so that the laborer as laborer will get more wages or less wages, the capitalist as capitalist will get more interest or less interest, the landowner as landowner more rent or less rent.
- The natural laws of production are physical laws and the natural laws of distribution are moral laws.
- That which we create with our own labor, belongs to us alone. That which God or Nature provides belongs to each of us and to all of us (my paraphrase).

In the final natural law, what exactly does "each of us and all of us" mean? The answer to that question is the heart of distribution theory. But first we look at distribution theory's soul, the intellectual property distribution.

Intellectual Property: Monopoly vs. Distribution

Today

Required Reading

Every author wants nothing more than their book to be widely read. Musicians want their music to be widely heard. Inventors want their invention to ease life's burdens. Chemists want their drugs to cure disease everywhere. The creator bares their soul to the world. But the tyranny of intellectual property law leaves them with no choice but to sell that soul to the highest bidder.

Rather than spread the fruits of creation, the owner of intellectual property today attempts to maximize profit by limiting supply. This can be done because they have a monopoly on the right to produce the product of the artist's soul, backed by the laws of the United States and every "civilized" country.

The intellectual property laws limit wealth creation, and distribute what wealth is created to the owners of the monopoly. The monopoly prices aren't so bad for copyrighted material. Despite its uniqueness, copyrighted material still competes with other copyrighted material; the songs from one artist compete with the songs from another. Patents, however, can lead to strict monopoly; a lifesaving drug costs $5,000 a pill, and there is simply no alternative. Extreme cases aside, patents add their monopoly pricing to every product we buy! This can be through patented parts, patented tools, and patented processes used to create the product. It is no stretch of the imagination to guess that the cumulation of these monopoly prices accounts for well over half the cost.

Profit from Location Value and Innovation

Required Reading

Besides unpaid labor (working on the cheap or for free) and the normal risk return on capital, there are two major sources of corporate profit: location value and innovation. In a sense, the soul of collection theory is the elimination of monopoly on location value. In that same sense, the soul of distribution theory is the elimination of monopoly on innovation.

Henry George used the metaphor of various armed highwaymen along the journey. What one doesn't steal, the others will. The monopoly of location value is the worst and will steal whatever is left. But the bandit who represents the monopoly on innovation is without question, second. Nowadays, he is vying to be the "baddest" thief of all.

There is a beautiful symmetry in the strategy to deal with these two forms of wealth destruction. It is an integrated solution in that the solution to the monopoly on location value – collection – gives us a solution to the monopoly on innovation – distribution.

Problem		Solution			
Name	Factor	Stage	Value	Terms	Use
Location Value Monopoly	Land	Collection	Uses	Pays	Exclusive
Intellectual Property Monopoly	Labor	Distribution	Creates	Paid	Shared

Figure 2A.1   An Integrated Solution to the two monopolies

We must collect ground rents from those who take exclusive use of the land. We must distribute ground rents to those who share their creation.

Currently artists and innovators make their money through profits on sales. Instead, creators should, by natural law, receive a return from the wealth they have created. That wealth increases both location value and the associated ground rents. The increase in rents should be distributed to the artists and innovators.

George would likely have been fascinated in how this distribution of wealth is directly tied to the distribution of product. He was not likely to have foreseen this solution, because the technology to implement it was unimaginable in the 1870s. Critical to the implementation is the internet and biometric identity, as well as computer modeling of myriad alternative and combinations of patents that comprise a product or tool.

Among other things, the biometric technology insures that:

1. The product is explicitly requested by the consumer, even if it is free
2. The same consumer requesting the same free product does not count as multiple requests

As of this writing, distribution theory does not predict what percentage of the distribution should go toward intellectual property. In the assumptions, the intellectual property distribution is set at \$92/person/month, larger than the distribution for national defense. That is \$320 billion annually for a population of 290 million. The money is used to reward inventors, artists, architects, authors, chefs, musicians, programmers, producers, engineers, and others who create intellectual property that can be shared. This is in addition to compensation for educational materials through the academic achievement annuities.

For most of recent history, business profits have come predominantly from location value. These profits derive from exclusive use of the land. The second most common source of super profits has been a monopoly on exclusive use of intellectual property. With the ground rents, the location value available for business profits is greatly diminished. Replacing profit from location value with this new form of profit from sharing innovation, will create new opportunities for personal and business wealth as it multiplies the wealth of the nation many fold.

Copyrights (Copyshares) and Patents

> Copyrights and patents will be consolidated under a single agency administered of the Library of Congress. There will no longer be any prohibition on the use of intellectual property in any product or document. It shall be encouraged. All products and processes will be patented and then given unique product ids, regardless of the amount, if any, of original intellectual property. Each patented product or process or copyrighted material will be broken down into its constituent intellectual property. Manufacturers will receive 1% of the intellectual property distribution simply for patenting their product or process or copyrighting the content they are distributing, in addition to receiving percentages for original intellectual property added.

A more appropriate name for copyright would be copyshare, but I will stick with the original term in this edition.

All copyrighted material must be on file at the Library of Congress. The cost to copyright is the $35 universal deductible per author/owner. It is up to the author or publisher to answer online classification questions, and supply an electronic copy in a standard medium. Ownership of the copyright is broken down by percent. VIP signature is needed by all authors/owners to copyright. Copyright ends 25 years after the death of the original author(s). Even if a copyright is owned in whole or in part by a business, it must be associated with a personal author.

There is some overlap between copyright and design patents, business process patents, and software patents. Less ambiguous are chemical patents, biological patents, and patents on machinery. Generally though, a patented item is a solution to a particular problem, while a copyrighted item is a document that might or might not contain a patentable solution. Patent ends 25 years after the death of the original creator(s). Even if a patent is owned in whole or in part by a business, like copyright, it must be associated with a personal creator.

Is the item already patented as a solution to a different problem, as a solution to a more general problem, as a solution to a more specific problem? Is the item a specific example of something more general that has been patented, or a general example of something more specific that has been patented? Is the item a working example of something that was patented only in theory? I won't attempt to answer how such problems are resolved today, only that future AFFEERCE solutions will allow the Library of Congress to incorporate new ideas into existing patents. Specific instances of general patents will be assigned percentage ownership. The composition of a patent can include processes, feature choice-sets, where each choice is its own patent, and even a choice-set describing the arrangement of features. Each element of a choice-set recursively includes the same elements. Rather than proprietary all or nothing solutions, solutions at the Library of Congress patent office will be constantly improving as new owners, processes, choices, and arrangements are added. Think of it as patent algebra.

To patent requires a search of other solutions and some proficiency in patent algebra. Unlike copyrights, patent search, and composition, alternation, and concatenation with existing patents might require many hours of work. Because the dimensionality of classification systems is always less than the infinite dimensionality of reality, clones (identical products) can develop along multiple branches of the classification tree. Library of Congress personnel have the expertise to resolve these ambiguities.

Every product is patented and given a unique product id. The product id is required if the product will ever be a capital expenditure exempt from consumption tax. This include all products in store inventories, so patenting the product is a business necessity. Even more beneficially, any intellectual property in the product that is not currently under patent or explicitly in the commons, becomes the intellectual property of the business obtaining the patent. If the business is owned by a large collective, the patent does not expire until 25 years after the death of the last surviving member of the collective at the time the patent was issued.

To encourage companies to patent every single product, or process, a 1% tranche of the intellectual property distribution is returned to the manufacturer of a product or the implementer of a process, even if that product or process is an exact copy of another patented product on the market, or process in use. Unless products are patented, the owner of the intellectual property within the product cannot be compensated, so this 1% is money well-spent and will insure patenting is part of any product roll-out. Like other tranches of the intellectual property distribution, this tranche is also based on distribution totals. If the tranche contains $2.8 billion, and 280 billion products are sold or downloaded during the year, the manufacturer will receive an extra penny for each patented item sold.

The cost to patent is the $35 universal deductible, however, several applications to the Library of Congress might be required. It is the duty of the inventor, or hired technical experts, to break the product down into the intellectual property it contains, and classify that property as patented, commons, or new. The public hierarchical database contains all patented and commons intellectual property. Library of Congress personnel will process the patent and correct minor errors. In the event of a classification error that halts the process, the patent will be returned to the inventor with the branch error identified and the correct branch supplied. Using the correct branch, the inventor will rework, and resubmit the patent for an additional $35 universal deductible.

Once the intellectual property breakdown is finalized, Library of Congress personnel will assign percentage of ownership to all the intellectual property in the product. There could literally be tens of thousands of owners of any given product. This is particularly true if the product contains software, heralding an age of universal object libraries that reduce redundancy thousands of times and reward independent developers of quality objects or agents.

There is a powerful motivation for manufacturers to patent every product. These are:

1. Most every product that is not a complete copy has unique intellectual property that is neither under patent nor in the commons. This might be a high level configuration of parts, or as trivial as surface art. Sale of this product or any other product that uses this intellectual property, produces income for the manufacturer from the intellectual property distribution.
2. 1% of the intellectual property distribution goes to the manufacturer, or implementer of a process, even if the product or process is a complete clone.
3. Without a product id, the product cannot be placed on a purchase path. This means the product cannot be sold in a retail outlet, unless the retail outlet is willing to pay consumption tax on the purchase of inventory. That is highly unlikely.
4. Product patenting costs only a small multiple of $35 (the universal deductible). It is a virtually free government service, and the Library of Congress guarantees that each $35 iteration will be closer to the goal of a patented product.

Tranches and Distribution

Equity requires a breakdown of the intellectual property distribution into tranches for such things as books and articles, robots, business software, TV programs, movies, architectural drawings, music, machines for the end user, various kinds of capital machines, and so on. Each tranche is distributed on tranche specific rules, such as quantity of distribution, number of viewers, items produced, or number of users. The rules for each tranche are set by an associated VSG (voluntary standards group). With the intellectual property distribution, all content will be free, creating a trillion or more dollars of wealth.

What will not usually be included in the rules are price or total sales in dollars. In other words, for copyrighted material, the distribution will be the same whether the item is sold or freely downloaded. For patented consumer items, it likewise doesn't matter whether the item is sold or given away for free. Assembly line machines might have been purchased or given to the enterprise for free. In either case, the intellectual property distribution will be based on the amount of desired goods produced by the machine. Patented processes and methods will always be free. The intellectual property distribution will be based on the output of those processes and methods. Copyrighted material like software, which is both a consumable and a capital good will have more complex rules.

Inventors will try to get major corporations to take their machines for free. Every song ever written will be freely available. Movie theater prices will be reduced to a fraction, as all films will be provided for free. All TV shows will be free to stream. Commercial television can reduce the number and length of commercials. The latest bestseller will be free to download as an e-book as soon as it is published. Hard copy book prices will be cut in half. Academic journals will be free, and all articles freely available. Innovators will gladly spread the secrets of formerly proprietary processes. Best of all, life-saving patented drugs will be as cheap as aspirin.

Suppose there are 20 billion book events in a given year, including book purchases, library check outs, and free downloads. A moderately popular author sells 100,000 copies of a book, has 150,000 library checkouts and 800,000 free downloads of the e-book, a total of 1,050,000 book events. Of the $320 billion intellectual property distribution, suppose there is a $9 billion tranche for book events. The author would receive $472,500 in royalties. Of course, VIP identity would be required to download an e-book, so the same person would not be counted more than once. It will be common for the author and publisher to take joint ownership of a copyright. The publisher can concentrate on high quality printed material, and publicity, without worrying about losing money from free downloads. The author and publisher get royalties from library checkouts and don't have to worry about pirating. The consumer gets free downloads. It is win-win-win.

Music events are also based on quantity of distribution. Suppose there are 40 billion music events and a $18 billion tranche. A hit song is included on 1 million albums sold, is downloaded 4 million times, is played on 1,000 radio stations, with 5,000 average listeners, is performed at several concerts with 1 million total in the audience. This is a total of 12 million events. The musician, record company, and other owners of the copyright would receive $5.4 million from that one song alone. Inclusion of the song in very large collections would not count as heavily. Performers at smaller venues might be honor bound to report the songs they had performed, although even tickets costing a penny could be tied to individual identities. A small time artist who sells 200 tapes and gets 500 downloads will get $314 in additional royalties per song. The exact method of calculating events will be determined by the industry VSG.

Movies, TV shows, recorded plays and concerts would follow a similar form of royalty distribution. The critical point is that content would be freely available to all. Consumers pay only for media, and media might be subsidized by content. The artists, authors, producers and studios would be paid from the intellectual property distribution.

Every machine sold or given away is a collection of many patents. Each patent is treated as a percentage of the product. Final percentages would be used to determine the distribution of the tranche.

A huge benefit of the intellectual property distribution for Americans is from the drug patents. Drug makers will have every incentive to distribute their drugs at the lowest possible price, if they hold the patent. It will be the generics, if they even exist, that are more expensive. The more widely the drug is prescribed and purchased, the greater the royalties.

If proprietary processes are not patented, they can be stolen and patented by the thieves. Profits from innovation that should have gone to the original company, will now go to the thieves. Of course, once a process is patented, sharing is encouraged. If the patenting company is trebled or a competitor produces the same product, the intellectual property distribution from those sales will still go to those who hold the patents, which is the owners of the corporation at the time the patent was issued.

It is clear that this distribution will save trillions of dollars. If all of AFFEERCE did nothing for the economy except this one distribution, AFFEERCE would still be worthwhile. For a feature creating trillions in wealth, a $320 billion allocation is a small price to pay.

It would hardly be equitable to use all of the ground rents to fund artists, inventors, and creators of all stripes, although we could do worse.

The Problem with Local Distribution

> **Local distribution of locally collected rents creates gross inequality between cities or communities. It makes only a slight dent in the Gini coefficient at the expense of giving the individual less power over their circumstances. It will lead to barbarism.**

Consider this Georgist dictum: Location value is created by the community and should be returned to its creators.

What is the community? Is it our neighborhood, our city, our county, our state, our nation, or the world? While the collection method using 150% ODV makes it impossible for a landowner to create location value for their own land with an improvement, neighboring lands see a sharp uptick in location value. In general, this location value decreases with distance from the improvement. Creation of location value is thus exceedingly local. Unfortunately, this is highly problematic.

In a sense, the distribution of ground rents on location value is currently "as local as it gets." What I mean is that the owners of the property receive the entire non-taxable distribution of the rent, also called the imputed rent. This trivial assertion is useful in understanding what happens when we slowly grow the size of the distribution domain.

Imagine if the distribution domains were each one square mile. Wealthy neighborhoods would receive all of their own ground rent and poor neighborhoods would receive little or no ground rent. If these rents were used to pay for police, schools, and other city services, the wealthy neighborhoods would have the best police and teachers money could buy, while the poorest neighborhoods would have no sewers, no police or fire protection, and no education. As certainly as night follows day, the wealthy neighborhoods would put up giant walls to keep out marauding gangs of the desperate poor.

There are two fundamental reasons why this is true.

1. Individuals with arbitrary wealth are not randomly distributed throughout the dominion.
2. Even if we could affect a one-time random distribution, the dynamics of any economy cause individuals to cluster together according to their wealth.

It might seem these problems would go away if the distribution domains were large enough to encompass entire cities. A city is certainly a reasonable definition of community. But the same principle holds to a lesser extent. There will be rich cities and there will be poor cities. Rich cities will have many city services and poor cities will have few. If this seems to be an acceptable distribution compromise, then you have not considered the dynamics.

Consider that deterioration of city services causes location value to drop. As location value drops, so does ground rent. As rent drops, the amount of money available for city services drops. As city services deteriorate, location value drops even more, causing rent to drop, causing city services to drop even further… Local distribution mirrors some of the problems of a land value tax.

Imagine two communities, one wealthy, one poor, separated by miles of prairie. On the eve of Georgism, the wealthy community has better roads, better schools, less crime, and far nicer homes. The location value and thus the ground rents will be considerably greater in the wealthy community. Rents paid by each community are returned to that community. Perhaps as much as 30% of the rents are sent on to some state or nation, whose capital is many hundreds of miles away. That is really immaterial. The rents received by each community are spent on new public goods and/or given to the citizens as a dividend. The poor community is more likely to favor the dividend to feed its people, while the wealthy community will favor public goods that have a bigger effect on land value. But even that is immaterial to the fundamental notion that land values must increase at a faster rate in the wealthy community, simply because more ground rents are returned to be invested.

Whatever the difference in wealth between the richest and poorest cities on day 1, that difference will continue to grow. Much as inequality between people grows with today's "local as it gets" distribution of the ground rents, inequality between cities will grow, if rents are distributed to the cities from whence they came.

The size of the domain of distribution is inversely proportional to the likelihood of chaos and gross inequality. By size, I mean the population, wealth, and diversity of industry, rather than land area. By chaos I mean the unpredictability of results from a miniscule change in initial conditions, although the more common definition would apply as well.

The distribution domain today is the landlords and their families. That is why we have the uber-wealthy 1% and the rest of us. In an economy that returns location value to the community that created it, we will have the uber-wealthy 1% of communities, and the rest of the communities, with perhaps as many as 50% of the communities in crime-infested blight; barbarism.

Keep in mind that an exogenous event, like the closing of a factory, can turn a virtuous cycle into a death spiral overnight. Fear of barbarism will be a self-fulfilling prophecy as people flee the jurisdiction while they still can afford to, driving land values down even faster. This is the chaos factor.

It is clear that the larger and more diverse the distribution domain, the less violent the creation or destruction of wealth from distribution of the ground rents. There is a light at the end of the tunnel. For one, the problem is virtually non-existent with distribution domains at the national level, especially for nations that are wealthy to begin with. Furthermore, with a distribution net cast over the entire world, the problem ceases to exist.

We conclude that the distribution domain be, at a minimum, national in scope.

However, there is a problem. "Why should a community invest in infrastructure that will raise ground rents when those rents are lost to a national distribution?" Citizens would be paying twice for their public goods. The answer is part of another integrated solution that will be covered shortly.

But first, two more land mines. The one on the right is labeled "Each of us". The one on the left is labeled "All of us."

Each of Us and All of Us

That which God or Nature provides belongs to each of us and to all of us. Ground rents are not a tax, but rent payments to the common owners of the land. Paying the entire distribution as cash to each of us will eliminate public goods and services. The poor will be forced to pay fealty to a wealthy landowner for protection and sanitation leading to a new feudalism. On the other hand, if all of the ground rents go for public goods and services, this is a regressive 100% head tax on the distributions. It will push the poor to the margin and lead to barbarism at the city gates.

What if we were to divide the ground rent equally between every citizen in the distribution domain? Paid out in cash. Those checks every month would be greeted with joy by those who were either not employed, or brought in a low wage. The wealthy would treat them as an insignificant source of income.

It sounds like a boon for equality, but what about police and fire protection, streets and sanitation, good government, education, and healthcare? Who will pay for those?

Part of the idea behind the ground rents is to eliminate taxes on production. But without a tax, who will pay for these important services. Some on the right say that with all this money coming in to each individual, taxes could be voluntary. However, the problem with voluntary taxation is summed up by a phenomenon that has come to be known as "the tragedy of the commons." It is a drama that plays out in so many contexts, that there is serious debate as to whether it is a natural law or not. There are those who believe as Garret Hardin, who coined the phrase, that it is natural law and those who follow Elinor Ostrom, who won a Nobel Prize, refuting that premise.

You can recognize the drama by its favorite slogan, "I won't be the sucker." For instance, common grazing land is shared by several ranches. If each rancher limits grazing, as agreed, to a few hours a day, the land can be used for grazing indefinitely. But two ranchers allow their cattle unlimited access to the land, depleting the resource. A third farmer then gives his cattle unlimited access, saying, "I won't be the sucker." Or the lifeboat that can hold only 20 but 30 are in the water from the sinking ship. A man volunteers to sacrifice his life until he sees someone in the boat "less deserving" of life than himself. "I won't be the sucker," he says, starting a free-for-all that sinks the lifeboat.

As for voluntary payment of taxes, nobody wants to be the sucker while others are not paying their fair share. Somebody might say, "Why should I be a sucker and pay, when he isn't, especially since he will benefit more than I?" Voluntary taxation does not work. This is especially true when no one expense benefits a majority. If one third benefit from spending on A, one third benefit from spending on B, and one third benefit from spending on C, good luck getting the two thirds who do not benefit to part with their hard earned cash or monthly cash stipend to pay for A, B, or C, especially if it is completely voluntary. Whether voluntary taxation might work at some time in the future, nobody can say for sure. But in our present culture, "the tragedy of the commons" is our national drama. Sort of like the bald eagle is our national bird.

The result of a 100% cash distribution is private ownership of these services. Although the wealthy receive much more benefit from public goods than the poor, everyone needs public goods and services. While private police forces, private roads, private fire protection, and so forth, might please libertarians, they force the average person to seek protection on lands controlled by a wealthy benefactor, in exchange for fealty and other rents to the lord of the manor. Like the land value tax of collection theory, the 100% cash distribution leads to feudalism.

Levying a tax would seem to solve the problems of private police forces and other manifestations of the commons tragedy. But it raises the question, "What kind of tax and how much?" One of the benefits of collecting ground rent is the elimination of all taxes. Income and profit taxes can cripple productivity. A consumption tax of sufficient size to fund these services would also hurt. While people will gladly pay a rent of their choosing to ward off treblers, particularly a redistributed rent, many will evade or dodge taxes, creating an enforcement problem.

We see that distribution to "each of us" leads to either feudalism, or taxes on productivity that serve to inhibit productivity.

Before looking at the "all of us" distribution, recall a statement of fact that is essential to the analysis: Ground rents are not a tax, but rent payments to the common owners of the land

This is a key to the entire theory of distribution. When a tax is paid, nothing is directly received in return. However, ground rent is a purchase of location value. The more rent you pay, the more location value you get. Location value is used to increase business profits or to have a more comfortable lifestyle. It can even increase social status.

When a wealthy industrialist purchases a large quantity of location value, it can hardly be called "a progressive tax." No more so than when that same industrialist purchases a private jet, or capital goods. To call paying ground rent for location value "a progressive tax," is to condemn the poor to the most heinous tax of all.

In the "all of us" distribution, 100% of the rents go for public goods and services. However, this is mathematically identical to the "each of us" distribution with an additional tax levied. In this case, the amount of tax is 100% of the distribution and the type of tax is a head tax, the most regressive of all possible taxes. In as much as public goods and services, particularly police and fire protection, benefit the wealthy over the poor, regression is plumbed to new depths. To claim that location value purchased by the wealthy somehow makes this assault on the poor "progressive" reminds me of Orwellian doublespeak.

Services are per person, so the money for public goods and services is divided equally between regions based on population. Those areas with the most density receive the most money with sparse areas receiving much less. Equity demands nothing less.

An equitable distribution of public goods and services, even with a national distribution domain, shows a high correlation of spending effectiveness with population density. This is a natural law because it can be no other way. It is simply economy of scale. $35/month/person for police protection can only buy the wilderness pioneer a down payment on a shotgun, while it can support a high-tech efficient police force in the populated downtown.

In the "all of us" distribution, a 3D graph of location value will evolve toward mountains that are steeper and higher, not unlike today, but they will grow faster and with greater efficiency. The poor will be pushed outward to the margin. It is a natural law that the more money spent on public infrastructure, the greater the value of the land; the greater the value of the land, the higher the ground rents; the higher the rents, the more poor are pushed to the outskirts of the city.

While money for goods and services will follow the poor out, a ring does not have the same density or efficiency as a circle. Despite free land at the margin, scarce capital will be commandeered to augment public goods and services. The inequality between the center of the city and the outskirts will continue to grow. The end result can only be barbaric raids on the inner city by poor and desperate bands.

A cash or benefit entitlement, not unlike the food stamp and other aid programs we have in place today, would nip the barbarism in the bud. However, these programs foster the cycle of poverty, by discouraging employment, thrift, and the economy of scale. They further class division and resentment. They encourage mendacity. Even if entitlements were sufficient to place poor children on a level playing field, the moral hazard would pull them down again. Distribution of the ground rents to the community was supposed to end the need for hideous welfare systems, not accentuate that need.

The symmetry is obvious. Distribution to "each of us" necessitates a tax to prevent feudalism, while distribution to "all of us" necessitates an entitlement to prevent barbarism. It is looking like the best theory of distribution is a hacked, backroom compromise, engineered by professional politicians, not unlike today.

The Solution – A Synthesis of Objectivism and Subjectivism

> **It turns out that a head tax is exactly neutralized by a personal distribution. Like sodium and chlorine, the synthesis is harmless. A head tax and a personal distribution cancel each other out. They detoxify each other. Public services have far more benefit to the poor when public service distributions move with the person. The intellectual property distribution, distinct from both a head tax and personal distribution, provides equal benefit to all social classes by lowering the cost of goods in the marketplace.**

Consider that police protection is a public good. Police protection benefits the industrialist qualitatively more than the pauper. An "all of us" distribution of $35/month/person for this protection would be a godsend to the industrialist. It would be, at best, irrelevant to the pauper, but to the exclusion of food, medicine and shelter for themselves and their children, it would be a tragedy. There is nothing more regressive than this head tax.

Consider that nutritious food, warm and safe shelter, cash, and basic medical care are private goods. If the pauper received $220/month for food, it would be a godsend. If the wealthy industrialist received $220/month for food, it would be irrelevant. There is nothing more progressive than this distribution.

Consider sodium, a toxic corrosive metal that would kill you if you ate it. Consider chlorine, a fatal poisonous gas. These are like the "each of us" and "all of us" distributions. Combine them and we have a necessary component of life; sodium chloride; table salt.

This is called a synthesis when two or more things combine to form something totally different. But how can combining the two forms of distribution create something qualitatively superior? The answer lies in neutralization. A head tax and a personal distribution cancel each other out. They detoxify each other.

Not only have we eliminated the progressive/regressive toxicity for the prince and the pauper, but every income class in between. For instance, as one's wealth increases, the food distribution becomes less and less significant, as police protection becomes increasingly necessary.

Nor do the distributions come with any stigma, propensity for class warfare, or moral hazards. Warren Buffet receives the same allocation for food as the street peddler. A family of 10 receives ten times the food distribution as a family of one. Economies of scale encourage family, commune, and collective.

Interestingly, public goods once irrelevant to the lower classes become highly valuable. Police and fire fighters are paid per life, not per property. Thus their priorities are apt to change. Most importantly, distributions for public goods and services move with the person.

Each person carries a portfolio of distributions for police, fire, streets, sanitation, and so on. Not only are strangers welcomed into families, and collectives because of the economies of scale they bring for food and housing, but they are welcomed into communities because of the economies of scale they bring to public services. This is the beginning of an epoch where people are truly valued by others; a world that welcomes refugees with open arms.

When public goods and services are paid per person, and not by the value of improvements, the trend toward mixed-use, family businesses, collectives, mutual organizations, and a general integration of home and work is accelerated.

A distribution scheme where every head tax is cancelled out by a personal distribution is ideal and utopian. The distribution scheme, which I call universal distribution, is so superior to anything we have now, that getting it perfect is not that important. Although a 50/50 split between basic income and public goods is acceptable, in the next section we will see that a bias in favor of basic income is preferable.

There is, of course, a third category of distribution that is the soul of distribution theory, the intellectual property distribution. This is the distribution that allows innovation to replace location as the primary source of business profit. Because food and housing and unlimited free education are part of universal distribution, all have an equal chance at the intellectual property distribution. The universal benefit of this distribution is also seen in this natural law: the greater the intellectual property distribution, the lower the cost of goods in the marketplace.

Despite the ultimately agreed upon allocation of say, $5/month/person for fire protection, the level of federation that receives a tranche of the distribution, allocated for a particular use, can, by a super-plurality change the allocated use. However, what can never be changed is the right to leave a community and take one's default distributions with them.

Personal Distribution Bias

> **A bias in favor of personal distributions is acceptable once minimum required public services have been met.**

Looking at the negative consequences of deviations from the two extremes, using all of the ground rent for public services, and distributing all of the ground rent to each of us, there is an asymmetry. Using the rent for public services constitutes a head tax. This tends to drive the poor from the city center to the margin, leading to barbarism at the gate. As personal distributions are slowly added, the effect of the head tax is lessened in a quantitative manner. The poor are driven to the margin at a slower rate, until personal distributions are equal to the head tax. At that point, the negative effects of the head tax are gone, but the poor still might be driven out of the city because they lack resources. So even as basic income exceeds the head tax, the rate of driving the poor to the margin continues to slow, until such time as the housing distribution is sufficient to afford a minimal efficient, warm, and safe dwelling near the city center.

Distribution of all the ground rent, on the other hand, forces the poor to purchase protection and other services from wealthy feudal lords. Slowly increasing head taxes for services does not lessen feudalism in a quantitative manner. Only when a critical juncture is passed so that city protection and sanitation services are sufficient for people to venture out on their own does the economic hold of feudal lords end. Additional head taxes do nothing to change that relationship.

While it is obvious that head taxes should never exceed basic income, there is no such constraint on basic income. However, if education and medical care are included on the public goods side of the ledger, there is close to a 50/50 balance.

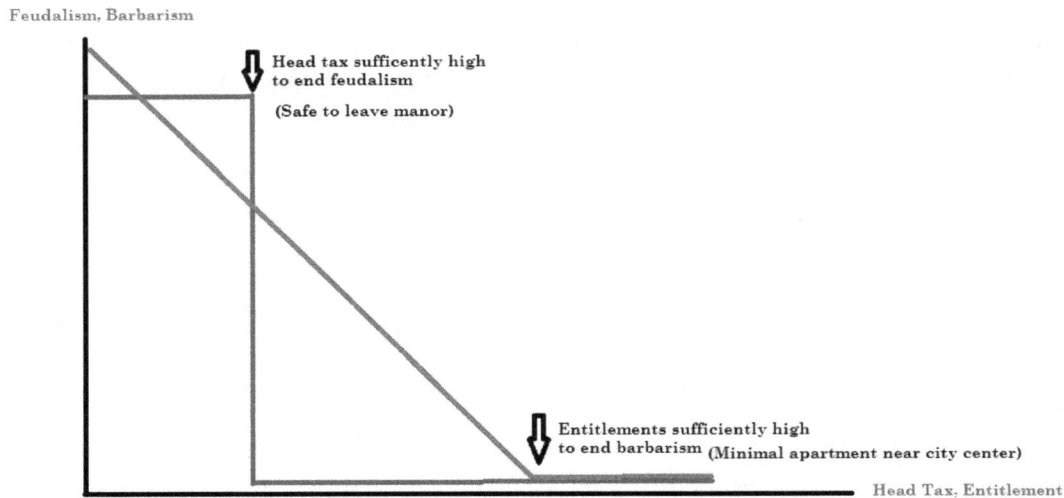

Local Land Capture

> **The national increase in land value is exactly equal to the requirement for additional currency to prevent deflation. This currency only exists for new wealth, not wealth transferred between dominions, so it can be justly used to compensate land value increases from local infrastructure investment.**

There is still a flaw in the distribution system. Suppose a locality decides to invest additional money outside of the distribution package for a new bridge, museum, rapid transit system, or something else that will make their town a nicer place to live and work. This will increase the desirability of the community and raise ground rents. However, since the distribution domain is national, an insignificant portion of those increased rents will come back to the community. In effect, they are paying for the public good twice; once for the original investment and a second time in increased rents.

When local ground rents are returned locally, as seen above, we end up with very rich and very poor cities. However, if local rents generated by locally financed improvements are not returned locally, the citizens end up paying twice. This is a counter-incentive for community improvement.

Localities should be repaid for these improvements only under these conditions:

1. The improvement can be shown to raise the location value in subsequent years, independent of other factors
2. The total location value of the nation increases
3. The amount paid is equitably divided between all localities registering investments based on the increase in location value generated by the improvement.
4. The total amount paid is exactly equal to the increase in national land value.
5. The money paid must not interfere with funding the distribution package and cannot involve the return of local rents, locally.
6. Payments cease after a cutoff of 150% of the initial investment.

There is an integrated solution where each of these requirements is not difficult to ascertain.

On points 2 and 4, *Chapter 6 – Balance if the RCs and the Treasury* shows how easy it is for the Treasury to determine the exact increase in national land value. This requirement arises because there is no social benefit to increasing land value in one location at the expense of decreasing it in another. For instance, if a factory is lured from one city to another, should the town that gained the factory be rewarded again with increased distribution, while the town that lost the factory be punished twice? This is especially difficult if the factory moved because of a public good funded by private investment.

On points 1 and 3, I will show directly below how easy it is to measure location value increases from an improvement with trebling/self-assessment. The natural marketplace of location value, self-assessment, gives us a good tool for statistically analyzing the depth and breadth of increase from any such public improvement that no assessor, with a natural bias for increasing local revenues, could possibly do.

The money paid for local land capture does not come from the ground rents as required by point 5. It comes instead from the Treasury. Amazingly, to prevent deflation, the new money that must be created by the Treasury exactly equals the national increase in land value.

National refers to the distribution domain, whatever that might be. It is assumed that the currency domain is the same as the distribution domain, and that the reserve ratio at banks is fixed by law at 50%. Notice that the natural law is true regardless of whether the land value increase comes from population or productivity. Although this law sets a lot of policy, the benefits reward localities for investing in public goods at the same time maintaining an exceptionally stable currency.

To determine the increase in location value from an improvement, the rent increase or decrease in all nearby properties is fed through statistical and other objective computer analysis. Frozen, modified, or trebled ground rents paint an accurate picture of the improvement's impact. Notice in the second drawing, the lack of information an assessor would have for this computation using sparse land sales.

Change in self-assessed value of every property from project approval to completion and signoff

Only 2 sales of nearby properties from project approval to completion and signoff

National land value is a simple function of the ground rent and will be covered in *Chapter 6 – Balance of the RCs and the Treasury.*

A Controlled Distribution

The more controlled the distribution, the more free the society. The stronger the safety net, the more risk people will take. An allocated distribution provides the strongest possible safety net.

This natural law will strike some as funny or ironic. As Nature provides food and shelter for all species, it is our inherited task to provide the same to humanity. Therefore it might not be constitutionally wise to allow a super-majority to override this bedrock of distribution theory, especially for children.

All of my examples have used earmarked distributions. This distribution is for food, this distribution is for housing, this distribution for police protection, and so on. The reason goes beyond simplifying the balancing of head taxes with personal distributions, although that is a benefit.

You might say, "What's with this nanny state? Why not just have half of universal distribution go for a basic guaranteed income in cash, and the other half go for public goods and services?" Well that would be very nice and qualitatively superior to anything that exists in the world today. But still, we could have so much more freedom by controlling the distribution.

Before your head spins off, let me explain. Freedom is enhanced by risk-taking. That is the case whether it is jumping out of a plane, starting a new business, or changing the direction of your life. A society that treasures freedom encourages risk-taking. What gives the acrobat the courage to first walk the tightrope? The safety net!

The best way to encourage risk-taking is to provide a safety net, below which none can fall. Most people will fail 4 or 5 times before they have a successful business. If the safety net had gaping holes, would you walk the tightrope with those odds? "Yes," you say, "but the cash comes every month. There are no gaping holes." But cash is good for all debts public and private, while earmarked funds are not. If failure leaves you in debt, how much of your family's food and housing money will go to the creditor? How much looser was the creditor's standards, knowing the cash would keep coming? Cash can be spent on alcohol and drugs. If things are bad, the temptation might be too great. How much of your family's food and housing money will go for alcohol, drugs, tobacco, or gambling? Housing money goes first to ground rent, mortgages, and apartment rent, before it can be spent on utilities. Is a landlord more likely to rent to an unemployed family with an allocation that can only be used for apartment rent, or one that receives the same allocation in cash? Education is vital for a prosperous society. It is both a public good and a private one. Given cash, how many would choose education over many luxury vacations? There are quite a few other similar conundrums. In terms of freedom, the basic equation is this: As long as hunger and homelessness are conceivable, there will be fewer entrepreneurs, less people who quit their day job to write the great American novel, or compose the next hit song, or invent the next big thing. Therefore, our job is to make them inconceivable.

This is not money that you produced with your own labor. In a free society, that is only yours to control. This is the gift from God or Nature that belongs to each of us and all of us. It is our right to demand of these ground rents, as a collective, that there be no hunger or homelessness, lack of medical care or access to education. It is our right to weave a safety net through which none can fall.

What follows is a detailed list of reasons why universal distribution is better than an unallocated basic income.

1. The right to life for children includes the right to nutritious meals. Though the intention of most parents is to provide for their children, a few would be tempted to spend the money elsewhere. The best way to insure all children are receiving nutritious meals without bureaucracy is to allocate a portion of basic income for food.

2. There are several valid reasons for a consumption tax, such as a discretionary tax, achievement annuities, and special sunset taxes approved by the voters. By exempting the distributions from this tax, the consumption tax becomes progressive. This is only possible with allocated cash.

3. In families, young adults and other family members will be reluctant to surrender a portion of their cash stipend to the family shopper. Either the family shopper will end up spending more of their own money for food, or large families will lose their efficiency as everyone does their own shopping. Accounting of who spends what is more difficult. A food distribution will solve many conflicts.

4. As citizens of Earth, we have a right to know that other citizens are not going hungry because they spent their food money on a drug fix, alcohol, or at the casinos. This is a choice people can make with the fruits of their own labor, not the bounty of the Earth. We have a right not to have mothers with children, or anyone for that matter, begging on the street for food.

5. A food distribution does not restrict anybody's freedom. Rebates are available for families without children.

6. A food distribution allows us to deal with the imbalances caused by crop subsidies. Using part of the revenue from trebled cropland to increase the food distribution will force that money into the hands of farmers allowing them to increase the ground rent on cropland and make it more productive. An increase in the general cash stipend would never efficiently find its way to farmers.

7. Food distributions encourage the growth of larger alternative families for economies of scale. As few as six people with six food distributions can enjoy a menu without regard to cost. A single person on a single food distribution will have to economize to stretch the budget. A cash stipend offers no manageable incentives for larger families or collectives.

8. The housing distribution allows mortgage lenders to make loans at low interest rates for families whose total housing distribution is more than sufficient to cover the mortgage. The automatic draws on the housing distribution are ground rent first, mortgage or tenant rents next, association assessment next. The household is then free to spend the remainder on utilities, repairs, or improvements as they see fit. Cash qualifications for a mortgage would be much tighter.

9. The housing distribution will encourage the development of efficiency studios with all utilities for those unemployed choosing to live alone. A fixed tenant rent equal to the $370 per month housing distribution is possible because landlords can rent these out to the unemployed without fear of default. A cash distribution is far more risky and will force the poor into homelessness or substandard housing.

10. This bears repeating for housing: As citizens of Earth, we have a right to know that other citizens are not homeless because they spent their housing money on a drug fix, alcohol, or at the casinos. This is a choice people can make with the fruits of their own labor, not the bounty of the Earth. We have a right not to have the homeless on our doorsteps, sleeping on rapid transit, under viaducts, and over vents.

11. The housing distribution can be used for vans, RV's and houseboats, including fuel. For families without children, the housing distribution could be used for a treehouse in the woods or a cave in the mountains. Excess housing distribution can be used for utilities and renovations. In the deep woods, it can be used for sleeping bags, lanterns and an ax. If there is still housing distribution remaining, it can be rebated at 50%. An acre of badlands at $12 a year can give a family without children a large rebate. One cannot justly claim that the housing distribution infringes on their freedom.

12. The housing and food distributions make a prospective new member of a family not a burden. Wherever a person might wander, they will tend to be welcomed because they bring added food to the table and new utilities to the home. The sum is greater than the parts due to economies of scale. This is a major cultural shift from the isolation and loneliness promoted by crony capitalism. A cash stipend will tend to be hoarded; not freely shared.

13. Cash is valid for the payment of all debts public and private. A single business mistake could leave a family hungry and homeless until bankruptcy is declared. It is illegal to demand food or housing distributions as

repayment for a debt. Credit for food or housing cannot be extended in promise for future distributions. Distributions can only be transferred within the family, or used at point of sale for their designated purpose. No matter what happens, there will always be food and shelter.

14. There is a $35 cash distribution, and it is especially easy to earmark this because it is unique. It acts as a universal monthly deductible for the emergency room, initial visit to a specialist, or court of law. These are all distributions, but overuse of these resources is discouraged. When confined to a penitentiary, $30 of this distribution is automatically given to the victim. (See, *Chapter 9 – Government, Law and Justice*).

15. The medical distribution is used to purchase a basic insurance policy. If this is an implied portion of an unallocated basic income, many citizens would opt not to buy the policy. Equity demands that they be refused service in the ER without adequate cash or credit. Even with the cash for emergency treatment and diagnosis, if they lack the cash or credit, surgery cannot be performed. If they are confined to a penitentiary, without cash, they can receive no medical treatment without having purchased the basic policy. This is an affront to civilized humanity. In an AFFEERCE economy, the medical distribution is a right.

16. Recently, there was news of a house burning down as the fire department watched. The family had not paid for fire protection. As with personal distributions, if police, fire, and defense distributions were paid from a cash stipend, chaos would reign. Moving into an AFFEERCE police or fire district, increases funding by one distribution and moving out, decreases it. This fosters good police-fire-community relations; each person is a valuable asset to their community. Hiding these distributions in a cash stipend does no such thing.

17. Education is the essence of culture, an open-minded liberal society, and a technological world. If you handed everyone a wad of cash and told them to get educated or party, most would party. Allocating money for childhood education does not guarantee that unallocated money will be spent on universities and trade schools. Most people would still forego an education. Yet, these are the places where people need to go to learn to program and operate the complex machinery of the future. Furthermore, education is the most complex distribution because it is not distributed equally, even with equality of opportunity. One cash sum would either be prohibitively large or cheat some students out of their complete education.

The Withering Away of the Allocations

By making it very difficult to increase or add to allocated distributions, increased production goes to lower rents and a variable cash distribution called a citizens' dividend. Over time, the citizens' dividend and other dividend accounts overwhelm the allocated distributions. This is called the withering away of the allocations.

Constitutionally, it will be very difficult to change the distribution package. This is a good thing. The AFFEERCE enlightenment predicts that over the decades humanity will shed the afflictions of fear and greed that mark our present era. With these afflictions gone, it is reasonable to assume that personal decisions on monetary allocation will become more rational. The distribution package allocations will have solved the problems they were intended to solve. Feudalism, barbarism, poverty and homelessness, will no longer be dangers. All people will have equal access to education and basic medical care. Further increases in land value should be distributed directly to the people.

The distribution package is distributed to or for every citizen regardless of age, income, assets, or family size. What will happen is that the distribution package will remain the same size (except for special situations like restoring free enterprise to farming), and added productivity will find its way into a citizens' dividend that is distributed to each adult as cash. (See, *Chapter 6 – The Balance of the RCs and the Treasury*) The process where the distribution package remains the same size, while the citizens' dividend grows with increased productivity is called "The withering away of the allocations."

Chapter 4 – Reproductive Freedom and Control

The MIT study comes a few weeks after a similar one by Stanford University researchers found that children from low-income backgrounds tend to have smaller brains, overall, than their wealthier peers. The brain of a child whose family earns less than $25,000 annually is 6% smaller in surface area than a child whose parents earned more than $150,000, according to the study, published in Nature Neuroscience.[FTN4.33]

Introduction

Required Reading

Reproductive control is shrouded in taboo and controversy. The notion that some people shouldn't have children is often equated with the Holocaust. This is not only an insult to the millions who perished in the genocide, but to the progressives of a century ago who saw eugenics as a means to social reform. We are fighting many centuries of religious teachings advocating as many children as possible without regard to the physical, mental, emotional, or financial ability to support them.

Initially, this chapter was in the part on funding, because reproductive control was my primary source of funds for a free and equitable society. I was thoroughly convinced of the rightness of two often contradictory principles. First, that taxes on productive labor was morally wrong and financially counterproductive, and second, that all children have a right to a level playing field in terms of nutritious meals, warm and safe shelter, medical care and unlimited free education. Years ago, my only solution to this "contradiction between objectivism and subjectivism" was to have parents fund an annuity for a lifetime of distributions for their child, before they can give birth. This expensive proposition required the poor to labor for over a decade, prime childbearing years, to afford a single child. Enforcement, no matter how gentle, would be a threat to freedom.

After discovering Henry George and the moral basis of ground rents, and satisfying myself with a consistent collection and distribution theory, the need for a baby tax disappeared. But not quite. In the penultimate chapter in this section, *Chapter 6 – The Balance of the RCs*, I show how the baby tax is a rarely needed tool to assure ongoing prosperity. But in this chapter, we examine some serious social issues, as well, that should not be swept under the carpet because it makes some people uncomfortable. There is plenty of time to debate whether a baby tax has a place in an AFFEERCE society, or not. Before taking a side, I only ask that you read this chapter.

Overpopulation today, is not the issue. Malthus' prediction of an uncontrollable world population explosion doesn't seem likely. In fact, the advanced industrial economies are already experiencing low, or even negative population growth, while both disease and war slow down population growth in impoverished nations. If that remains the case, that is, if the fertility rate remains under 2.1, the size of the tax would be nominal, or non-existent. The tax might even go negative as a baby credit.

Critically, no country today has universal distribution. To use current examples of birth rates is like comparing apples with oranges. It is like arguing for a 55 mile per hour speed limit in the 1800s. Even countries like Denmark which has excellent family benefits, provides many of those so-called benefits only to the poor. If the condition of a benefit is that one remains poor, it is not a benefit but a stigma. Denmark also has high taxes on productivity that can serve to discourage bringing children into this world[FTN4.35]. And while Denmark's fertility rate is under 2.1(1.73), it is still higher than many other developed nations that provide fewer enticements. It is the undeveloped nations that have devastating fertility rates above 4[FTN4.36]. There is a common belief that developed nations have low fertility rates and undeveloped nations have high ones, and that is the complete story. Why then do all the Scandinavian countries have a higher fertility rate than all the Eastern European countries, even heavily Catholic Poland (1.33)? That question is answered next.

The Means of Reproduction

Reproduction in Pre-Modern Times

> **Most of the reasons for having children in pre-modern times increased the wealth of the family, church, and state. The means of production were the means of reproduction, and it was the responsibility of the woman to have as many children as possible.**

Let's make a list of answers to the question, **"What motivated people to have children in pre-modern times?"** Some answers will apply only to certain periods, but that isn't important.

Although certainly a motivation, sexual pleasure was not likely a primary one for having children in pre-modern times[FTN4.18]. Inheritance was more important. Children provided a means for the upper class to pass on the family name, wealth, and position in society. However, the majority of families had neither wealth nor position. So inheritance was not the primary motivation, either.

The most important reason for having children in pre-modern times was to supply the labor pool[FTN4.19]. Twenty kids would grow up to bring down a mammoth much easier than one. If you had twenty children harvesting grain, and three died, with a little added effort, the crop could still be brought in. If you had four children working the fields, and three died, the harvest would be in jeopardy. Children, by and large, were not expected to reach adulthood.

As long as each child produced more than they consumed, there was a profit. And, those profits might be used to support parents in their old age, to support a temporarily sick or injured worker, or to pay tribute to the overlord, the king, or the church[FTN4.11]. The more children, the more profit.

Early on, mankind learned to protect itself from wild beasts. But later, when we developed agriculture, we needed armies to protect our land. The size of armies depended on population. Bigger armies allowed more land to be protected – and conquered. Conquered lands brought in still more profit.

The dominant equation for family, tribe, and state were identical. Children = Wealth. The more children one had, the wealthier one was, as was their tribe, manor, or kingdom.

The financial instruments to generate this wealth, the means of reproduction, the baby factories, were women. Their worth was measured by the children they bore. From puberty to menopause, pregnancy was expected. If women produced enough children before menopause, they could expect to be fed and honored in old age. But very few made it that far[FTN4.20].

Here is a list of reasons motivating people to have children in pre-modern times, with some overlap.

1. To feed the labor pool
2. To provide security for old age
3. Children were not expected to survive to fertility.
4. To provide security for temporarily sick or injured workers
5. To insure stability in the face of a loss of a few workers
6. To generate profits for overlords, tribes, and kings

7. To build large armies
8. Not enough sons
9. To allow for inheritance of family name, family wealth and family class
10. To combat loneliness and provide spiritual enrichment
11. God commands you to be fruitful and multiply
12. People want to be mothers and fathers
13. The pleasure of procreation

Children = Wealth, was enshrined in Biblical law: be fruitful and multiply. A woman was to obey her husband and submit to sex with him whenever he desired. Powerful men could acquire many wives and mistresses continuing to procreate when others were pregnant.

Wealth brought more than multiple wives, particularly better conditions for the household; improved sanitation, abundant foods, warm and safe shelter. Thus children born in wealthier households were more likely to survive. Natural and sexual selection improved the species and evolution moved forward.

By the end of the pre-modern period, Children=Wealth was well-established in law, and in scripture. Reproduction was a woman's responsibility, her raison d'être.

Reproduction in Modern Times

> **The gap between the means of production and the means of reproduction has been widening since the Enlightenment. Children throughout the period brought increasingly less wealth to family, church, and state. By the end of the period, it was a woman's right to choose whether or not to have a child.**

With the Enlightenment, chinks developed in the equation, Children=Wealth. We ask a similar question. "What motivated people to have children since the 1600s?" Not surprisingly, the answers this time come with qualifications.

Prior to the industrial revolution, economic growth was primarily a function of population and territory. I.E. Children=Armies, Armies=Territory, Territories=Wealth➜Children=Wealth. Technology played a small role, in the weapons of war, military strategy, and tool innovation, but Children=Wealth drove productivity. With the industrial revolution, however, technology began to drive productivity. At some point in the nineteenth century, technology surpassed population as the main driver of economic growth [FTN10.19].

Child labor laws, a great humanitarian step forward, by their very nature served to decrease the value of children as members of the labor force.

As all habitable lands were occupied by the start of the Twentieth Century, territorial growth became increasingly difficult. Following the tragic outcomes of WWI and WWII, and the development of nuclear weapons, territorial growth was outlawed internationally[FTN4.02].

Recently, economists began to speak of an acceptable unemployment rate. Feeding the labor pool was no longer a reason to have children.

Among, early innovations of the modern era were financial markets and banking systems. Instead of having children to provide security in old age, people were increasingly relying on their savings and investments. With the Social Security Act of 1935, this incentive to have children all but disappeared.

Medicine significantly lowered the infant mortality rate. Children were expected to survive until fertility.

Labor fought to improve the lot of sick and injured workers through contracts, sick days, long-term and short-term disability insurance, workman's compensation, health insurance, SSI, and SSDI[FTN4.21]. The need to have children to fill in for, or provide security, when another child is temporarily disabled, is not relevant to many households.

Having children to insure the stability of the workforce ended with the demise of feudalism. Free men could travel and contract their services. If workers were lost, new ones could be hired.

The late eighteenth and nineteenth centuries brought revolutions that changed the relationship of the people to church and state. Head taxes all but disappeared[FTN4.22]. Mandatory church tithing was mostly abolished during the same period[FTN4.23]. By the twentieth century, governments often ran deficits, spending more than available tax revenue.

Very possibly, the Vietnam War was the last time the military would rely on the general population for soldiers. Today's army is a professional outfit. There is no draft and military leaders prefer it that way[FTN4.24]. Technology is the driving force for military superiority.

Women's equality in the West all but eliminated the need to have more sons. Inherited aristocratic title lost any recognition in law. Rights gained through inheritance no longer existed. There was still motivation to have children to pass on the family name and family wealth, but that too was weakening.

Motivations for having children today (**with qualifications**) include:

1. To allow for inheritance of family name and family wealth. (**Some would rather leave a legacy to a charity or institution than ungrateful children.**)
2. To combat loneliness and provide spiritual enrichment. (**Social and spiritual organizations often provide the same benefit.**)
3. People want to be mothers and fathers. (**Adoption is no longer taboo and has social benefits.**)
4. God commands you to be fruitful and multiply. (**Increasing rejection of organized religion.**)
5. The pleasure of procreation. (**Contraceptives and alternative sexuality allow for the pleasure without children.**)
6. Achieve immortality by passing on genes. (**If you examine the statement, it has no meaning. It is a secular variant of "Be fruitful and multiply."**)

Pre-modern age	It is a woman's RESPONSIBILITY to have children
Modern age (end of)	It is a woman's RIGHT to decide whether or not to have children

The Postmodern Era

Today, the withering thesis that children bring wealth comes face to face with its antithesis: children bring poverty. With the passage of time, the thesis grows weaker and the antithesis stronger. Most synthetic outcomes are terrible and frightening. However, requiring men and women to pay for the privilege of having children in an environment of AFFEERCE distributions brings back the notion that children are valuable and increase the wealth of family, collective, and state, without putting an undue burden on women to reproduce.

Postmodernism is a movement that began in the second half of the 20th century. The invention of the microprocessor, the most important technological development of the postmodern age, is essential to AFFEERCE. Reproductive freedom and alternative families reached public consciousness with the sexual liberation movements of the 1960s and 1970s; women's liberation and gay liberation. Betty Friedan's 1963 book *The Feminine Mystique* and the June 28, 1969 Stonewall riots being the seminal events.

Deconstruction, the tearing down of all narratives, is the heart of postmodernism and must precede the weaving of a new natural story. But it is in the process of deconstructing the roles of women, family, and sexuality that the reasons not to have a child become more obvious.

At the end of the pre-modern era, there were at least twelve reasons for having a child. Today, only six remain, and all of those qualified. Now, postmodern deconstruction has given us a new question. **In the postmodern era, what are the reasons NOT to have children?**

The planet is filling up. Resources are being depleted[FTN4.03]. Technology might extend the life of our limited resources; it might also fail to do so. Why risk it? So a person can have an heir; not be lonely despite billions of people in the world; enjoy the pleasure of procreation without contraception because some preacher tells them that several thousand years ago it was commanded we be fruitful and multiply?

What about the labor pool? Jobs are becoming increasingly complex, requiring lengthy education. The "acceptable" level of unemployment goes up all the time, causing parents to ask, "What if the child isn't smart enough? What if there is no money to pay for an education?"

Then there is the length of childhood. The age of maturation is going up. The length of education is increasing for those who can afford one. After graduation, economic necessity often sends young adults back to the nest, where they remain a burden well into adulthood.

Today, it is considered child-abuse if children do not have access to health care, education, nutritious food, and sanitary conditions[FTN4.25]. This added financial burden is both a motivation for AFFEERCE, and a reason not to have children in the postmodern age.

Working with children can also be scary. A simple hug could be misinterpreted and result in loss of employment or even incarceration. Children become untouchables[FTN4.26, FTN4.27]. There is even a grey area for parents who often cannot figure out what is "appropriate." Although probably uncommon as a reason not to have children; the ever-increasing fear of intimacy might add weight to this reason in the future.

Some parents have children only to please their own parents, their church, or to fit in with society. Children born to unloving parents are more susceptible to negative influences. There is no longer an army that wants to straighten them out or free clinics where they receive help with addiction.

Every child could be considered a burden on society. If the parents are poor, society must pay for the healthcare, housing, clothing and nutritious meals. Even if the parents are wealthy, society must still pay for all education through high school. An increasing number of these children fail to become productive citizens.

For children that don't make it, society must pay for minimal healthcare, minimal housing or prisons, and food stamps in perpetuity.

Children, rebel. Some see the world they are about to inherit, and take a stand. Others see the world they are about to inherit and turn to drugs, alcohol, and other dangerous pursuits. Most parents do not look forward to teenage rebellion.

With all of these motivations not to have children, the middle class and more educated realize that having many children is no longer practical. Most of the population growth is occurring amongst the poor and religiously indoctrinated[FTN4.04, FTN4.05]. Very few of these kids stand a chance. Our society, as a whole, is in jeopardy.

Reasons Not to Have Children in a Postmodern Society

1. Overpopulation.
2. Each additional child reduces the resources to educate the others.
3. My child might not be smart enough to get a job in a high-tech world.
4. My child might remain a financial burden to me well into adulthood.
5. I want to have a successful career. A child will hold me back.
6. I must insure my child has proper healthcare, healthy meals, appropriate clothing or seek assistance from the state.
7. I must be careful how I touch or punish my child to stay clear of child abuse laws.
8. If I fail to raise my child properly, they might end up in an underworld of criminals and addicts.
9. I'll have to deal with a teenage rebellion which might be nastier than those of earlier generations, considering the state of the world.
10. Taxpayers will foot the bill for my child's basic education at the very least, and at most, for all necessities for the rest of his or her life.
11. Because sex with contraception, or alternative sexual expression is also pleasurable.

So the postmodern age gives us a new equation: Children=Poverty. It is every bit as fundamental to society as Children=Wealth was five hundred years ago.

And the trend is only going to accelerate. Any job that can be completely described in a manual or two can be coded and executed by machines. Large assembly lines can be reduced to a few highly skilled technicians and a host of robots. While I do not believe it is conceivable for machines to possess human consciousness (See *Volume III - Philosophy*), there is no question that given enough innovation, a single skilled human being can operate a machine that will do the work currently done by tens of thousands of workers. Massive wealth will be created. Where should it go? To build prisons for the unemployed underclass whose clergy instructs them to reproduce?

In pre-modern times, having a child was the best thing you could do for yourself, for your neighbors, for your overlord, for your church and for your king.

Having a child today can be an act of aggression against your neighbor and country's space, wealth and security. It is a thankless task that leaves one with little reward and many burdens. The church still claims it is good, but to listen is to condemn one's heirs to a cycle of poverty.

The thesis, reasons to have children, grows weaker, as the antithesis, reasons not to have children, grows stronger. Here are some conceivable outcomes:

1. We will cease reproducing and cease to exist (unlikely).
2. The middle class will cease reproduction, but the poor will not, because:
   A. In the impoverished community, child labor laws are ignored
      1. Assassins and drug runners as young as six or seven are in high demand due to short sentences for juveniles.
      2. Selling young girls into prostitution is high profit.
   B. There is still entitlement since mothers with their children are supported by the state.
   C. There is no place for children to fall, already at the bottom.

      D. Religion is the only thing that supplies any comfort in a miserable life.

      E. There already is poverty and children are the only hope, however remote, for a way out.

3. Technological advances create the need for an ever more skilled workforce as low skilled jobs are replaced by automation.

      A. Children are increasingly born to the very families that do not have the means that allow their children to compete in this high tech world.

      B. Education costs are leaving behind the middle class, too. It is forcing many into lifelong debt. Scholarships and grants only reach a small percentage of those who cannot afford school.

4. More and more children are born to families without the means to educate them.

      A. When nobody understands the technology, the technology will collapse.

      B. A reversion to barbarism will revive the need for an unskilled workforce.

      C. An unskilled workforce will bring back many of the reasons to have children.

5. The direction of evolution will reverse (whether cultural or genetic).

      A. An idiotocracy will develop (from a movie by the same name).

      B. Those with the best genes will have the fewest offspring.

      C. Those who live in the worst environments will have the most offspring.

It is not a pretty future. Only by abruptly reversing the trend toward Children=Poverty and reestablishing Children=Wealth, can these abominable consequences be avoided. Only then can humanity enter a new enlightenment. Everything about AFFEERCE is designed around this now revolutionary notion that Children=Wealth.

Today, a baby tax would be a disaster! The middle classes would have even less children, while the tax would be ignored by the poor. The baby tax would be unenforceable, except by the most draconian of measures. Universal distribution is a required precondition for any reproductive control.

In a truly free society, many of the reasons to have children in pre-modern times will come back in a thoroughly modern context. All children will be precious and valuable.

Can a society really be completely free if one has to pay to have children? I'll turn that on its head: Can a woman be completely free if she is under constant peer pressure to produce wealth by having babies?

Pre-modern age	It is a woman's RESPONSIBILITY to have children
Modern age (end of)	It is a woman's RIGHT to decide whether or not to have children
Postmodern age (end of)	Men and women must pay for the PRIVILEGE to have children

Women's Rights

> **The fight for women's right to choose was hard fought, but victory was made easier by the poverty children bring to families in the postmodern age. When children once again bring wealth through the distributions, women's freedom to choose a career will be jeopardized. A baby tax can act as a valve to relieve this reactionary pressure.**

Women have successfully eschewed the forcing of motherhood upon them in the industrial West. Today, it is a women's right to choose between motherhood, career, or both. The days when women were treated as baby factories are long gone; barefoot, pregnant, and chained to the home and hearth.

"Margaret Sanger (founder of Planned Parenthood) was well aware of the emancipatory potential of reproductive rights...Birth control she argued "is no negative philosophy concerned solely with the number of children brought into this world. It is not merely a question of population. Primarily, it is the instrument of liberation and human development [FN6.710]."

Today, the ability of women to land careers is no longer threatened by pressure to bear children, and the hard-won freedom to choose would seem to be the ideal situation.   But this freedom is viewed through the myopic lens of the equation: Children = Poverty. As long as children bring down the standard of living of any family, the rights of women in the workplace are secure. This is not to minimize the efforts of those women who took to the streets to demand equality. Their efforts won the day. But suffragettes and even feminists from the mid twentieth century are long gone. Because women's rights have become custom and because we live under the banner of Children=Poverty, those rights are preserved.

In an AFFEERCE economy, children will bring a family wealth. Once the child is born, there is an instantaneous increase of $625 per month in the household income. Every additional child increases the wealth of the family through the economies of scale. Six children can pay for a swimming pool and bring a bountiful table at every meal. With eight, a gymnasium or bowling alley might be added. Chores can be more easily divided with large families. Family businesses are easier to start. Children no longer add to the family burden of medical insurance or college funding. Every additional child increases the odds that one of them will become a multi-millionaire.

Children=Wealth puts new pressure on women to produce family wealth by having babies. Two hundred years of progress will begin to erode in a few short years. Although women will fight back, social pressures will be relentless and only a few brave souls will survive in the workforce. Over the centuries, natural selection will eliminate working women from the species. Even worse, young girls at puberty will be recruited into producing new infants; new wealth for the family.

What might be a utopia for men would be hell for women. Nor would the utopia for men last very long either, as resources became exhausted and productivity growth fell behind population growth.

This entire nightmare is nipped in the bud by a baby tax. The baby tax acts as a valve to release pressure on women to reproduce; the greater the tax, the less the pressure. However, a small baby tax might just suffice.

Those that fail to pay the tax will find themselves oppressed by the same tax we have today: the income tax. It will be levied at 40% on all family members, including all paternal family members if different. Furthermore, no citizens' dividends for family members will be issued. If the tax is not paid up by the time the unfunded child is able to make purchases, the child will pay an additional 5% in consumption taxes. This is also true for all citizens who were born before the capitulation. This will continue until the baby tax plus interest plus a small penalty is collected. In no case will this ever affect universal distribution and thus jeopardize the life, health or opportunities of the child or any family member.

The Baby Tax as the Best Investment Ever

A baby tax as a one-time premium for a lifetime of distributions outperforms every known investment class over time.

Today, it costs $245,340 to raise a child through the age of 17[FTN4.12]. Here is a breakdown of that spending and how much is saved by the distributions.

	Percent[FTN4.12]	Total Spending	Covered by Distribution	Actual Distribution
Food	16%	$39,254	$39,254	$47,520
Housing	30%	$73,602	$73,602	$79,920
Health Care	8%	$19,627	$19,627	$25,920
Education/Child Care	18%	$44,161	$10,800	$10,800
Transportation	14%	$34,348	$3,240	$3,240
Other	14%	$34,348		
Totals	100%	$245,340	$146,523	$167,400

Investing $10,000, the baby tax, returns $146,523 in 18 years. More is returned for food, housing, and health care than spent by the average family today. As much as $167,400 is returned on that $10,000. The amount saved on education and child care is somewhat ambiguous. The education distribution is amortized over a lifetime, with additional funding from achievement annuities. Child care is better managed by large families and closer knit communities, saving for many the complete cost of child care. Private schools tap into most of the same funds as public schools, so they too are less expensive.

The distributions continue over a lifetime, not just 18 years and significantly, the $245,340 expense does not include a college education – free in AFFEERCE. The cost of a 4-year degree at a public institution is $60,000 including room and board[FTN4.13]. The $10,000 initial investment returns $227,400 in 22 years, a return of over 16% if the money were paid out at age 22. But the money is paid out constantly giving a real return of well over 20%. Over the course of 22 years, such an investment beats every investment class hands down. The state will be coercing you into making the best investment of all time. There are worse fates.

How Feminists Define Reproductive Rights

AFFEERCE reproductive freedom and control and the feminist definition of reproductive rights are almost identical, despite the baby tax (or perhaps because of it).

In *Reproductive Rights and Wrongs*, Betsy Hartmann describes a list of demands that feminists associate with full reproductive rights. Here is a comparison with AFFEERCE and its reproductive control. [FTN4.17]

Feminist Demand	AFFEERCE Response
The right to economic security through the opportunity to earn equal pay for equal work, so that women can adequately care for themselves and their family.	The right to economic security through the distributions, so that women or men can adequately care for themselves and their families.
The right to a safe workplace and environment for all, so that women are not exposed to hazards that threaten their ability to bear healthy children, or forced to choose between sterilization and jobs.	The right to be warned of any hazards in the workplace and the right and financial ability to refuse work under those conditions, so that women or men are not involuntarily exposed to hazards that threaten their ability to bear healthy children.
The right to quality child care so that women can enter the work force secure in the knowledge that their children will be looked after.	The right to form large alternative families, with full distributions for all family members, so there are always plenty of people home to look after the children, as other parents go off to work.

The right to abortion, free and informed contraceptive choice, and other forms of reproductive health care.	The right to free abortion on demand in the first trimester, free contraception and informed contraceptive choice, free reproductive and other health care.
The right to sex education so that women and men of all ages are better able to understand and control their own bodies.	Ditto.
The right to decent medical care, necessary not only to insure contraceptive safety, but a basic human right.	Ditto.
The right to choose how to give birth and to have control over the development and use of new reproductive technologies.	Ditto.
The right of lesbian women and women with disabilities to be mothers.	The right of any human being or family of human beings to be parents who pay the baby tax
The participation of men as equal partners in future-baby, housework, and birth control, so women no longer have to shoulder the 'double burden.'	The right to union into any family whose charter meets one's expectations, and the right and economic ability to leave any family that does not.
The right to be free of all forms of violence.	Ditto.
An end to discrimination so that all people, regardless of race, sex or class-can lead productive lives, and exercise real control over their own reproduction.	Zero tolerance for discrimination by a governing body outside of a rogue state. (See, *Chapter 9 – Government, Law, and Justice*) All people, regardless of race, sex or class who choose to lead productive lives, can. Every aspect of society will be designed so families can raise the funds to exercise real control over their own reproduction.

On the Natural Right to Bear Children

There is scarcely anything more tragic in human life than a child who is not wanted – Martin Luther King

The worst problem is to possess plenty of children with inadequate means. – The Prophet Muhammad

Planned parenthood is an obligation of those who are Christians. Our church thinks we should use scientific methods that assist in family planning – Archbishop Desmond Tutu [FTN4.06]

Today, an unaffordable child will either be entitled to food, shelter, medical care and education at the expense of the taxpayer, a violation of the right to property, or be denied these things which is a violation of the child's right to life.

The baby tax could be viewed as contrary to the historically held view that procreation is a fundamental and natural right. The United Nations Declaration of Human Rights of 1948 proclaiming the right to found a family, free from constraint [FTN4.08], upholds procreation as a natural right. In the case of Eisenstadt v. Baird (1972) the Supreme Court ruled that the individual, married or single, has the right to be free of unwarranted government intrusion into...the decision whether to bear or beget a child. In Griswold v. Connecticut (1965) the Court ruled the state can interfere with marriage and procreation only upon proof of compelling state interest [FTN4.09].

It will not be a question of arguing "compelling interest" for the AFFEERCE baby tax. This is a new concept and requires constitutional protection, even if the baby tax is nominal and rarely used in amounts exceeding $10,000. However, it cannot be said to violate the United Nations Declaration of Human Rights, when the only penalties restore current conditions: an income tax and no citizens' dividends.

The right to have a child is a fundamental violation of the child's rights. The child is a human being who has the right to nutritious meals, warm and safe shelter, basic medical care and unlimited free education. Unless this is affordable, at least one of two crimes is being committed.

The first crime is not providing adequate food, shelter, etc. necessarily placing the child at a severe disadvantage to others. There is no level playing field. One child in a hundred will defy the odds and achieve greatness. This is used as an argument to "prove" the above factors are not so important. Instead, I argue, it is a case of the exception proving the rule.

The second crime is against society. Today, having a child is armed robbery. Because we insist the child receive some food, some shelter, some medical care and some education, the taxpayer is forced, at the barrel of a gun, to pay for that child.

A person's supposed right to have a child is a violation of the right to life of the child and a violation of every person's right to property. What has been held up as the essential natural right is in fact the most unnatural of rights. It is the right to create human suffering and steal the fruits of other's labor. The greatest threat to natural rights is also the greatest blessing of mankind, so it is hard to discuss this without generating powerful emotions.

Rage and the Apocryphal Racist Narrative

The following narrative is apocryphal, which means it is false. Nevertheless, it is often told around the world. In the United States the narrative usually applies to African-Americans and occasionally other minorities. So why bother repeating such a racist account?   There are several important reasons.

1. There is a holocaust in poor African-American communities that is ignored, even by our President. Middle class African-Americans, who have made it out of the ghetto, often don't want to look back. Some move to the far right, attributing the dismal situation to a lack of morals. But no personal moral code can save the vast majority who are victims of our corporate welfare state, an economy with neither livable entitlements nor free markets; an economy that seeks to strangle the middle-class and leave the impoverished in a wasteland.
2. Such stories are often harbingers of the future. They are told as a plea to change course. Today's apocrypha is tomorrow's truth.
3. A significant minority of the population believes the story is true today. It is indeed true for a very small percentage from all communities regardless of ethnicity.
4. The story illustrates the question of procreation and natural rights as a parable.

Sensitive readers might choose to bypass this parable.

What will the average child born today cost the taxpayer? A lifetime of education, food, shelter, and medical expenses, runs upward of $600,000. While the successful adult earns much of that in the marketplace, a considerable portion comes directly from the taxpayer's pocket.

Look first at the fortunate child. Even in a well-to-do family, giving birth to a child is tantamount to billing neighbors at least $27,000 for education. These neighbors had no say in the decision to have a child. They were not asked if they had $27,000 to spare for education. But they foot the bill anyway. Perhaps this family has a priest who instructs them it is God's will to have one child after another; to bill their neighbors $27,000 + $27,000 + $27,000 + $27,000 + ... What can their neighbors do to stop this theft? Absolutely nothing! Churn out babies, one after another. They have no recourse.

Of course, not all families are well-to-do. And when mothers feel it is their religious duty to have as many babies as possible, even middle class families might find themselves short on cash. But no worry! The taxpayer will pay for post-natal hospital care if there is no insurance. The taxpayer will pay for a bigger house for the family, if it is too crowded. The taxpayer will pay for food, if there is not enough to feed the children. What can citizens do to stop this theft? Absolutely nothing! Families can churn out babies, one after another. There is no recourse.

And the biggest bill is yet to come. First there is daycare, then preschool, then thirteen years of regular schooling; $27,000+ per child. Worse than taxation without representation, it is taxation without any input at all. No way to even petition your grievances; no king to beseech. They have a child, you pay, no say, period.

You are being extorted, paying tax dollars under threat of imprisonment, for the fruit of someone else's womb. Your property is being seized, with no redress, and with no offense committed by you. Your natural rights are under gross attack.

But it gets much, much worse. For what I have described is the system at its best. Extortion that you can be proud of. After all, you're helping the next generation. And aren't we all really a village and so on?

But no, there is no bar to having a child if one lives in abject poverty. Many religious leaders will still tell Mama it is God's will to reproduce. Now the taxpayer has the privilege of paying for pre-natal, delivery, and post-natal care for mother and child. Now the taxpayer is assured the privilege of paying for nutritious food, and for the social worker who will make certain the child is being fed properly. But the social worker only comes twice a month, and Mama can feed the kids well on those days. In the meantime, she can get 75% on her link card for crack. Now the kids are screaming because they're hungry, but it doesn't bother Mama. She doesn't have a care in the world, feeling oh so nice on the taxpayer's dime. She figures if she had enough kids, perhaps there would be enough to get high every day of the month, and still fool the social worker. What can citizens do to stop this theft? Absolutely nothing! Families can churn out babies, one after another. There is no recourse.

But it gets worse. After paying for Mama's crack, there are the educational expenses. Here the taxpayer gets a little break. These kids usually drop out of school early. But it is not really a break at all since the taxpayers have already paid so much more for food (Mama's crack), shelter, and medical expenses. It is when the child drops out of school, and hits the streets that the extortion kicks into high gear.

The natural rights of the taxpaying public are not the only rights that are being trampled on. Our child, born to these circumstances is likely to have nothing to live for except drugs and gangs. They are born to a world that could never employ them. With none of the requisite skills, they are denied the right to life, liberty, and property, let alone the pursuit of happiness, unless that happiness comes in a hypodermic needle.

Malnourished and under-educated, these kids can turn only to crime. And it is here that you pay for extra police. It is here that you pay higher insurance premiums for stolen merchandise. It is here you pay higher medical bills for the overdoses that fill the ER.

But the story gets worse. A huge percentage of these kids will go to prison. There is no other option.

Prison costs from $40,000 to $60,000 per inmate per year; even more in some states. That's per year! And you're paying for it! Don't you feel proud? You supported this child from birth to adulthood. You've already spent $200,000 for this treasure and now you have the privilege of paying maybe 2 million dollars more to keep this precious gift to humanity behind bars, perhaps for the rest of their life.

For in prison our child will have close contact with the best teachers around: murderers, armed robbers, and rapists. And just in case our child was not fully proficient in crime, just in case our child had an ounce of humanity left after starvation and crack mama and gangs, the teachers will make sure our child comes out of prison a cold, calculating killer.

What about prison reform you ask? It can't happen! Do we give our prisoners nutritious food when law-abiding citizens are not entitled to nutritious food? Do we give our prisoners free psychiatric care when law-abiding citizens are not entitled to free psychiatric care? Do we give our prisoners free continuing education when law-abiding citizens are not entitled to free continuing education? Do we make prison a ticket out of poverty while the victims of crime have no ticket out of poverty? Prison reform cannot happen. It is inevitable that our child comes out of prison a cold, calculating killer. There are no other options.

And in the final scene, as the curtain falls, one special taxpayer, one who helped with the millions of dollars, needed to raise our child from birth, meets our child, and meets with the bullet from our child's gun, and falls along with the curtain, along with our society, along with the world as we know it.

In the United States, the situation is worse than other Western industrial societies. It is sucking the blood from our nation. It is laying out the battlefield for race war or class war. It is dividing families, friends and neighbors. And all because of the real crime: having an unentitled child.

End of story! This is an extreme exaggeration at best. Statistics show that welfare mothers have only two children on average, and the vast majority of them do not take crack, or other addictive drugs, nor do they use their child's food money for drugs[FTN4.31, FTN4.32]. Furthermore, most children raised in poverty do not become criminals. These children are far more likely to be the victim of a criminal than a rich suburban taxpayer is likely to be the victim of a criminal.

But the diatribe is important because of the truths that it contains. It is a fear hidden not far below the surface in many of us. In less developed countries, the situation is more apparent. In India, for instance, there are children who have been blinded or dismembered by criminals, or have done it to themselves, to increase begging profits and their chances of getting something to eat[FTN4.30].

Robert Blank, in his book *Regulating Reproduction* argues that even if procreation is an inalienable right, it can be regulated by a society which is concerned about the welfare of the child to be born and his survival in society. He argues that reproduction in these terms is a right shared with society as a whole and is part of a larger complex of rights, responsibilities and obligations[FTN4.10]. Blank quotes Ribes (1978) indicating that the right of procreation cannot be exercised without "due respect for the vital requirements of the child to be born, and those of society." [FTN4.10]

The Tragedy of the Commons

Required Reading

The claim of those who support universal distribution, yet oppose population control is that each family will respect the common wealth by exhibiting maturity in reproductive affairs, averaging two children per two adults, or slightly more when growth is desired. That is, the wealth of everyone will be enhanced, if no family tries to hoard all the wealth for itself.

Unfortunately, it is a simple fact of human nature: If having a child increases your wealth, some people will have as many children as they can. This is demonstrated by a game called prisoner's dilemma, a classic game in game theory.

In prisoner's dilemma, two are arrested. If each of the accused remains silent, they will each receive 1 year in prison. If one rats out the other, the one who rats will walk free and the other will receive 3 years in prison. If both rat each other out, they will each receive 2 years in prison.

Game theory shows us that the rational decision is to rat out the other party. If you do, your potential sentence is 0 or 2 years. If you do not, your potential sentence is 1 or 3 years. Assuming that the goal of the commons is to limit total prison time, the choices being 2 years, 3 years or 4 years, if the individuals behave rationally then the best case scenario, 2 years total, will rarely occur and the worst case, 4 years total, will usually occur.

The same is true when Children=Wealth. If each child brings a family increasing wealth, even though it is quite clear that if too many families have too many children, everyone's wealth will suffer; families will tend to have as many children as possible to maximize their personal wealth, even as the common wealth decreases. This same principle applies to recycling, littering, global warming, pollution, cattle grazing, and, in general, failure to return things in nature to the state in which they were found. In 1968, in an article for *Science Magazine*, Garrett Hardin termed this phenomenon, "the tragedy of the commons.[FTN4.07]"

By tragedy, Hardin means an unfolding of events that can only lead to bad ends, especially as used in drama where escape is futile, but the drama in this tragedy is real life. He notes that it is the rational position for each cattle farmer to graze as many head of cattle as possible on common land, even though if all farmers did this the land would become barren. It is rational for each of us to pollute and maximize our own profits, even though we destroy the air. It is rational for maritime nations to relentlessly fish the seas, even though species will become extinct.

> *Ruin is the destination toward which all men rush, each pursuing his own best interest in a society that believes in the freedom of the commons. Freedom in a commons brings ruin to all*[FTN4.07].

> *...natural selection favors the forces of psychological denial. The individual benefits as an individual from his ability to deny the truth even though society as a whole, of which he is a part, suffers* [FTN4.07].

The essence of the commons tragedy: **If I don't do it somebody else will. I won't be their patsy!**

But even these tragedies of the commons, Hardin ties to the bigger tragedy, population growth. He notes that there is no problem dumping your waste as you please in a wilderness, as opposed to the inner city. That is, the ratio of people to land is the genesis of much of the tragedy.

> *The pollution problem is a consequence of population. It did not much matter how a lonely American frontiersman disposed of his waste. "Flowing water purifies itself every 10 miles," my grandfather used to say, and the myth was near enough to the truth when he was a boy, for there were not too many people.* [FTN4.07]

I'll now quote extensively from Hardin, whose eloquent words are inimitable.

Freedom to Breed Is Intolerable

> **If children of improvident parents were allowed to starve to death, there would be no need for a baby tax. But without the baby tax, universal distribution sets us onto a tragic course of action.**

> *In a world governed solely by the principle of "dog eat dog"--if indeed there ever was such a world--how many children a family had, would not be a matter of public concern. Parents who bred too exuberantly would leave fewer descendants, not more, because they would be unable to care adequately for their children....If each human family were dependent*

only on its own resources; if the children of improvident parents starved to death; if, thus, overbreeding brought its own "punishment" to the germ line--then there would be no public interest in controlling the breeding of families. But our society is deeply committed to the welfare state....In a welfare state, how shall we deal with the [group] that adopts overbreeding as a policy to secure its own aggrandizement? To couple the concept of freedom to breed with the belief that everyone born has an equal right to the commons is to lock the world into a tragic course of action [FTN4.07].

Conscience Is Self-Eliminating

Those with a conscience who treat reproduction responsibly must be replaced by those who do not

It is a mistake to think that we can control the breeding of mankind in the long run by an appeal to conscience. Charles Galton Darwin made this point when he spoke on the centennial of the publication of his grandfather's great book. The argument is straightforward and Darwinian.

People vary. Confronted with appeals to limit breeding, some people will undoubtedly respond to the plea more than others. Those who have more children will produce a larger fraction of the next generation than those with more susceptible consciences. The difference will be accentuated, generation by generation.

In C. G. Darwin's words: "It may well be that it would take hundreds of generations for the progenitive instinct to develop in this way, but if it should do so, nature would have taken her revenge, and the variety Homo contracipiens would become extinct and would be replaced by the variety Homo progenitivus".

The argument assumes that conscience or the desire for children (no matter which) is hereditary--but hereditary only in the most general formal sense. The result will be the same whether the attitude is transmitted through germ-cells, or exosomatically, to use A. J. Lotka's term....To make such an appeal is to set up a selective system that works toward the elimination of conscience from the race.

Mutual Coercion Mutually Agreed Upon

Coercion to halt a commons tragedy is easy if the majority can see the problem. A baby tax would have the same effect as parking meters on downtown traffic.

The social arrangements that produce responsibility are arrangements that create coercion, of some sort. Consider bank-robbing. The man who takes money from a bank acts as if the bank were a commons....That we thereby infringe on the freedom of would-be robbers we neither deny nor regret.

The morality of bank-robbing is particularly easy to understand because we accept complete prohibition of this activity. We are willing to say "Thou shalt not rob banks," without providing for exceptions. But temperance also can be created by coercion. Taxing is a good coercive device. To keep downtown shoppers temperate in their use of parking space we introduce parking meters for short periods, and traffic fines for longer ones. We need not actually forbid a citizen to park as long as he wants to; we need merely make it increasingly expensive for him to do so.

Coercion is a dirty word to most liberals now....As with the four-letter words, its dirtiness can be cleansed away by exposure to the light, by saying it over and over without apology or embarrassment. To many, the word coercion implies arbitrary decisions of distant and irresponsible bureaucrats; but this is not a necessary part of its meaning. The only kind of coercion I recommend is mutual coercion, mutually agreed upon by the majority of the people affected.

To say that we mutually agree to coercion is not to say that we are required to enjoy it. Who enjoys taxes? But we accept compulsory taxes because we recognize that voluntary taxes would favor the conscienceless [FTN4.07].

Recognition of Necessity

Once we stop a commons tragedy, our freedom increases.

> *What does "freedom" mean? When men mutually agreed to pass laws against robbing, mankind became more free, not less so. Individuals locked into the logic of the commons are free only to bring on universal ruin; once they see the necessity of mutual coercion, they become free to pursue other goals. I believe it was Hegel who said, "Freedom is the recognition of necessity."*

> *The most important aspect of necessity that we must now recognize, is the necessity of abandoning the commons in breeding. No technical solution can rescue us from the misery of overpopulation. Freedom to breed will bring ruin to all. At the moment, to avoid hard decisions many of us are tempted to propagandize for conscience and responsible parenthood. The temptation must be resisted, because an appeal to independently acting consciences selects for the disappearance of all conscience in the long run, and an increase in anxiety in the short.*

> *The only way we can preserve and nurture other and more precious freedoms is by relinquishing the freedom to breed, and that very soon. "Freedom is the recognition of necessity"--and it is the role of education to reveal to all the necessity of abandoning the freedom to breed. Only so, can we put an end to this aspect of the tragedy of the commons* [FTN4.07].

A Georgist Perspective

Required Reading

Many Georgists consider Hardin's prophecy to be false. Not only has Malthus been proven wrong, but it is generally accepted that people produce more than they consume. There is also the argument from nature: every species has the natural right to bear children. It would be absurd to deny this to mankind.

Every species also has predators, yet it is the goal of mankind to eliminate all of his predators. This changes the equation, but more importantly, the "economic law" that "people produce more than they consume" needs to be questioned. Henry George himself believed this so-called law of nature would fail.

> *All I wish to make clear is that even without any increase in population, the progress of invention constantly tends to give a greater proportion of the production to landowners. Therefore a smaller and smaller share goes to labor and capital. Since we can assign no limits to the progress of invention, neither can we offer any limits to the increase in rent – short of the entire output. If wealth could be obtained without labor, there would be no use for either labor or capital. Nor would there be any possible way either could demand any share of the wealth produced. If anybody but landowners continued to exist, it would be at their whim or mercy – perhaps maintained for their amusement, or as paupers by their charity.* [FTN4.34]

Because the people will be the landlords in an AFFEERCE economy, the fruits of progress will be theirs. That does not alter the tendency for a lessening of the amount of production that goes to labor before distribution of the rents. The tragedy of the commons does not go away.

A Gentle Response

Required Reading

In the chapter on distribution theory, we saw how the tragedy of the commons makes voluntary taxation impractical. There is little doubt that the tragedy is behind many of our social problems. But is the tragedy endemic? Is it a natural law or something that can be overcome?

I don't think there is a black and white answer to this question. But one thing is certain: the susceptibility of humanity to the tragedy of the commons can be reduced. Elinor Ostrom showed how the commons tragedy can be reduced for resources in common, such as pastureland and rivers, but some of her remedies, such as peer pressure, and graduated sanctions could apply to childbirth, as well.[FTN4.37]

The AFFEERCE Enlightenment, a new humanity arising from an economy where objectivism ("Your life is not my fault. My life is none of your business") and subjectivism ("We are all one") are synthesized, results in a fundamental belief system where one's own welfare is intimately tied to the welfare of others. In prisoners dilemma, it becomes more natural for neither prisoner to rat the other one out. The tragedy of the commons is more easily averted.

That is why we begin with a baby tax of $10,000 and hope that it can only move in one direction: down. The fertility rate can be as high as 3.6 (Namibia, Pakistan) before there is any financial need to consider raising it. That is because the $10,000 as well as interest on the 1 year advance payment of ground rents provides funds for positive population growth. This is discussed in more detail in the next chapter.

The Fundamental Relations of Reproductive Control

> **The three fundamental relations of reproductive control are FR5, which shows how universal distribution can lead to Hardin's tragedy of the commons; FR7, which shows how entitlement is a precondition for reproductive control; and FR6, which shows how eugenics of the marketplace prevents genocide by obviating any other kind of eugenics.**

Reproductive control is at the heart of a number of AFFEERCE fundamental relations. The fundamental relations are some of the original tenets from which AFFEERCE was born.

FR5:   Prevents Social Collapse – Universal distribution means children add to the wealth of a household. For those households with little wealth, children might be the only way to obtain more. The balance of the RCs insures that the productivity of the nation grows faster than or equal to population growth. Otherwise, should automation push marginal productivity below subsistence, barbarism would result.

This is a restatement of Hardin's tragedy of the commons and a major theme of this chapter.

Interestingly, just as reproductive control is a requirement for distribution, the basic income of universal distribution is a prerequisite for reproductive control. Betsy Hartmann in her book, *Reproductive Rights and Wrongs*, notes that once villagers in third world countries have enough children to meet their needs, they often want to limit family size. In societies where children are entitled to go to school, not only are they no longer a source of labor, but parents must pay for their education and other needs. When the labor value of children decreases, male heads of household are more willing to let their wives work outside the home. Their wages are more valuable to the family than household work, thus spurring a fertility decline [FTN4.11].

It is also well established that high infant and child mortality rates are major underlying causes of high birth rates. [FTN4.14] In third world countries, more so than the United States, it is precisely want for the necessities of life that deny women the right to control their own reproduction. For these backwards countries, Children=Wealth is still true for the old reasons, i.e. labor source and social security. Only when families are secure in the necessities of life is reproductive freedom possible.

FR7:   Precondition – Entitlement is a precondition for any kind of reproductive control. Without entitlement, children provide the poor with many of the same necessities as in pre-modern times or in the third-world today, such as income, social security, and safety. Likewise, without entitlement, a parent cannot always afford to stay home and provide care for the child. Entitlement is the engine that allows for both an orderly increase and decrease in population.

Together, FR5 and FR7 show that entitlement is not only an engine of population growth, but population control as well. As a counter to Hardin, an abundance of opportunity or an enlightened population are likely to tip the scale in favor of responsible reproduction.

In an AFFEERCE economy, any family with sufficient funds can adopt a child. A single person constitutes a family of one. Today, some states prevent adoptions by gays and lesbians, or frown on single person adoptions. Adoption agencies use prejudice when screening applicants. Even in more liberal states, agencies put a value on the children themselves. Ozzie and Harriet get David and Ricky. "Problem" families get the "problem" children. FR6 eliminates this discrimination against families and children. Fitness to be a parent is defined as the ability to raise the requisite funds. Fitness is realized through family wealth or size, or benefactors. Fitness can simply be realized by the ability to win hearts. Suppose there is a mentally challenged woman who is a joy to behold. Her family decides she should be a genetic parent because her love and joy are too valuable to waste, despite her mental challenges.

FR6:   Prevents Genocide – By using market forces and projected future population needs to set the baby tax, and by allowing equal access for all to pay the tax, control of reproduction is taken away from politicians and bureaucrats, who might base decisions of who could reproduce on a whim, ethnic loyalties, personal and popular prejudices.

Blank talks about two potential futures. The first future, the Brave New World scenario puts all reproductive choice in the hands of the state[FTN4.15]. In the second future, the reproductive choice of individuals is expanded.[FTN4.16] He never considers AFFEERCE, where there is expanded reproductive choice and reproductive control is market control.

Procreative Law Should not be Complex

Required Reading

Hardin was concerned about the tragedy of the commons in a welfare state. With universal distribution, the benefits of having a child are far greater than in any welfare state we have today. Will a baby tax of $10,000 be sufficient? What about some other form of coercion, such as a two child policy, or some combination of the two, such as $10,000 for the first child, $20,000 for the second, $40,000 for the third, and so on? We won't know until we get there.

The consequence of policies is that they lead to increasing amounts of administrative law in their implementation. It would be a blow to freedom for a bureaucracy to make decisions on reproductive rights. A flat baby tax, "eugenics of the market-place," is preferable to any decisions made by corruptible men. But even with the baby tax, is there wiggle-room for corruption? What if a child lives only two minutes and then dies? Is the baby tax forfeited or not? Does that depend on the amount of the tax? For instance, if the tax was smaller than the money spent on medical care for mother and child in this tragedy, should it be returned?

What about late term abortions? The baby tax leaves no mechanism to discourage them. If a mother decides that a luxury Vegas vacation beats having a baby in the eighth month of pregnancy, what is to prevent her?

These questions seem daunting, but in a free society, none of them pose any real problem. Late-term abortions cannot be prevented beyond charging the universal $35 deductible, and perhaps a few hours of mandatory preliminary counseling, at most. Penalties beyond that encourage backroom abortion (which is completely legal) to the detriment of both mother and fetus. Medical rebates can be prohibited for money-saving abortions. (See *Chapter 11 – Medical Distribution*)

Families could save toward a child in a future-baby fund, maintained, let's say, at the Treasury. The future-baby fund would be exercised when mother and child leave the hospital. If the child dies in the hospital, the fund is not exercised. In another case, if the family does not want the child, the fund is returned to the future-baby family only to the extent adoptive parents are willing to pay. For instance, if the baby tax is $10,000 and the highest price the adoptive parents are willing to pay for this child, perhaps born with a serious defect, is $3,000, then $3,000 of the future-baby fund is returned. It works very much like the return on advance payment of ground rents.

If the child dies soon after leaving the hospital, families can make an appeal for new future-baby funds through the discretionary tax. (See *Chapter 5 – 2% Discretionary Tax*) These heartfelt appeals will be quickly rewarded.

Sterilization and Wrongful Life

Required Reading

A mother can choose to have a disabled child. It is argued that heightened discrimination of the genetically disabled will occur as prenatal technologies are widely accepted. Torts for wrongful life might strengthen the attitude that only pristine pure health is tolerable [FN6.40]. Some claim that if the freedom to choose whether or not to have a child is limited by the threat of civil liability for having a genetically defective child, then our posterity will be the beneficiaries. We will have decided that there is no absolute right to reproduce and that instead it is a limited privilege to contribute one's genetic heritage to future generations[FN6.41]. It is also argued that present generations are 'causally' responsible to some extent for the genetic health of future generations and thus it can be argued that they have a moral responsibility to them. [FN6.43]

In *Regulating Reproduction*, Henry Blank argues that due to genetic advances, sterilization no longer represents a permanent destruction of a person's reproductive capacity but rather a less intrusive and presumably temporary cessation of fertility. [FN6.42]

It is impossible to say how future voters will deal with sterilization. A baby tax is sufficient for reproductive control. It is my personal feeling that there will be no concept of "wrongful life" in an AFFEERCE society, as many charities will be anxious to take-in and love severely disabled children. During pregnancy, the mother of a disabled fetus decides how to proceed. While forced sterilization is a violation of human rights, voluntary sterilization, using the latest technology, is provided as a free medical procedure.

A more difficult problem is the ethical dilemma in extreme cases. What of the crack-addicted, heavy smoking, alcoholic mother who bears children illegally and repeatedly? If enough damage is done to the fetus, even a loving home cannot erase all the scars.

While there are many unfortunate reasons such children are born today, there is reason to believe this will not occur in a free society. For one, men are equally, if not more, responsible for unfunded births than women. Heterosexual men will get the on/off vasectomy (See *Contraceptives* below) because that will represent sexual liberation without the fears of unintended paternity. It will give them the control they want.

Addicts who become pregnant will gladly take advantage of free abortion on demand. The pregnancy will only interfere with their quest for drugs. It will be a very rare child born to such circumstances, one that the innumerable charities will be anxious to love anyway.

One place that sterilization might be needed is in the pharmaceutical isolation centers, discussed in *Chapter 9 – Government, Law, and Justice*. The unlimited supply of free drugs requires the prevention of childbirth. Society must decide whether that should be through forced sterilization, forced contraception, or forced abortion. Inasmuch as sterilization eliminates the possibility of abortion, it might be the most humane choice. Charities might offer a $2000 sterilization award for those who opt for sterilization upon entry to an isolation center.

In the penitentiaries, there must never be forced sterilization nor forced abortion. Prisoners are kept physically isolated from one another, and conjugal visits can proceed as they would in the home. The AFFEERCE penitentiary is bound by law to treat their inmates humanely.

People with serious disorders do not want to bring a suffering child into this world, although often religious zealots will argue that every possible child should be brought into the world. Hopefully, the AFFEERCE enlightenment will end the spiritually bankrupt concept of procreation trumping all.

Being voluntarily sterilized will no longer preclude having biological children due to advances in genetics. It will simply mean you cannot accidentally get pregnant the old fashion way.

Contraceptives

Contraceptives must be freely available. Emphasis should be on contraceptives that do not impair health. The vasectomy with on/off switch shows considerable promise.

It is vital that all forms of contraception, from condoms to sophisticated medical procedures, be freely available. There must never be a co-pay or deductible for contraceptive pharmaceuticals or procedures. Nor can there be a co-pay or deductible for the reversal of any such procedure.

There is an important question as to whether contraceptive side-effects are a violation of natural rights, in an AFFEERCE society. For instance, the Norplant implant has several drawbacks:

1. It causes changes in your menstrual bleeding.
2. It may cause other side effects like headaches or acne.
3. It must be put in and taken out at a clinic
4. You may be able to see the implants or a small scar on your arm.
5. You can feel the implants when you touch your arm. [FN6.49]

In particular, changes in menstrual bleeding, headaches, and acne constitute violations of natural rights if the implant were to be required by law. With the imposition of the income tax on families with unfunded births, women might feel forced to use contraceptives, or even undergo sterilization, that would affect their physical and mental health.

As Betsy Hartmann points out in *Reproductive Rights and Wrongs*, safer methods such as condom and diaphragm have been grossly neglected, both in terms of lack of funding for research and their promotion and distribution. [FN6.5]

In an AFFEERCE society, emphasis should be on prophylactics that are mechanical and do not cause changes in hormone levels, or carry side effects (Although all options must always be available at no charge.) The granddaddy of mechanical contraception, the vasectomy with on/off switch, is the killer technology that will allow full sexual freedom without any risk of accidental pregnancy. The first story appeared in 2008, from Australia[FN6.51], but here is the latest (2016) from Ben Taub at IFLScience.com:

A German carpenter has spent the past 20 years developing an idea for a male contraceptive consisting of a switch that sits inside the testicles, in order to control the flow of sperm through the urethra. Having already attained a patent for the product and created a working prototype, inventor Clemens Bimek is now awaiting the start of an upcoming clinical trial on his product.

Made from PEEK-OPTIMA – a polymer that is regularly used to manufacture implants – the so-called Bimek SLV is surgically inserted into the spermatic ducts during a half-hour operation. Once implanted, the switch can be felt through the skin of the scrotum and physically flipped in order to open or close the flow of sperm.

The device is inserted into the vas deferens as a blockade of sorts. When the switch is in the open position, sperm is able to pass through the vas deferens – the duct that conveys sperm from the testicle to the urethra – before exiting the penis via the urethra. However, when the switch is flicked to the closed position, sperm is blocked from passing through, therefore eliminating the possibility of pregnancy arising from sexual intercourse.

According to the manufacturer's website, the Bimek SLV is preferable to other contraceptive techniques, such as having a vasectomy, wearing a condom or using the female pill, since it offers a solution to many of the drawbacks pertaining to these options. For instance, it provides greater flexibility than a vasectomy, enabling users to control their own ability to impregnate their partner rather than permanently disabling this. Also, unlike condoms or pills, it cannot be forgotten, since it is constantly present within the user. [FTN 3.38]

Jill Michelson of Marie Stopes International, designers of a similar device, said, "women tended to bear the burden of preventing unwanted pregnancies and men needed to take more responsibility. Any new form of contraception is always a good thing. [FN6.51]"

Abortion

Required Reading

Deaths from illegal abortion and the number of abortions in general, are caused both by lack of entitlement and the anti-life actions of the religious right. In Latin America, during the 1980's, when abortion was outlawed in most countries due to opposition from the Catholic Church, one fifth to one half of all maternal deaths were due to illegal abortions. In 1978, six years after enactment of India's relatively liberal abortion law, there were one million legal abortions in the country, compared to five million illegal ones. [FN6.52] Failure to use contraceptives is probably the leading factor in most abortions.

In an AFFEERCE society, there is full and free access to all contraceptives, and there is free abortion on demand in the first trimester. After that, if approved by a super-majority, several hours of mandatory options counseling and payment of the $35 universal deductible would be required. Abortions will likely be exempt from medical distribution rebates.

Transgenic Babies

Required Reading

Blank argues that the very meaning of reproductive rights must be expanded in light of recent advances in genetics and medicine. No longer is the genetic linkage unambiguous. Virtually any combination of germ material is now possible. [FN6.6]

The sexual revolutions that accompanied the postmodern age removed reproduction as the sole purpose of sex. Blank termed the removal of reproduction from sex, the first revolution. [FN6.61] The second revolution, which is happening today, is the removal of sex from reproduction. [FN6.62]

This will be a great benefit to the AFFEERCE family. In large, less affluent, families, should we be forced to raise the baby tax above $10,000, there might be only enough money for a few children. Determining who will be the biological parents could be divisive. Soon, these advances in genetics will offer a solution. Everyone can be a biological parent!

In a process called sperm mediated gene transfer one or more chromosomes from each prospective parents can be added to a single sperm cell. What is absolutely amazing is that each of these chromosomes, finds its complimentary chromosome, and exchanges DNA[FN6.64]. It is as though the sperm is taking the best features from each of the many parents and building a super-sperm. When this super-sperm fertilizes an egg, we have a child with many fathers, both male and female. This is still science fiction for humans, but it is being done in animals, and the process might be perfected soon.

Surrogacy

Required Reading

Blank describes the complete mother-woman as one who fulfills all three roles: genetic, carrying, and rearing. Without transgenics, a child can have up to five parents, with transgenics, many more [FN6.65].

Surrogacy is a critical component of reproductive rights. Blank discusses how surrogacy can be an alternative to abortion.

> *Artificial placentas and surrogate mothers are available to women who either cannot, or choose not to carry their fetus to term. Fetal transfer has been perfected as an alternative to abortion and there is an adequate supply of childless women who are anxious to adopt these embryos and fetuses. Abortion is no longer an issue, except in cases where the embryo is identified as defective. Because this determination is made by four weeks gestation in most cases, second trimester abortions are unnecessary. As an alternative to natural gestation, a mother might choose to have her fertilized egg removed and grown artificially in a laboratory.* [FN6.66]

In AFFEERCE, there are no real issues involved with surrogacy, as there are today. Bearing a child without penalty requires a fully funded future-baby account. The family that owns that future-baby account is the real family of that child. A surrogate outside the family has no relationship to the future-baby account. If the surrogate is inside the family, she has the same mothering responsibilities and privileges as the biological mother, the biological father(s) and other adults in the family.

Some argue that surrogacy is designed for the financial exploitation of needy women. But they deny a woman's right to do what she wishes with her body, and the right of less wealthy women to earn a living. Because of the distributions, no woman or man is forced into any job they do not want. Carrying a baby can be emotionally rewarding and there is no reason it should not be financially rewarding. In an AFFEERCE society, before or after the baby is born, it is likely that the surrogate will be invited to join the family. Surrogacy can lead to union with a wealthier family, perhaps in a role as surrogate and nursemaid.

In Vitro Gestation

Required Reading

In vitro gestation (IVG) is the idea that an egg is fertilized and then able to develop through birth outside of the human body. Today, this is science fiction. However, ectopic pregnancies (outside the womb) have already resulted in healthy babies.

The very possibility of IVG is reason enough for a baby tax. With Children=Wealth, the mass production of children, untaxed, would lead to the collapse of society. The invention of IVG would necessitate an increase in the baby tax to insure it is used only for loving parents and not to produce an army of entitled clones.

Social Imbalance

Required Reading

Other problems caused by an inadequate baby tax are social in nature and do not show up in the formulas and tools found in the next chapter. They include:

1. Women are pressured to be mothers at the expense of a career.
2. Girls at the age of 14 are pressured to become pregnant.
3. Poor families are having children solely to increase their standard of living.
4. Churches and charities are picking up the baby tax for addicts and imbeciles.
5. Polygamous households become the normative alternative family for wealthy men.
6. Children are viewed as financial instruments.

If these problems reach a point where they become a nuisance to a super-majority, the electorate can vote to increase the baby tax regardless of Treasury formulas.

Summary

Required Reading

Reproductive Control through the baby tax is a new coercive power of the state. Even if the tax is an affordable $10,000 (all income is somewhat discretionary with universal distribution), the promise of freedom and prosperity in exchange for such power will make some uneasy. Here I summarize all of the reasons for this tax and hopefully assuage those fears. A few will be discussed in more detail in the next chapter.

1. Relieves pressure on women to be baby-creating wealth machines.
2. Stops young girls from being forced into pregnancy at puberty.
3. Prevents attempted domination by any community, theology, or creed through procreation.
4. Holds productivity and population in balance assuring prosperity for all of humanity's reign.
5. Eliminates fears of future population control based on race, creed, religion, or whims of tyrants.
6. Works in harmony with evolution, and not against it. Prevents an idiotocracy.

7. Eliminates the need for authoritarian government, predatory war and even disease to control allocation of limited resources.

8. Allows for universal distribution without the tragedy of the commons and barbarism.

9. Lays to rest the apocryphal racist narrative for those who believe it.

10. Increases profits from location value by decreasing the ground rents or adding to the citizens' dividend.

11. Promotes the idea that every child is valuable.

12. Reduces the fetishism of commodities by directing savings toward the greatest possible non-material acquisition – a child.

13. Reduces disease by encouraging safe sex.

14. Protects against in vitro gestation and an army of entitled clones.

15. Discourages those who are addicted to drugs or alcohol, gambling, or other habits that prevent savings, from being parents.

16. Prevents wealthy men with many wives and mistresses from building empires through procreation.

17. Within the reach of all working people, because all earned income is discretionary.

18. Is an investment with an over 20% annual return.

19. Creates a sense of entitlement for the distributions. They are no longer handouts. They are paid for.

20. Encourages new family structures to facilitate procreation

Chapter 5 – The Consumption and Other Taxes

Introduction

Required Reading

A tax is required to fund public services beyond the distributions. But what form should it take? A consumption tax that excludes the distributions is both progressive and somewhat voluntary. Accounts to be funded can be easily added and subtracted from the tax. A consumption tax is tied to the consumer and not where they consume. All funding is related directly to the consumer or their dominion.

A just consumption tax is a tax on consuming natural resources that is passed along the chain of production to the ultimate consumer. This is a tax on land and not on added labor beyond the labor of extraction. Products made from recycled materials would be tax free. Unfortunately, a just consumption tax is highly regressive. The same tax would be paid on a drab outfit as a designer original at 50 times the price. After all, they both contain approximately the same amount of natural fiber. The same is true for expertly cut gemstones and other luxury goods.

To remain progressive and tax ostentation, the consumption tax must not only exclude the distributions, but be a tax on the final price. Because the final price includes a significant amount of labor, the consumption tax has a damper effect on productivity, although not as much as an income tax, because it is partly a tax on land, and is additive. However, there are over 40 AFFFEERCE features that increase productivity listed at the end of *Chapter 10 – The Amazing List*, some several times. A slight damper on productivity might prove more beneficial than expected.

There is another consideration in deciding between a just consumption tax, and a progressive one. Taxes are levied by the citizens of a dominion for infrastructure and other projects that increase land value and are eligible for local land capture. If taxes are repaid at 150% from local land capture currency, the most progressive schemes become the most regressive and vice versa. In that case, the just consumption tax is also the most progressive. This requires further study. For the time being, the consumption tax used in the examples is a simple progressive one.

Most of this tax is personal, rewarding the consumer's teachers and schools, and distributing funds at the discretion of the consumers. Producers do not pay the consumption tax on registered (patented) capital goods or raw materials with a product id. This includes all natural resources and produce patented in the commons. Should an entity, as opposed to an individual, purchase items for consumption, the proceeds are parsed out to the accounts of entity members.

Critics say a consumption tax is regressive and discourages consumption. It is neither. Because the distributions are exempt from this tax, it is progressive. As for discouraging consumption, one could only wish that were the case. Despite large sales taxes, many spend themselves deeply into debt. 300% taxes on cigarettes have made only a small dent into consumption. Wanton consumption is nothing a society should encourage. Even Henry George saw no harm in taxes on ostentation. While there is a big difference between spending above the distributions and ostentation, evidence suggests that absolutely no harm comes from such a consumption tax, provided it is not large.

Service is never taxed. In packages where the service and product are bundled together, the price of the product, for purposes of a consumption tax, can be the minimum of the price under an objective theory of value. (See *Chapter 10 – Subjective, Objective and AFFEERCE Theories of Value*) This can be the Georgist theory where the price of the product is the price of the product alone in an active market, or if there is no active market for the product alone, the labor theory where the price of the product is determined by the sum of the labor that went into it.

Furthermore, there are certain social benefits that can only come from a consumption tax, such as rewarding persons and institutions who contributed to the consumer's financial success. That financial success is almost perfectly correlated with consumption. Teachers and schools that instill knowledge and values of greatness might reap these rewards. This will be discussed later with the education distribution.

The discretionary tax comes out of a consumption tax and favors the preferences of those who have achieved financial success, in relation to their success. Evidence suggests that a discretionary tax increases consumption. For instance, charities often have "dine out" nights at certain restaurants where a small percentage of the tab goes to the charity. People go out of their way to eat out on those nights.

When a governing district requests funding from the citizens for a special project, those funds must come from a consumption tax. As we saw in distribution theory, a local land tax has far too many dangerous side effects. Consumption taxes must be approved by a 2/3 plurality of the dominion, be specifically earmarked to a public business plan, and have a maximum two year duration.

A consumption tax is levied when funds are moved from a corporate account to a spending account. When payment of the tax has been waived, funds are transferred between corporate accounts.

Notice that all suggested uses of a consumption tax apply to citizens; financing a special project, usually local; rewarding teachers from years past; a discretionary tax for the consumer's favorite cause. Foreign nationals do not pay the consumption tax. Where would it go if they did? This increases the competitiveness of AFFEERCE exports, and favors a balance of trade surplus.

Baby Tax

Required Reading

Future generations will decide whether there is an initial baby tax, and whether it is nominal or larger. In this book, we assume that the tax will be $10,000. These taxes are added to the distribution package and as discussed in the next chapter, are likely output to a dividend fund. For those born before the capitulation, or otherwise unfunded children, an additional 2% is added to the consumption tax. This tax accumulates and will end once the baby tax is paid in full. Corporations, and those whose birth was funded by a baby tax, are exempt from this portion of the consumption tax.

The achievement annuities are covered in *Chapter 11 – Education Distribution*.

Excise Taxes

Required Reading

Excise taxes can be structured as either consumption or sales taxes or a combination. The difference between a consumption tax and a sales tax is that funds from a consumption tax go to the dominion of the consumer while funds from a sales tax go to the dominion of the enterprise. Unlike consumption taxes, sales taxes are paid by tourists, and on export. The determination will be based on how the excise tax is to be used. Excise taxes must be earmarked and approved by a 2/3 plurality of the dominion.

Pigovian Taxes

There are costs associated with polluting the earth, air, or water; failing to reforest after a timber cut; depleting a lake of fish, or the earth of minerals. Taxing the perpetrators of these offenses, and returning the revenue to the victims is meant to both discourage the activity, and compensate for the damages.

These taxes, Pigovian taxes, named for British economist Arthur Pigou, who argued that industrialists seek their own marginal private interest. When the marginal social interest diverges from the marginal private interest, the industrialist has no incentive to internalize the cost of the marginal social cost[FTN2.25]. Pigovian taxes force the industrialist to consider the social costs.

With a purchased covenant that is designed to protect the environment or valuable resources (See *Chapter 2 - Covenants*), the rent surcharge paid for violation of the covenant is Pigovian, with the proceeds returned to the community. Pigovian taxes, in the form of excise taxes, land surtaxes, or taxes levied on certain activities by a super plurality of the community, can also be directed back to the community.

2% Discretionary Tax

Payment of this tax is mandatory, but how the tax is spent is at the discretion of the individual paying the tax.

Two percent of the consumption tax is a discretionary tax. Every citizen can divvy it up however they wish. For those portions an individual chooses not to allocate or neglects to allocate, default allocations will come equally from all seven levels of dominion. For instance, level 1 might allocate the money to the building employee holiday fund, level 2 to upkeep of the neighborhood parks, level 3 to parks and recreation, landmark maintenance, and a fund for victims of crimes. Higher levels would have much more complex allocations. Level 7 might have an allocation for the national parks, and a UN approved war in Africa.

These tax dollars can be directed to any corporation with a VIP account number. People, charities, causes, organizations, businesses, public places such as parks, bike paths and beaches, governments, families, and any other unit of society, are corporations with VIP account numbers.

There is a caveat. The VIP looks for cycles, and cycles void the tax usage. Here is an example of a cycle. Suppose you direct all of your 2% to person A and Person A directs all of their 2% to you. That is a cycle and the entire 2% allocation is voided and reverts to default allocations. On the other hand, suppose you direct all of your 2% to person A, and person A directs their tax in such a way that after going through several people, .01% of their tax comes back to you from Person Z. Then only .01% from Person Z is voided and only .01% from you to Person A is voided. Your direction of 1.99% to Person A is a valid allocation. Funds cannot be given to family members or to organizations where family members hold more than a .01% financial interest.

In addition to allocating funds, you can allocate your allocations. In a sense, when you do nothing, you allocate your allocations to the seven levels of dominion. But you can also allow one or more of other people's allocations to control the transfer of your money as well, by allocating portions of your allocations to them. Funds are transferred at the moment money is moved from a personal corporate account to a personal spending account either explicitly or as a personal corporate account taxable debit.

Discretionary allocations are secret. A contract that dictates how or where to allocate discretionary funds is not enforceable. It is illegal to use force or threats of force to control how you allocate your discretionary tax. The discretionary tax cannot be used in the pricing of goods. When funds are received through a discretionary tax allocation, there is no record of who sent the money.

There are an untold number of good uses for the discretionary tax. This list gives examples.

1. National, state, and local museums and galleries
2. Local department of parks, recreation and beaches
3. Charitable organizations
4. Your favorite political or social organization
5. Funding for a new monument, a new school, a new bridge, a new highway
6. Your favorite author or artist, or the author or artist that most recently inspired you
7. A local hero, reward for a good deed
8. The tireless leader of your organization who foregoes a job for the cause
9. Your local beat cop. A law officer or prosecutor who succeeds in sending the bad guy to jail
10. A new business that moves to your community or a struggling business important to you
11. Reward a social worker or spiritual leader who helped you through a difficult time
12. Fund relief efforts for disasters
13. Reward a corporation for environmental policy (unless you own more than .01% of the stock)
14. Fund another child for a family that lost a child at a young age
15. Reward someone who was unjustly imprisoned or your hero imprisoned for civil disobedience
16. Reward a crime victim
17. Support public television and radio, or your favorite show on TV
18. Help maintain a local jogging path that you use daily
19. Donate to foreign aid organizations or U.S. military bases abroad
20. Help finance a foreign war if approved by a super plurality of the population (or majority if UN sanctioned)

There is no limit to the number of people and places in your allocations, and you can change the allocations whenever you wish. People and places can be added through the VIP reader on your personal computer, phone or other VIP device.

If you make a request for funds (which is perfectly legal as long as there is no force or threat of force) you must set up a special corporate account. Receipt of discretionary tax funds in answer to a request for funds is consideration (that is, you have made an enforceable contract with the public.) Suppose you do not believe in contraception or abortion and are requesting $10,000 to fund a future-baby account. Once the $10,000 is received the account is closed to new discretionary tax funds or private donations. Furthermore, the money can only be used to fund a future-baby account. Anything else is fraud and breach of contract.

Stopping Choke

Required Reading

In the next chapter, we look at a likely rare phenomenon called choke. This occurs when all ground rents are too high to be trebled. If the system comes to a complete halt, funds at the rate of $350 billion/year will very quickly restart the system. If consumption tax generates $86 billion per percent, a 4% tax will generate the funds to restart trebling.

Totals

All of these uses for the consumption tax are optional, and will be decided by a super-majority. For purposes of illustration, on the day after capitulation, the consumption tax will total 8% and be broken down as follows:

2% - Teacher achievement annuity (Rewards teachers, tutors, professors, authors, etc. for your achievement)
2% - School achievement annuity (Rewards schools, publishers, producers, for your achievement)
2% - Discretionary tax (Charity, foreign aid, disasters, culture, heroes, approved wars, military bases)
2% - Temporary substitute for the missing baby tax

Social Constructivism and Taxes

Beyond the collection and distribution of rents, taxes in AFFEERCE, with rare exceptions, are optional. They are used to encourage certain behaviors. This is called social constructivism.

Collection of the ground rents frees humanity from the burden of taxation altogether. And yet AFFEERCE is littered with little taxes. Why is this?

First, let me say that with the possible exception of the baby tax, none of the taxes are fundamental. They can all be abolished, and some no doubt will be over the 60 embryonic years leading to AFFEERCE. However, the taxes are designed to nudge us in certain directions. This is called social constructivism. The effects are subtle, but real. Some people hate social constructivism and others think it is a really good idea. They will both make their opinions known during the course of the embryo. My goal in this section is to list the elements of social constructivism, and show how dominions with Class II, and Class III legislation, along with an alternative currency, can avoid social constructivist taxes, altogether.

Elements of Social Constructivism

Tax	How it works	Social Constructivism
2% Discretionary	This consumption tax can be directed by the consumer, in any combination, to any person, place or thing. Support for local heroes, crime victims, charities, local organizations, poor families, parks, beaches, foreign wars, etc. Cycles are not allowed and are computer checked to prevent money from being returned to consumer.	Empowers the population to solve problems. Encourages consumption for a good cause. Encourages crowdfunding. Allows the people to rally to the aid of a victim of injustice or natural disasters in a manner that helps.
2% + 2% academic / school annuity	This consumption tax is divided with 2% going to the consumer's teachers, tutors, online instructors, textbook authors, and anyone else in the role of sharing knowledge, and 2% going to the schools and publishers that host these transfers of knowledge. Made possible through the VIP and high speed computing.	Enhances the education distribution. Rewards teachers for creating students who go on to become very successful consumers. Encourages the sharing of information and an economy based on each of us teaching others what we know. Discourages information monopoly and secrets.

50% rebate of food and housing distributions	Unused food and housing distributions are rebated only at 50%. This is a head tax on unused distributions which rightfully belong to the people.	Eliminates hunger and homelessness. Prevents spending of food and housing money on addictions and other vices. Encourages proper nutrition for children. Encourages economy of scale and the formation of mutual organizations. Discourages loneliness.
Excise taxes	These are consumption taxes placed on certain items. Also called sin taxes. Can be passed with Class II legislation.	Discourages alcohol, tobacco, recreational drugs, gambling, prostitution, and so forth. Proceeds must be earmarked for rehabilitation and related services.
Pigovian taxes	These are taxes on minor pollution or extraction of collectively owned resources.	Encourages care for the environment. Protects collectively owned resources. Proceeds must be earmarked for environmental cleanup, reforestation, or other forms of renewal.
Baby tax	Generally $10,000, payable when mother and child leave the hospital. Enforced with an income tax on paternal and maternal families. If fertility rate exceeds 3.6, or productivity falls behind population growth, the baby tax can increase significantly.	Discourages addicts and others who cannot save money from having children. Protects women from the peer pressure of having children in order to increase distributions. Protects against tragedy of the commons. Clinches distributions as a right by mandating "pay-in" from each person.

Avoiding Taxes

Certain types of social constructivism might be opposed by some dominions and rogue states. Depending on the tax, alternative currencies, super pluralities, and super-duper pluralities can be employed to avoid the tax.

Many of the ideas in this section will be better understood after reading *Chapter 9 – Government, Law, and Justice*, and *Chapter 10 – Economic Principles*. I decided to include them here in the general discussion of taxes. The interested reader can return to this section after reading those chapters.

The VIP$ is backed by land value. It is the only currency used in the collection and distribution of rents. Beyond that, dominions can establish alternative currencies. These currencies are automatically exempt from the discretionary, academic/school, and excise taxes. However, every dominion with an alternative currency will maintain a treasury account of VIP$ for import of foreign goods (i.e. AFFEERCE goods from outside the dominion.), funded by the distributions and exports. These imports, including those of capital goods are subject to consumption taxes. For purposes of discretionary and academic payouts, the purchase is equally pro-rated between all members of the dominion. Thus, the constructivist right of individuals to reward local heroes and teachers is relegated to a proration of collectivist spending.

A dominion can mimic this effect of alternative currency with Class II legislation. Like an alternative currency, this will only be a positive, if commerce within the dominion exceeds the import of capital goods. Countercultures convinced of their superiority will likely opt for this and might be surprised by the bottom line.

The 50% rebate on food and housing distributions can be overwritten in a dominion through Class III legislation with the treble option, or by a rogue state. It is predicted that these dominions will use all of the housing distribution to protect and grow their territory. The VIP$ from the food distribution can be stored in the Treasury for capital goods purchases and territory protection, and used as collateral for the issuance of alternative currency. Reallocation of distributions at levels of dominion higher than the individual, such as law enforcement, sanitation, and so on, requires only class II legislation, so all of this money can be placed in the Treasury account and used as collateral at the pleasure of the dominion.

The ground rent, baby tax, and Pigovian taxes must be paid in VIP$. The baby tax and Pigovian taxes can only be initially allowed or eliminated by a 2/3 majority constitutional amendment of the entire nation, or ultimately international in scope. Rogue dominions pay these taxes from their Treasury accounts. Rogue states or Class III legislation can maintain local controls on childbirth. Exit rights, however, limit the availability of punishment beyond banishment. In general, rouge states will wish to maximize population within the constraints of their Treasury account. Failure by a rogue state to pay the baby tax or Pigovian taxes will create an income tax on exports and all residents who earn VIP$ outside the dominion or on citizens' dividends, place liens on property improvements, end ground rent freezes, and as a last resort, debit the Treasury account. In this regard, rogue states receive the same treatment as large, alternative families.

Chapter 6 - The Balance of the RCs and the Treasury

Philosophy

Required Reading

AFFEERCE marks an epochal change. The Children = Poverty of the modern era will be replaced by Children = Wealth, not seen for centuries in the West. More significantly, land ownership by the community, a relic of prehistoric society, returns.

In the postmodern era, through genetic engineering, we are taking the process of evolution away from Nature. Just beyond our grasp, but fast becoming a global necessity, is the end of disease and war.

Standing on the brink of the mother of all epochal changes, these seemingly disparate concepts, children bringing wealth to the family, land owned by the commons, controlling evolution, and ending war and disease, are intimately connected. For the past several billion years, all of them have fallen under the umbrella of what is commonly called, "The Balance of Nature." Over the past several thousand years, governments have existed to usurp nature in some of these areas, often with negative results.

Predators and prey, territorial boundaries, disease, evolutionary change, and the rate of reproduction are tools used by Nature for these billions of years to keep the world in balance. The epochal change is marked by the passing of the baton from nature to humanity, where, at least for our own species, we agree to maintain the balance of nature. It has been termed the Anthropocene Epoch[FTN4.01].

Essential to AFFEERCE is "the balance of the RCs" which honors the contract with nature, and provides abundance for the people of Earth, eons into the future. When the balance of the RCs replaces government as the human implementation of the balance of nature, trebler wars replace violent ones, with all of the excitement and none of the injury. The loser walks away richer because of the war, and the plunder is divvied up amongst the citizens of Earth.

"The RC" refers to two concepts, rental of the commons, and reproductive control, both of which can be abbreviated RC. The combination of the two, rental of the commons through collection of the ground rents, and reproductive control through the baby tax are the normal source of distribution funding. Current thinking is that the baby tax will play only a tiny role in funding the distribution package. It is not expected to exceed $10,000 unless there is an explosion of fertility at the expense of production. If there is less than zero population growth, the baby tax could become a baby credit.

The real issue in managing the balance is in controlling the rate of fall of the rent multiplier.

The Distribution Package

Private Distribution   **Public Distribution**

Food   **Police**
Housing   **Fire**
Medical Care   **Government**
Education   **Streets/Sanitation**
                                                                                        National Defense

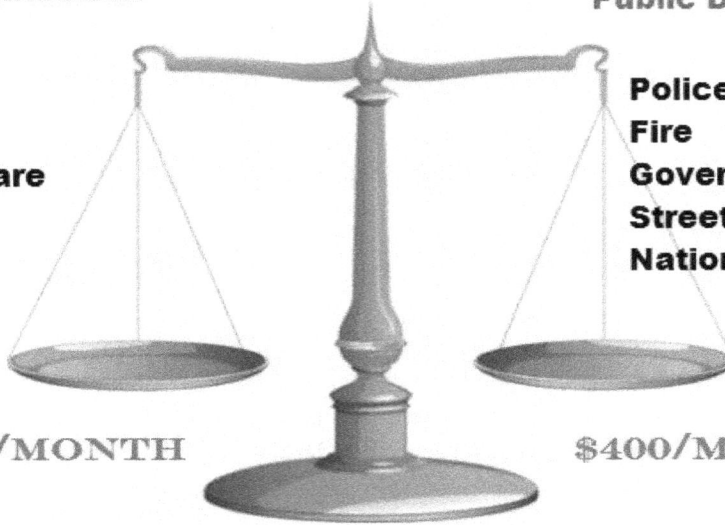

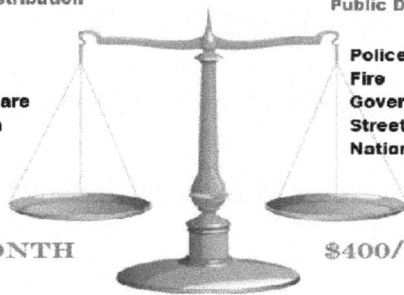

$800/MONTH $400/MONTH

According to distribution theory, personal or private distributions should be greater than or equal to public distributions. In this way, each head tax is neutralized by an entitlement. In the package being presented, based on 2002 population and U.S. land usage statistics, personal distributions exceed public distribution by 2 to 1, although education, like the intellectual property distribution can be considered both a public and a personal distribution.

$1,200/person/month * 12 months * 290,000,000 persons = $4.2 Trillion

Basic Flow

$4.2 Trillion Dollar Container (2002 pop. x $14,400)

Private Distribution   **Public Distribution**

Food   **Police**
Housing   **Fire**
Medical Care   **Government**
Education   **Streets/Sanitation**
                                                                        National Defense

$800/MONTH $400/MONTH

⬆ **Trebles and self-assessment increases**   ⬇ **Lower rents to those who accept them**

The distribution package contains the one year of advance ground rent payments, or $4.2 trillion. Should anyone increase their rent, or treble a property, the distribution package will hold too much cash. If we think of that metaphorically as adding pressure to the walls of the distribution package, the typical way to alleviate the pressure is to lower the rents of all properties whose ground rents are not frozen, or already at a minimum, restoring the container to $4.2 trillion.

Interest on the Distribution Package and Fertility

Interest on the distribution package can support a fertility rate above zero population growth without raising the baby tax.

Funds in the distribution package are loaned to collectives, and other small businesses by the citizen investors (See *Chapter 10 – Citizen Investors*) for purchase of capital equipment. These loans become part of the distribution package and the interest adds pressure to the walls. Assuming an interest rate of 1%, it is reasonable to ask what is the fertility rate supported, assuming there is no trebling or increase in ground rents.

We know that a fertility rate of 2.1, zero population growth, is supported with no interest as the number of deaths equals the number of births. However, we can support a 1% population growth rate. Using the formula:

Growth rate = log(fertility rate/2)/mean woman's childbearing age[FTN4.39], and assuming a mean child bearing age of 27, the interest on the distribution package can support a fertility rate of 3.6. That is an average 3.6 children for every two parents. I assume that ecologists and feminists would object to such a high rate, and would demand an increase in the baby tax, in conjunction perhaps with an advertising campaign, to bring the fertility rate down closer to 2.1.

The sociological issues behind the fertility rate are of little interest to the Treasury. In general, interest on the distribution package, along with baby tax revenue, if any, will add pressure to the sides of the distribution package, as long as the fertility rate is below 3.6.

The Rent Multiplier

Required Reading

There is a multiplier maintained by the Treasury. The multiplier drops from 1 (100%) to .01 (1%), lowering all ground rents that are tied to the multiplier to equal the funds from trebles and self-assessed rent increases. At any time, a tenant can freeze their rent, raise it, or reattach it to the multiplier at the current level. When the multiplier hits .01, all rents tied to the multiplier are renormalized and the multiplier is set back to 1.

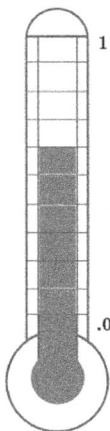

Fixed Rent – Ground rent explicitly set by the land rights owner
Float Rent – Ground rent that is allowed to shrink over time
Using these definitions, the rent multiplier is a number such that:

(Rent Multiplier x Float Rent) + Fixed Rent = The Distribution Package

Productive Event – Any treble, self-assessed increase or other increase in rents.
Choke – The complete absence of productive events
Meltdown – An unstoppable cascade of productive events

Trebling is Inevitable

Required Reading

There is a common belief among reviewers of earlier editions that the system will choke frequently; that trebles will be few and far between. However, this is on par with the notion that given a free market, there would be no buyers or sellers of goods, because the parties could never agree on a price. Henry George revealed a natural law that assures frequent trebling. **People seek to satisfy their desires with the least exertion**

If trebling occurs infrequently, people will allow their ground rent to fall and neglect to improve their properties. This, of course, increases the probability that the property will be trebled. Even with frequent trebling, people will desire to pay the lowest possible rent that still avoids the trebler, thus making them vulnerable to any change in conditions, including increases in population, increases in productivity, or innovation to increase profit from location value.

Meltdown and Choke

Meltdown and choke are equivalent to boom and bust in today's economy, although much easier to control. The Treasury maintains a constant rate of fall of the rent multiplier by channeling excess distribution package funds or deficits into or out of citizens' dividend accounts. In choke, trebling can be restarted with an increased baby tax, sales taxes, or Treasury monetization feeding the distribution package.

The rate of fall of the multiplier, which mathematicians would call dm/dt is the critical variable in determining the percentage of profits from location value that constitute treble safety. After all, if the rate of fall is fast enough, it doesn't matter if trebling costs you over 100% profits from location value, as profits will return in short order. The problem is the faster dm/dt, the more people will freeze or raise their ground rents. And the more people that freeze or raise their rents, the faster dm/dt. This creates an explosive condition where the rate of change of the rate of fall (d^2m/dt^2) is a function of the rate of fall. Ideally d^2m/dt^2 should equal 0. This is not possible without an intervention policy.

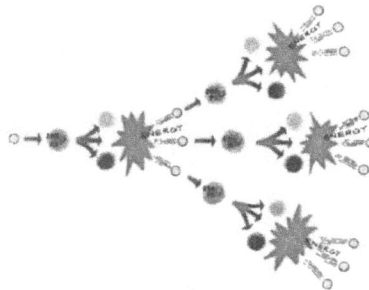

With little relief from the massive amount of funds pouring in, the distribution package is filled with more cash than it can hold, metaphorically causing the sides to bulge.

- The meltdown will not stop until average ground rent is well over 100% location value and choke occurs

- Because of 150% ODV well-kept residences paying fair rents will likely escape

- However, most commercial enterprises will be seriously hurt

- Meltdown followed by renormalization increases the likelihood of future meltdowns

The goal of the Treasury must be to keep the rate of fall of the rent multiplier constant. The Treasury can avoid meltdowns by keeping $d^2m/dt^2 = 0$.

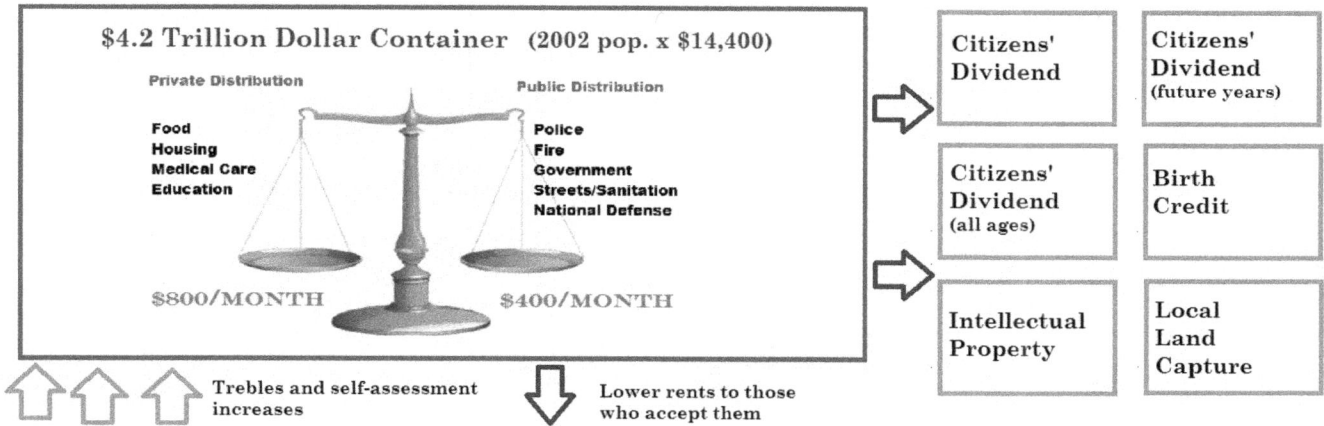

- Move excess funds into a citizens' dividend for those over the age of majority

- Absorb liquidity by moving funds into accounts for future citizens' dividends

- Handle minor population shrinkage by extending CD (citizens' dividend) to all ages

- Handle serious population shrinkage by moving excess funds to a birth credit

- Increase profits from non-location value by increasing the intellectual property distribution

- Reward local land capture over and above currency created

It is essential that the flow between these various dividend accounts and the distribution package be bidirectional in order to keep the rate of fall constant. This rate of fall will be determined early on, by closely monitoring the rate of trebling. Rapid changes in the rate of fall will diminish trust as well as trebling.

The Treasury creates new currency at 20 times the net increase in ground rents. As seen in the chapter on distribution theory, the new money is used to fund local land capture. Any funds placed in the local land capture dividend account rewards local land capture over and above this newly created currency.

The Treasury will control the amount of funds into and from the various dividend accounts. However, choosing which dividend account in particular to add to or withdraw funds from, is as much related to cultural and social norms as it is to financial conditions. All of the dividend accounts benefit large constituencies, although everyone does not benefit equally from any particular account. In a normal economy, the treasury feeds cash into these dividend accounts or very temporarily reverses the flow.

In the event of a crisis, certain extraordinary measures might be needed to prevent choke.

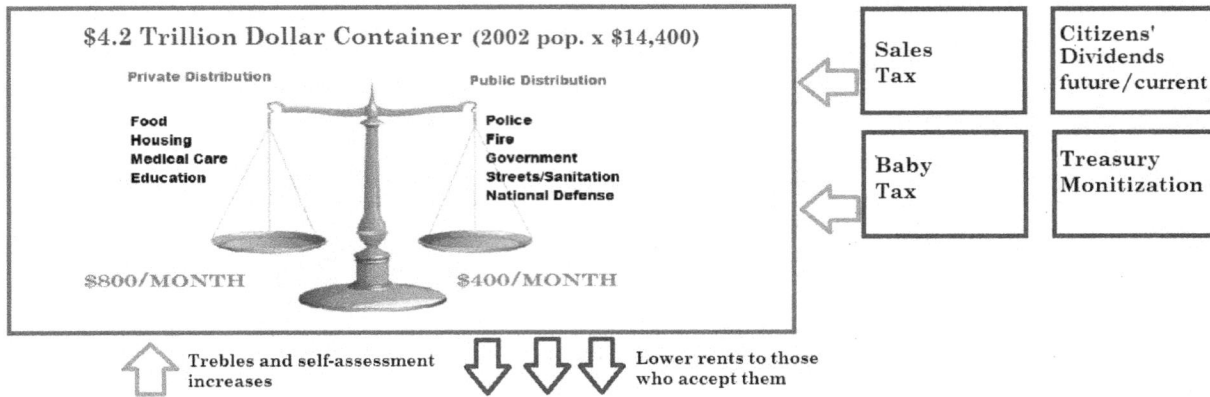

Meltdown and choke are the AFFEERCE equivalents of boom and bust. By keeping the rate of fall constant and reasonably low, meltdown is avoided. Without meltdown, choke is unlikely. But it is almost a law of nature that if things go too well for too long, people let their guard down and get greedy. Perhaps greed will disappear with the AFFEERCE enlightenment, perhaps not. In any case, the Treasury needs the tools to stop a financial crisis, should one occur.

There is probably nothing left in the present or future citizens' dividend accounts should a financial crisis arise, but a box is included for completeness.

In choke, location value is dropping everywhere. Ground rents are making up an increasingly higher percentage of location value and nobody is trebling. Therefore, once the citizens' dividend accounts are exhausted, nobody's rent can fall further. The goal of the Treasury is to feed money into the distribution package, driving down ground rents until trebling restarts. The source of the money depends on the nature of the crisis. If lack of liquidity is caused by excessive savings with no corresponding investment opportunities, funds to restart the trebling engine should come from a consumption tax. If the problem comes because the population is disproportionately favoring reproduction over production, with fertility rates exceeding 3.6, funds must be generated by a steep increase in the baby tax.

Choke itself is a remote possibility. Savings will be high and population growth assured. In such an environment, land value will tend to increase. Even if the rent rate of fall is 10%, land value need not increase by nearly that much as most rents will be frozen. However, should the perfect storm occur, the Treasury is left with no choice but to mint the virtual currency and feed it into the distribution package until trebling restarts.

The Withering Away of the Allocations

Required Reading

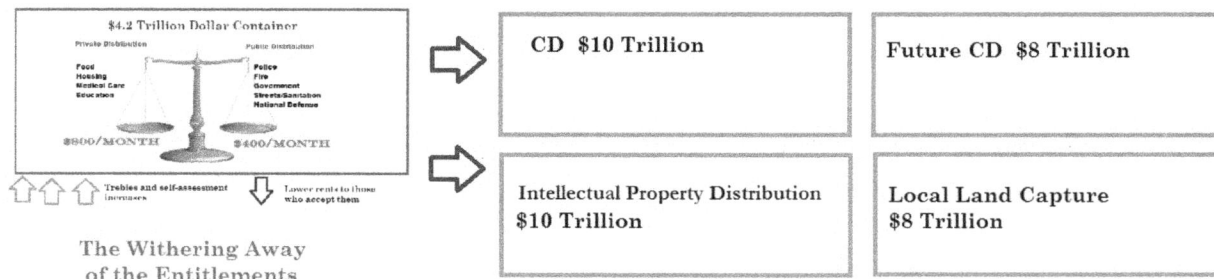

The Withering Away
of the Entitlements

Over the decades of an AFFEERCE economy, productivity will grow much larger than the distribution package, since

126

the distribution package is constitutionally protected from increase without concurrence of a 5/6 majority. The vast majority of collected rents will find their way into the dividend accounts. The citizens' dividend will provide cash that can be spent freely. The intellectual property distribution will turn all of us into inventors and artists, and local land capture will encourage every little town to build infrastructure, heretofore seen only in sci-fi books about the future. These will be the trends.

- The rate of fall of the rent multiplier, dm/dt, will slowly increase, pushing average ground rents over 90% of location value as business collectives rely less on location value for profit.

- Population less susceptible to "tragedy of the commons" behavior

- Most profit will come from innovation and creativity

- The distributions will be dwarfed by CDs, rewards for innovation, and return on local infrastructure investment.

- Revenue for public goods and local infrastructure investment , beyond the distributions, will be raised from consumption taxes approved by a supermajority.

- Local land capture funds will motivate a change in the consumption tax from progressive to just.

The 10% Assumption

Required Reading

Although a thorough mathematical analysis is needed to determine the optimal rate of fall of the rent multiplier to minimize the possibility of either meltdown or choke, a 10% rate is used throughout this book. With a 10% rate, a trebled ground rent will return to its original value in under 12 years. Given an active trebler market, a 10% rent rate of fall will insure that over 85% of natural resource and high luxury location value goes to ground rent. Likewise, over 70% of prime office/retail/apartment location value will go to rent.

Future-Baby Accounts

Special savings accounts for future children increases predictability of changes to the distribution package and can be used by the Treasury as a tool.

One does not associate the Treasury with baby services, although this one could be useful as a tool in balancing.

Citizens are encouraged to save for children in future-baby accounts. Once the account reaches the level in the baby tax/ground rent ratio, it is fully funded and entitles the account owner(s) to a child through birth or infant adoption at any time in the future. Once the account is fully funded, it can never be "unfunded" due to an increase in the baby tax. Should the baby tax be lowered, money will be returned to the family owning the fund. This remains true until the day both mother and child are released from the hospital and the fund is exercised.

A bigger encouragement for saving is that the Treasury, without approval of the electorate, can for a brief instant, lower the level of full funding. In that instant, partially funded accounts can become fully funded. Excess funds will be returned to families, creating unexpected windfalls. This encourages savings in future-baby accounts as opposed to raising baby tax funds in the months preceding delivery. Banks will pay interest on future-baby accounts. Public banking, through the citizen investors, will likely pay 1% on these deposits.

Future-baby accounts are heritable. They will remain fully funded in perpetuity, and can be passed from generation to generation.

If the number of fully funded future-baby accounts is growing, and they are not being exercised, the Treasury can create a surplus dividend account in anticipation of their exercise, rather than moving the money to other dividend accounts.

If the citizenry consistently uses future-baby funds, any possibility of shock to the system from unexpected population booms is removed. A fully funded future-baby account bestows the right to have a child, not the obligation. Families might fund multiple accounts before bearing or adopting to have better control over spacing of their children.

Cropland Imbalance

Cropland imbalance is the Treasury program to reverse the negative effects of farm subsidies and restore the free market to farming. It was described in detail in Chapter 2.

In summary, there is a surcharge on ground rents of cropland converted to residential/commercial. The surcharge and other rent increases on that land, increases the size of the distribution package by increasing the amount of the food distribution. This extra money finds its way to farmers, due to the decreasing supply of cropland, who use much of it to raise the ground rent on their fields which further increases the food distribution and allows the surcharge to be lowered.

The program is a success when the creation of cropland is equal to the conversion of cropland and the surcharge is eliminated. At that point, funds from trebled cropland are treated no differently than the ground rent funds from other lands in lowering the multiplier. Barring drought, insects, dust, or other natural disasters, the percentage of cropland should remain stationary or slowly drop with increased farm productivity.

Immigration and the Treasury

Required Reading

Open borders are essential for free trade and human dignity. There is no such thing as an illegal immigrant. The abolition of the minimum wage in conjunction with distributions will tend to bring capital home. With all essentials covered, many will be eager to take low paying jobs working the fields at harvest time, to pay for a Caribbean vacation come winter. It will be family fun and good exercise.

All adults over 14 years of age are welcome to visit and work in the AFFEERCE nation. Ironically, the situation for migrant workers will be much different than today. It will be harder for non-citizens to compete with citizens excited about earning discretionary income. Because immigrants do not come with a food and housing distribution, they cannot live in the dormitories without sacrificing $370 a month. Nor can they partake in the bountiful farm cooking without paying $220 a month. All visitors must purchase a $5 a day medical insurance policy or be denied any medical treatment without payment upfront. Foreign workers automatically have a $740 per month disadvantage.

Foreign tourists and workers will have VIP accounts. Because foreign workers and tourists have no teachers or schools to receive their annuity, these, and funds from the discretionary tax, could be rebated against a medical policy. At $150 per month, in increments of as little as $5 a day, the medical policy might be deemed mandatory for all foreign guests.

Citizenship Tax

> **Like a baby tax, those who wish to become citizens and partake in the distributions must pay a citizenship tax. The amount of this tax is determined by public policy.**

How much should it cost to purchase citizenship and the universal distribution that comes with it? Is it fair to associate different rates with proficiency in different languages or skill sets? Would price discrimination against certain nationalities require a 5/6 plurality of the nation to implement?

The Treasury might want the leeway to lower the citizenship tax if there is less than zero population growth.

It is likely there will always be a surplus of job openings in an AFFEERCE economy. People will tend to do what they love to do, and others will pay them to do it. The fear of immigrants "taking away jobs" will disappear from the radar.

With nothing to fear on the employment front, the tax should be as low as possible, yet still large enough to achieve a net increase in national productivity. If it turns out that immigrants are almost always hard working entrepreneurs, there is no reason why the tax should be much greater than the $10,000 baby tax. However, unlike babies, immigrants don't usually begin life in the new country at the age of zero, so the tax should be pro-rated for age.

In this table, the citizenship tax is $95,000 prorated for age.

Age	Approximate Cost
0-9	$95,000
10-19	$85,000
20-39	$65,000
40-59	$45,000
60+	$25,000

Many have died paying "coyotes" this much for a dangerous attempt at illegal immigration. In an AFFEERCE society, all can enter freely; the borders are open. Any immigrant can pay this tax (plus plane fare) at the nearest embassy or consulate   to become a citizen fully entitled to the distributions. A social worker will be meet them at the arrival gate and help them get settled.

It will be difficult for the average immigrant farm laborer to fund citizenship. With wages for migrant farm labor at $1000 a month, $740 will be spent on medical, food and shelter. Skimping on food and shelter, it would still take a 20 year old laborer almost 14 years to fund a citizenship.

It would also be illegal for a foreign worker without proper funding to bring children into the country on a permanent basis without risking their being taken away for child abuse (Failure to provide children with universal distribution's nutritious meals, warm shelter, education and medical insurance, will constitute child abuse).

Technical professionals could earn a citizenship much more quickly. Assume a couple of trained computer programmers get jobs in the United States, with salaries of $75,000 each. Ground rent, food and other necessities cost them $2000 a month. So $24,000 of their income goes for survival. That leaves $126,000 for funding citizenship. If they are both in their 30s, they can become citizens in a years' time, and two months later fund a child at the citizen's rate of $10,000.

Chapter 7 – Summary of Part I – Funding Freedom through the Collection and Distribution of Ground Rents

Collection and distribution of ground rent is essential AFFEERCE. Readers should be familiar with the ideas summarized here.

Collection Theory

Required Reading

- Land is objectively worthless
- All land was initially seized through violence
- The subjective value of land is arbitrarily high
- All profits of companies that own their own land, save the profits from risk return, innovation and unpaid labor, come from location value
- Like art, location value cannot be measured outside of a market
- For sales prices, it is always the location value of the less efficient seller and not the location value of the more efficient buyer
- Because a low land price is in the interest of both the buyer and seller, there is not a market in land, but collusion.
- Objective scoring is grossly inefficient, leaving land idle in places, with super-profits from location value in others.
- If only comparable sales or objective scoring is used to determine location value, all land prices approach as a limit the objective value of land, which is $0, as individuals are forced to engage in immoral behavior.
- If a land assessor uses only subjective criteria in determining land value, all land taxes approach as a limit the subjective value of land which is arbitrarily large (subsistence for all "non-connected" exclusive users). Assessors are forced to engage in immoral behavior.
- In a Georgist economy, there is no market for land
- If ground rent is based on 100% of location value, then all land is free. As soon as such land develops a price, it is undervalued
- If a buyer pays a price for land which causes an upward reassessment then they are paying for the land twice.
- Land must not be owned, assessed, and taxed, but rather rented from the commons
- With self-assessment and land seizure, people will always pay what the land is worth to them. For the most efficient user, this is, by definition, the true ground rent.
- Whenever the ground rent is raised on a property, all the other ground rents in the nation drop by a small amount – unless they were explicitly frozen by the land rights owner.
- Ground rents feed a distribution package that is constant in size for zero population growth
- Once established, the ground rent for any property will drop on a regular basis, ultimately down to the minimum. Only the land rights owner can raise their ground rent.
- Trebling requires that the current ground rent be tripled and 150% be paid on the objective depreciated value of the improvements in order to gain ownership of the land rights
- Trebling and land seizure give location value monopoly to the most efficient user of the land
- When location value of the most efficient business is unclear, the greatest benefit to both the individual and society is too allow ground rents to fall without fear and either match or accept the treble when it comes

- Trebling ground rents extracts near the maximum possible revenue of any conceivable system of taxes. Furthermore, it succeeds at doing this by enhancing, rather than curtailing productivity, and it is, in a sense, completely voluntary.

- A trebling system automatically leads to the highest possible ground rent for depleting the Earth's resources

- Well-maintained improvements and increased efficiency will lower the ground rents on a property. Failure to maintain a property is an invitation to treblers

- The most efficient use of the land is rarely the tallest possible building

- The existence of neighborhood blight is virtually impossible with trebling/land seizure.

- Vacancies do not allow the ground rent to fall! While a regional supply glut will drive down ground rents, a supply glut in one building will do no such thing.

- Trebling deplores inefficiency and will drive down tenant rents to achieve 100% occupancy.

- When initializing ground rents, there is no benefit from assessing anything but a fair rent to one's land. A ground rent too high or too low can be financially devastating

- Improvements must at least equal the rate of depreciation to prevent the ground rent of the improved property from rising due to depreciation

- Homeowners should allow their ground rents to drop to the minimum, use all extra funds to maintain their property, and match or accept trebles when they come

- Jurisdictional covenants can be broken by a dominion treble.

- Ground rents are not a tax, but distributions to the common owners of the land

- Ground rents are paid one year in advance with the first one year advance payment paid by the Treasury as compensation for the land.

Distribution Theory

Required Reading

- Human law is utterly powerless directly to alter distribution so that the laborer as laborer will get more wages or less wages, the capitalist as capitalist will get more interest or less interest, the landowner as landowner more rent or less rent (Henry George).

- The natural laws of production are physical laws and the natural laws of distribution are moral laws (Henry George).

- That which we create with our own hands, belongs only to us. That which God or Nature provides belongs to each of us and to all of us.

- For art and innovation, the greater the distribution of product, the greater the distribution of wealth

- Content, apart from the media, will always be available at no charge to maximize profit for the creator.

- The size of the domain of distribution is inversely proportional to the likelihood of chaos and gross inequality.

- An equitable distribution of public goods and services, even with a national distribution domain, shows a high correlation of spending effectiveness with population density.

- Ground rents are not a tax, but distributions to the common owners of the land

- A head tax and a personal distribution (basic income) cancel each other out. They detoxify each other.

- Distributions for public goods and services move with the person.

- A distribution scheme where every head tax is cancelled out by a personal distribution is ideal and utopian.

- The greater the intellectual property distribution, the lower the cost of goods in the marketplace.

132

- While head taxes should never exceed personal distributions, there is no such constraint on personal distributions
- The more controlled the distribution, the more free the society

Balance Theory

- We agree to maintain the balance of nature for our own species.
- RCs: Revenue from renting the commons and reproductive control
- Because the rent rate of fall tends to be much faster than changes increasing business or location risk, defaults for businesses with viable plans will be practically unheard of.
- The national increase in land value is exactly equal to the requirement for additional currency to prevent deflation. (land value = ground rent/.05)
- The biggest issue in managing the balance is in controlling the rate of fall of the rent multiplier.
- The rent multiplier must be made to fall at a constant rate
- Cropland should be trebled away at the same rate it is created
- The distribution package for the nation contains more personal distributions than head taxes and remains constant for zero population growth.
- Interest on the advance payment of ground rent supports a fertility rate that significantly exceeds zero population growth.
- (Rent Multiplier x Float Rent) + Fixed Rent = The Distribution Package
- The Treasury can avoid meltdowns by keeping $d^2m/dt^2 = 0$ by channeling excess funds into dividend accounts
- The dividend accounts include current and future citizens' dividends, a baby credit, additional intellectual property and local land capture accounts.
- The increase in ground rents times 20 is exactly equal to the increase in total land value nationwide and exactly equal to the amount of new cash the Treasury must mint to prevent deflation.
- A consumption tax, high baby tax, or the creation of inflationary currency are tools the Treasury could employ in the unlikely event of choke.
- By remaining constant against increasing productivity the allocated distribution package will wither away in favor of dividend accounts over time
- If approved by the electorate, a cropland surcharge can be converted into increased food distribution to increase the location value of farmland and thereby eliminate the surcharge

Final Thoughts

The equitable collection and distribution of ground rent is a requirement for all freedoms envisioned by the objectivist right plus the basic shared wealth imagined in the wildest dreams of the socialist left. Yet it is profoundly neither right nor left but a synthesis of individualism and collectivism, part of the grand synthesis between objectivism and subjectivism.

From our wresting of the balance of nature, comes a world without underpopulation or overpopulation, isolation or loneliness, hunger or homelessness; a free society where people seek their own opportunities, with families, collectives, and mutual organizations beyond our imagination, and personal freedom beyond anything we have ever seen. Healthcare, education, food and shelter will be rights, not privileges. And children will be both valuable and abundant.

By keeping the collection and distribution of rents at the highest level, equality of opportunity is assured, panarchy can blossom, wars are replaced by trebler wars, mobility is enhanced, and people are welcome wherever they might roam.

Implementation of such a society by dictate, vote, or revolution would likely lead to chaos, as the machinery of the new economy is precise and must be in perfect working order before the changeover.

AFFEERCE begins its life as an embryo, and succeeds because it is able to capture a sufficient amount of land to be self-sustaining and thriving within the existing political order. Only then can capitulation take place. While the Chinese Communist Party, for instance, might be tempted to implement the collection and distribution of ground rents from above, particularly since Sun Yat-Sen gave us the basic principle of rent collection, they would do far better to establish a viral community, similar to that described in Volume II, and allow it to grow organically. As the cliché goes, "Nine women cannot have a baby in one month."

In Part II of this volume, we look at a political system that follows naturally from a viral city and embraces freedom in new ways. While the Chinese might have the advantage of expediency, the United States has a history of freedom, and likely respect for the economic success of the embryo. The frontier culture in U.S. heritage plays very well with the integrated solution.

Part II – A Free Society

"Poverty, therefore, is a thing created by that which is called civilized life. It exists not in the natural state. On the other hand, the natural state is without those advantages which flow from agriculture, arts, science and manufactures." – Thomas Paine

"I am now convinced that the simplest approach will prove to be the most effective — the solution to poverty is to abolish it directly by a now widely discussed measure: the guaranteed income." – Martin Luther King

"The fact is that the work which improves the condition of mankind, the work which extends knowledge and increases power and enriches literature, and elevates thought, is not done to secure a living. It is not the work of slaves, driven to their task either by the lash of a master or by animal necessities. It is the work of men who perform it for their own sake, and not that they may get more to eat or drink, or wear, or display. In a state of society where want is abolished, work of this sort could be enormously increased." – Henry George

"Productiveness is your acceptance of morality, your recognition of the fact that you choose to live--that productive work is the process by which man's consciousness controls his existence, a constant process of acquiring knowledge and shaping matter to fit one's purpose, of translating an idea into physical form, of remaking the earth in the image of one's values--that all work is creative work if done by a thinking mind, and no work is creative if done by a blank who repeats in uncritical stupor a routine he has learned from others--that your work is yours to choose, and the choice is as wide as your mind, that nothing more is possible to you and nothing less is human" – Ayn Rand

Chapter 8 – The Natural Rights of Mankind

A man's natural rights are his own, against the whole world; and any infringement of them is equally a crime, whether committed by one man, or by millions; whether committed by one man, calling himself a robber, (or by any other name indicating his true character,) or by millions, calling themselves a government. – Lysander Spooner

Philosophy

Required Reading

A definition of natural rights, is very dependent on the philosophy of the person giving it. I define those rights from an AFFEERCE perspective in *Volume III – The Philosophy*. Here it might be sufficient to define natural rights as this:

1. Every person has a natural right to the product of their own labor (the right to property).
2. That which God or Nature provides belongs to each of us and all of us (the right to life, entitlement).

The AFFEERCE right to property leads to all the natural rights of mankind as many on the political right have argued for centuries. The AFFEERCE right to life generates all the nutritious food, warm and safe shelter, free education, and health care that many on the political left have demanded.

The AFFEERCE vision of natural rights, is profoundly Georgist. To touch on philosophy, it can be considered the synthesis of objectivism and subjectivism. It marks the end of left and right, the end of war and misery, and thus the end of history as we know it.

More on the Right to Property in an AFFEERCE Society

Required Reading

The right to property has a different meaning for different types of property. The basic types are land and its natural resources, land improvements, financial instruments, possessions including currency, intellectual property, and yourself. It is the job of the state to protect the owners of property from theft.

The labor theory of property advocated by John Locke [FTN8.13] and extended by Henry George [FTN8.14] is the basis of exclusive rights to land and natural resource property. In the labor theory of property, ownership of land is maintained through some combination of using labor to improve the land and paying a rent to the inhabitants of Earth to use the land. The more improvements made to the property, the lower the rent; exactly opposite the property tax philosophy.

The right to the fruits of our labor including portable possessions and financial instruments is absolute. The right to intellectual property is revolutionized in an AFFEERCE society to maximally benefit both society and the innovator.

The right to trade one's body and labor is absolute. However, in no case can this be a remedy of an enforceable contract. Suicide, drug use, working in a bar where patrons smoke, and selling organs, are all natural rights. However, only portable possessions as collateral, financial instruments and currency can be demanded in lieu of performance.

The Right to Life and Insurrection

Required Reading

Every human being has a right to life, including the right to defend against attack. The right to life trumps all other rights including the right to property and gives the starving person the right to steal food. The owner of the property has a right to defend his property. Thus there is conflict today between the right to life and the right to property absent the right to share equally in the gifts of nature.

Should a group of people be starving, homeless and feeling there is no way out, the right to life gives them the right to foment insurrection. This is a natural right, as is the right of the propertied class to defend themselves. This conflict, in its catastrophic form, ever present in our thoughts, but unspoken, is at the root of political economy. Whatever the outcome, there is little to be said for either the right to life or the right to property prevailing, one over the other.

Nevertheless, the right to life and the right to property are both natural rights. What are not natural are the so-called "rights" society has put in place to stop insurrection; notably, the right to a job, regulations, and even the minimum wage.

Stopping insurrection is not necessarily bad, if fundamental solutions are forthcoming. Perhaps artificial fixes, such as minimum wage, are better than insurrection, although they do tend to increase contradictions in society and make matters worse in the long run.

Childbirth and Natural Rights

Required Reading

Many consider having a child to be the greatest blessing, and AFFEERCE does everything it can to encourage childbirth, save violating the natural rights of mother or child.

The child's birthright is to live in a free society. A free society is only possible with a free market, and a free market is only possible with universal distribution. It is the child's birthright to have nutritious meals, warm and safe shelter, and quality healthcare. This is the natural right to life and it is only possible with universal distribution. Most importantly, it is the child's birthright to have an equal chance at greatness. No brilliant mind should suffer for lack of education. This too, is only possible with universal distribution.

Finally, it is everyone's birthright not to be subject to taxation so that others can bear children. One of the most fundamental principles of a free society is that one is free to take any action, as long as others are not forced to pay the price. So it is with childbirth. If you have a child, and place the burden of supporting that child on others, you have committed a theft.

In an AFFEERCE society, the privilege of giving birth to a child is contingent on demonstrating the ability to be a parent by raising a small portion of the child's future distribution. This commitment leads to a counter-commitment from the commons to pick up the remainder of the tab. But the money does not come from the taxpayer. It comes from ground rent on commonly owned land.

The Gun Control Debate

Fears that arise from a conflict of natural rights disappear when those rights are no longer in conflict.

From the right to property, follows the right to defend oneself. From the right to life, follows the right to be free from acts of violence. In the gun control debate, we tackle the contradiction between being allowed to have a gun and being free from gun violence.

In an AFFEERCE society, where the right to life and the right to property are not in conflict, will the rights that follow, the right to be free from acts of violence and the right to self-defense also be not in conflict? AFFEERCE clearly defaults to the side of the gun owner. The right to self-defense is a natural right, while the right to be free from acts of violence is subjective. A super plurality can change this in any dominion; however, the point of this discussion is to examine the associated fears on both sides and see how AFFEERCE changes those fears. In an AFFEERCE society, will the fear that causes conflict between the right to be free from acts of violence and the right to self-defense be eliminated?

In regard to this debate, here are the fears, and an AFFEERCE society's stance?

	Fear	AFFEERCE Response
1	Fear of the government seizing all arms.	The right to property is a fundamental natural right.
2	Fear of the government imposing marshal law.	The trimmed-down government will have incentives to reduce incarceration and increase productivity. The AFFEERCE government is created by the citizens to protect natural rights,.
3	Fear of criminals breaking into the home.	Poverty and the war on drugs are eliminated. Larger families will be a more formidable threat to an intruder. The VIP increases the odds of capture. Prisons will no longer be criminal factories, but penitentiaries that have an incentive to reduce recidivism.
4	Fear of race and class warfare.	Class conflict eliminated when all share in the Earth's bounty. Wealth goes to the enterprising. The importance of gene pool diversity in certain family structures will eliminate racial and ethnic identity over time.
5	Fear of the mentally ill going on a rampage	Current society is so beset by contradictions that I wonder why there are so few rampages. At times I have become so enraged by the state of affairs that random violence has crossed my mind. Luckily, my moral code and self-preservation prevent that from happening. In recent attempts to preserve property rights at the expense of entitlement, mental health services have been all but eliminated [FTN8.09]. To make matters worse, materialists have tried to extinguish all vestiges of a moral code [FTN8.10]. A majority of citizens likely have fantasies of random violence, but sublimate those needs in violent movies, violent music and violent games. AFFERCE will end most of these conflicts in society. There will be ready help for the mentally ill, loneliness will be supplanted by a rich family life, and children, the most valued members of large families, will not be likely to form street gangs. Wars will become trebler wars. Moral codes will return when the universe is once-again viewed as purposeful. (See Volume-III)

One side of the gun control debate has fears 1-4. The other side has fear 5. In an AFFEERCE society, the fears will evaporate, and so will the gun control debate.

The Smoking Debate

> **In an attempt to resolve conflicts in natural rights, the current polity has created artificial rights, such as the right to a job, and an obligation to live.**

There are parallels between gun control and the right to smoke; the right to smoke versus the right to be free from second hand smoke. In this debate, non-smokers have prevailed in that exposure to second hand smoke is not subjective. In a free society, the conflict would go no further. Our society is not so free and that has led to a new problem.

It is the right of smokers to have bars and restaurants where smoking is permitted. More exactly, in terms of free choice, it is the right of proprietors to own bars and restaurants where smoking is permitted and the right of customers to choose to patronize such establishments. These are natural rights, and in an AFFEERCE economy, there are no conflicting natural rights.

Workers have the right to work in a smoke-free environment. This is a natural right in a free society. But tyrants, who are especially fond of false logic, have twisted this right into an abrogation of rights. "The worker has no right to work in a smoke-filled environment." The law does not actually say this, but proprietors in many places are forbidden from running a bar or restaurant where smoking is permitted.

Implementation of this smoking ban violates the natural rights of entrepreneur, worker, and customer. The state responds that the worker has a right to life, a natural right, and therefore they have a right to a job, since without a job they could not survive, and they have a right to a safe workplace, since without a safe workplace, they might not survive. So the state is framing the worker's right to life, a natural right, improperly, and with several artificial rights, to justify violating other natural rights.

For one, when the state invokes the worker's right to life, with no consent from the worker, it is no longer a right to life, but an obligation to live. Historically, the suicide laws make it abundantly clear that there is no right to death; the right to choose life or not.

The "right" to a job is not a natural right in a free society. Implicit in the right to a job is the obligation for someone to hire. This obligation is a clear violation of the natural rights of the business forced to do the hiring. They are forced to use and pay for unwanted services; similar to extortion by the mob.

While the right to a safe workplace is a natural right, the right to risk safety for perceived gain is also a natural right. Rather than acknowledge these rights, the state resorts to arbitrary or corrupt inconsistencies. It is illegal for someone to work in a smoke-filled restaurant, but not to work in a coal mine or atop a skyscraper. Which businesses are allowed to operate and which are shut down is not based on natural rights at all, but rather the whims of politicians and their financial backers.

When Natural Rights are in Conflict

Required Reading

Without universal distribution, the right to life and the right to property are in conflict,. AFFEERCE resolves this conflict. Nonetheless, conflicting rights are part of human nature and will not be completely eliminated, as long as two humans inhabit the planet.

When analyzing rights in conflict, it is important to distinguish between a right and a privilege. The right to be intoxicated and the privilege to drive an automobile are not in conflict, because driving an automobile is not a right. Beyond privileges such as driving, intoxication can lead to various illegal behaviors, most notably domestic abuse. However, the distributions allow victims of domestic abuse to remove the abuser from the family without serious financial difficulties. Furthermore, large alternative families will tend to eradicate domestic abuse altogether. So, is being intoxicated a right? What about a child's right to be protected from intoxicated adults? Do children have a right to be intoxicated?

These are rights in conflict, but remedies vary. A family is governed by a charter that might or might not be a democracy. Even if it is, children under 14 will not likely have the deciding vote. Thus intoxication within the home is likely a decision matter for adult family members. In a community, outside the home, intoxication can be outlawed by a 5/6 plurality. (See, *Chapter 9 – Government, Law, and Justice*) However, no punishment can violate an adult's right to leave that community.

Although parenting is a privilege, it nonetheless gives many rights to the parent that are in conflict with the natural rights of the child. These include the right to property, right to association, right to free speech, and even the right to liberty, itself. The privilege of parenting bestows on children only a privilege of property, although the child's right to life is constitutionally protected.

The age of majority in an AFFEERCE society is 14, as the distributions allow young people to form families early without major economic consequences. Because Children = Wealth, there are also many diverse families willing to take in these youth. By the age of 14, each child's individuality emerges and each individual has their own needs. Some paths chosen include drug abuse and indiscriminate sexuality, and things even more unfathomable. As painful as it might be for parents to watch, respecting this freedom will often bring rewards down the road.

Does a community have the right to curtail these freedoms by law? Can a community restrict the rights of property through the age of 21? Can a community restrict the right of property regardless of age? Suppose an individual builds nuclear weapons in their basement. Certainly the community should be able to restrict this right to property in direct conflict with the right to life.

Procedures for passing legislation are designed around the natural rights of man. Legislation designed to protect natural rights is called Class I legislation. It can be passed by a governing council. Legislation designed to handle a conflict in natural rights is called Class II legislation. Bills raising additional revenue in accordance with strict guidelines are also in Class II. They must be passed by a direct vote of a super plurality of the electorate. Legislation that infringes on natural rights, Class III legislation, must be passed by a 5/6 plurality of the electorate. In the next chapter on *Government, Law, and Justice*, you will see the importance of Class III legislation in community freedom and how the right to leave (exit rights) protects individuals against local or family tyranny.

Chapter 9 – Government, Law and Justice

To prevent government from becoming corrupt and tyrannous, its organization and methods should be as simple as possible, its functions be restricted to those necessary to the common welfare, and in all its parts it should be kept as close to the people and as directly within their control as may be. – Henry George

Introduction

Required Reading

At the end of Phase-IV of the embryonic AFFEERCE nation described in *Volume II*, U.S. voters are expected to approve a package of constitutional amendments to enshrine freedom, limit and shrink the government, and implement the collection and distribution of the ground rents. In this chapter, we examine the government, legal, and, judicial system, although the final structures of government, law, and justice that emerge from citizen and scholarly input over 60 years will likely look different than what follows below.

The government I will describe is both government and government framework. The default government protects natural rights and maximizes freedom, but critically protects the natural right to sacrifice freedom. Within the government framework can be many different types of governments and cultural biases. This is called a panarchy. Equality of opportunity is maintained by the collection and distribution of rents at the highest possible level. The constitution protects the right to life of children and exit rights of adults, that is, the right to leave.

Thus in the distant future, the entire world can share equally in the fruits of the Earth (the ground rents), and still have different nations, with very different governments and laws. In such a world, trebler wars will replace violent ones.

Implementation of a panarchy, requires a very rigorous legal framework, as well. A framework that protects natural rights, and eschews injustice within an environment of arbitrary governments is a tall order. Elegance, simplicity and logical consistency are critical to success. Over the 60 years prior to capitulation, great legal minds will test and debate facets of the legal framework presented below. The final result will look very different. But we need never compromise our principles, or sacrifice elegance. I believe there is always an equitable solution to every conundrum if the framework is correct. While either inconsistency or incompleteness are inevitable according to the laws of mathematics, they can be subtle and of no material consequence.

The legal framework fits within a government framework, so it is there we begin. The AFFEERCE government framework and default government is a cellular democracy. This organization was inspired by the work of Georgists Fred Foldvary and Edward Miller. Cells are organized hierarchically, with representatives chosen from the councils of cells one level down, or discrete individuals at the lowest level. The cellular democracy is not a substitute for direct democracy but augments it to save the population from the tedium of maintaining adequate business, civil, and criminal law. However, the cellular council is constrained by the one principle that defines its mission.

It is the sole job of government to protect the natural rights of its citizens.

Protecting these natural rights is protecting the citizens from theft, murder, rape, fraud, extortion, and so forth. It is only these laws that can be passed by a cellular council without ratification by the direct democracy. These laws are called Class I laws. Class II laws are concerned with conflicts in rights and Class III laws violate natural rights. They are ratified by super-pluralities of the direct democracy and are discussed in detail, below.

The cellular levels are well defined at levels 0-7 in the United States, or 0-9 in an international framework. Every distribution is divided into one or more tranches. Every tranche is earmarked for one of these levels. Personal distributions are earmarked for level-0. Although distributions are allocated to such things as police, fire, streets, sanitation, and national defense (See, *Chapter 11 – Universal Distribution*), a cellular council, with ratification by a 2/3 super-plurality of its citizens can change the allocations.

Cellular Federation

Required Reading

Federated government is a world-wide phenomenon. In the United States today, we expect government at the municipal, county, state, and federal levels. Lower levels of "pseudo-government" include neighborhood councils and condo boards. These are representative democracies. Direct democracy, though now technologically feasible, is all but absent from our current political systems. These federated levels have an ad hoc feel about them, arising as they did from centuries of common law, and canonized a quarter of a millennium ago. Cellular democracy is a new way of implementing federation that is attuned to today's technology and utilizes the best in both representative and direct democracy.

"All politics is local," famously quipped former Speaker of the House, Tip O'Neil, but in a cellular democracy, all politics really are local. Consider the Wikipedia description of Dunbar's number:

> *Dunbar's number is a suggested cognitive limit to the number of people with whom one can maintain stable social relationships. These are relationships in which an individual knows who each person is and how each person relates to every other person. This number was first proposed in the 1990s by British anthropologist Robin Dunbar, who found a correlation between primate brain size and average social group size. By using the average human brain size and extrapolating from the results of primates, he proposed that humans can only comfortably maintain 150 stable relationships*[FTN9.11]

In a cellular democracy, the average total constituency of a "state" representative is slightly less than Dunbar's number. Even at the national level, the average total constituency of a member of congress is 169, and that includes children. Remarkably, representatives are able to maintain relationships with their entire electorate!

A small group of 69-141 immediate neighbors, both adults and children under 14, is called a level-1 cell. The cell might have a name like 'Floors 4 thru 7 of Park View North Apartments.' One of the cell members, who is especially civic minded, trustworthy, and good with numbers, is elected to represent this group of neighbors on a level-2 council. The 9-19 members of the level-2 council make up a level-2 cell, perhaps named 'Parkview North and South Tenants Council.' That is the usual extent of electoral politics in a cellular democracy. The level-1 council can recall or replace their representative at any time, though typically only for failing to act in the community's best interest, as the seniority of a representative has its benefits.

Direct democracy is different than electoral politics. In a direct democracy, citizens vote on issues, not politicians. When the citizens at level-1 elect a representative to level-2, their electoral duty is done. However, their representative is only empowered to protect their natural rights. Many issues, such as the raising of revenue, changes to the distributions, or conflicts in natural rights, fall outside the representative's power (unless a 5/6 plurality of the citizens in this dominion changed the nature of its government). While representatives craft proposals of this nature and submit pro and con written opinions for the voters, only the direct democracy can ratify these proposals, and usually by a 2/3 plurality.

The thrust of representative government is protecting natural rights, and implementation of the proposals passed by both the representative and direct democracy is a natural right. It thus falls on the representatives to create an executive branch to implement these proposals, and to closely monitor this branch to insure the natural rights of the citizens are protected.

How does the representative democracy form beyond the election of representatives to a level-2 council? Recall the level-2 council contains from 9-19 representatives. One of these representatives is elected to represent them on the level-3 council. The level-3 council contains 7-15 representatives. They will elect a member to the 7-15 member level-4 council, who will elect a member to the 7-15 member level-5 council, and so on. Within a nation, levels can go as high as 7. If the United States were a cellular democracy, the Congress would be at level 7. In an international cellular democracy, the UN would be at level-9. Levels are assigned functions by constitution, negotiation, and treaty. Although there is added prestige, responsibility, and salary in being a higher level representative, power in an AFFEERCE society is concentrated at the lower levels, primarily with individuals (level-0) through direct democracy.

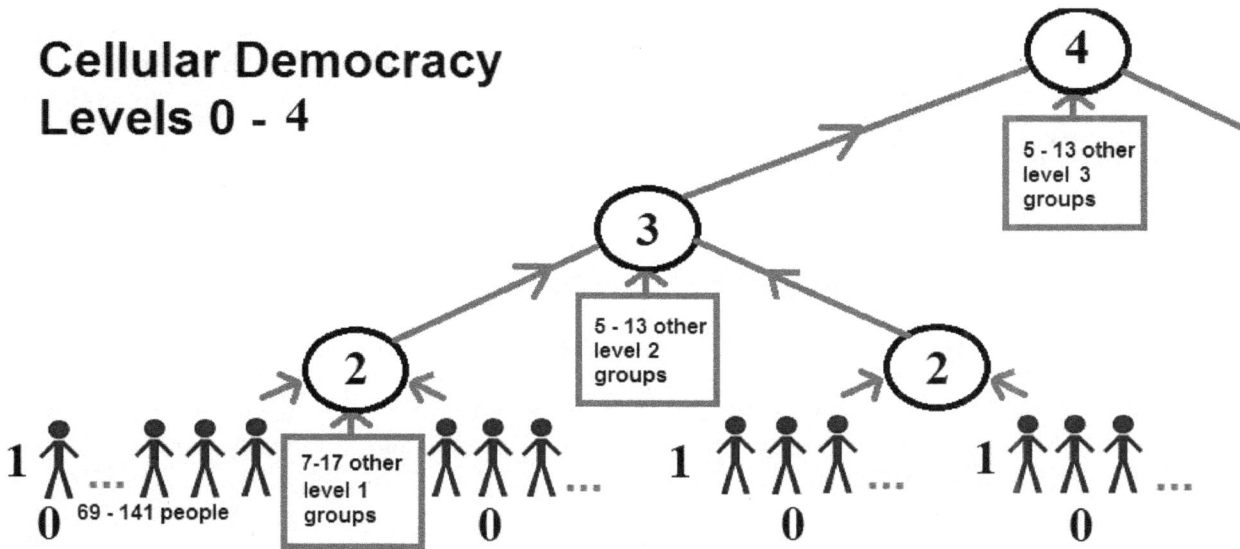

Cellular Democracy Levels 0 - 4

A series of free university courses at each cellular level would act as a voluntary standard prerequisite for election to a higher level. In a democracy, there is no obligation to use successful completion as a criterion for election.

We have the "Law of the Single Partial" to guide in the creation of top down cells. That is no cell can contain "part of" more than one physical or acknowledged building, neighborhood, or district. So a cell cannot contain part of one building and also part of another. It can contain an arbitrary number of complete entities, but only one partial.

Constitutional Rights

> **The basic constitutional rights are these: The right to life of children under the age of 14 cannot be surrendered. The right of an adult to leave a family or any jurisdiction cannot be surrendered. Other constitutional rights can be nullified in a dominion through Class III legislation.**

The right to life is the most basic of all rights, but very general. Within the plethora of rights that spring from the right to life, what laws can be chiseled into the constitution that do not turn the right to life into an obligation to live?

It is not such a tragedy if children under 14 years of age are obliged to live. In fact, society has come to demand it. They are too young to choose suicide, or consensual torture, or even consensual sex with an adult. They are denied the right to property and obliged to live.

Customs can and will change. The ambiguity of the right to life of children makes it subject to varied judicial interpretation which is precisely as it should be.

What about adults? What simple constitutional law forms the basis of the legal system for adults? The rights to life, entitlement and property are too general. An adult legal system cannot be built on the ambiguity afforded children. The following bedrock of the AFFEERCE legal system might come as a surprise.

The right of an adult to leave a family or any jurisdiction cannot be surrendered!

This might seem a bizarre basis of a legal system. How does this put into law the right to life?

Victims of domestic abuse understand it well. In many situations, there is a theoretical "right to leave" while the reality is that victims are often financial prisoners. Universal distribution breaks down the walls of that prison. But the principle goes far beyond domestic abuse. It is the basis of the legal system, yet would have no real meaning without universal distribution making it possible.

Preventing the right to leave is a component of all crimes of violence against persons. Equally important, it is the basis of contract law. A contract where I agree to be an indentured servant for 4 years is not enforceable. But one where I agree to pay $10,000 should I fail to serve is enforceable for $10,000.

Exit rights unambiguously include the right to leave with portable personal property. But what of improvements on land? The constitutionally enshrined treble option gives those who vote no on Class III legislation the right to 150% compensation on the objective depreciated value of their improvements before the law can go into effect. However, those who neglect to take this option and choose to leave later, due to prosecution under local law, can dispose of the property only in a manner allowed by local law.

The real beauty of this constitutional law is in the freedom it gives diverse cultures to create their own environments.

The constitution can be amended by a proposal from the highest level council and ratified by a super-majority of the entire population. This is not a super-plurality, but requires the actual approval of 2/3 the voting population, regardless of turnout.

Elements of a Bill

A bill consists of three elements: a prohibition, extent, and penitentiary punishment. The prohibition is standardized at the Library of Congress and the penitentiary sentence is used for ordering identical prohibitions by severity, even though the actual punishment might be a fine and further subject to judicial discretion.

Prohibition

The **prohibition** is a phrase in the natural vocabulary whose definition is stored at the Library of Congress or higher level equivalent. It could be "premeditated murder," "assault and battery," "grand larceny" and so forth. The phrase used in the prohibition is standardized across the entire AFFEERCE nation. The definition can only be changed by the highest level council (the Congress). To effect the change, there must be unanimous consent of all councils that use the prohibition in their statutes. If consensus cannot be reached, those adhering to the old definition, will add the current year to their prohibition. i.e. "premeditated murder 2016." The unadorned "premeditated murder" will carry the new definition going forward. Without consensus, the definition cannot be changed more than once a year.

Extent

The **extent** is optional. It is usually numeric, but can be other limits that define the size of the criminal domain. For example, blood alcohol level for DUI prohibitions, dollar amounts for grand larceny, or specific instances of a general prohibition. The extent refers to the size of the criminal domain. Extent often moves in the opposite direction as the numbers that define it. For instance a lower blood alcohol level increases the number of violators, as does a lower threshold for grand larceny.

Punishment

Standard punishment is always a penitentiary sentence, or a penitentiary sentence in lieu of fine. Most people will pay the fine in the latter case, but the government has no right to seize assets, so the accused can always choose the penitentiary over a fine. With victim approval, the judge can also replace all or part of a penitentiary sentence with a fine for actual and punitive damages. Any other punishment beyond this must be mandated through Class-III legislation. All penalties are constitutional, and can be passed through Class III legislation, although exit rights negate the effectiveness of a death penalty.

The **punishment** is a maximum sentence, or sentence range, and acts as a guide to the judiciary. Highest numbers are always used for comparison.

By defining laws in this manner, class, scope, and nature of a veto are also well defined. These will be examined below.

The AFFEERCE Principle of Judicial Review

Required Reading

When a governing council passes a bill, it undergoes judicial review before it can be implemented as law. This is different from today, where the court rules on a law's constitutionality, only after it is enforced.

The bill will be classified as class I, II, or III. It can also be declared unconstitutional if it violates the adult's right to leave or the child's right to life, the collection and distribution of rents, or the government framework as defined in the constitution. If the bill fails to have a single prohibition, optional extent, and punishment, it will also be declared unconstitutional.

The court can rule a Class II bill as a prohibition of an actual or potential incursion (see *below*).

The Three Classes of Law

Class I legislation protects natural rights. Class II legislation resolves conflicts in rights. Class III legislation restricts natural rights. A rigorous definition of these classes is included in the constitution.

Class I bills:

The first class, mentioned above, consists of those laws that protect the natural rights of its citizens. These laws are usually passed by governing councils at some level of the cellular democracy. Class I laws are not ratified by the direct democracy because the courts have ruled that they do not violate natural rights in any way. They only protect natural rights. Thus ratification would violate general principles of the division of labor by placing an unnecessary burden on the population.

Assume a Class I bill is passed by a governing council.

If it has a unique prohibition in the hierarchical chain, then it becomes law.
If there is an identical prohibition at a higher level:
    If the punishment is greater than or equal to the higher level punishment
    If the extent is absent, greater than or equal to the higher level extent
then the bill becomes law
    If the extent is less than the higher level extent
then the bill is reclassified Class III and requires ratification by a 5/6 super-duper majority w/treble option
    If the punishment is less than the higher level punishment
then the bill is reclassified Class III and requires ratification by a 5/6 super-duper majority w/treble option
If there is an identical prohibition at a lower level:
    Regardless of punishment level or extent of the lower level
the high level bill becomes law. However, the extent and punishment defined in the lower level bill is in effect for that dominion.

It is easy to understand the rationale for these rules when examining the prohibition against premeditated murder. If the sentencing guidelines from the higher dominion call for a 20 year sentence, and the lower dominion decides to increase this to a 30 year sentence, they are entirely within their rights. However, if they lower the sentence to 1 day in jail, or lower the extent to only include murders done with an icicle, they are more or less legalizing murder. If the court decides this violates the rights of ordinary citizens, the bill is reclassified as Class III.

Class II bills:

Legislation requiring ratification by a 2/3 super-plurality of the citizens, is called Class II legislation. These include all laws where natural and other rights are in conflict. Particularly, this applies to public spaces. The constitution might also define public accommodations, housing for rent or sale, and places of employment to be subject to Class II legislation. These pit a natural right (the right to property) against a more subjective right (the right not to be humiliated or disrespected as defined by the prevalent culture). Taxing the citizens through a consumption tax can resolve a conflict in natural rights if the distributions are insufficient for necessary services in a crisis, but not for infrastructure or special projects in general. Still, it is reasonable that consumption taxes, for well-defined projects, and with strict sunset clauses be Class II. Due to local land capture (See, *Chapter 3 – Distribution Theory*) these taxes will likely be increasingly popular as citizens' dividends grow over time. Class II legislation is used for injunctions against incursion. Incursion occurs when a lower level dominion corrupts the public space. Incursion is most often associated with the myriad types of pollution.

Class II laws resolve conflicts in natural rights , e.g. the right of teachers to carry a gun, and the right of parents to send their children to a gun-free school. By default, there is no law preventing teachers from carrying guns to school. The right of parents to send their children to a gun-free school is not a natural right, but it is a right parents might rationally demand.

A Class II bill that has a unique prohibition in the hierarchical chain, will be placed on the ballot to be approved by a 2/3 super-plurality of the dominion.

If there is an identical prohibition at a higher level
If the punishment is greater than or equal to the higher level punishment
    If the extent is absent, greater than or equal to the higher level extent
then the bill will be placed on the ballot to be approved by a 2/3 super-plurality of the dominion.
    If the extent is less than the higher level extent
then the bill is reclassified Class III and requires ratification by a 5/6 super-duper majority w/treble option.
    If the punishment is less than the higher level punishment
then the bill is reclassified Class III and requires ratification by a 5/6 super-duper majority w/treble option.

Once approved by the voters, a Class II bill becomes law after 30 days. Before or after it becomes law, a Class II bill can be vetoed by a lower level dominion with a 5/6 super-plurality. The treble option is not used, if the veto occurs before the bill becomes law. This is called an "up veto."

At any time, a Class II law can be repealed by a higher level dominion with a 5/6 plurality. The treble option is never used. This is called a "down veto."

If the court rules the Class II legislation to be a prohibition against a material incursion, vetoes are not permitted. Class II legislation regarding material incursion is only constitutional if passed by a direct ancestor of the offender. Otherwise, the incursion must be resolved in civil court.

Class II bills for raising revenue must meet the conditions specified in the constitution, or they will be reclassified as Class III with the treble option.

Class III Bills:

Class III legislation restricts natural rights and requires a 5/6 super-duper plurality of the citizens and the treble option for "no" votes. This legislation includes all forced obligations except those explicitly designated as Class II under the constitution. Citizens are constitutionally protected from Class III tyranny through exit rights and the right to life. Class III is the "heart of panarchy."

Class III laws allow violations of natural rights for no rational purpose. We associate such laws with prejudice, ritual, ignorance, and superstition. Many freedom lovers would prohibit such laws. Today, the Supreme Court of the United States declares most class III legislation unconstitutional. But ritual is an important part of many cultures. We can reasonably ask if women should have the freedom to live in a community where wearing a burka is required of all women.

But we do not live today in a society where "an adult's right to leave cannot be surrendered" is the basis of all law. Even if this is so for the wealthy, the poor are usually trapped in the financial prisons of their inheritance. AFFEERCE universal distribution turns the right to leave into reality. The emigrant not only has the wherewithal to make it on their own, but universal distribution fosters an environment of welcoming families and communities.

Class III bill will be placed on the ballot to be ratified by a 5/6 super-duper plurality of the dominion with the treble option. Appearance of the same prohibition in the hierarchical chain is irrelevant. For more on the treble option, see below.

Once the Class III bill has been ratified by Dominion R, and the treble option satisfied it will become law in 30 days. Before or after it becomes law, a Class III bill can be vetoed by a lower level dominion, Dominion V with a 2/3 super-plurality. This is called an "up veto." If vetoed, the lower level dominion, Dominion V, inherits the law in effect for the parent of Dominion R.

Before and only before the Class III bill becomes law, a Class III bill can be vetoed by a higher level Dominion H, with a 2/3 super-plurality. This is called a "down veto." The Class III bill will not become law.

However, Dominion H cannot exceed level-4. That means Class III bills cannot be down-vetoed at level-5 and above. Realistically, this means a rogue state set up in the local forested areas is likely to be down-vetoed, while an orphaned cell in the middle of the wilderness has no obstacles in forming into a rogue state. (See also, *Judiciary and Rogue States, Chapter 11 – Rogue States and Distributions*)

Panarchy

Class-III legislation turns AFFEERCE into what is known as a panarchy. That means people of a dominion can have any form of government they choose. The right to leave, the right to life of children, the collection and distribution of ground rents, the independent judiciary, and balance of the RCs are the only barriers to complete independence.

Although originally envisioned by Belgian political economist Paul de Puydt to be independent of where a person resides[FTN9.12], panarchy in an AFFEERCE polity must be associated with a cell of arbitrary level of federation. Because cells are associated with dominions, so too must any local/regional form of government.

De Puydt felt that governmental competition would allow as many regularly competing governments as have ever been conceived and will ever be invented to exist simultaneously. [FTN9.12]

Diverse government will mostly form as rogue states in the hinterlands. Some with only a few Class III laws will function as a laboratory for experimental ideas in political economy.

Rogue States

Rather than pass a laundry list of Class III bills, each with the treble option, a dominion, Dominion R, can choose to "go rogue." A bill to "go rogue" is Class III with the treble option. However, once rogue, Dominion R no longer functions as an AFFEERCE cellular democracy. It is guided by its own internal constitution or other powers. The treble option and class nature of legislation are gone, unless those features are maintained by the rouge constitution.

The right to leave a rogue state is protected by the AFFEERCE constitution. However, the right to property is not. What property an emigrant from a rogue state can take with them is at the pleasure of the rogue state, once the treble option no longer applies.

The rogue state has total control of internal distributions. All tranches, including personal distributions for each member of the rogue state can be disbursed at the highest level, although the rogue state can also allow its members to receive personal distributions directly.

Trebling within the rogue state can be disallowed. Property and land transfers are subject to internal rules. Most importantly, the rogue state is not protected against capture by dominion treble. If ground rents are allowed to fall too low because of a prohibition on internal trebling, rogue state land will be easily captured by outside forces.

Distributions go to a Treasury account, as rogue states likely maintain an alternative currency. A highly successful rogue state will tend to import in its alternative currency, export in VIP$, and use its expanding Treasury account for "land and babies."

A rogue state can appoint or elect one or more representatives (depending on district size) to a parent level council, if it is not an orphaned dominion. Rogue state members can participate in the direct democracy for constitutional amendment and laws for recognized jurisdictions, provided the secret ballot is respected. The rogue state can prohibit members from such participation. In no case can the rogue state confiscate or alter votes in the direct democracy.

Treble Option

Required Reading

Because class III legislation violates natural rights, the right to leave is protected in extraordinary ways. There are three ways to vote on class III legislation: yes, no, and no with the treble option. In the third case, the voter is vetoing the legislation unless supporters treble the voter's land within the dominion. The voter is demanding 150% compensation for improvements to their land, so they can presumably get out of town before the repressive legislation goes into effect.

Those voting no with the treble option remain anonymous. The voting application interfaces with the online land system and gets both ODV and ground rents for the property. 150% of the ODV and 3 times ground rent are summed together and combined with the ODV and ground rent of other voters who voted no with the treble options. Should the class III legislation be ratified supporters will have 30 days to raise the funds to buy out those who demand exit rights with compensation. If supporters fail to raise the funds, the measure will be considered defeated and the identity of those who voted no with the treble option will never be known.

Direct Democracy

Required Reading

Other than class I bills, passed by a governing council, all other questions are placed before the voters. This should not be overwhelming. Special taxes will be local. Such proposals at cellular levels above 4 are unlikely. Class III bills will be very rare outside of specialized communities and class II bills will be sufficiently controversial as to limit their frequency.

It would be best to name a day of the week, such as Sunday, voting day. Every Sunday, issues requiring a vote, are available online for voting during the entire 24 hour period. Because a VIP identity is needed to vote, there is no possibility of fraud. Whether a person voted or not is public information, but how they voted is secret.

The Right to Leave

The right to leave allows freedom pending trial and allows the accused to face trial under the laws of different dominion in exchange for banishment from those dominions with the same prohibition and a harsher punishment. It allows the right to leave rogue states and escape prosecution altogether. It allows people the opportunity to experience different cultural communities, without fear. It prohibits contractual remedies of indenture.

There are no ideologically pure positions. There are times, such as during an arrest, or when defending your comrades in a military battle that the right to leave is indeed surrendered. Nevertheless, AFFEERCE is designed to minimize those situations.

In the event of an arrest, after booking, the non-dangerous suspect is charged and released pending trial. There is no way to actually flee, unnoticed, because of the VIP.

However, there are several forms of being on the lam enshrined in the constitution. The first is a refusal to stand trial. Suppose you live in a dominion where the extent of blood alcohol for a DUI is .01, and you were arrested with a blood alcohol level of .02. You declare your intention to refuse trial, and your VIP is disabled in all dominions where the extent of blood alcohol for a DUI is .02 or less. You will not be able to live in these dominions, nor will you be able to do business in these dominions outside of an alternative currency, until such time as you return to stand trial for the DUI, if ever.

Another option is to stand trial, but stand trial under the law of another dominion, where the punishment is less. The venue is up to the accused and can be the arresting dominion, or the dominion whose law will be applied. If found not guilty, complete freedom is restored. However, if found guilty, the lesser punishment is used as a guideline for judicial sentencing. The VIP is also disabled in the arresting dominion, and any other dominion where the same law has guidelines for punishment that are more severe. The accused will not be able to live in these dominions or do business in these dominions, until such time as they appear before a judge in the arresting dominion and complete the remainder of the sentence handed down. However, "time served" is possible if the accused has led a productive life in the interim.

If the dominion of the crime is a rogue state, and the infraction is Class I, the accused can choose to be tried in any non-rogue dominion, regardless of severity of punishment. The VIP will only be disabled in the rogue dominion.

Refusal to stand trial for Class II and Class III infractions can at most result in disabling the VIP in the accusing dominion. The accused is free to live and work in any other dominion, and the charges will bear no weight in other dominions. If the accused wishes to return to life in the accusing dominion, they must return to face justice.

For a class I infraction that is universal to all dominions within AFFEERCE, the right to leave is contingent on an outside country willing to accept the accused. If a country so agrees, the AFFEERCE nation will pay the airfare and extract the maximum possible fine for the infraction from the VIP, leaving the accused with a minimum of $1000 to be converted into the currency of their choice. Citizenship of the accused will be cancelled and their VIP disabled throughout the AFFEERCE nation. The procedure for restoration of citizenship will involve repayment of all costs associated with the emigration, and facing justice. All distributions for the intervening months will be permanently lost. Once the entire world shares in this constitution, this option will be gone.

It might seem odd that rather than extradite, offenders are almost encouraged to flee the jurisdiction. That is because unlike the deplorable conditions of prisons today, offenders receive their full distribution of nutritious meals, warm and safe shelter, quality medical care and unlimited free education (to the extent possible) in AFFEERCE penitentiaries. The difference is they are no longer at liberty. The penitentiary is a place to get one's soul in order, to be penitent, to learn a new career, and plan a new life. There are social workers, psychologists, and trainers to help. Incarceration begins a new chance at life, and if one chooses to flee the jurisdiction with seared conscience, so be it.

As for military service, outside of the heat of a raging battle, where individual freedom is sacrificed, there can be no contract that holds one in a state of involuntary servitude. Enlistees are free to resign at any time, although there can be a stipulation in the signup documents for monetary penalties that might be kept in escrow.

The right to leave allows one to take risks in their personal life they would not ordinarily take. Immersing oneself in the rogue state of another culture where the laws and customs are difficult to understand, is much easier when you can just leave. If you are curious about joining an S&M community or want to live in a village under sharia law, the right to leave is a critical ally if things get difficult. If you sell yourself as a slave or prostitute, the right to leave is there, should you have a change of heart. You can be sued for monetary damages, but can never be forced into involuntary servitude.

The right to leave enhances individual freedom and the freedom of communities to pass class III legislation. But can it be carried too far? What about consensual dueling, or mortal combat between consensual soldiers from consensual communities? If the right to sacrifice one's natural rights is a natural right, then even these should be tolerated. The down veto will likely prevent such behavior in all but the remotest of wilderness. In reality, the Hatfield's and McCoy's are not likely to rise again, except in peaceful trebler wars or on the athletic field.

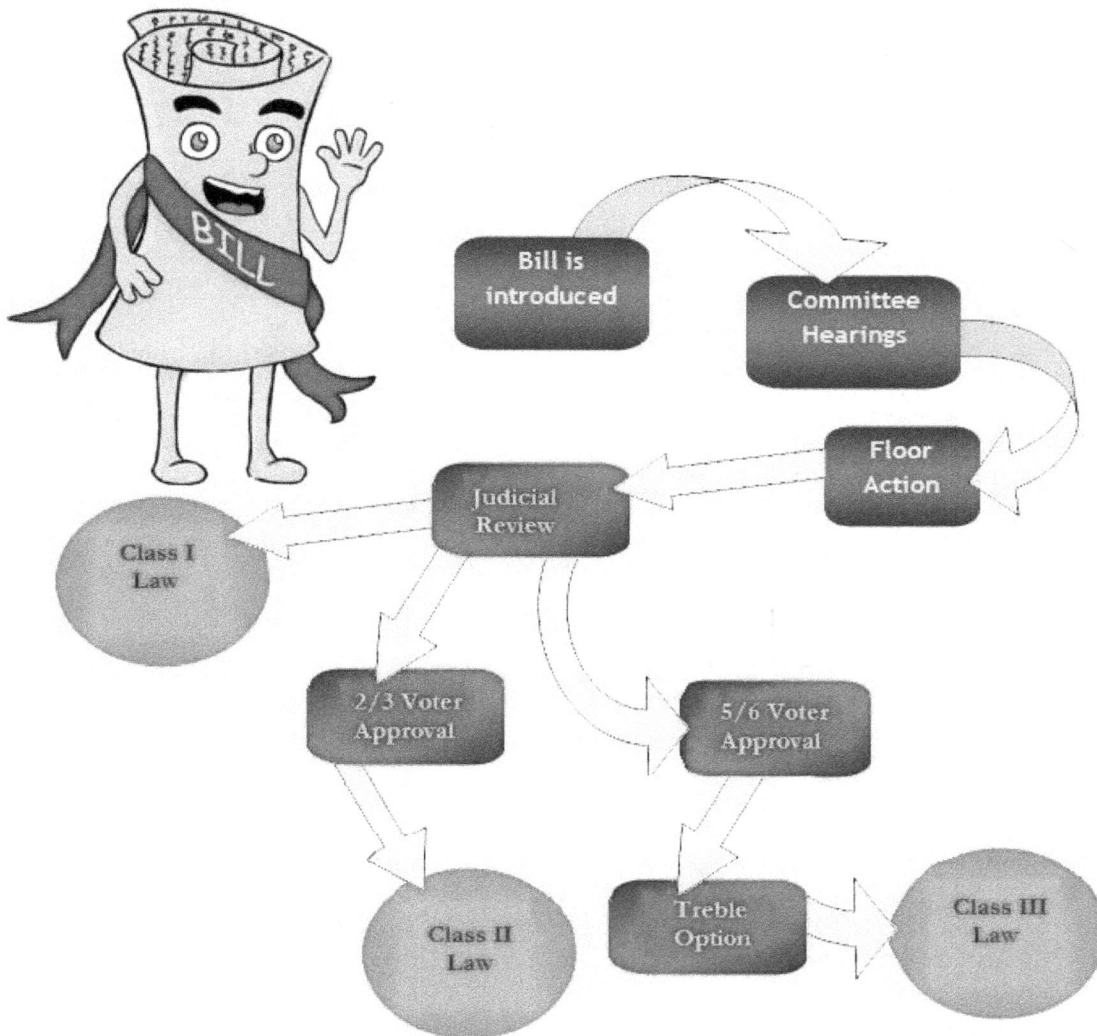

The Three Ways an AFFEERCE Bill Can Become Law

The Cellular Democracy

Definitions

Browse Entries

Cellular democracy has its own language. Some is borrowed from graph theory in mathematics, some from cellular biology, and some from political economy. To understand the concepts, one must understand the language.

Definitions	
Level N	Refers to any arbitrary level of the cellular democracy. When N = 0, it refers to an individual.
Level N-1	Refers to the level directly below level N
Level N+1	Refers to the level directly above level N
Parent	The cell at level N+1 that has an elected representative from the cell at level N is the parent of the cell at Level N.
Sibling	A cell at level N that shares the same parent as another cell at level N is a sibling of that cell.
Child	A cell at level N that elects a representative to a cell at Level N+1 is a child of the cell at N+1.
District	A cell at Level N or a voluntary association of sibling cells at level N
Governing District	A district that performs the functions of government at level N, usually named.
Geographic District	A district at level N based on geographic form over function
Special Governing Districts	A governing district with a particular responsibility, such as school district, sanitation district, transportation district, park district, police district, etc.
Cellular population	The cell population at Level N is the sum of child cell populations at level N-1 or the number of individuals at Level 1. This is a recursive definition. If you think of a cell at level N as being the upside down root of a tree, the cell population of N is the total number of people in all of the branches whose ancestor is the cell at level N.
District population	The combined cell populations of the one or more cells that constitute the district.
Disbursement District	A governing district that receives a monthly disbursement of a tranche of a particular distribution for each person in the district population.
Enterprise District	A district that manages an enterprise for the benefit of the district population. Unlike free enterprise, district enterprise operates under a set of constraints. Most district enterprises are natural monopolies such as utility supply and delivery, street parking, waste and recycling, but the enterprises can engage in other ventures with approval of a super-plurality of the district population.
District Council	If a single cell constitutes the district, the cellular council and district council are one and the same. Otherwise, each cell appoints the same number of representatives to a district council.
District Executive	District councils can hire an executive to manage the business of the district for a term in office. The executive can optionally be reappointed at the end of the term. The executive can be terminated by a 2/3 vote of the district council, or elimination of the district through distribution.
Cellular Dominion	The cellular dominion at level N is the combined adjoining dominions of child cells at level N-1 or the adjoining land of individuals at level 1, plus unclaimed land completely surrounded by children at level N-1 (See Encirclement Capture below). This is a recursive definition.
District Dominion	The combined cellular dominions of the one or more cells that constitute the district or unclaimed land completely surrounded by district cells.

Orphaned Cell	If a cell or district at level N is surrounded by land whose minimum dominion is level N+2 or greater, the cell is orphaned. It has no representation above level N. If its immediate parent is at level N + m, then it collects all distributions for levels N + 1 through level N + m - 1.
Encirclement Capture	Contiguous regions consisting of properties with no residents, unclaimed land, or orphaned cells will be captured into the dominion of any cell or district that completely encircles the land. If the encircling region or district is at level N, any orphaned cells at level N or higher, are adopted into the cellular democracy. Otherwise, orphaned cells remain orphaned in the new dominion. If no orphaned cells are adopted, the process is 100% reversible with a breakout.
Breakout	A contiguous region consisting of properties with no residents, unclaimed land, or orphaned cells is in the dominion of the cell or district that completely encircles it. If the dominion of one or more encircling cells is altered, the dominion of the region is raised to the dominion of the higher level district or cell that completely encircles it. It is impossible to orphan a cell with a breakout operation alone.
Daughter Cell	A cell that results from the splitting of a cell.
Distribution	[Distribution of a cell is unrelated to universal distribution]The breaking apart of an undersized cell at Level-N. The parts are distributed to neighboring sibling cells such that the resulting cells have a valid cellular dominion. When a cell at level-N is at its lower limit, a 2/3 plurality of that cell's council can agree to a distribution. When a cell falls below its lower limit, distribution is engineered by the level-N+1 parent council. Distribution can cause a breakout and lead to orphaned cells.
Mitosis	The splitting of an oversized cell at level-N into two daughter cells at level-N. When a cell reaches its upper population limit, mitosis is optional. When a cell exceeds its upper population limit, mitosis is mandatory. Each of the daughter cells must have a valid cellular dominion (all land must be contiguous). Districts are always maintained, even if this results in a distribution of the smaller daughter cell. Optional mitosis is approved by a 2/3 plurality of the level-N council. Mandatory mitosis will be engineered by the level N+1 parent council, if the level-N council fails to act in a timely manner. Mitosis can cause a breakout.
Switching Allegiance	A cell, district or individual resident land rights owner at level-N bordering another cell at level-N that is not its sibling, can switch allegiance to the parent of that bordering cell at level N+1. The cellular or district dominion, or the individual landholding becomes part of the dominion of that parent cell, as does any unclaimed land that is now fully surrounded. The allegiant cell becomes a member of any districts that the N+1 parent is a member of. Mitosis, encirclement capture, breakout, and/or distribution can result. A reasonable fee to cover costs can be charged only by the common ancestor.
Dominion Trebling or Conquering	If borderlands are trebled, the trebler can conquer that land for their own dominion, as if a resident land rights owner on that land had switched allegiance to the trebler's dominion. The trebler need not move to the land and need only be a resident of the dominion. A dominion treble at level 2 or above can orphan cells.
Rogue State	A cell or district can vote itself a rogue state with class-III legislation. Nobody can switch allegiance to a rogue state if they do not meet the criterion. Enemies of the rogue state can treble away at its borders. A rogue state surrounded by land with no residents, or unclaimed, will be orphaned.
Titled Position	A district at level-N can create a set of service positions, in order of prestige. Service to the district includes hosting meetings and receptions for the local council, as well as for outside dignitaries. It includes sponsoring of boondoggles including room, board, travel, entertainment, and receptions. It includes ribbon-cutting, parades, groundbreakings, and boosterism. It might include providing rent-free office space in a palace.

Cellular Aristocracy	The aristocracy will literally save the taxpayers over $100 billion without any sacrifice of freedom or democracy. The first aristocrat in a dominion is the dominion resident paying the highest total ground rent for dominion land. The second aristocrat is the dominion resident paying the second highest total rent for dominion land, and so on. Registered aristocratic families, beginning with the family of the first aristocrat can voluntarily select from titled positions. One member of the family can use the associated title at level N, while other members of the family must use the associated title at level N-1. Titles are either gender neutral or masculine. Title holders can use the feminine form at their preference.

National Cell Populations

Required Reading

Table 9.1	Low	High	Avg.	Natural Population Low	Natural Population High	Population - Target	Executive Title	Aristocratic Title
Level - 0	1	1	1	1	1	1	Parent	
Level - 1	69	141	100	69	141	100	Manager	Sir
Level - 2	9	19	14	621	2,679	1,400	Manager	Lord
Level - 3	7	15	11	6,831	29,469	15,400	Manager	Baron
Level - 4	7	15	11	75,141	324,159	169,400	Manager	Count
Level - 5	7	15	11	826,551	3,565,749	1,863,400	Chairman	Duke
Level - 6	7	15	11	9,092,061	39,223,229	20,497,400	Governor	Prince
Level - 7	7	15	11	100,012,671	431,455,519	225,471,400	President	King

In the language of cellular democracy, an individual is a level-0 cell. An association of one or more cells at a given level N is a district at level N. The vast majority of families are districts at level-0. So too, are most floors of apartment buildings. Multiple family districts are properly contained within an apartment floor district. Proper containment is the requirement that a child district has only a single parent. In real life that is not always true. If a family lived in the only bi-level apartment in a building, and districts were organized by floors, it would be ambiguous which floor the family was in. When people self-organize into districts, ambiguities are unlikely. If assigned districts based on geographical and topological features, ambiguities will be more common. Retrofitting existing districts into a cellular democracy, will cause problems, too.

A level-1 cell contains from 69 to 141 level-0 cells. Since a level-0 cell is an individual, the level-1 cell contains from 69 to 141 individuals. The level-1 cell might consist of three mutually exclusive level-0 districts, perhaps three floors of a condominium, containing 37, 34, and 35 residents respectively, a total of 106 members in the level-1 cell. That is close to the desired average of 100. The level-1 district for a 12 story building might consist of 4 such mutually exclusive level-1 cells. The members of a level-1 cell are called the level-1 council. Everyone over the age of 14 in this building is a member of one of the 4 level-1 councils. The members of each level-1 council elect one or more members to the building district council, in this case a condo board. The condo board hires an executive, the building manager, to oversee the building. They also elect a single member to represent the building at level-2.

As introduced earlier in the chapter, the level-2 council consists of the 9 to 19 elected level-1 representatives, who represent a population of 621 to 2,679. They might come from four districts representing three condominiums and an apartment building, a total population close to the expected target of 1,400 individuals. The level-2 council elects a representative to the level-3 council, and organizes into level-2 district councils as well. Level 3 consists of 7 to 15 level-2 cells, and the council consists of representatives from each of those cells, representing a population from 6,831 to 29,469.

Table 9.1 shows population ranges and targeted populations for cells at all levels.

The Government Distribution
Required Reading

Every citizen is entitled to a government that protects their natural rights, by administering distributions for police and fire protection, transportation and sanitation, as well as passing class I laws that protect natural rights.

To that end, every person carries with them a $20/month government distribution divided into tranches for each level of the cellular democracy.

There is nothing fundamental to the distribution scheme shown, other than to make a good fit with the existing U.S. federated republic.

Table 9.2 Government Distribution	Tranche	Average Population	Monthly Revenue @$20/population
Level – 1	0%	100	0
Level – 2	10%	1,400	$2,800
Level – 3	50%	15,400	$154,000
Level – 4	10%	169,400	$338,800
Level – 5	10%	1,863,400	$3,726,800
Level – 6	10%	20,497,400	$40,994,800
Level – 7	10%	225,471,400	$450,942,800

The money at level-2 is mostly a token appreciation for community service, although along with the distributions, it could easily support a building manager. At level-3, representatives are expected to work full-time. Each level-3 cell assumedly receives monthly government distribution income of $154,000. Suppose three level-3 sibling cells form a governing district called Springfield. Springfield has a population of about 45,000. The district council receives about $450,000/month for salaries and supplies from the government distribution.

Figure 9.3

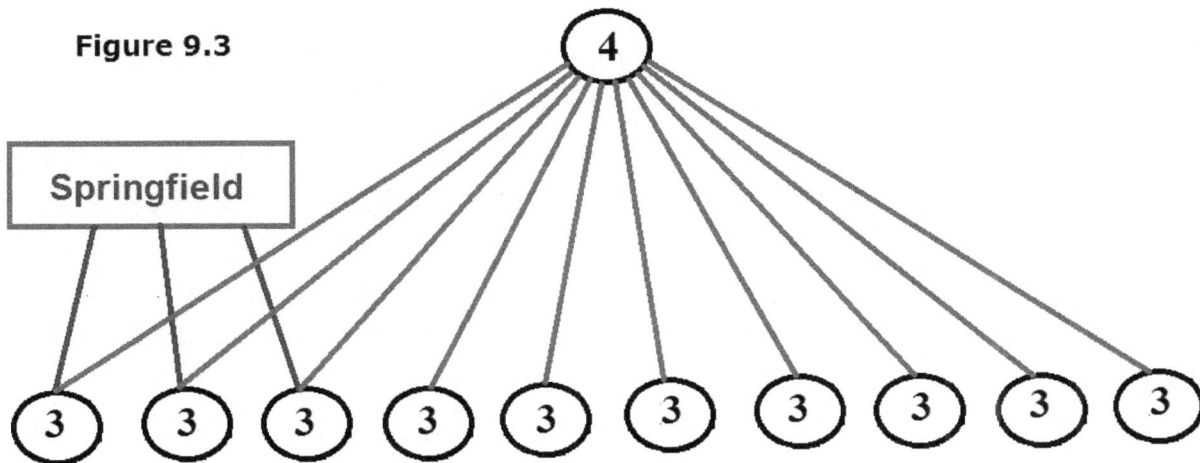

District council members are expected to hire a city manager, who in turn hires a city clerk, city treasurer, and city attorney with the consent of the council. Each of these departments needs staff, as well. Since all Springfield employees, and their families, have universal distribution, nominal salaries can be lower, even though real wages are greater. There are about 30 level 3 cellular council members in the Springfield district. Each cell elects one member to the level 4 council, and perhaps three members to the Springfield district council.

Junior members of the level 3 cells in the Springfield district might be expected to fill certain lower level positions in city hall to get hands on city experience. As they gain in seniority, they are moved through a wide variety of city hall jobs. At cellular council meetings, they learn more about Springfield issues. When a slot opens up on the district council, the most qualified is elected to the position.

Council members should not take a high salary from the government distribution. It should be allocated primarily to executive functions. Council members, who are not otherwise employed, should fill executive roles for extra income. In an AFFEERCE polity, the line between the executive and legislative branches of government is far more blurred than under most governments today. The judiciary, however, is far more independent.

In a way, the government distribution protects our right to efficient government. Once established at $20/month, it cannot be changed except by a 5/6 majority of the entire nation. The government is not funded from the ground rents, per se. It is funded from the distribution package. All of the proceeds of ground rent go to this package, where it is divided up between the citizens. Every person has a distribution for government services of $20/month. The $20 is used wherever a citizen resides. If a person moves to the middle of the wilderness and becomes an orphaned level-0 cell, a few of the lower level tranches of that $20 will go right back to the person. They will be their own local government!

Draws on the Government Distribution

> **Before government employees can take a salary the distribution pays for penitentiary security, judgments against the dominion, uncovered building expenses, or scheduled payments on pre-capitulation debt.**

There are additional draws on the government distribution before it can be used for salaries and supplies, some of which also help to protect our natural rights.

The first draw on this distribution is the security cost for penitentiaries. This does not include food, housing, medical, education, counseling and other rehabilitative measures for prisoners. Those are distributions that everyone has. It does include guards and their equipment, bars, electronic locking, and other expenses explicitly designed to deny liberty. For efficiency, a draw on the this distribution might go into effect when confinement exceeds 24 hours. This use of the government distribution is restricted to the common dominion in which both the crime and incarceration occur.

The second draw pays the expense of any judgment against the district resulting from injury, death or improper confinement caused by fraudulent or incomplete VOS (See Regulation, below), police brutality or misconduct, or malicious prosecution. As always, this use of the government distribution is confined to the governing district being sued. Liability is limited to 2 weeks' pay of those found responsible, to the extent of their responsibility. The proceeds of universal distribution are exempt from all judgements. Public goods and services cannot be impacted by a judgment.

The third draw is used to fund government buildings, ground rent, furniture, technology and the utilities to run them. However, this draw comes after exhaustion of a distribution for capital expenditures equal to the government distribution. And that distribution comes after those expenses covered by the cellular aristocracy, discussed below. Thus, the third draw against the government distribution is unlikely to be used.

The fourth draw on the government distribution is for any scheduled payments on local, regional, or state debt. As in all uses of the distribution, this draw only applies to the governing district created from the older levels of federation in which the debt occurred. For example, Iowa citizens would never pay for Illinois debt and Peoria citizens would never pay for Chicago debt. In the cellular democracy, citizen investor investments in cellular enterprise (see below) are paid from sales. Ordinary debt will either be constitutionally prohibited for governing districts and cellular enterprise, or permitted only through Class III legislation.

The fifth and final draw on the government distribution is used for salaries and supplies. No government distribution in one dominion shall go to government employees in another.

Because penitentiary security draws on the government distribution, and because fines go only to police, prosecutors and victims, there is no incentive, and every disincentive, to pass or encourage passage, of superfluous, petty, or tyrannical laws.

Police brutality must never be allowed to happen in a free society. Police and prosecutors are under constant scrutiny from the judiciary (see below) through the judicial distribution. All internal affairs investigations are conducted by the judiciary, usually at the recommendation of the public defender's office, also part of the judiciary.

Liability must be limited, however. One expensive judgment in a medium-sized city could wipe out the salaries of governing council members, civil servants, a majority of the salary of police officers and prosecutors, for a long time. For purposes of public safety, a two week limit of liability would likely be both necessary and sufficient. Having elected officials, civil servants, and fellow officers, forced to live off the distributions for two weeks because of police brutality or malicious prosecution, is a very good incentive to keep police officers and prosecutors from going haywire. The draw on salaries and fines up the chain of command is determined judicially. Because of the medical distribution, medical expenses are irrelevant to the settlement. If the extent of brutality calls for additional compensation, the victim should make an appeal to the populace for the discretionary tax. Thanks to universal distribution, lawsuits against governing districts do not affect city services. Aberrant behavior on the part of law enforcement is also far less likely in a society where poverty has been eliminated and families are strong.

Here is a summary of what the government distribution does:

1. Discourages superfluous and tyrannical laws.
2. Discourages police brutality and misconduct.
3. Discourages malicious prosecution.
4. Pays off local government debt.
5. Discourages governing councils from violating standards they have promised their citizens.
6. Encourages the sale of unused buildings and moving to smaller more energy efficient sites.
7. Discourages bureaucracy and waste.
8. Supports a government.

On the website, there is a full discussion of how the federal government in Washington D.C. (cellular level-7) can be effectively run with its 10% tranche of the government distribution and 10% tranche of the government capital expenditure distribution.

Enterprise Districts and Distribution

...experience goes to show that better results can be secured, with less risk of governmental corruption, by state management than by state regulation. – Henry George [FTN11.33]

Dominion owned enterprise is more efficient than dominion regulated enterprise. They can return profits to the dominion, reducing taxes for special projects. Natural monopolies are good candidates.

Regulated monopoly is a can of worms. It is far better for these natural monopolies to be run by the state for the benefit of the people. Unlike state-run industries in communist countries, the cellular democracy keeps these companies efficient and vital.

Simply moving to a district gives a citizen a share of the profits of a district enterprise. This will cause an inflow of people and a rise in rents until equilibrium is reached. Ground rent will rise as treblers pick off the weakest properties. Because there is no local distribution of rents, there will be no feedback loops causing violent shifts from equilibrium.

A district enterprise is a net positive if the citizens dividend paid from enterprise profits is greater than or equal to the increase in ground rents, and the increase in density does not exceed the desired rate of growth. If both are true, the government services from enterprise profits come for free.

In addition to density, a profitable cellular enterprise will attract territory.

The primary force of equilibrium is the reduction in the citizens dividend due to increased population. However, if the cellular enterprise is a natural monopoly, the increase in population will also increase profits.

There are several ways an enterprise district is naturally associated with a governing district.

1. Many enterprises will be firmly integrated with executive departments of a governing district. For instance a utility delivery business is likely to be part of a roads and infrastructure department.
2. Unlike free enterprise, cellular enterprise employees can receive salaries from other sources, such as the government distribution, other distribution disbursements and profits from other enterprises.
3. The online voting infrastructure of a governing district is in place, so citizens can approve revenue generating licenses, permits, assessments, excise taxes, and fees. The same voting infrastructure allows citizen approval of class-II regulations for cellular enterprises dealing with alcohol, narcotics, psychedelics, tobacco, gambling, prostitution, and firearms.

Here are some candidates for cellular enterprises.

1. Utility delivery and supply
2. Recycling, refuse, and materials recovery
3. Sports teams, stadiums, theme parks
4. Prostitution, gambling, narcotics (class-II restriction on competition is possible)
5. Parking garages and metered street parking
6. Railroads and public transit
7. Jitney dispatch
8. Hospitals and schools in remote territory
9. Penitentiaries and rehabilitation
10. Monopoly restaurants, gas stations, motels and advertising on highways within the dominion.

11. Mining and refining of local monopoly resources (Treble-safe ground rent can be as high as 56% profits on unimproved mineral deposits with a 10% rent rate of fall)
12. Satellite launches, space tourism, and industry sponsored experiments
13. Scientific laboratories that both partner with private industry and are innovation generators (See, *Chapter 11 – Intellectual Property Distribution*)

Distribution Disbursement

> **A particular distribution, such as the law enforcement distribution, is divided into a set of one or more tranches directed at various levels of federation. Like the government distribution, these tranches add up to 100% of the distribution.**

Table 9.4 Law Enforcement Distribution @$30/person/month			
Traditional Role	Tranche	Directed Cellular Level	Probable Monthly Disbursement/cell
Building/Community	9.5%	1	$284
Local Police	80%	3	$369,600
County Sheriff	7%	4	$355,740
State Police	2%	5	$1,863,399
FBI	1.5%	7	$101,462,130

Suppose a co-op with 630 residents has a level-1 governing district consisting of 6 level-1 cells, each with 105 residents. Their monthly law enforcement distribution would be 6.3 * $284 = $1,789.20. This would pay for a single shift of door security, especially if two of the district council members assume the role. With universal distribution, salaries can be this low, especially in service to your neighbors. Interestingly, there does not need to be a condo, co-op or gated community, to take advantage of the building/community law enforcement tranche. An apartment building of the same size might have the same sized governing district (although it would be called a tenants council, rather than a condo board). They could use the tranche to hire building security independent of the landlord or in partnership with the landlord. If the building/community law enforcement tranche is unused at level 1, it is directed to level 2 for community policing. If there is community policing, it is likely further subsidized from the level-3 local police tranche. If no community policing is in effect, the tranche is directed to level-3 where it is merged with the local police tranche.

An average cell at level 3 has a population of 15,400, a reasonable size for a police district. The governing district of Springfield in Figure 9.3 has three such districts, each receiving an approximate monthly disbursement of $369,600. The exact amount is a function of the cell population.

There is no requirement that a police district be equal to a level 3 cell. Springfield could have chosen to have a single police district identical to the governing district, or combined the two smallest cells into a police district with the larger cell standing alone. While the local police tranche is directed at level 3, it can, by consent of the level 3 council, be disbursed at levels 2 or 4, with their consent. The former works for rural areas and the latter for highly dense urban areas. In the case of an extremely isolated population, the local police tranche might be disbursed at level 1, or if an individual lives alone in the wilderness, at level 0. The tranche can also be apportioned. For instance, a portion of the level-3 disbursement can be apportioned to level-2 cells for community policing programs, or a portion of level-7 (FBI) can be apportioned to level-4 or level-5 for regional field offices.

Nothing can prevent a 2/3 plurality of any dominion from using the allocated tranche for an altogether different purpose. Of course, when a person moves out of the dominion, their public and private allocations move with them.

Whatever the cellular composition or cellular level of districts, the cellular democracy is dynamic and that composition will change with mitosis and distribution, those a function of population migration, switched allegiances, and dominion trebling.

The district or cellular council can hire and fire the chief executives of distribution funded departments and approve the budgets of how they will spend the distribution funds. Shortfalls are not allowed, and must come out of salaries if they inadvertently occur. Budgets are public and disbursements beyond petty cash are VIP enforced, making shortfall unlikely. An increase in land value that forces the distribution funded department to raise its ground rent will almost always be caused by increased population density, and thus higher distribution revenue. Furthermore, councils can modify budgets at any time and provide the distribution funded departments with government distribution, or enterprise revenue, provided that revenue is not used to make up a budget shortfall.

With the approval of the council, a distribution funded department can create a cellular enterprise related to its function. All fees, fines, licenses, permits, and excise taxes that are revenue for the enterprise must be approved by a 2/3 plurality of the cell or district population.

The Cellular Aristocracy

Introduction
Required Reading

The cellular aristocracy is not an invention of diverse governments in a panarchy, although it can be integrated with any of those governments. Instead, it is a constitutionally defined feature of the cellular democracy. For those dominions embarrassed by such a feature, it can be dispensed with by a vote of the cellular council.

Although promoting an aristocracy is much ridiculed, it is hard to fault an idea that will literally save the taxpayers as much as $100 billion. As the late Senator Everett Dirksen would say, "That's real money." What exactly does aristocratic title mean in a free and democratic society?

1. Title is only a function of paying the highest total ground rent within the dominion. For example, the grand baron of a given district will lose their title, if a resident of the district, paying a higher rent, wishes to assume the title.
2. Title is completely voluntary. If you do not wish a title, it passes to the next highest renter. If at a later time you change your mind, and you are still paying a higher ground rent than the current holder of the title, you can usurp the title at will.
3. Title carries with it many responsibilities of a pecuniary nature. Most members of the aristocracy enjoy these responsibilities. They include hosting parties for legislators, sponsoring fact-finding trips out of state or out of country, paying for airfare, and hotels for your delegation, hosting evening entertainment, choosing restaurants, serving as a social ambassador, arranging schedules, leading sightseeing expeditions, and significantly, maintain government office buildings as palaces.
4. Registered alternative family members can assume a title one level down from the main titleholder, and can assume aristocratic duties ahead of the next aristocratic family.
5. At the federal level, the highest aristocracy will serve as U.S. ambassadors, maintaining the embassies and hiring staff. The Royal Family will host parties and state dinners at the White House for the President of the United States.

6. Title can be removed by a 2/3 vote of the associated cell or district, if the aristocrat is deemed an embarrassment to the district, city, state, or nation.

The aristocracy saves the taxpayer a fortune in financing boondoggles, entertaining visiting dignitaries, and maintaining embassies. Perhaps the biggest savings comes from maintaining government office buildings as palaces. Not only will this provide government with free office space, but the palaces, as a point of pride for the aristocrats, will be stunning architecturally and maintained beautifully. The ground rent on the palace itself is kept low through a jurisdictional covenant. The aristocrat will treble the palace upon assumption of the title. If they remain titled for 12 years, ground rents will return to the minimum.

In a cellular democracy, higher offices will tend to be filled by the best qualified person. Expected course work at each level promotes a meritocracy. Knowledge of spreadsheets and budgeting will be far more important than charisma and good looks. To put it simply, in an AFFEERCE polity, our legislators will be a rather boring bunch. And the higher they get, the more boring they will be. Rising through 7 cellular levels they will not be part of royal families with names like Clinton, Bush, or Kennedy, but talented people first elected by their neighbors. This will be very, very, good for democracy and good government, but kind of lifeless. Enter the aristocracy, with no real power except to make our boring nerds look good; to surround them with enough fluff and falderal to generate an aura of importance.

Obtaining Aristocracy

Title is based on paying the highest ground rent and willingness to assume the duties.

Aristocracy is very much a family affair. The 1st aristocratic family is defined as a registered or biological family residing in the district dominion whose members pay the highest ground rent on properties within the dominion, have at least one member who volunteers to fulfill the duties of cellular aristocrat and is not prohibited from carrying out that service by a 2/3 majority of the governing council and is not otherwise titled at a higher level of the cellular democracy. In the same manner, the 2nd aristocratic family pays the next highest total rent, and so on down the line.

Many districts have need for more than one aristocrat. The titled positions are ordered by prestige. Titled positions are offered first to members of the 1st aristocratic family, then the 2nd, and so on, until all titled positions are filled.

The first aristocratic family member to volunteer in a particular district at level N can choose the title gender variant at level N or lower, they feel most comfortable with. Other family members of aristocrats when they volunteer for service can choose a gender variant title at level N-1, or lower. For instance, the first family member to volunteer in a level-6 dominion might be, Princess Sally Jones, Ambassador to Spain, while the second family member to volunteer might be, Duke Harry Jones, Ambassador to Monaco. Sally Jones might have chosen any lower level title of either gender she felt most comfortable with. She might have gone with Count Sally Jones, Ambassador to Spain.

These are the default titles at different levels of the cellular democracy.

Level 1 – Sir or Madam
Level 2 – Lord or Lady
Level 3 – Baron or Baroness
Level 4 – Count or Countess
Level 5 – Duke or Duchess
Level 6 – Prince or Princess
Level 7 – King or Queen (only 1 royal family allowed)

Aristocracy can be obtained by raising one's own ground rent, purchasing or trebling other properties within the dominion, or by capturing territory that borders the dominion with a dominion treble.

The quest for aristocracy in a successful city-state plays an important role in cellular democracy dynamics, allowing innovative and efficient governments to grow and prosper as poorly managed dominions disappear. The quest also raises the general citizens' dividend, saving the citizens billions of dollars even before aristocratic contributions.

Aristocracy Hosts Government
Required Reading

Let's look at the typical duties of the Grand Baron of a medium sized level-3 city.

1. Pays for travel, meal, and hotel accommodations for district council members on jaunts and boondoggles, accompanying them as a social ambassador.
2. Hosts meetings of the district council at his/her palace or estate.
3. Entertains visiting officials from other cities, states, and countries and hosts meetings between local and visiting officials.
4. Offers to match tax receipts of district residents for pet projects.
5. Boosts the city
6. Hosts ribbon cutting ceremonies and groundbreakings.

The Baron of Public Safety could be responsible for such things as public safety promotion, hosting police and fire balls, entertaining visiting police chiefs, retirement parties, funerals, dress uniforms, police-fire-neighborhood sports competitions, and matching taxpayers for a new police and fire station.

Grand aristocrats can also maintain a mixed use palace that functions as the offices for government as well as home to the aristocratic family. This wipes out budgets for maintenance, ground rent, utilities, depreciation, and interest. Another option would have the district, perhaps with matching funds from an aristocrat, build such a palace. The Grand Aristocrat and family can call the palace home, as long as they maintain their title, and meet their responsibilities of paying maintenance, ground rent, utilities, depreciation, and interest, as well as all the hosting and boosterism required of the district's Grand Aristocrat. Aristocratic duties can be shared within the family. The Grand Baroness Monica Travers might be hosting a reception while her son Lord Joseph Travers is running a ground breaking ceremony on the other side of town.

The travel and entertainment budgets of every city, county, and state are eliminated. It is a revolutionary concept and so simply true: **People will pay for the privilege of paying for the social expenses of government.**

At the highest levels, the largest land rights owners in the nation can volunteer to be ambassadors or consul generals. Responsibilities include paying for maintenance, upkeep, utilities, depreciation, and interest on the embassy, hosting all embassy receptions and dignitaries, hosting State Department and military employees using the embassy as an office/home. Security and military travel is paid for by the national defense distribution, however, travel to and from the embassy or consulate by State Department officials should be covered by the ambassador. Like a Grand Aristocrat, the duties of an ambassador can be shared within the family.

An ambassador who shirks their responsibility, or is otherwise an embarrassment to the nation, can be removed by a 2/3 vote of the level-7 council.

In the United States, the Grand Prince of the Congress hosts the level-7 council, and maintains the U.S. Capitol Building as a palace. One half of the building (There is only a house of representatives. The ratifying body is the direct democracy.) will be converted to a large palatial residence. Congressional office buildings will either be sold or converted to palaces for lesser princes and princesses. Because the federal government will be half of its current size or smaller, there is plenty of room for palace/office mixed-use in existing buildings.

The Royal Family lives in the White House, along with the president who is the chief executive hired for a term by the level-7 council. The Royal Family will host all White House dinners, entertainment, receptions, balls, and so on, as well as maintain the White House. While presidents have terms, and come and go, the Royal Family, should they continue to pay the highest total ground rent in the nation, and assuming they are not removed by a 2/3 vote of the level-7 council, can reign in the White House for many generations. Executive department buildings are also converted to palaces for their sponsoring aristocrats. The aristocracy will rule the Washington social scene.

Of course, beyond the prestige and social power which can be immense, the aristocracy has no power (unless granted by a 5/6 plurality of a dominion) , outside of advocacy, to write laws, raise revenue, grant pardons, or declare war, sign treaties, or any other non-social function of government.

It is likely that the aristocracy, as a well-established social class, will be threatened by corruption, and will consider it their duty to report possible transgressions of the legislators and executives they so closely work with, to judicial investigators.

Chancelleries

> **Universities and hospitals can create chancelleries to fund buildings and generally support the campus. The chancellor need only be the highest bidder or trebler for the chancellery, to attain aristocratic status. All chancellery rent goes directly to the institution.**

VOS certified (See, *Regulation* below) universities that accept the tuition and fees provided by the education, food, and housing distributions without additional charge, and VOS certified hospitals that administer a self-insured HMO provided by the medical, food, housing, and disability distributions without additional charge, are eligible to convert their land into chancelleries.

A chancellery consists of a mixed use building/residence that is home to a chancellor or vice-chancellor. Ground rents do not go to the high-level distribution package. Instead, they go directly to the institution.

The chancellor is considered a member of the aristocracy, even though their only holding might be the chancellery. They are responsible for the institution's social scene, charity balls, graduations, ribbon cutting, etc. Being a chancellor is also a ticket to the general aristocratic social scene. In addition to paying a ground rent directly to the institution for the mixed use home, they pay maintenance, utilities, and grounds keeping on the building. Typical chancelleries would be a penthouse on the top floor of a hospital, or the student union building. Universities might also have vice-chancelleries, homes integrated with lecture halls and labs, and associated with a particular college.

Chancelleries are created by the institution's board of trustees and the chancellors and vice-chancellors must be approved by the board before their bid is accepted. They can be subsequently removed by the board, as well.

Community Dynamics

An AFFEERCE society is conducive to the formation of cultures and subcultures, tribes and panarchy. People join with others of similar interests. Families can be very large and integrated into larger mutual organizations such as a commune or collective. Mutual organizations can organize into enterprise districts. Large cultures can fill many branches of a cellular democracy. There are three ways to achieve these lower levels of a cellular democracy: existing, bottom-up or top-down.

Existing refers to those counties, cities, and communities that pre-date capitulation. Residential buildings self-organize as a cell or district. Because all distributions are apportioned, there is no financial penalty or reward for cell size. Level-1 representatives organize into cells which select a level-2 representative. An attempt should be made to turn existing districts, such as school districts, into legal districts that group siblings, and not cousins. The process works from the bottom up. The primary goal should be to match existing cities, counties, and states. Of course, the cellular democracy is very dynamic and all of these districts will change dramatically over the years, but the objective of starting with a known structure is a good one to reassure people in the face of a new system.

Bottom-up cellular democracy forms from collectives of like-minded pioneers who organically build cells and districts from the ground up, designed to optimally utilize the government distribution and the various lower level tranches of distributions such as transportation, sanitation, police, and fire. These communities will also make optimal use of the educational and medical distributions with such things as home schooling and community health care initiated as a cellular enterprise.

These cellular democracies will often be orphaned from the national cellular democracy due to one or more missing levels. Some of them will be rogue states. Any distribution tranches to those missing levels will be disbursed at the highest level of the orphaned cellular democracy. Even with apportionment, orphaned cellular democracies will have access to funds that usually go to the missing levels. While these orphaned democracies will have no representation on higher level councils, they will have direct democracy in all of their dominions.

Top-down cellular democracies are planned on land owned by a single land rights owner or consortium. Covenant patterns can be used to exactly place homes and businesses. Zoning restrictions on such land cannot be broken without a dominion treble extending from the borderlands. Dominions are planned in advance, their cellular and district levels determined by the ultimate number of residents. Despite land rights ownership in a top-down community, the cellular democracy is constitutional law, and the passage and repeal of class II and class III legislation cannot be tampered with except by a vote to go rogue. A core group of true believers will likely define the culture with class-III legislation early on. Newcomers can be subjected to arbitrary tests and initiations, as long as the right to leave and the right to life of children are never violated. No matter what restrictions are placed on visitors, the constitution demands access for an independent judiciary to protect both the constitutional rights of citizens and the class-III created culture. If the punishment for theft is to lose a hand, the judge will so sentence the convicted, but inform them of their right to leave the community permanently and be sentenced to a standard AFFEERCE penitentiary from a higher dominion, or go to a welcoming dominion where the act is a lesser crime or not a crime at all.

Like bottom-up communities, top-down communities will rise in the hinterlands and are likely to be orphaned cellular democracies, with all the disbursement benefit that entails.

Top-down communities aren't only the domain of religious or racist fanatics. The environmentally conscious can design a top-down community centered on solar bricks, electric autos, bicycles, green homes, yards, and waste disposal.

Extra land seized from heathen farmers

Come to Beautiful Christ County!
Spend a lifetime of quiet devotion in The City of Our Father. Solve Biblical mysteries, riddles and numerological relationships in the Village of the Holy Spirit. Praise the Lord and spread the good news from the county seat, Jesustown. Free dormitory living. Award winning estates for unwed mothers. Reasonably priced single family homes. Plenty of full and part-time job opportunities at 3 farm collectives, doll factory, theme museum and town businesses.

Mothers! Our elders will give unto Caesar his satanic birth tax so that you are free to be fruitful and multiply.* No waiting list for spacious family dorms for married couples, estates for unwed mothers.

* Requires a 4 year commitment to Christ County

Jesustown

City of Our Father

Village of the Holy Spirit

Christ County Kansas
Rev. Herman Thirdword,
Count of Christ County

Advertisement for a Top-Down County

Civil Rights

In the battle against racism, sexism, and homophobia, attaining civil rights legislation was a good focal point for action. This battle was partly responsible for creating the African-American middle class. From a natural rights perspective, civil rights legislation is unfair. It violates the entrepreneur's natural right to hire/contract who they wish.

Discrimination is essential in allocating human resources. Not discrimination based on race or sex, per se, but discrimination based on compatibility, knowledge, and other subtle factors used to build a successful working environment.

Racism, sexism and homophobia, fit this model of discrimination only when prejudice blurs the vision of employers and other employees. Exclusion breeds more exclusion and thus perpetuates these types of discrimination. As a result, only members of the "old boy's network" can work together.

In an AFFEERCE economy, work is more of an avocation than a vocation. Many will be partners in mutual organizations. People will tend to work where they are needed and loved, in answer to a calling. Universal distribution allows each of us to be selective.

Unlimited free education can turn arbitrary and capricious discrimination into a challenge. Ridding the world of bigoted corporations is a noble endeavor. Spend years learning about the business. Use the citizen investors to get started. Undercut, collude, and use every competitive advantage to put the bigot who refused to hire you out of business. In common cause, there will be other workers who share those goals and are willing to work for less money to see them achieved.

The civil right to be served in a public accommodation is also a question of contradictory natural rights. It is the proprietor's natural right to refuse service and the patron's natural rights to be free from harassment and pursue happiness. How the proprietor implements this natural right is determined by community standards and the

165

appropriate VSG. In an AFFEERCE society, Class II regulation should generally not be used to shut down businesses. Instead, deviations from fair business practices are prominently posted on the VOS (violation of standards). Save for acceptable hygiene standards, intended discrimination must be prominently posted. Prominent posting protects the natural right to be free from humiliation when turned away. It notifies friends that this is not a welcoming place for the group.

Why is discrimination even legal? Freedom of association is a natural right, as is the right to refuse service. In some cases, the community might even approve of discrimination; for instance, ethnic clubs, men's clubs, women's clubs, or perhaps transgender female clubs. It is not uncommon for people to need support from others like themselves.

It becomes far more heinous when certain groups are singled out for exclusion. While freedom to refuse service is a natural right, that doesn't mean the community has to take such discrimination without fighting back. There are plenty of other freedoms that can be used to fight back. The freedom of speech is a natural right. That includes the right to picket, boycott, leaflet, and otherwise express one's disapproval in front of the establishment. There is also civil disobedience; sit-ins and occupations. This can't be classified as a right, since there will be arrests—but then, that is the whole point. Perhaps civil disobedience can be classified under the natural right of insurrection that naturally follows from the right to life and the only natural right not protected by the state.

The fight for civil rights led by Dr. King and others was a noble effort. The Civil Rights Act of 1965 dismantled that effort; far better that the civil rights movement had continued until there was truly no more discrimination. The same was true in the gay rights movement, where some of the leadership cautioned gays to avoid rocking the boat in hopes of "sneaking" through civil rights legislation. They missed the whole point of using visibility to advance LGBT integration into society.

AFFEERCE communities will be quite diverse. Outside of the major urban areas there will be enclaves of just about anything you could imagine. As long as natural rights are respected, in particular, freedom of movement (right to leave), and the rights of children to their full distribution and to be free from physical and sexual abuse, these enclaves can operate under their own customs. Some of the more remote communities will no doubt incorporate racism, sexism, and homophobia into their lifestyle. Unless neighboring communities rise up with pickets, boycotts or dominion treble, the offending enclave will probably be left alone.

Although I felt differently earlier in life, I do not think anything good can come from civil rights legislation. I would much rather see the tools of freedom employed to confront bigotry head on. However, if the situation is particularly acute, a super plurality can pass class II legislation, such as civil rights laws, that restrict the right to property.

Large, diverse, loving families will prosper and be fruitful. Bigoted, ignorant, families will isolate themselves. They will tend to live off the distributions, and thanks to the baby tax, soon fade away.

Penitentiaries

Prisons today are crime factories. For the entire time of their incarceration, inmates are taught, influenced, and learn morality from each other. Inmates are subjected to a violent hell that often leaves them ready to terrorize the general population. Prisons have every incentive to create criminals, as there is a prison industry in this country[FTN9.02]. Prison reform is impossible because victims have less rights than prisoners in terms of food, housing, medical care and education. The AFFEERCE penitentiary is concerned primarily with rehabilitation and incentivized for non-recidivism. Following conviction, the defendant is given time to get their affairs in order.

There is no possibility of prison reform in the United States. The reason is simple. Because of our current prison and economic system, those who steal, maim, and murder, are entitled to quality healthcare, but their victims are not. Those who steal, maim, and murder, are entitled to three square meals a day, but their victims are not. There are even programs to find jobs for ex-offenders, while their victims often have no employment opportunities. Under these conditions, further prison reform is impossible.

Prison is a barbaric society where the strong and intimidating rule. The culture encourages the most despicable behaviors. Rehabilitation is very difficult. In fact, 67.5% of those who are released from prison are hardened criminals. FTN9.03 Prison can be no other way, as long as prisoners are given entitlements that law-abiding citizens are denied.

In an AFFEERCE economy, every citizen is entitled to nutritious food, warm and safe shelter, medical care and unlimited education. This is a basic requirement for prison reform. In such a society, and only in such a society, will prisoners have fewer rights than the ordinary citizen. Prisoners have exactly the same distributions for food, shelter, education, and medical care as their victims. What prisoners do not have, is their liberty. Penitentiaries will likely be small, often family-run, businesses. They will be designed for rehabilitation and education. Each of these penitentiaries will specialize in a specific problem, such as drugs, alcohol, gambling, and domestic abuse. Facilities are graded by the VSGs on their recidivism rate. More importantly, they receive a non-recidivism annuity as long as former inmates do not return to crime or unmanageable addiction.

In addition to the standard food and housing distributions, penitentiaries are funded by the $300 per inmate per month disability distribution. There is also the additional $300 security stipend. This isn't part of a regular distribution, but comes from the government distribution before the politicians get their share., giving politicians a strong incentive to not enact superfluous laws. Institutions can generate additional revenue through commissary profits and inmate work programs.

In an AFFEERCE society, the penitentiary, (the word prison is too reminiscent of today's hellholes), is concerned exclusively with rehabilitation. This will be brought about by two powerful incentives. Both of them have to do with recidivism. First, once the inmate is released, the penitentiary will continue to receive $25 per released inmate per month, for the rest of the released inmate's life, or until such time as the inmate is convicted of a penitentiary offense, or seeks refuge in or is sentenced to an isolation center, such as might exist for the severely addicted and child predators. It is unlikely that an inmate would be sentenced to the same penitentiary twice. The second incentive is that any recidivism of a released inmate goes on the penitentiary VOS. Judges, with many competing choices where to sentence a prisoner, will certainly use recidivism on the VOS as a criterion.

The lack of liberty in a penitentiary means the inmate can be denied freedom of association with other inmates. It means that meals are taken in the room alone, with social workers, visiting family, tutors, or spiritual guides as companions. When inmates are allowed together in small groups for activities like chess, Scrabble, drama club, calisthenics, library, and prayer, they will be video recorded from many angles and indications of violence, secret societies, or gangs will result in loss of all such privileges for a period of time. Conjugal visits with friends and family members are allowed, but inmates are confined to single rooms, and there shall be no sex or physical contact of any kind between inmates. If the inmate can afford it, the penitentiary can allow in outside prostitutes, wrestling coaches, and trainers for physical contact needs. A fundamental principle of the AFFEERCE penitentiary is the less contact inmates have with other inmates, the less likely recidivism. This goes back to the earliest ideas about penitentiaries. Unlike early penitentiaries, inmates will not go stir crazy, but have plenty of contacts with positive role models, particularly private teachers who have strong economic incentives to teach prisoners trades FTN 5.10.

When the accused is convicted of a crime and sentenced to a penitentiary, they are given anywhere from two weeks to six weeks to get their affairs in order, move their possessions to storage, if need be, or make other arrangements with their landlord or mortgage holder. If family members cannot afford the ground rent or mortgage they should find smaller quarters. Every attempt should be made to avoid foreclosure (See *Chapter 11 – Housing Distribution*.)

Because of the VIP, there is little danger of escape. In fact, if a convicted person is willing and able to convince another country to take them, the state will pay for the plane fare, and revoke their citizenship (See, *Right to leave*, above). However, if a judge determines that the convicted is a physical threat to others, this privilege of getting their affairs in order will be denied.

Penitentiaries can be a blessing. It is a time to gain a spiritual foothold, to train online or with a tutor for a new career, or design the ultimate business plan. Halfway houses allow the inmate to spend as long as needed working with a social worker, landing the right job, finding an apartment or unioning into a family, commune, or other mutual organization. In the halfway houses, ex-prisoners regain liberty to associate with each other.

Isolation Centers

> **Isolation centers are minimum security facilities, preferably miles from the general population, for special conditions where rehabilitation is difficult or unlikely.**

There are additional freedoms for those who voluntarily commit themselves to one of these centers. Drug addicts have a strong incentive to voluntarily enter an addiction isolation center. There they will be supplied with unlimited free opiates, benzodiazepines, amphetamines, tobacco, alcohol, coffee and marijuana. Inmates have a tiny private room with bed and bath, and a supervised 24 hour buffet (both nutritious food and munchies) at the communal dining hall. There also can be a library, gymnasium, television rooms, game rooms and so forth. There is an infirmary and rehabilitation center funded by the medical distribution.

Isolation centers for child predators will provide free virtual child pornography and art, and be otherwise similar to the addiction centers. Those who commit acts of violence at isolation centers can be sentenced to a penitentiary where they will not receive intoxicants or virtual pornography.

Isolation centers make their money off the food, housing, $300 disability and $300 security stipend. They also get a $25 per month annuity from those who are rehabilitated and leave the center. The food cost for addicts tends to be much lower, although the money saved will be used to purchase intoxicants. Centers can raise additional funds by underpaying inmate labor and overcharging at the commissary. There is not likely to be much inmate labor at an addiction center possibly leading to a curtailing of services. That problem should not exist at an isolation center for child predators. Isolation centers can only be profitable with several hundred inmates. Those who enter an addiction isolation center voluntarily or remain in one after their sentence is complete will likely spend half their remaining lives in and out of such centers. Thus a center serving 400 inmates will likely receive an additional $10,000 per month in annuities. Child predators today are less likely to be rehabilitated, though new treatments in the future might change the odds. Child predators are much more likely than addicts to engage in productive labor, and this labor can be exploited to fund a profitable isolation center.

How AFFEERCE Eliminates Crime

Required Reading

What is the state of crime in a free society? Assume 100 arrests today in any given region of the United States over a certain period of time. Arrests remaining = 100

From 2002 through 2012, the NYPD has spent approximately 1,000,000 police hours arresting people for marijuana possession. In that time, they arrested over 440,000 people for minor marijuana charges, costing taxpayers over 75 million dollars in 2012 alone[FTN9.04].

All told, in the past 40 years, the U.S. government has spent over $2.5 trillion dollars fighting the War on Drugs. Despite the ad campaigns, increased incarceration rates and a crackdown on smuggling, the number of illicit drug users in America has risen over the years and is estimated at 19.9 million. At least 25% of all arrests are for the possession and/or sale of narcotics[FTN9.05].

The war on drugs spawns additional crime, gangs, and in Chicago, one of the worst homicide rates in the nation. In an AFFEERCE society, intoxicants are legal and taxed for ordinary citizens. There are isolation centers where addicts, convicted of theft or DUI, who refuse rehab, receive free drugs in exchange for loss of liberty to leave the centers. There is no war on drugs. The legalization of drugs and prostitution will significantly reduce gang-related crimes. Estimated reduction of crime is 25%.   Arrests remaining = 75

Ending the war on drugs is not the only area where AFFEERCE cuts the cost of fighting crime. Domestic violence-related police calls have been found to constitute the single largest category of calls received by police, accounting for 15 to more than 50 percent of all calls.[FTN9.06]

In an AFFEERCE society, there are no real financial roadblocks to leaving an abusive situation (the right to leave). Housing and food distributions allow the abused spouse to leave the family. Sometimes it is the abuser who feels trapped, and they too can now easily leave. Because AFFEERCE families will tend to be quite large, abusers can be quickly expelled, often without any police intervention. Every family has a social worker who serves as a first responder for many of the non-violent problems that might tie up police time. Estimated reduction of crime is 20%. Arrests remaining=60

Poverty is a major cause of crime. In one study of cities with populations over 100,000, every one percent increase in the population below the poverty level led to an increase of about 135 total crimes and about 25 violent crimes [FTN9.07].

The housing distribution, food distribution, cash distribution, economies of scale of large families, free unlimited education, and quality medical care put an end to the crime caused by poverty, latch-key kids, lack of educational opportunity, poor nutrition or unsafe, unsanitary, unheated shelter, or lead-based paint. Estimated reduction of crime is 20%. Arrests remaining = 48

It has long been recognized that repeat offenders commit a large number of the serious and violent crimes. In Florida, one study revealed that upwards of 70% of crimes are committed by 30% of the offenders [FTN9.08].

AFFEERCE penitentiaries are incentivized to reduce recidivism. Without universal distribution, prison reform is impossible. After all, why would society tolerate nutritious meals, quality medical care, job training and education for the incarcerated criminal, when the victim is entitled to none of this? Estimated reduction in crime is 30%. Arrests remaining = 34

A significant amount of police work will be eliminated by the VIP. No citizen can make a purchase, pay their ground rent, or even take public transportation without using the VIP. AFFEERCE is a cashless society. It is difficult to survive without revealing where you are. Criminals, once identified will be caught. There is no way around that. Estimated reduction of crime is 30%. Arrests remaining = 23

There are also AFFEERCE intangibles that should reduce crime; the end of loneliness due to large families, the AFFEERCE enlightenment, and the opportunity for everyone to live their dream. It is my belief that this will provide a further reduction of crime of 10%. Arrests remaining = 20

Very conservatively, 100 crimes have been reduced to 20, or an 80% reduction in crime. But the estimates of crime reduction are based on treating the percentages as dependent variables. Treating them as independent variables gives an impossible reduction of crime of 135%. The true number is somewhere in between. It is reasonable to conclude that AFFEERCE will reduce crime by 85 to 95%, and more over time. This will allow police time to pursue cases they would otherwise ignore, providing more time for detective work and getting convictions, and less time in dangerous situations. Police officers must never be fired when crime drops. To motivate successful crime-fighting, only attrition should be used in response to lighter loads.

Penalties

> An AFFEERCE society places a higher priority on victim compensation than incarceration. The judge can convert all or part of penitentiary time to actual and punitive damages that go to the victim, police, and prosecutors, based on the assets of the convicted. The victim can veto any such arrangement and the convicted can demand penitentiary time versus asset forfeiture. Special investigators in the judiciary play close attention to convictions where large penalties are involved. Police and prosecutorial misconduct is penalized at twice the severity of the law in which the accused is tried.

Every person incarcerated in a penitentiary, drug rehab, or mental health facility has a $35 cash distribution. When involuntarily confined, $30 of that $35 goes to the victim. With the approval of the victim, the rewards are much greater when the convicted buys years off their sentence. The judge sets the price for the accused to avoid a year in the penitentiary, based on the assets of the accused, the sentencing guidelines in the law, and the nature of the crime. The victim can veto any fine the judge sets, in lieu of the penitentiary. However, the victim is less likely to approve a $1,000 per year payoff, than a $100,000 per year payoff. The wealthy are more likely to avoid the penitentiary, but also more likely to be prosecuted.

Unless the assets of the accused were stolen, they cannot be seized. This practice, currently, in the United States, often without due process, clearly constitutes unreasonable search and seizure. Those who profit from the drug wars have told the courts to see it otherwise.

The convicted always has a right to the penitentiary over the surrender of assets. This will keep victims from demanding too high a payoff in exchange for years off a sentence. Typically the cost of avoiding each year of incarceration would increase exponentially. Given a five year sentence for fraud, the judge might set the cost of one year off the sentence at $10,000; the second year would cost $20,000; the third year $40,000; the fourth year, $80,000; and the final year at $160,000. The judge would divide this money into actual damages and punitive damages. Actual damages all go to the victim. Punitive damages are equally divided between the police, the prosecution, and the victim.

The investigating and apprehending officers split the proceeds of any fines or stipends going to the police. Prosecutors can likewise split the proceeds of any fines or stipends with assistants, according to their own formula.

Compensating the victim is very important in a just society. A $30/month annuity while the offender is in the penitentiary is not much compensation. It is in everyone's interest to allow the exchange of penitentiary time for actual and punitive damages. Therefore the judge can convert any portion of the penitentiary sentence to actual damages and any portion to punitive damages, in accordance with the worth of the offender. It is the right of the victim or the family of a deceased victim to insist that penitentiary time be served and no monetary alternative be offered. And it is the right of the accused to take the penitentiary over forfeiture of assets, beyond $30 of the monthly cash distribution.

Some might complain that this is unfair to the poor, but they are wrong. If anything, it would be unfair to the rich. Today, police tend to target the poor and give the rich a break. There is no incentive to target a wealthy person. In all likelihood, they will hire an expensive lawyer and get off. In AFFEERCE, where the wealthy can avoid the penitentiary by paying a fine, that is not the case.

For instance, suppose a multi-millionaire is convicted of a violent rape. While this offense could mean 8 years in the penitentiary, the multi-millionaire is given an option of paying 1 million dollars in actual damages and 1 million dollars in punitive damages in lieu of 7 years. In that case, the victim would get $1,333,000. The prosecutor would get $333,000. The arresting officer would get $167,000 and the investigating officer would get $167,000. The convicted would spend a year in the penitentiary.

In AFFEERCE, law enforcement has every incentive to target the rich over the poor. However, targeting should not be confused with the manufacturing or withholding of evidence. Malicious prosecution is punishable by a sentence up to twice the length demanded for the accused. Fellow prosecutors, police, and government officials could suffer a liability of up to two week's salary.

Even "honest mistakes," by police and prosecution, when the liberty of a defendant is at stake, are very serious offenses. Those who sacrifice personal ethics for the allure of high fines will, at the very least, be terminated and likely find themselves in a penitentiary.

Regular investigations of the police and prosecutors are conducted by the judiciary, with its departments of internal investigations and special prosecution. Public defenders are also part of the judiciary. AFFEERCE judges will have a bias toward the defense. This is how it should be. Police and prosecutors are under constant scrutiny. In exchange for the higher standard, and the high likelihood of special prosecution, both police and prosecutors have the opportunity for high income from fines in lieu of prosecution. The common career path today, from prosecutor to judge, will not exist.

What about compensation for a person unjustly imprisoned? If unjust imprisonment is due to withholding, or modifying evidence by police or prosecutors, a lawsuit can be initiated for up to 2 weeks salaries and fines due government officials. Without official malfeasance, the unjustly imprisoned can request funds from the discretionary tax, perhaps accompanied by a plea from the governor.

In an AFFEERCE society, there is no concept of, "not guilty by reason of insanity or impairment." Mental illness, intoxicants, addiction, and any other circumstances are considered by the judge in choosing a penitentiary that will best aid the offender in overcoming their problems. Because of the importance of drug rehabilitation and mental health care, fines will not be an option for the portion of the sentence deemed critical to rehabilitation. If this leads to inadequate victim compensation, the victim can request funds via the discretionary tax.

The AFFEERCE philosophy of justice is very different than the one in force today. Dishonesty is fraud. There is no plea bargaining. If lawyers believe their client is innocent, they have an obligation to do everything possible to get their client found not-guilty. That includes appeals, and if new evidence is found at any time post-sentencing, a hearing to reopen the case will usually be made in the defendant's favor. If a client has committed a crime, their lawyer has an obligation to do everything possible to argue any mitigating circumstances, to argue for lower damages, and to have their client sentenced to the best possible program for rehabilitation. If a lawyer believes a client is lying about innocence, or the evidence reveals that a client has knowingly lied, the lawyer should convince the client to change their plea or drop the client. There is little room for moral relativism in an AFFEERCE society. The accused is either guilty or innocent. There should be no protection from double jeopardy when significant new evidence is uncovered after a not-guilty verdict. By the same token, prosecutors will be severely punished for malicious prosecution if there is no current evidence of guilt. The penitentiary is no longer a horrible place. It is a chance for the criminal to get a new start in life and no criminal should be denied that right.

Judiciary and Public Defense

The single judiciary is organized along cellular levels. Judges are selected at random from respected legal scholars nominated by law schools. The judiciary consists of the jurists and staff, public defenders, internal investigations, and special prosecution. It is completely isolated from the legislative and executive branches, and the direct democracy, outside of impeachment. It is responsible for judicial review and classification of bills prior to passage, as well as appellate functions.

Generally, there is one judge for every 9000 citizens, today [FTN9.09]. Because the crime rate should be significantly reduced in AFFEERCE, and what constitutes liability more clearly defined with the VOS, judges will have time to wisely adjudicate cases. Still, with the radical redefinition of family and land, family and chancery law cases will increase, filling much of the gap from reduced crime and liability.

The judiciary will organize itself primarily along cellular levels. Initially this will likely be at level-4, corresponding to the old idea of county. Different kinds of courts, such as family and chancery court, will be organized at lower levels. Appellate courts will be at levels 5, 6, and 7, with the Supreme Court at level-7. There is, however, only one judicial system, regardless of how the courts self-organize.

New tasks include the classification of bills prior to their passage into law (Class I, II, or III) and a greater role for chancery and family judges with assumedly a smaller role for judges in criminal court.

It is essential that judges be highly paid legal experts with records of exceptional honesty, and extreme respect from their peers. They cannot be elected as popularity among the citizenry is not a desirable quality. Furthermore, only a minute portion of the electorate has any knowledge at all about which judges to retain. Political appointments are tainted with corruption, and represent a gross conflict of interest. The judiciary must be completely independent, yet structurally tied to the cellular democracy.

The AFFEERCE philosophy eschews legislating certification. However, even with medical deregulation, diagnosticians must be AMA VSG certified, even if you ultimately choose to have your surgery done at Joe's Brain Surgery Shack for the rebate. (See, *Chapter 11 – Medical Entitlement*) However, the idea of deregulating the judicial system is anathema. There is no concept of saving money by going with a street corner judge.

New criminal and civil judges must come from long-time faculty at law schools, selected by their peers. They should have no arrests, except perhaps for civil disobedience cases. Their merit testing scores should be in the upper quartile and they should have at least 10 years of teaching experience. Wisdom and fairness should be qualities that students and fellow faculty members ascribe to the prospective jurist.

Each law school should have a prospective judge in each judicial category (civil, criminal, family, etc.), as agreed upon by the faculty and approved by the students. When a vacancy opens up in the judiciary, judges at level N+1 will fill a vacancy at level N, by selecting a sitting judge at level N-1. This will create a new vacancy that will ultimately appear at the lowest level of the judiciary for that category. This vacancy will be filled by randomly selecting a law school and filling it with their prospective jurist from that category. The actual method will be determined by the judiciary.

It might be decided that family and probate judges should come from the ranks of social workers, who have achieved very large families (See, *Chapter 11 – Social Worker Distribution*), have no arrests, and have both passed the bar and received high scores on their certification. They should be selected by their peers. Perhaps they can sit with a co-judge selected from a law school to avoid any possibility of corruption.

The distribution for the judiciary also pays for public defenders appointed by the court. Lawyers go into the public defender's office because they are dedicated to fighting injustice. Winning percentage as a public defender must be posted on their VOS.

Associated with the judiciary and the judiciary distribution is a branch of law enforcement dedicated to investigating police brutality, manufacture of evidence, government malfeasance, and malicious prosecution. This branch includes a special prosecutor's office to prosecute these infractions. Investigations are initiated by public defenders or jurists. The fines and annuities police and prosecutors receive for successful convictions is an incentive for corruption. The penalties for such corruption will be severe. For minor infractions, after due process, the judiciary investigators might receive double indemnity from the offending officer or prosecutor. Medium infractions might also result in termination of employment and major infractions will result in a penitentiary sentence. Judiciary oversight is found at all levels of the cellular democracy.

The judge is the highest paid public servant, earning $18,000 per month on average. They will administer huge fines that could make police officers, prosecutors and victims rich. There must be no temptation for corruption. They must decide on competing penitentiaries for sentencing based on the needs and personality of the accused. The decision must be based on the best interest of the accused and society, again with no temptation for corruption.

A judge can be impeached by a majority vote of the district council and convicted by a 2/3 vote of the voters in the associated district dominion. An impeached and convicted justice is forever barred from the judiciary.

The judiciary distribution is $9/person/month. How this is allocated is determined by the judiciary, not the citizens. At today's population, the distribution is $2.8 billion/month or $34 billion annually. The federal judiciary today has a budget of about $5 billion, with judiciaries of the larger states around $1 billion. Court costs are also covered to a small extent by the universal deductible of $35 to bring a civil case, family case or to treble land. The proposed judiciary distribution should be sufficient.

The Judiciary and Rogue States

The primary role of the judiciary in rogue states is to insure the right to life of children and the right to leave of adults are protected. At a minimum jurists must be present and have access to the accused at all times during a trial, to the convicted at frequent intervals for non-corporal punishment and at all times corporal punishment is meted out. The right to leave is always an option. Jurists, if permitted, will serve as judges in the rogue state and follow local laws in sentencing, even as they inform the defendant of their right to leave.

Judges do not make law, but adjudicate the laws passed by a council, direct democracy, or other body. That is also the case in a rogue state. Judges will do their best to follow the law, even if that law is riddled with contradictions, arbitrary clauses, and favoritism. They will also inform any defendant of their exit right options. Exit rights are never waived, so before and during the execution of the punishment, the judge will frequently inform the accused of the right to leave.

In some rogue states, the judge must be a member of a religious order. Such a judge will not be a member of the judiciary. However, a member of the judiciary must be present throughout the trial and must be able to inform the defendant about their exit rights, frequently, before, during, and after the trial.

Interference with the judicial obligation to inform the accused of their right to leave, or preventing the accused from exercising their exit rights is a federal crime defined in the constitution. The FBI will make arrests, and if needed the military will be brought in.

The judiciary will supply public defenders for the accused in a rogue state, or for those accused under Class III legislation, unless such defense is prohibited by the laws of the rogue state. The judiciary will investigate rogue state police and prosecutors for corruption and malfeasance unless this too is prohibited by the rogue state law. Although the judiciary offers the rogue state its full set of services, the only service it must accept is the frequent notification of exit rights by the judge to the accused.

Regulation

Required Reading

What about consumer protection? No worry, say some, fraud is illegal and will be prosecuted. But what is fraud? If someone sells an ice cream cone that is 90% lard, is that fraud? What about 2% lard? If you buy a cereal called "bugs bunny" and it contains rabbit shaped wheat clusters and dead cockroaches, is that fraud? Cockroaches probably have more nutritional value than wheat clusters.

Suppose an inexperienced worker is hired to work on the exposed girders of an office tower being built. His boss throws him a safety harness, and then says, "You should wear the safety vest, but some of the guys say that only wusses wear it." So the newbie goes up to work, sans harness, and is blown off to his death. Is that fraud? Is there criminal liability? What if the guys really do say, as a standing joke, that only wusses wear the harness?

You're driving 12 hours and see a sign for a motel 20 miles away. "We have small rooms but cheap prices only $18 a night!" You check in exhausted, hit the sack, and wake up with rats crawling all over your blanket. In your underwear you run screaming to the front office. "I thought your rooms were cheap because they were small," you yell. "That too," says the manager.

There are literally billions of cases where fraud is ambiguous. An industry can collude on a set of standards, and even display an "Underwriter's laboratory" type of seal, but nothing prevents another business from producing the product at less cost by violating those standards and selling to customers who have no knowledge of the standard and neither the time nor energy to study labels.

Even as the objectivists say "Caveat Emptor," if the motel has rats, don't go back (ignoring the endless supply of suckers who think they're getting a deal because the rooms are small), the entire equation changes with children: "La Cucaracha, baby food with a Spanish flair;" you-know-what in mild salsa.

Changing "Buyer Beware" to "Buyer be very, very, afraid," hardly sounds like the motto of a free society, but when it comes to children, failure to adhere to standards is nothing less than child abuse. Adults can choose to live with rats, but if they raise their children in such an environment, they are abusers.

In principle, regulations attempt to resolve contradictions between the right to life and the right to property. Objectivist economists argue that the right to life and the right to property are rarely in conflict as long as each person operates according to their "rational, self-interest." However, according to the subjective theory of value, self-interests are infinitely varied making it disingenuous to assert that "rational, self-interest" is nothing more than the desire to make money.

In the real world people are far more likely to take a loss in exchange for trading with someone they are sexually attracted to. They are far more likely to give better deals to their friends and compensate by overcharging those who are very different from themselves. They are far more likely to take significantly less pay in jobs that provide sexual, aesthetic, or social satisfaction. In an extreme example, open bidding for the job of grammar school teacher could result in the exclusive hiring of pedophiles. Open bidding for the job of pharmacist could result in the exclusive hiring of drug addicts.

Some proprietors get their jollies secretly watching customers in dressing rooms, bathrooms, and motel rooms. Self-interest can also take a mildly sadistic bent, with the proprietor getting off on jokes and gags played on the customer; rodents in the motel room, spiders in the panties, pilots yelling, "We're going to crash," doctors giving you just days to live, worms in the spaghetti, porn on a new computer.

There are also decided advantages in cutting corners that are not obvious to the consumer, such as not fixing lead-based paint, asbestos, and contaminated water in public accommodations. If there were no regulation, imagine what could be done to processed food in order to save money.

Some companies are designed around short-term profit; make their money and leave, the owners having no compunction about exhausting natural resources. Companies planning for the long-term are concerned about natural resources. Cleaning up pollution almost never pays unless the company must pay rent on the air or water it pollutes.

The argument that bad practices will quickly destroy a business is false. Companies change names. People are mobile and do not spend their time researching companies. Even major news exposés can be lost amongst the information overload. Some wealthy persons, bored with their lot, don't give a whit about profit, as long as they can engage in practices that suit their fancy. Getting the most from life and making a profit are often two very different things.

Regulation acts as a headwind to a free market economy. Without safety inspection and quality control, prices can drop significantly. But do we want a society where "made with the highest quality beef," means the hotdog is 1% high quality beef and 99% offal and floor sweepings?

Headwind or not, without regulation, there is no right to life.

Today, regulation is delegated to bloated bureaucracies. Regulations are arbitrary, confusing, often in conflict with one another, and thus impossible to apply without corruption and cronyism. Businesses can face regulatory nightmares and only wade through the mire with political contributions and lobbying. Codes constantly change, so buildings are out of code soon after construction. The only way to pass inspection without significant capital outlay is to grease the palm of the inspector.

Bureau of Standards

In an AFFEERCE economy, there is only one regulation. It is called the VOS or Violation of Standards document. It simply lists standards violations, some in bold and some requiring customer sign-off. Once you have properly revealed how your entity deviates from acceptable standards, you are no longer liable for that deviation. For this reason businesses are as anxious for standards as consumers. The Bureau of Standards is supported by its business members and consists of voluntary standards groups (VSGs) that specify standards and how deviations are to be reported.

Every corporation, family charter, product, and offer of employment must have a VOS. So too must requests for funds, contracts, medical procedures and proposed legislation..

The VOS is typically a public document available through a VIP reader, accessed through signatories, by date, by region, by type, and by the name of the entity, such as business, product, or offer.

When selling products, to or for children under the age of 14, the VOS must say: NO STANDARDS VIOLATED and be signed by the appropriate signatories.

Perhaps you are thinking this sounds every bit as bad, if not worse, than the regulatory quagmire we find ourselves in today. But that isn't so. All parties will take the initiative to have an accurate and honest VOS. The reason for this can be summed up in three words: **release from liability**.

The AFFEERCE philosophy on regulation is to satisfy the universal demand for protection. This is a demand from businesses, consumers and employees. Consumers and employees demand protection from undisclosed or fine-printed gotchas, while businesses demand protection from liability.

The AFFEERCE Bureau of Standards is not a bureaucracy that writes regulation, but one which oversees the writing of standards. It is similar to the private American National Standards Institute (ANSI). It is envisioned as a government agency, because unlike ANSI, it has law enforcement powers. While ANSI standards are completely voluntary, violation of VOS display requirements are violations of civil or criminal law. There is not an endless maze of regulation, but a simple law describing how to display standard's violations. It is important to reiterate that these standards do not prohibit any business activity. Rather, they are concerned with the nature and extent of disclosure for violating standards. Unlike ANSI, certification is done by third party agencies and not the bureau itself [FTN10.10]. The groups making these standards are called Voluntary Standards Groups or VSG's.

Bureau of Standards – Employees and Members		
Title	How Paid	Function
Consumer senators	Member dues, government distribution	<ul><li>Elected from each level-5 cell.</li><li>Should have a respected history in consumer advocacy</li><li>Hire/fire consumer advocates</li><li>Coordinate, create and merge the VSGs.</li><li>Set policy for democratic procedures within the groups</li><li>Set formatting standards</li><li>Publish and distribute the latest standards to affected enterprises and inspection agencies.</li></ul>

Members	By sponsoring institutions	• Pay dues to support BOS and consumer advocates • Sit on VSGs and lobby for VOS standards • Sponsored by corporations, trade groups, schools, special interest groups, and wealthy interested parties • Each sponsor can seat a delegate and alternate in a VSG, but only one can vote. • VSG can unseat shadow corporations, wealthy interested parties, and disruptors by 2/3 vote.
Consumer advocates	Member dues	• One consumer advocate for each member in a VSG • $2000/month salary per VSG • Normally sits on two VSGs • Technical certification in VSG subject matter required • Access to Library of Congress for research • No financial or family ties to any members on the VSG.
Regulators	Fines from improper or fraudulent VOS, Member dues	• From 1 to 6 per VSG • Investigate complaints • Report complaints of inconsistent language, or inadequate or contradictory standards, to the VSG. • Prosecute in court if need be • Overseen by the judiciary

Functions and Features of the VSG
Required Reading

1. Create and update one or more VOS requirements documents.
2. Create test questions for membership certification (assembled/administered by Department of Education)
3. Create test questions for career certification (assembled/administered by Department of Education)
4. Create curriculum standards for the subject and focus of the VSG.
5. Recommend class II legislation for child standards (requires majority of district council, judicial classification, and 2/3 vote of dominion)
6. Recommend class II legislation for standards that conflict with freedom (requires majority of district council, judicial classification, and 2/3 vote of dominion)
7. Meets one day each week. Dues-paying lobbyists, as well as paid consumer advocates can theoretically sit on a maximum of five VSG's, although the heavy workload would be prohibitive.
8. Ranges in size from 20 to 200 not including alternates.
9. All decisions require a majority vote. Because consumers have different philosophies and businesses are in competition, a straight vote along business/consumer lines is unlikely.
10. VSGs in excess of the maximum size can be broken-up into multiple VSGs by the consumer senators.
11. Dues paying membership is $2500/VSG/month, with $2000 paying the salary of a consumer advocate and $500 supporting the consumer senators and Bureau of Standards generally. Dues entitle delegate and alternate to Library of Congress research privileges.

12. Dues can be raised, if there are an insufficient number of qualified available consumer advocates to match industry supply. Shadow corporations, not actively engaged in research studies or education programs, can be removed by 2/3 of the VSG to prevent a raise in dues. With an excess supply of consumer advocates, dues can be lowered back to the base, shadow corporations and wealthy interested parties can be welcomed back.

13. Can be created by a majority of institutions in an industry, or an act of Congress (level-7 governing council).

The VSG's set the standards and businesses implement the standards they choose, listing violations of those standards on the VOS in a manner specified by the VSG document. The business pays an inspection agency, such as a legal or accounting firm, or a myriad of other types of inspection agencies, modeled like an accounting firm, to certify the VOS, assuming liability for an improper VOS at the time of inspection, but not subsequent violations. A change in business circumstances often will require an amendment to the VOS to prevent liability.

The relationship of businesses with inspection agencies will be similar to their current relationship with accounting firms. Although there is potential for abuse, such as was the case with Enron and Arthur Anderson, the transfer of liability to the inspection agency provides a powerful check.

VSGs at Lower Levels of Dominion
Required Reading

Any dominion at level 3 or above, can sponsor VSG's whose VOS applies if all parties to the transaction are members of the dominion. VSGs at level-5, loosely corresponding to states, might be common. Educational standards can be set by any dominion that encompasses the entire school district. Unlike the federal Bureau of Standards, VSGs at lower levels will only be self-funding to the extent there is incentive for businesses and other dues-paying members to join.

Lower level VSGs can always add more restrictive requirements. Looser requirements are only valid if permitted by the high level VSG, and if all parties to the transaction are members of the lower level dominion.

Spending several years in lower level VSGs might be a requirement for employment as a consumer advocates at the Bureau of Standards.

Functions and Features of the VOS
Required Reading

1. Protects the entrepreneur against liability for any listed violation of standards.
2. Inspection protects the entrepreneur against liability for any unlisted violation whose cause preceded the inspection. The liability is transferred to the inspection agency. The entrepreneur remains liable for any unlisted violation whose cause occurred after the last inspection.
3. Has the date of the latest certification, inspector name, and agency, as well as the date of the latest amendment.
4. Where violations could otherwise result in liability, the customer is almost always required to sign the VOS, acknowledging the violations, before the transaction can take place.
5. Children under the age of 14, and those who demonstrate temporary or permanent serious mental impairment cannot sign a VOS.
6. Can be required by a contract at the completion of a service. Contract can demand inspection and even by a particular inspection agency.
7. Any contract can specify acceptable and unacceptable violations.

8. Can be required by a retailer from suppliers. Failure to do this could constitute a violation of standards for the retailer.

Here is a simple example of a business that a VOS allows.

Suppose you have a room painted with lead-based paint, and not insulated against the cold. The room is unused and you want to rent it out for $150 a month. With a monthly housing distribution of $370, this represents a $220 savings. The tenant will use $40 for running a space heater and other electric, and have $90 of the $180 rebated every month. Since a standard apartment will not have lead-based paint and will be insulated against the cold, the VOS will specify these two violations, the prospective tenant will sign the VOS, and the transaction can take place.

Deregulation

Required Reading

Regulation via VSG, VOS, and inspection agency, opens up many enterprise opportunities not currently possible. In highly regulated areas such as medicine, deregulation will dramatically bring down costs. The desire to save money and get a cash rebate will drive prices lower.

Deregulation will be a major factor in driving down medical costs. Perhaps the biggest test of the VOS and the free market would be Joe's Brain Surgery Shack. For this and more on medicine and medical deregulation, see *Chapter 11 – The Medical Distribution.*

Deregulation will allow people to exchange large risk for large reward. Perhaps the easiest way is to be a human guinea pig. Early trials of untested pharmaceuticals will command top dollar. Drug companies will likely be required by the VSG to accurately spell out all the risks based on animal trials and past data. Perhaps a 20% risk of death will earn $200,000. For someone hell bent on suicide, an average of 5 trials will bring their family $1,000,000 as a bequest. It sure beats running out into traffic and hoping for a medical rebate by using low-cost options.

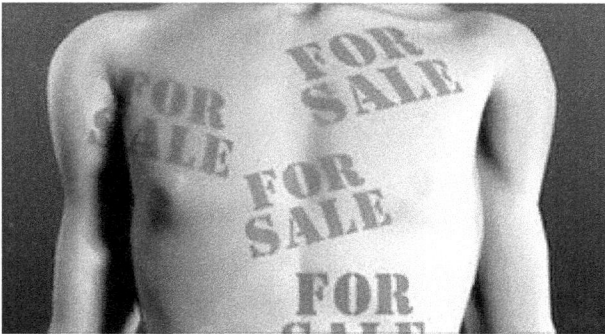

Deregulation allows for the oldest option in high pay, available mostly to the young and attractive. Full-time sex workers, with a VOS attesting to health and safety measures, can expect to earn good money for several years.

The Right to a Safe Workplace

> The right to a safe workplace is also the right to knowingly work in an unsafe workplace, as long as there is VOS sign-off.

The right to a safe workplace follows from the right to life. However, the right to property, and the right to pursue happiness imply the right to work in an unsafe workplace, as well. If you want to hunt the Great White Shark with a spear gun, and you claim to be aware of the dangers, and if someone hires you to do just that, there can be no liability in a free society.

Deregulation benefits both the company with hazardous jobs and the worker willing to work in dangerous occupations. Although OSHA (Occupational Safety and Health Administration) is replaced by VSGs and private inspection agencies, one assumes that workplace health and safety standards in a free society will be as strict, if not stricter, than they are today. The employer, however, is also free to post a workplace VOS with the violations and hire employees only after they have signed the VOS.

Because of the distributions, nobody is forced to work in any job that does not meet their minimum safety requirements. Deregulation opens new opportunities without forcing anyone to violate their own standards or put themselves in a dangerous position.

In today's world, the right to work in an unsafe workplace is often ignored. It is ignored at great cost to business, the worker, and the economy. Often the job simply disappears because it cannot be made safe. The worker loses the right to take on greater risk in exchange for a much higher wage.

Along with the right to an unsafe workplace, is the obligation on the part of the employer to post and explicitly inform workers of industry standards violations. You should expect a safe workplace, just as you would expect the toilet to flush in your hotel room.

Regulators in a free society will not close down businesses that fail to meet a reasonable person's expectation. But they will insist that any workplace deficiencies are prominently posted and are conveyed to the potential worker/patron both verbally and in print. This is all done with the VOS, a violation of standards certificate signed-off by a private regulatory industry, and happily financed by the business to eliminate liability. Failure to meet the terms of your own VOS, however, is fraud, a criminal offense.

Although the workplace or place of business is free from state sanction and legal liability once the deficiencies are properly posted and otherwise conveyed, the right to strike, picket, and leaflet may be exercised, and thus these institutions might not be free from worker/community sanction.

Labor Unions

Required Reading

Freedom of association guarantees the right to form unions and trade organizations of any kind. However, in a world where entrepreneurs will soon outnumber workers, it is hard to imagine any real purpose for these unions beyond camaraderie and the exchange of knowledge. Most new enterprises will be owned by their workers.

There is no right to a job, so a worker can be fired without giving reason, including union organizing. On the other hand, because of the personal distributions, labor practices deemed unfair by the majority of workers, can be met with strike and pickets without fear of starvation or homelessness. Depending on the skill of the striking workforce, the strike can result in, replacement and termination of the striking workers, or the failure of the company, or worker victory, or some combination of these.

The government should not take any position in a labor dispute beyond upholding the natural rights of the participants. "Binding" arbitration requires the voluntary cooperation of all parties. It is not enforceable.

Harassment of replacement workers and sabotage are serious violations of the right to life and the right to property respectively. The state will deal with these severely. Sit-ins and occupations are violations of the natural right to property but have some standing in that the people are the real owners of the land. They are treated as misdemeanor civil disobedience. Massive occupations by the majority of the community pit the natural right of insurrection against the natural rights of the business owners. Under such circumstances the state and ultimately the electorate, have the option to treat the occupation as civil disobedience and make arrests, facilitate negotiation, or allow the insurrection to run its course.

AFFEERCE should bring about a greater mutual respect between labor and management than exists today. What constitutes labor and what constitutes management will be much more fluid due to a radical shift toward family businesses, mutual partnerships, and entrepreneurship in general. Because of universal distribution, nobody will need a job. This hopefully will end both the deference and condescension often seen today in worker/management relations.

Denial of Service

Required Reading

Denial of service is an important right in a free society. While a VSG for restaurants might allow, as standard, the denial of service to those with poor hygiene, or no shirt, no shoes, no service, in general, a policy to deny service must be explicitly stated on the VOS.

Inclusive discrimination is traditionally more tolerated by the community than exclusive discrimination. Far fewer would be offended by "bookstore for university students only" than "no blacks," "no gays," "no Hispanics," "no Jews," or "no Irish." While both forms of discrimination will be legal if specified clearly on the VOS, the latter is apt to provoke community action, boycotts, civil disobedience and denial of service to the proprietors or those who work in the establishment.

Denial of service to individuals can also be done through the VOS. If the proprietor suspects a customer of shoplifting, defacing, or is engaged in a dispute with that customer, the customer's name can be added to the denial of service section of the VOS. No reason should be listed to prevent libel, while listing the name without a reason might need to be constitutionally protected.

In a free society, denial of service acts more as a deterrent. I suspect it will be infrequently used.

Contracts with the Public – A Legal VOS

Required Reading

In order to have a valid business contract, consideration is required. Mutual consideration holds that both sides must be required to perform an obligation, or there is no contract. For instance, if we both sign a contract where I promise to give you 1 million dollars for no particular reason, that contract is not valid. However, if the contract stipulates that I give you 1 million dollars if you take my garbage out to the curb, and you do in fact take out my garbage, the contract is valid (although a judge might modify the terms based on the objective theory of value). The act of taking out the garbage is called in legal parlance, consideration. In other words, you did something for the money. It was a legal trade.

In AFFEERCE, the scope of consideration is expanded to include two new ideas: votes in an election and requests for anonymous funding.

The secret ballot will be enforced by high security software. Whether or not you voted, however, is public information. Being elected as representative to the N+1 cell is a social contract, in other words, consideration in an AFFEERCE society.

For instance, a cellular representative could sign a VOS, pledging she will direct a portion of the transportation distribution to be used for a rail extension. The pledge can be contingent on a citizen investor loan to a cellular enterprise or a voter approved tax levy, as long as these are clearly stated in a public position paper. With a signing witness attesting to the politician's sobriety and soundness of mind, a contract will be created. This is not an idle promise of a politician, but an enforceable contract should she win. Failure to implement the plan is fraud, and could result in a heavy fine or penitentiary sentence, although unforeseen obstacles could be mitigating factors.

In addition to votes, the receipt of anonymous funds in response to a plea for funds constitutes consideration in AFFEERCE. With the 2% discretionary tax, everyone will have the means to be charitable. It is important that recipients who solicit donations state exactly what they will do with the money and follow through with their pledge. At times, a specific amount of money may be requested, and the VIP will cancel incoming donations when the limit has been reached. Anonymous donations are consideration. This applies to any charitable organization. Their VOS must specify how the funds will be allocated, especially administration costs. This does not apply to unsolicited donations.

Accuracy of Information

Increasingly, people are getting their news and information online. There is no sure way to identify outright lies, propaganda, distortions, or disguised advertisements. It helps to know the source, but even that, logo and all, can be forged. Yet, the ability to discern accurate information is vital for a free society. There is a technical solution that insures a valid VOS for all online information.

Responsible media and consumers in the appropriate VSG will be in strong agreement that VOS certification is required for all information sources. An inspection agency can determine the accuracy of facts in the previous year's publications. Predictions either come true or they do not. Unverifiable information is problematic.

The information source and its VOS are encrypted with the private key of the inspection agency and further encrypted with the private key of the information source along with a checksum as metadata with every news story, photograph, or opinion piece. The browser decrypts the metadata with the public key of the information source, verifies the checksum to insure the item has not been modified, and then decrypts the VOS to find the accuracy of the information displayed.

Using the technique described above, the internet browser can report on the authenticity and probable accuracy of any news story, photograph, or opinion piece. Technically, this is easily done today. However, ANSI standards are not enforceable; nobody wants Washington regulators dipping their hands in another pie, costing the taxpayers more money. The self-supporting Bureau of Standards, and AFFEERCE requirements for full disclosure on a VOS, will restore truth to online information.

Chapter 10 – Economic Principles

We are free to imagine an ideal society in which all other tasks are almost totally automated and each individual has as much freedom as possible to pursue the goods of education, culture, and health for the benefit of herself and others. Everyone would be by turns teacher or student, writer or reader, actor or spectator, doctor or patient – Thomas Piketty

Introduction

Required Reading

In an AFFEERCE economy, free enterprise means laissez–faire; government has little if anything to do with business except to protect the natural rights of those who engage in commerce. The people, in their wisdom, can by a super plurality, modify this from time to time and place to place, but nothing that cannot be repealed by a simple majority. No legislative body shall ever have the power to modify laissez–faire.

The ownership of private property is absolute, so much so that there is always the option of serving time in a penitentiary rather than surrender a nickel in fines or submit to seizure of personal property (unless such property was obtained by theft).

Although land is owned by the commons, a land rights owner has exclusive control of "their" land if sufficient ground rent is paid to the people. Nobody can seize another's land unless they treble the ground rent paid to the people, and unless the current land rights owner is unable or unwilling to match that ground rent, and unless the trebler pays the current land rights owner 150% of the depreciated value of land improvements.

AFFEERCE is based on the philosophy that free markets are the most efficient way to run an economy, that every human being has a right to sell their labor and the products of their labor, their property and the products of their property for any price they wish, on any terms they wish, with the proviso that contracts that can only be satisfied by violations of natural rights are not enforceable. Fraud and coercion are such violations. So is mandatory indenture. That is, you can sell yourself as a slave, but if you change your mind after a while, no court can force you to satisfy the remainder of the contract in that manner.

AFFEERCE free enterprise is not watered-down free enterprise. Precisely because of universal distribution, free enterprise can do no harm.

I will remind leftists that no other political economy guarantees the right to nutritious meals, the right to warm and safe shelter, the right to unlimited free education, and the right to quality medical care.

There are many rights that spring from the right to property. Despite the claim that the United States is an economy based on the free enterprise system, many property-based rights are abrogated. As shown earlier, the right to property in this and other systems is toxic and conflicts with the rights to life. Abrogated rights include the minimum wage laws. Minimum wage laws not only deny the worker the right to sell their labor at a lesser but competitive wage but extort money from the business paying the tab. Laws requiring more pay for overtime do the same. Regulations that make it difficult to fire a worker make employers reluctant to hire new workers, effectively pushing out of the workforce, retired workers who want to return, and those who wish to learn on the job. Corporate income tax (along with all of the above) causes capital to be expatriated and attacks domestic productivity. Workplace safety standards deny workers the right to take on dangerous jobs in exchange for higher pay. Liability is vague, ambiguous, and unlimited, diverting large amounts of capital into insurance premiums. Small businesses are legally denied the right to cooperate in any manner, even when up against a giant monopoly. In some states, businesses are forced to shut down based on a vote (rarely even a secret ballot) of their workers. Government regulations are often so complex that bribery and clout become the only way to establish a business.

Beyond regulation to protect children and the mentally disabled, all of this is an attack on freedom. It is a fear of losing everything that causes people to surrender their freedom. Such fear is a western industrial extension of the adage that when people are cold and hungry, they will choose tyranny if it means a warm bed and a full stomach for themselves and their children. With AFFEERCE and universal distribution, those fears will wane, and free enterprise shall reign.

The Wealth of the Nation

Required Reading

Your personal wealth is a measure of how much you have of the things in life you find important. If having a cooked meal waiting for you every night after work is important to you, and you have that, you are certainly wealthier than if you did not. If going water skiing every day is important to you, and you can, then you are certainly wealthier than if you could not. If having two dogs and a house in the mountains are important to you, and that is what you have, you are certainly wealthier.

Subjective, Objective, and AFFEERCE Theories of Value

A subjective theory of value says that a product is worth whatever somebody will pay for it. Objective theories use objective criterion for determining value such as the labor that went into the product, or the price realized for the product in an active market. The AFFEERCE theory of value is that the value of a commodity is subjective to the extent that there is no fear, pain, desperate need, ignorance, or other serious distress on the part of the subject. To the extent that these emotions are present, objective theories hold sway. For any transaction, the wealth of the nation increases by the difference between the buyer's subjective valuation of the goods and the seller's objective valuation. Productivity is a measure of these winning transactions, and it is the best measure of the national wealth.

Money has value because it can be traded for something that is important to you, something that will increase your wealth. You save money because a future trade is more important to you than a present one. In a sense, money only increases your wealth when you spend it. A billion dollars will not buy a man dying of thirst in the dessert a drink of water if there is no water. A homeless man sipping at the water fountain is far wealthier.

The subjective theory of value holds that the value of a commodity is equal to the value the owner places on the commodity. This is in contrast to the labor theory of value which holds that the value of a commodity is equal to the sum of all the labor that went into it, or other objective theories. Both seem to tap into deep truths[TN4.01]. In an AFFEERCE economy, we recognize that the subjective theory drives most transactions, while the objective theory is the primary tool of judicial equity. These are combined in an AFFEERCE theory of value.

There are emotions attached to money. The critical emotion is fear; fear that you will not have money to trade for something important in the future. This fear leads to the emotion of love for money in and of itself. We can picture Ebenezer Scrooge, picking up a handful of coins, letting them fall through his fingers as his face lights with joy. There is also the profligate use of money, we might consider hate, such as throwing money away gambling on long shots that are really no shots, or spending all one's money on things that have no importance at all. At the root of this, we find Karl Marx's fetishism of commodities.

As against this, the commodity-form, and the value-relation of the products of labor within which it appears have absolutely no connection with the physical nature of the commodity and the material relations arising out of this. It is nothing but the definite social relation between men themselves which assumes here, for them, the fantastic form of a relation between things... I call this the fetishism which attaches itself to the products of labor as soon as they are produced as commodities, and is therefore inseparable from the production of commodities. — *Karl Marx* FTN10.02

Some claim the fetishism of commodities is not a problem. If Scrooge values the money, in and of itself, in a free society, he has every right to do so. They confuse having a right and what is good for society. Some say, what people do freely is good for society, and what is good for society is people doing things freely.

Suppose Warren Buffet were drowning and a passerby had ready access to a life preserver. "Help," cries Warren, "throw me the life preserver!" "Will you give me all your money?" asks the passerby. "Yes," cries Warren, "just throw it, please!"

The subjective theory of value correctly asserts that at the moment of drowning, the life preserver was worth to Warren Buffet his entire estate. And in a free society, the passerby is not obligated to throw the life preserver. So is this contract valid?

It is absolutely clear, in this extreme case, that the objective theory of value has some merit. The labor of throwing in the preserver is worth no more than a few cents. No judge, in a sane society, would ever consider the contract valid, even though it meets the definition of a valid contract perfectly.

The motivation for the fetishism of commodities is the fear of not having money to trade for something important at a later date. The motive of the contract with Warren Buffet's was his fear of drowning. In both instances the motive was fear.

The AFFEERCE theory of value is that the value of a commodity is subjective to the extent that there is no fear, pain, desperate need, ignorance, or other serious distress on the part of the subject. To the extent that these emotions are present, the objective theory of value holds sway. That objective theory, however, is not the labor theory, if possible, but one where value is determined by the outcome of a large number of similar transactions in the marketplace.

The free market works because the value of what you have is worth more to me than anything else the money you are charging would buy. You can get something worth more to you from the money you are charging than the thing you are selling. AFFEERCE theory tells us it is good to eliminate fear, pain, ignorance, desperate need and serious distress, both to enrich our souls and help the market operate more efficiently.

Selling a mentally disabled person the Empire State Building for $100 and handing them a mini-replica after they agree to the sale, might not be fraudulent, but a judge will invoke the objective theory of value, if he or she does not revoke the entire contract. Unlimited free education will help to reduce ignorance, but ignorance can never be completely eliminated. In the vast region between fraud and the subjective theory of value lies judicial application of the objective theory. This is how it should be.

It is also worth noting that because pain and suffering will always be a part of illness, the objective theory of value has a role to play in quality healthcare. Charging $20 for an aspirin, because the market will bear it is unacceptable. However, deregulation will drastically bring down the high cost of health care. (For more, see *Chapter 11 - The Medical Distribution.*)

Although complete elimination of these negative emotional/physical states is not possible, AFFEERCE deals a knock-out punch to the fundamental underlying economic fear. The distributions put the full force of society behind the notion that tomorrow, come what may, there will always be food, shelter, unlimited education, and quality medical care.

With the fear of not having enough money for the future gone, AFFEERCE transactions become mostly win-win transactions. Each party to the transaction increases their wealth. While it is logically impossible to measure the cumulative subjective wealth, we can measure when wealth increases, by counting transactions; the more transactions, the greater the increase in wealth.

For any transaction, the wealth of the nation increases by the difference between the buyer's subjective valuation of the goods and the seller's objective valuation. This wealth increase is independent of price. Price determines how the buyer and seller share this increased wealth, but not the wealth itself which is fixed at the difference between the two valuations. This is impossible to compute, since the size of the win is subjective, but a count of the number of transactions is objective and measureable.

For the business consumer that buys labor, machines, and tools, the size of the win can be measured by the amount of product that these workers, machines, and tools produce. What is the win from the transaction of purchasing a machine? It is the thousands of wins from the transactions of goods produced using the machine. Productivity is a measure of these winning transactions, and it is the best measure of the national wealth.

The traditional components of productivity, the generators of winning transactions, are investment, innovation, skills, enterprise, and competition. [FTN10.03] Unlike today, there are two other major contributors to productivity in an AFFEERCE economy: the family division of labor, and the family economies of scale.

How Does AFFEERCE Contribute to National Wealth?

Required Reading

Investment

Government borrowing + total investment = savings + foreign investment.

This well-known equation describes the big problem with total investment in the U.S. Since government borrowing is high and savings so low, only by the grace of foreign investment do we have any investment at all. Investment is the main driver of productivity and productivity the main driver of national wealth. To make matters worse, regulatory obstacles to business might create situations in some industries where there would be no incentive to invest regardless of how low the interest rate is.

In an AFFEERCE economy, savings in a future-baby account are the only way to fund a child. With an estimated funding level of $10,000, this will be a major component of personal savings. Employees and entrepreneurs are further enticed to save wages and profits because these are not taxed until spent. The AFFEERCE Treasury will have a baby-tax reserve fund and one year advance ground rent payments of over $5 trillion, based on a 2002 population of 290 million. Excessive savings will not only satisfy our wildest investment needs, but provide considerable capital for investing abroad and spreading AFFEERCE to other nations.

Innovation

In an AFFEERCE society, like no society before, innovators of all social classes will have the free time to exercise their genius and love of craft, research and develop ideas, and partake in free education. There will be freedom to implement an innovation without fear of catastrophic failure leading to loss of one's home and medical care. With this freedom to pursue one's dreams wherever they may lead, working in the arts and crafts can lead to unexpected innovation.

The rewards for innovation are large and equitable with the intellectual property distribution. This distribution makes all content free (e-books, software, music, videos, e-zines, etc.) and greatly reduces the price of medicine, machinery, theater, and hard-copy. Innovators are rewarded based on demand and sharing, not monopoly and restriction of supply.

Spending as much on intellectual property as we do today, could easily result in wealth that is 5 to 6 times greater than today.

Skills

Unlimited free education allows anyone, with the ability, to acquire whatever skills they want or need. Abolition of the minimum wage can make on-the-job training a profitable venture for business. Lifetime academic royalties will encourage businesses and trade organizations to establish specialty schools and online courses (See, *Chapter 11 – The Education Distribution*).

Enterprise

Large families, with the distributions, division of labor and economies of scale, are ripe for the creation of new enterprise. Unpaid labor is the main building block of new enterprise. Because of universal distribution, all labor in the initial stage of a new enterprise can be surplus (unpaid) labor.

Citizen investors control $5 trillion of capital for small and medium enterprise. This money is available for capital expenditures outlined in a business plan. It cannot be used, and is not needed for salaries. This is VIP enforced. With the only risk being depreciation risk, interest rates for these mutual collectives are very low.

The ability of small businesses to collude in the division of territory and setting of prices further encourages their formation. Enhanced worker mobility, no right to a job, no minimum wage, and the elimination of financial fear, not only serve to foster the formation of new enterprise but to reorient existing firms.

Competition

The large family business or mutual organization has a competitive advantage over established larger businesses because all workers directly benefit from ownership. The distributions provide an additional marginal advantage that cannot be matched with a more traditional organization.

Trebling provides a new form of competition in the base case where diversity is limited by population. For example, if a community of 300 supports a single grocery store, rather than the folly of opening up a competing store, the trebler competes for the single store, providing citizens with the full benefits of location monopoly.

The Family Division of Labor

The family division of labor and family economy of scale play an even larger role in wealth creation than simply enhancing enterprise and competition. We defined personal wealth as having those things that are important to you. If engaging in creative activity, education, relaxation, meditation, and play are important to you, then time is important to you.

If you live alone, you are shopper, cook, dishwasher, launderer, bill payer, fix-it person, otherwise employed worker, and housekeeper. Either you are wealthy enough to pay for domestic help, and/or retired with income, or there is little or no time for solitary pursuits. Some can engage in their art only at the expense of living poorly.

Nothing frees up time like the division of labor. In large AFFEERCE families, chores can be divided based on ability and intra-family markets. Suppose the only task for a creative member of such a family is doing 4 hours of family laundry a day. During those four hours, the innovator could take notes and engage in deep thought. The rest of the day is free for personal pursuits. Meals are prepared and served, the bed is made, and all shopping is done by others. This particular family member, currently bringing in no income to the family beyond the distributions, is probably wealthier than the vast majority of people today. And should the innovator be successful, the fruits of his labor will add significant material wealth to him and his family. And it will add even more to the wealth of the nation.

In large families, the division of labor can create immense wealth by using members for home schooling, elder care, and home business. Very large families and communes can tap into distribution dollars that go to higher levels of dominion.

The Family Economy of Scale

Even with AFFEERCE distributions, it is tough for a single person to find a small studio with utilities for $370 a month. It is much easier, however, for a couple to find a nice one bedroom for $740 a month. It is even easier still for a couple with two children to find a three bedroom apartment, with rec room, and utilities for $1480 a month. In an AFFEERCE economy, ten people can live in large homes with private bedrooms. Twenty could afford a swimming pool and gym, and perhaps even a ballroom with the $7400 distribution. Universal distribution radically changes the culture in favor of very large families. Although the freedom to live alone is inviolable and something that many will wish to do at some points in their lives, the cultural shift to large families is unstoppable due to the economies of scale.

Once upon a time there lived a pair of monks, one old and one young.

'What are the differences between Heaven and Hell?' the young monk asked the learned master.

'There are no material differences,' replied the old monk peacefully.

'None at all?' asked the confused young monk.

'Yes. Both Heaven and Hell look the same. They both have a dining hall and tables laden with a bountiful feast' said the old priest. 'The diners are seated in comfort with huge chopsticks attached to their arms at the elbow to reach the delicious food.'

'In the case of Hell,' continued the old priest, 'people are always starved because no matter how hard they try, they fail to get the food into their mouths.'

'But doesn't the same thing happen to the people in Heaven?' the junior questioned.

'No," explained the old monk. 'They feed each other.' [FTN10.04]

The economy of scale, in conjunction with the division of labor, creates an unbelievable benefit in the food distribution. At $220 per person per month, the family of ten has a $2,200 per month food distribution. The family shopper will buy raw foodstuffs in bulk, and the family chef will convert these meats, grains, produce, and spices into daily banquets, turning a single person's meager food distribution into bountiful abundance by the economy of scale. Wealth is created!

Extremely large families can employ economy of scale and division of labor to bring in additional distribution money by handling municipal duties within the family compound such as law enforcement and sanitation. Fire protection and transportation distributions are available to smaller families in rural areas.

Profit and Location Value

All profits for companies that own their own land, save the profits from normal risk return, innovation and unpaid labor, come from location value!

For that matter, even companies that do not own their own land, get the majority of their profits from location value uncollected by the landlord. Most business owners will deny the majority of their profits come from location value, insisting that it is excellent service or efficient processes. But excellent service is paid for with wages. To the extent it is unpaid, it is time donated to the corporation by the employees; unpaid labor. Although unpaid labor does contribute to profit, it tends to dissipate as employees catch on and either demand full compensation, resign in anger, or engage in subtle sabotage. Only the owners gladly engage in unpaid labor, which is why employees are often compensated with stock options. Efficient processes lead to profits from innovation. But unless that innovation is patent protected as an intellectual property monopoly, competitors will quickly adopt the innovation, likely improving on it as they benefit from non-first use.

So while unpaid labor and innovation, can temporarily boost profit, the bulk of ongoing profit is from location value. As always, the best way to prove this is by placing the identical business in the Wyoming badlands. How profitable will the business be then?

Consider 2 identical factories, one 50, the other 200 miles from a major city. The more distant has a higher cost to import raw materials, export product, and attract skilled labor. Profits at the closer factory are due to location value.

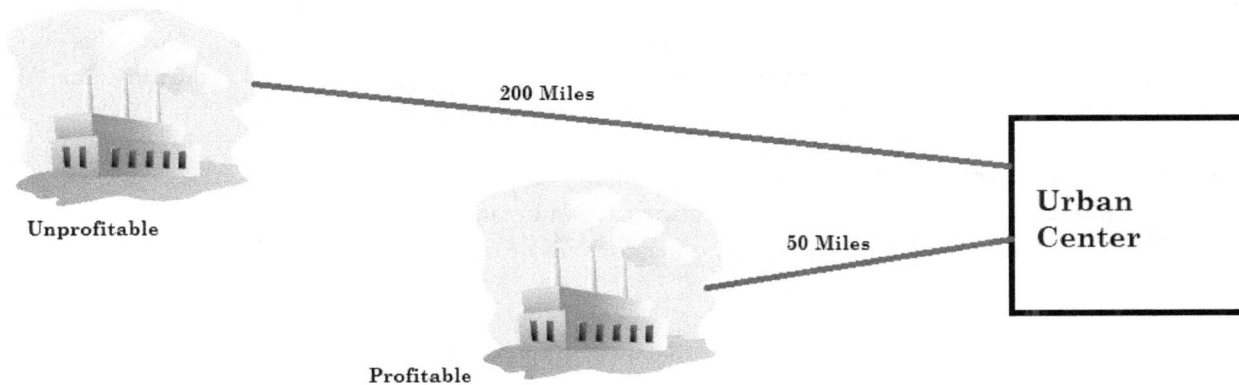

The risk rate of return can generate significant profit (or loss), but only at the metaphorical cost of being unable to sleep at night. The risk-free rate of return is rather paltry. At the time of this writing it is very close to 0% or even negative after inflation.

In an AFFEERCE economy, how will a business generate profit? Not insignificantly, unpaid labor will play a larger role. Unpaid labor is driven by emotion. Certainly, there are the negative emotions; fear of losing one's job, fear of the boss, fear of asking for a raise. But in a Georgist society, it is the positive emotions that will predominate; belief in the company and wanting to make it strong, desire to help a coworker, team spirit, shared goals. Because the distinction between workers and owners will be blurred in a world of collectives and large family businesses, unpaid labor will be gladly given, helping to create the profit needed for growth.

More significantly, AFFEERCE will see a major transformation in the source of business profits. Over the decades, or even centuries, the major source of profits will shift from location value to innovation. The intellectual property distribution will increasingly add directly to the bottom line of businesses that patent their products and processes. As other companies freely copy those good ideas, the patenting business's intellectual property distribution will grow even larger.

Trebling leaves significant profitable location value for those who compute a fair ground rent. If the rent is too low, matching a treble could temporarily boost the rent to over 100% location value until it drops back into a profitable range at the rate of 10%/year. A company that sets a fair ground rent, however, should still be able to profit from location value.

Competition, Collusion, and Monopoly

> **The right to try and form a monopoly or collude with competitors is not only a protected natural right, but an essential tool to enhance competition. Predatory practices that do not violate laws against extortion or fraud, can still be fought through community action, or Class II legislation.**

Businesses can decide in collusion to raise prices. However, there can be no enforceable contract of collusion. If one of the businesses decides they are not going to raise their prices, they cannot be forced to do so. Businesses can agree to a division of territory, but once again, there can be no enforceable contract of collusion. Thus, despite the agreement, all businesses are legally free to sell in every territory.

The big, evil monopoly is a mythological beast. Every business is a monopoly of some kind, even if it is only a monopoly on location or brand. No business is an "evil monopoly" unless it engages in extortion or other forms of violence to stop competition, or is protected from competition by law. In the case of the medical or pharmaceutical industry today, that protection takes the form of imprisonment of the competition. However, perhaps the biggest form of government protection against competition has to do with intellectual property. AFFEERCE blows this out of the water in a way that protects the innovator better than current patent and copyright law and at the same time provides maximum benefit to society. (See, *Chapter 3 – Intellectual Property Distribution*).

Another common form of government violence in support of monopoly is the law against collusion. Recently we have seen small booksellers fall one by one to the online giants, in part because these booksellers have been unable to fix prices, combine catalogs, have a joint website, or any other cooperative effort the government has deemed illegal[FTN10.22]. Divided they fall.

Collusion by small producers is a powerful weapon to insure competition in a free market. It favors competitive markets that keep monopoly costs down and prevents inefficiencies from developing. AFFEERCE family businesses will be primary units of collusion. The members of these families, as owners of the business, will work for little pay and can take advantage of the household economies of scale, thereby gaining a competitive advantage. In collusion, these family businesses can divide territory and fix prices.

Monopoly of one kind or another, cornering some market, is a worthy aspiration for business. It increases the likelihood of a handsome profit. Trebling leaves a small monopoly on location value that can be exploited. That is particularly true if one is able to use that location value better than everyone else. If there is not even a monopoly of brand, then the product is merely a commodity, subject to commodity pricing.

Because monopolies often supply goods and services on a very large scale, they can take advantage of the economies of scale. These cost savings lead to both lower prices for the consumer and an increase in monopoly profits. Those increased profits are often invested in research and development, leading to even more economic growth. A higher ground rent is required to protect profits. Monopolies, by virtue of their market ownership, are in the position to set uniform standards. Such uniformity encourages new businesses to develop (e.g. applications for Microsoft's Windows, or applications for Apple's iPhone.)

For a business to achieve monopoly status, it must successfully navigate through a sea of competitors and potential competitors. Only then, has it proven itself so efficient that others could not hope to compete. This makes monopolies very beneficial. However, that benefit is lost completely, if other businesses do not have the right to compete in collusion. That benefit is certainly lost if the full force of the law is not brought down swiftly on business agents who use extortion, fraud, and other forms of violence to promote their business.

Community action can also be brought to bear against predatory business practices. Pickets, leaflets, strikes and rallies can be used. If the situation is acute, peaceful civil disobedience can be employed. A super plurality can pass a law if this is a case of a conflict in natural rights.

A hard-fought fight between the community and the predatory business may lead to a far better solution than the passage of a law. This goes against current wisdom. "We are a government of laws, not men." However, the friction between business and community, either today, or in an AFFEERCE society, does not go away, but is pushed into the background by the passage of the law. It can fester for years to come.

Citizen Investors

> The ground rent is paid a year in advance. This is over $4 trillion, for a population of 290 million. Money from the $10,000 baby tax is amortized over the life of an individual. After several generations, there will be an average of at least $5,000 per person or about $1.5 trillion dollars for a population of 290 million. Thus, at any given time the AFFEERCE Treasury will hold about $5.5 trillion dollars. This money must be invested and any growth above about 1% annually will exceed objectives. It is invested in small business, and collectives by the citizen investors.

How can this $5.5 billion be equitably and successfully invested? The cellular government can't do it without showing favoritism. Cronyism, corruption, and low returns would inevitably follow. Such a large purse in the hands of a few is a real danger to freedom.

Any citizen can become an investor of the Treasury's accumulated funds. It can be a very profitable, yet stressful, career choice. The following account is, of course, speculative. The actual requirements will not be set by me.

There will be a 6 month intense course (all education is free and unlimited) on investing, reporting, searching for opportunities, evaluating business plans, diversification, safety, and so on. This will be followed by an internship.

The interns research new enterprises seeking venture capital. Filling this need is the prime mission of citizen investors. However, cultivating these enterprises often takes years before the business plan is perfected, so the intern will be assigned to seek out and work with a promising enterprise, perhaps earlier rejected by other citizen investors due to a poor business plan. The student intern will work together with the entrepreneurs to perfect the plan. When the plan is approved by the school, the investment will be made.

With $5.5 trillion in available funds, there will be more capital than promising business plans. The citizen investor must be proficient in trading standard financial instruments. Interns, following completion of the 6 month course, are given $500,000 of the Treasury's money to invest in a portfolio of stocks and bonds of existing companies, bank instruments, and so on. Students discuss their portfolios daily and learn how to react and not react to changing conditions. At the end of the year, portfolios are priced. Students with portfolios priced under $500,000 are eliminated from the program until they make up the difference from their own funds or longer term notes appreciate in value. Those students who show a profit will sell their assets (investor years are completely staggered) and take 50% of the profit for themselves. The remaining profit and principle is returned to the Treasury. Half of that remaining profit is an insurance policy against future losses. Intentional losses and schemes to defraud will be prosecuted.

Annual portfolios are repeated until the business plan of the small enterprise is approved and the loan made. With successful repayment of that loan, the intern becomes a full-fledged citizen investor and is given funds from the Treasury based on relative performance over the previous year. Excellence is a consistent 4% return or better. Citizen investors should expect capital under management to double every year a 4% or better is returned. Capital under management will stay nearly constant from year to year with a consistent 2% return. With a 4% return, $500,000 under management will become about $500 million in 10 years and max out at $5.5 billion five years later, the maximum under management per citizen investor being 1/1000 of the total Treasury assets. Payout for citizen investors can be enormous. $500,000 at 4% pays a 50% commission of $10,000. Ten years and a consistent 4% annual return later, the annual commission is over $5 million. Commissions will be greater if returns exceed 4%.

Possible Investment Returns	
Insured bank deposit	.5%
Highest quality corporate bonds	2.0%
Distribution assured 23 year mortgage	3.0%
Income assured 23 year mortgage	4.0%
Best business plans	5.0%
Business plans where venture is at high risk, but principle recovery is fairly certain.	6.0%
Risky but well thought out business plans	7.0%

Losses up to half of profits turned into the Treasury will not lead to expulsion from the program, but might result in a considerably smaller portfolio in the following year, based on formulas used and relative performance. Losses greater than half the profits turned into the Treasury must be made up from the investors own funds, or they will be expelled from the program. Throughout the citizen investor's career, they have free access to professors, research tools, and ongoing apprentice daily discussions, investor discussion groups, resources they are encouraged to employ at the slightest concern, and for networking or socializing. Professors and personal tutors will go out of their way to help former students due to achievement annuities (See, *Chapter 11 – The Education Distribution*).

Because this is the citizen's money, investment rules for different asset classes will be strict. There will be rules for trading stocks and bonds on the secondary market, issuing mortgages, and foreign ventures. Most important are the rules for domestic startups – family businesses, communes, and collectives – the primary focus of the citizen investor as venture capitalist.

AFFEERCE is a nation of entrepreneurs and the legion of citizen investors will scour the nation providing venture capital to those whose business plans pass muster. The primary rule is critical: **Venture capital can only be used for approved capital expenditures.**

Significantly, this DOES NOT include paying for services, wages or salary. It does include ground rent, machinery, tools, raw materials, and inventory for sale. One or more credit accounts are established that are VIP-constrained to allow purchase of only specific items. A sinking fund for debt repayment is automatically funded with an agreed on percentage or amount of revenue at time of sale. Failure to meet agreed objectives could result in a repossession of capital. Unjustified shrinkage could result in prosecution. The rules are tough, but the availability of capital for the small business is unprecedented.

FAQ – Citizen Investor Start-Up Capital	
What if I need to hire workers?	Invite them into the collective as limited part owners, or pay with scrip.
Before there are earnings, my owners are having a tough time on the distributions. We need a raise.	Form a family or tight-knit community where economy of scale and division of labor create wealth. This increases business synergy. Trade limited ownership to an outside-employed spouse for wage capital. Accept charity.
We need to hire someone with a special skill that none of the current owners possess. What if no skilled laborer wants to join our collective?	Education is free and unlimited. Send some of your owners to school. It costs nothing but down time.
If we fail, and the capital goods repossessed, are we liable for the rent which cannot be refunded?	No. It came from the citizens and has already been returned to the citizens.
What if the business is trebled?	Typically the sinking fund will exceed the capital depreciation so the loan will be repaid and you will receive cash back of 50% or more of the loan amount. Restart at half cost or just retire rich.
My customers expect me to drive up in a BMW wearing a custom-tailored suit. Are these legitimate capital expenditures?	No! I'm sorry. The citizen investors are not interested in funding your business at this time.

With a $5.5 trillion pot and a million citizen investors, the average capital under management will be $5.5 million, earning the average successful citizen investor $110,000 per year. With one citizen investor for every 300 people, the streets will be awash in capital. A good citizen investor will be a free business consultant, building a network of small businesses, collectives, large families and other potential entrepreneurs, suggesting capital improvements for existing businesses and helping new businesses develop a sound business plan, as well as suggest courses for skills acquisition. Until a good opportunity is developed, capital under management can be invested conservatively in traditional portfolios.

Successful citizen investors with large capital under management will find it highly profitable to invest in the developing world. This neo-colonialism is the major ingredient in bringing AFFEERCE and prosperity to the Third World. Shuddering leftists should repeat the mantra, "In AFFEERCE, the right to property can do no harm."

Scrip

Required Reading

When a small business has an outstanding loan from citizen investors, or when a for-profit cellular enterprise is not profitable, salaries cannot be paid from revenue. For collective owners, universal distribution allows them to work for nothing, until the loan is repaid and the business is profitable. This kind of risk is impossible in today's economy for those who aren't wealthy to begin with.

For private enterprise with a citizen investor loan, paid services from non-owners is sometimes a necessity. For cellular enterprises, workers are not owners, and must be paid in good times and bad. This is done with a virtual currency called scrip. Scrip is denominated in VIP$ and held at the Treasury in personal accounts. Scrip is backed by faith in a particular enterprise. Thus all scrip is different. Scrip backed by Company X would be held in a separate account than scrip backed by Company Y.

Scrip must be redeemed from profits before any salaries or dividends can be paid. Scrip is senior to all loans except citizen investor loans. Scrip will be redeemed at random by the Treasury assuring equity. Redeemed scrip will be transferred from a scrip account to a corporate account.

Trickle-down and Bubble-up Economics

Required Reading

Trickle-Down

With so much money concentrated in the top 1%, why isn't more of it being invested in the U.S. today?

Trickle-down economics is the simple idea that concentrated capital has no other use than to be invested in new businesses, and hence increase wealth. However, it is not the wealth of the nation, but the wealth of the world. With labor so much cheaper abroad, all that money has instead been trickling down into former third-world countries that now experience tremendous growth[FTN10.05].

In small doses, building-up third world countries is a noble thing, but not at the expense of dragging millions of Americans into poverty, and destroying the very foundations of our economy. Furthermore, rapid redistribution of global wealth carries the high price-tag of culture shock. Third-world countries have a hard time reconciling primitive superstition with nuclear reactors. As we have seen, the rapid evaporation of wealth in the industrialized countries has also been accompanied by "culture wars."

Bubble-Up

Bubble-up economics is the simple idea that by providing monetary resources to the poor, small business will be attracted to the poorest neighborhoods, and thus increase the wealth of the nation. However, any stimulus is only a stimulus inasmuch as small businesses are created. One time payments do little or nothing in creating an incentive for businesses to form. Since 1980, there have been significant cuts to entitlements outside of the more universal Social Security and Medicare.

> By the end of Reagan's term in office federal assistance to local governments was cut 60 percent. Reagan eliminated general revenue sharing to cities, slashed funding for public service jobs and job training, almost dismantled federally funded legal services for the poor, cut the anti-poverty Community Development Block Grant program and reduced funds for public transit. The only "urban" program that survived the cuts was federal aid for highways – which primarily benefited suburbs, not cities.

> These cutbacks had a disastrous effect on cities with high levels of poverty and limited property tax bases, many of which depended on federal aid. In 1980 federal dollars accounted for 22 percent of big city budgets. By the end of Reagan's second term, federal aid was only 6 percent.

> The consequences were devastating to urban schools and libraries, municipal hospitals and clinics, and sanitation, police and fire departments – many of which had to shut their doors.[FTN10.06]

With few exceptions, these cuts have continued through the Obama administration[FTN10.07]. This has caused a shuttering of businesses in the poor communities, and a decrease in the national wealth.

Strangling the Economy
Required Reading

Between the loss of trickle-down capital to third-world nations and the loss of bubble-up capital to the budget deficit, America's economy is being strangled from both ends. Nowhere is this felt harder than in the African-American community where youth unemployment hovers around 49%[FTN10.08]. This is a holocaust, which if left unaddressed, can only have revolution or an unspeakably monstrous reaction as its outcome.

AFFEERCE is the answer. Entitlement spawns new business in formerly poor and lower-middle class areas. As a result, the wealth of the nation will increase dramatically. This is bubble-up on steroids. But amazingly, the more we practice bubble-up, the greater the effectiveness of trickle-down!

In a free market, capital that is more efficiently used in this country does not go abroad. In a free market, without a minimum wage, there is always full employment! Jobs are available at every skill level. Universal distribution ensures there will be domestic workers anxious to fill low-paying jobs. Capital will not go abroad. In fact, universal distribution is a form of protectionism. No non-AFFEERCE nation could hope to compete with an AFFEERCE economy. This is called the mercantile advantage. It is the dynamic force that spreads AFFEERCE from the viral community to the entire world.

The Detroit Auto Bailout - Too Big to Fail

> **The distributions end too big to fail by dampening the effects of failure. Falling ground rents allow industry in a temporary setback to catch up. They also allow more efficient users of the machinery to treble and take over the business.**

The auto industry bailout of 2008 was a classic example of the conflict between modern liberalism and classical liberalism. Failure to bailout the auto industry in 2008 would have resulted in disaster. Let's look at why bailouts are wrong, yet necessary, today, and how the same situation would unfold in an AFFEERCE economy.

There are a number of reasons why it is a violation of natural rights for the state to bail out an industry. They are:

1. Money is being taken from the taxpayers, without consent, and invested in a company from which the taxpayer will receive no profit.
2. Other companies, which receive no funds, are being placed at a disadvantage by a government whose job it is to protect their right to property.
3. A company using technology and methods that failed them in the open market is being rewarded for these bad decisions, while the efficiencies of the free market would have caused that company to fail.
4. Bailouts protect a company from competition. Protectionism by one country leads to protectionism in other countries and serves as a barrier to free international trade.

For these reasons, libertarians and libertarian-oriented Republicans were against the Detroit auto bailout, and to a lesser extent, the Wall Street bailouts of 2007 and 2008. And yet they happened. Why?

It is not as though Democrats were blind to these fundamental economic facts, even if the terminology of natural rights they use is different. It's just that they saw something obvious, something that most of those who call themselves conservative or libertarian or objectivist refuse to acknowledge. They knew that allowing the free market to take its course for companies that are "too big to fail," will result in major economic depression, probable revolution, or worse still, a complete breakdown of society.

The best possible outcome, were Detroit allowed to fail, would be workers seizing the auto industrial plants, and re-opening them under collective ownership. In the worst case, feudal enclaves would be established and armed raiders would go on missions to steal food and other supplies. It is unlikely that any national consensus could be reached to deal with either of those outcomes. Barbarism would ripple out from Detroit and envelop the nation.

Perhaps this is exaggeration but that can't really be known until it happens. I agree with the far left that the greatest contradiction of the free market, absent universal distribution, is that it will create the objective conditions to terminate itself, and do so with "extreme prejudice."

What would happen in AFFEERCE?

In every region, a significant portion of AFFEERCE productivity is generated from the distributions, as food and shelter are a large part of consumption. Family-based small business, shielded from catastrophic failure and with a competitive advantage from family based division of labor and economy of scale, will in all likelihood flourish.

There is no longer the concept of "too big to fail." Depressions are impossible on the bedrock of the distributions. Instead, business failures are an opportunity.

As the auto industry began to lose money, ground rents would drop to help support the bottom line. Depreciation funds would be spent elsewhere. If the company does not recover from these advantages, both depreciation and lower ground rents increase the likelihood of a treble. Bondholders will welcome a treble since 150% ODV will likely pay off most of the outstanding debt, although liens from non-payment of ground rents would be excluded.

Instead of seizing the plant, several hundred workers might temporarily forego children and move their future-baby accounts into a joint business corporate account, in exchange for shares. Given a good business plan, they could then obtain a trebler mortgage from the citizen investors.

If the workers have a plan for a new company direction, there is no catastrophic risk in foregoing future-baby or risking other savings. The distributions form a safety net through which none can fall.

Starting fresh, and with new insight, this worker collective could start up a lean and profitable auto enterprise. The local economy would barely miss a beat and, a year or so down the road, would be healthier than before the failure.

Minimum Wage

There is no natural right to a minimum wage. It is a violation of an employer's natural rights, to demand, under force of law that they pay more for services rendered than those services are worth. It is a violation of every worker's right to negotiate a fair contract of employment. With universal distribution, any wage is a living wage.

The current fight for a higher minimum wage is a logical consequence of the destruction of the middle class. The consequences in today's economy go beyond denying the employer's natural rights. After all, they have no problem denying worker's rights. However, a higher minimum wage turns the poor against the very poor in a bid for the fewer jobs that remain. Forcing an increase would be beneficial to the more educated of the poor, but would reduce the total number of jobs overall. It isn't even a Robin Hood type regulation that takes from the rich and gives to the poor. Instead, it takes from the very poor, shut-out of the labor market, and gives to the poor. By shutting out the unskilled worker, a minimum wage lowers productivity, and decreases the wealth of the nation, stealing from everyone. It also reduces the solidarity of the working class and hence the chance of insurrection. The only other beneficiaries of the minimum wage are a few unions that want to keep out poor and minority workers, or protect their jobs from competition.

Piketty argues that if the minimum wage is less than the marginal productivity of the worker, increasing the minimum wage will not result in increased unemployment provided it stays below the worker's marginal productivity. Various studies in the United States between 1980 and 2000 showed that the minimum wage had fallen so low it could be raised without any loss of employment[FTN10.19].

Even if few jobs are actually lost, the "final robber," as Henry George put it, will steal all that was gained. In the introduction we saw that if the minimum wage goes up in a city with low unemployment, workers will be attracted to the city and rents will rise to steal all benefits of the increased wage.

There is no minimum wage in an AFFEERCE economy. Universal distribution renders the idea of a "living wage" moot. This will expose a whole new class of jobs whose marginal productivity is far below today's minimum wage. Classically, this includes the artist who takes a break of a few hours a day to pick up litter at a corporate site for $3 an hour and much needed exercise.

Elimination of the minimum wage in an AFFEERCE universal distribution economy creates guaranteed full employment. It means that business must pay workers what they are worth in order to keep them, leading to wage increases for competent workers. It allows unskilled workers to compete with machines. It offers wage cuts as a possible solution for otherwise competent but very laid-back workers; the ones who have a life beyond work and are perfectly happy getting by on the lower wage. In today's world, the laid-back are fired, and only those who sell their soul to the company can keep their jobs.

Elimination of the minimum wage makes it easy for anyone to enter their chosen field, even if it will take them several years to get up to speed. And it makes it easy for bored retirees to come back and dabble in their old professions, even though technology has moved on.

All income is discretionary in an AFFEERCE economy, so employment for wages is optional. However, for those with addictions, with no worries over food or shelter, as little as $2 of discretionary income an hour, or even less, can seem a bonanza.

For the vast majority, lack of a minimum wage will be irrelevant. Developing skills through unlimited, free education allows the best students to set their own price. It is a simple formula. The more useful one's skills, the greater that person's worth in the job market. There is no necessity to work until one's skillset is commensurate with the salary demanded. The only time lack of a minimum wage might directly affect the salaries of those who seek professional careers through study, would be for internships taken early on to get one's feet wet in a chosen profession, or when returning many years after retirement.

Elimination of the minimum wage is a great liberator. It stops legislated overpayment for services, and it creates 100% full employment. The likely trend toward mutual organizations in business, should have little effect on the wages of apprentice or part-time labor.

Because of universal distribution, the concept of a living wage is gone. No wage, no matter how small, is in conflict with the natural right to life.

Trust

Honesty and trust are essential for the smooth operation of free markets. As Joseph Stiglitz points out in *The Price of Inequality*, the system would fail if most contracts had to be enforced in a court of law, or if individuals cheated on every contract, so long as they could get away with it. We expect honesty in those we deal with. Without that expectation, markets could not survive[FTN10.23].

As an example, Stiglitz points to the collapse of the Soviet Union. Trust was completely lost under the Communist dictatorship. In the sudden change from a planned to a market economy, people expected the worst from their trading partners. It was cheat or be cheated. Output declined from Soviet days, and organized crime grew much stronger[FTN10.23].

This also demonstrates a key failure of objectivism. Objectivists believe that trust follows from objective market conditions. They find it inconceivable that objective market conditions could follow from something as subjective as trust. At the very least, the Soviet experience demonstrates that trust is a learned value that follows from objective market conditions only after a significant period of time. In that time, horrendous things can happen.

In the United States, too, Stiglitz points out, trust has been declining as Wall Street, the banks, politicians, and the wealthiest 1%, engage in unfair, unjust, and even criminal behavior with impunity[FTN10.23]. This is one more marker of the U.S. decline into barbarism.

An AFFEERCE society places high value on honesty. There is a criminal penalty for providing false information on a loan application, should the loan go into default. Lawyers are prohibited from lying in court, even in defense of their clients. Prosecutors too, must meet a higher standard of honesty than today. They are obligated to produce all information relevant to the case. Many AFFEERCE businesses will be family businesses where lying would poison the family environment. VIP identities and a significant reduction in crime also increase social capital. Most importantly, the AFFEERCE enlightenment will dispense with moral relativism. It suggests our time on Earth is blessed with meaning and purpose (See *Volume III – The Philosophy*).

As it was years ago, a simple handshake will once again seal a deal.

City Passes

Like the universal auto pass, cities can raise revenue for beaches, parks, zoos, museums, libraries, and other attractions with a city pass. It allows free or reduced price admissions to these attractions. The pass is a VIP application, so no actual physical pass is needed. A city pass will be especially useful for revitalizing Washington D.C., following capitulation. The pass can also be used for reduced or free admission to private businesses, as well. Like the auto pass, the patrons are VIP identified upon entering the venue. The time spent at the venue until the next VIP identification determines funding from the pass. Passes can be used by tourists for free rides on public transit.

Corporations and Why They Pay No Tax

The wealth of a nation is a function of the total value of goods and services produced. Value is determined by the importance each individual puts on those goods and services. In a free society, the natural wage of a worker is equal to their productivity. The more powerful a worker's tools, the more the worker earns. Even in a semi-free society, neither unions, nor bosses, nor politicians can set the wage of a worker for very long before that wage snaps back to the natural wage equal to the worker's productivity.

It is one of government's most important tasks in a free society to insure there are no obstacles placed in the way of making the worker more productive. To this end, nothing shall be done to impede fully investing corporate profits in the development of more productive tools. Such tools not only increase wages, but add to the wealth of the nation. Corporate profits must never be taxed.

Each person in AFFEERCE, upon reaching the age of 14, is automatically given a corporation. They are the sole controller of this corporation through the VIP. The VIP keeps track of all transfers in and out of a personal corporate account. Stocks, bonds, and any other instruments that produce income, interest, dividends or capital gains are purchased in the corporate account, as all income accrues to the corporation consumption tax free.

Capital Expenditures and Purchase Paths

Required Reading

Purchase paths, created on the corporate account, are used to list products that can be purchased without payment of the consumption tax. Separate purchase paths for inventory, machinery, raw materials, furniture, utilities, and supplies, can make the process easier to manage, but only a single purchase path is required. Purchase paths can be associated with subaccounts for particular departments.

Products to be purchased without consumption tax are explicitly placed on a purchase path using the product id assigned to every product. Regardless of where these products are purchased, retail or wholesale, consumption tax will not be paid.

Consumption taxes are geared to the individual. Only individuals can pay a discretionary tax and only individuals have teachers and schools that are to be rewarded for the individual's achievement. An organization is considered the sum of the claims of its individual owners. In the same manner, a cellular enterprise is owned by the dominion's population. The VIP handles the complex computation of the tax for non-exempt purchases.

Products such as meals and lodging will generate red flags at the IRS, when placed on purchase paths. Because the corporate consumption tax is so low to begin with, the VSG might restrict waivers for these products to employees on the road full time.

Foreign capital expenditures, like ordinary foreign spending, require consumption tax payment and purchase of the foreign currency at the current market premium. For non-rogue states, this will automatically disappear when currency, collection, distribution, and intellectual property are at the highest international level.

Rogue states and other dominions using an internal alternative currency, will have distribution income routed to a Treasury account. Capital expenditures imported from this account are subject to the full consumption tax to compensate for 100% rebates on the distributions. Purchase paths do not apply.

Gold and Barter

Required Reading

Transactions paid with gold, foreign or alternative currency or barter are not subject to consumption taxes and invisible in an AFFEERCE economy. Foreign currency in a corporate account must be moved to a spending account or converted to physical notes, through payment of the consumption tax and possible premium, before it can be spent. However, foreign currency can be held in a private bank, and spent on imports without paying the consumption tax.

Gold and barter are actually rather useless for domestic transactions outside of a rogue state. The same tax-free transactions for personal property and labor can be done with VIP dollars in corporate accounts. Personal property from a neighbor can be purchased, completely consumption tax free (it has already been paid), using VIP dollars from one's personal corporate account. It is a simple transfer of VIP dollars from one account to another, along with the personal property exchange. No taxes or alternative currencies are involved. There is no implied contract for personal property exchanges. When you buy from a retail or wholesale outlet, you are protected by their VOS, but there is no such protection for alternative transactions. These types of transactions are best done with friends and neighbors, not strangers.

An advantage of using corporate VIP$ over barter, is the option to permanently record the contract where each of the parties gives the other party an equal but fair market value for their services. This protects both parties from a default and is completely consumption tax free.

If gold, barter, or alternative currencies are used for labor or personal property, it is essential that land improvements get recorded to protect the land from treblers. This is automatic with VIP transactions. For bartered labor, receipts and specifications must be scanned and downloaded to the online land system. A monetary value must be imputed and a depreciation schedule assigned.

Foreign Exchange and Implications

> **AFFEERCE has a competitive edge over non-Georgist nations and maintains a balance of trade surplus with them. Just as this mercantilist policy was used to expand the embryonic viral land trust, it is used to spread AFFEERCE throughout the world. After that, a balance of trade and comparative advantage, not mercantilism, is the best trade policy with other AFFEERCE or Georgist collection and distribution domains.**

No polity has ever had universal distribution, a form of protectionism. With universal distribution, foreign companies cannot hope to compete with AFFEERCE enterprise. AFFEERCE workers will have lower nominal wages given that free food, housing, education, and medical expenses are included in real wages.

An AFFEERCE nation is designed to have a massive balance of trade surplus. This policy, called mercantilism, has many benefits [FTN10.09]. For one, AFFEERCE nations are able to buy and hold the debt of other nations which gives AFFEERCE nations leverage. For another, all investment capital will "trickle down" into AFFEERCE nations [FTN10.09], while natural resource exploitation will happen abroad. The mercantilist policy of the embryonic AFFEERCE nation is called "the dollarnado;" U.S. dollars are sucked into the AFFEERCE Central Bank and they can't get out.

To meet mercantile objectives, all spending in foreign currency must be done from spending accounts or physical notes. That is, the consumption tax is always applied before the exchange of VIP$ into foreign currency, unless held as a financial instrument in a corporate account. In the latter case, it is applied when moving the foreign currency from a corporate account to a spending account, using market exchange rates. This is far less arbitrary and discriminatory than specific tariffs, but serves the same purpose.

There is no consumption tax for "earned imports." That is, goods can be exported in exchange for a foreign currency held outside the AFFEERCE Treasury. The currency in this account can be traded for imported goods without payment of the consumption tax. However, banks might charge a fee for these accounts, while the Treasury charges no fees.

Citizen or not, one can always move a return-of-capital back into a spending account without paying the consumption tax. If a foreign investor moves 10 million dollars into an AFFEERCE corporate account, that money can be expatriated in whole or in part, at any time in the future without taxation.

While there is no consumption tax for capital expenditures abroad if the foreign firm accepts VIP$, there could be additional local taxes. If an AFFEERCE citizen wishes to emigrate, their personal spending account and property move tax free, but corporate accounts are subject to the consumption tax before that money can be converted into a foreign currency. Distributions are suspended for emigrants, although the housing distribution might continue for two months to allow time for property disposal.

In the unfortunate circumstance that the collection and distribution of the ground rents is not done at the highest level, emigrants to other AFFEERCE nations can, by treaty, move from one set of distributions to another, with a balance of payments deficit or surplus accumulating for unequal emigration rates between the two countries. A balance of trade, not mercantilism, is the logical outcome of trade between AFFEERCE and other Georgist nations.

The effectiveness of a mercantile policy in spreading AFFEERCE is not confined to nations. In *Volume II – The Plan*, it is used to expand the borders of the embryonic nation; to foster the viral nature of the land trust.

See *Appendix II – Anatomy of AFFEERCE Mercantilism*

Foreign Investment and the Spread of AFFEERCE

> **Exploitation of natural resources pays a very high percent of location value in a trebling environment. Neo-colonial exploitation by AFFEERCE nations provides a vehicle for third world nations to become prosperous by instituting the collection and distribution of rents. Exploitation returns a high profit before the transition and a high profit to humanity after the transition.**

Significantly, the best investments might be abroad. This is especially true of underdeveloped nations that have yet to move to an AFFEERCE economy. Citizen investors might buy bonds of foreign nations, build plants, and exploit resources. While this has all the trappings of neo-colonialism, it has the opposite dynamic. It provides a sufficient capital base for the underdeveloped nation to prosper with AFFEERCE.

The colony of old would rise up to expropriate the capital, and institute a leftist government doomed to failure. The exploiters would return after paying homage to corrupt leaders.

Today, the standard of living in former colonies is far below their colonial level. Under AFFEERCE, the third world nation will no longer need to expropriate the foreign capital. By instituting the collection and distribution of rents and the balance of the RCs, over 33% (or more for mineral exploitation) of the return on foreign capital, feeds, houses, and educates the nation. This move is not entirely unwelcome by the exploiting firm. It eliminates political risk, strengthens local markets, improves workforce productivity, reduces security costs, eliminates bribes, and increases the personal safety of the foreign workforce's families in day-to-day living.

To facilitate this, citizen investors will not be penalized for investment losses in a third world country that adopts the collection and distribution of rents. Bonuses can be paid on investments that remain profitable.

Once the exploited country has built up a sufficient level of national wealth, they can join the international AFFEERCE community sharing in the collection and distribution of rents. Given a 5/6 plurality, countries are free to keep their own laws and forms of government within the framework of the cellular democracy. However, exit rights allow people the freedom to leave. Unlike refugees today, these refugees would be welcomed everywhere as they bring with them all of the public and personal distributions.

There is every reason to believe that once a single nation practices the collection and distribution of ground rents, the rest of the world will soon join in.

Failure to Pay a Debt

Required Reading

While there is no debtor's prison in AFFEERCE, fraud is an offense punishable by the penitentiary. Because the necessities are all provided by the distributions, there is no reason to seek funds to preserve life. If there was, the right to life trumps the right to property and that would make fraud acceptable as some would argue it has become in the United States today.

Because all debts are taken on for discretionary items or business expansion, which could be considered discretionary, a failure to repay opens the door to charges of fraud or failure to act in good faith.

Honesty is critical. A person who took on a loan in good faith and answered all questions honestly cannot be held criminally liable if the loan goes bad. However, lies found to be material will result in penitentiary time. Bankruptcy does not protect a person who answered fraudulently. On the contrary, it places all documents from other loans into the review process, even those not currently in default.

Inheritance

Required Reading

Although there are no estate taxes per se, 1% of the deceased person's estate will be levied for every three months they spend in a nursing home, hospice, or long term care. Penitentiaries, hospitals or mental health facilities entitled to either the $300 security stipend from the government distribution, or drawing the majority of revenue from the medical distribution, do not qualify for this levy. The levy is distributed as part of an average disbursement to protect wealthy invalids and prevent discrimination against indigent ones.

With advances in genetics including multiple paternity, egg fusion, and surrogates, the default estate disposition for those who die intestate is tied only to family, and not to biology.

If one dies without a will, as a member of a family, the personal corporate account is transferred to the family corporate account. The personal spending account is divided equally between the personal spending accounts of the remaining family members. The title for all personal property is transferred to the family.

All distributions will cease a month after death, except the housing and disability distributions which will continue for two months to provide severance for landlords and caregivers.

The Redistribution of Wealth at Death

Required Reading

Interestingly, redistribution of wealth at death tends to be a great equalizer in AFFEERCE. Due to the cost of funding a future-baby account, small, well-to-do, families might have many children, while those at the lower end of the economic spectrum, might organize into large alternative families, and have fewer children.

For instance, the head of an upper middle class family, who bore 10 children, leaves an estate of 1 million dollars. Each of the children inherits $100,000. On the other hand, an alternative family of 10 adults working sporadically for low pay can afford only 2 children and as each of the adults passes on, they leave an average estate of $20,000. Over time, each of the children inherits $100,000.

Banks

In order not to interfere with a land value backed currency, banks must maintain a 50% reserve ratio. If deposits are not insured, the bank must post a VOS. The citizen investors engage in public banking.

The monetary base, MB, is the fixed number of VIP dollars in circulation. To counter the natural deflation, additional VIP dollars will be created by the Treasury based on a net increase in land value and distributed as local land capture. (See, *Chapter 3 – Local Land Capture*)

Today, when banks loan money, the borrower deposits the money in another account. That deposited money can itself be loaned which increases the money in circulation, called M1. A bank could loan 10 different people $100,000, but it turns out to be all the same $100,000, loaned over and over again. Still that leaves a million dollars in circulation, all based on a single $100,000 of MB. This is called reserve fractional banking. If your paper currency says "Federal Reserve Note," it was created this way. Since this money is created from debt, without banks making loans, all money would disappear, except the coins in your pocket. This reliance on debt for our money is a moral hazard that leads to gross inequality and decay of good business values[FTN10.24].

It also creates inflation as a way of life. By virtue of the banks making a loan, there is more money in circulation chasing the same amount of product. Before this kind of money became common worldwide, about 100 years ago, inflation was rare, and a function of gold or silver discoveries, or printing currency faster than the rate of growth.[FTN10.25].

The VIP$ is Treasury currency backed by land value. It is called debt-free currency, since it is not backed by debt.

Banks maintain their VIP$ accounts at the Treasury. Because checks are no longer useful and Treasury accounts are free, banks will pay a small interest rate to attract corporate and spending accounts of businesses and individuals. Because only 50% can be loaned out, the interest rate will be quite small. It is transparent to personal transactions whether the account is a free Treasury account, or a bank account at the Treasury paying a small interest rate.

$M1 = MB * MM$

MM is the money multiplier. Since AFFEERCE is a cashless society,

$MM = 1/R$ where R is the reserve ratio or the fraction of deposits that cannot be loaned out.

If R were zero, banks would have an infinite amount of money to lend, regardless of the size of MB. Inflation would be unstoppable. On the other hand, if R were 1, banks would not exist, since they could not loan their deposits.

However, the standard formula for MM is deceptive. Money that the bank must keep locked in a vault, R, is not really money in circulation. So a better formula for MM is:

$MM = (1 - R)/R$

We see that an R of .5 or 50% reserve, does not change the money supply at all. If $100,000 is deposited, $50,000 is placed in the vault and $50,000 is loaned out. Subsequently, the borrower of the $50,000 deposits that money. $25,000 is placed in the vault and $25,000 is loaned out. When all is said and done, a deposit of $100,000 produces $100,000 more in deposits, $100,000 in loans and $100,000 placed in the vault. Even though a single $100,000 deposit produced $200,000 in deposits, only $100,000 is put to work in the economy. The second $100,000 in deposits could be used to pay off the loan, so they cancel each other out. In such an economy, savings will tend to equal investment, and government borrowing will not likely exist.

Critics might argue that a 50% reserve ratio will grind the economy to a halt. But that would be incorrect. In today's economy, a reserve ratio of 10% and a savings rate of 5% allows for bank loans of 45% of national income. Should the savings rate fall to 2%, banks would only be able to loan 18% of national income. However, in an AFFEERCE economy, with no tax on savings in a corporate account and with child funding being an important use of money, the savings rate will be close to 60%. This will allow for bank loans of 60% of national income. Changes in the savings rate will cause only minor fluctuations in the amount of money banks have to loan, without the risk of catastrophe that we live with today.

Another problem is default. Although banks usually require collateral to make a loan, collateral can fall short, and defaults do occur. With the collapse of the real estate market in 2008, defaults were common. If money is multiplied, then the amount of money in default is likewise multiplied. Without government intervention, bank failure is inevitable. The lower R, the more inevitable is bank failure from a wave of defaults.

With a 50% reserve ratio, excess defaults will cut into the bank's profit, but bank failure, absent very imprudent risk taking is highly unlikely. Because the economy is designed for no inflation, the rate of return will be low, but safety is essential. The VSG will probably require VOS certified banks to insure their deposits under $500,000 with a VOS certified private insurer. There is no FDIC. The insurer will examine the banks past and present loan portfolio to determine the appropriate rate.

Because people can move their money so easily with the VIP, banks will have to dip into their reserves from time to time. Banks are prohibited from making new loans until the reserves are restored. If reserves fall below 25% of outstanding loans, banks must borrow. No new loans can be made until reserve loans are repaid, and reserves are restored.

Any person or family can start a bank. The only major legal requirement will be a 50% reserve ratio. Unlike citizen investors, banks are not prohibited from loaning wage capital. VSG standards will probably require insurance on deposits up to a certain amount, but that amount is up to the VSG. Banks with a VOS disclosing no insurance will pay higher interest rates, but let the depositor beware!

The citizen investors and cellular enterprises can also engage in banking, including deposits. Whether banking is most efficient in the public or private sector remains to be seen. Citizen investors will only loan out advance payment of ground rents and baby tax reserve funds. Free Treasury funds not transferred to a bank account will remain idle.

The 50% reserve ratio for banks should put an end to the massive, high frequency trading in derivatives. Derivatives exist mostly because of fear, fears that are generated by the financial sector so that it can amass profits. Such fears include interest rate fluctuation and fear of financial collapse. Small banks with a 50% reserve ratio generate confidence, not fear. Universal distribution eliminates fear. Zero inflation encourages savings. Risk is taken by the innovative and enterprising. Complex financial instruments will tend to disappear as people increasingly invest in their own companies.

The Concentration of Capital

Required Reading

The rich get richer and the poor get poorer. The cliché is centuries old. And to make matters worse, when times are tough, the trend only accelerates. In 2008, politicians threatened us with financial Armageddon if we failed to bail out Wall Street. So having to choose between catastrophe and the rich getting richer, we chose the latter.

Studies in the last 100 years prior to the 1980s showed the idea that the poor get poorer to be false. Throughout most of the twentieth century the amount of wealth inequality was either decreasing or steady. The evidence seemed to prove Marx wrong. Then in the 1980s inequality began to tick up again. Capital was concentrating. People attributed this to the conservative revolution of Reagan and Thatcher and nothing fundamental[FTN10.19]. But the trend continued through Republicans and Democrats alike. It also began to spread to other countries in Europe. By the 2000s, the pace of concentration was accelerating and that continues to this day.

There are different theories as to what is going on. Thomas Piketty showed in his seminal work Capital, that if the return on capital is greater than the economic growth, capital will concentrate: the rich will get richer and the poor, poorer. Why was this not the case from 1914 through 1980? From 1914 to 1945, there were two world wars, serious inflation, and a great depression. In the wars, wealth was physically destroyed. Inflation created a negative return on capital for non-real assets. Depression allowed politicians to place a heavy tax on capital for public works and social welfare. Following WWII, massive rebuilding led to a rate of growth greater than or equal to the still heavily taxed return on capital. When the super growth ended in the 1960s, taxes dropped, return on capital became greater than growth, and slowly capital began to concentrate. It wasn't until the 1980s that anyone noticed, and it wasn't until the 2000s that people realized this was more than the normal ebb and flow of data. Thus the only thing that prevented doom was doom itself. It took tens of millions killed and cities destroyed to halt or reverse the concentration of capital. Now with peacetime growth, the rich, once again, grow richer and the poor, poorer[FTN10.19].

The Georgists would argue that the world wars and depression drove down the price of land, while the automobile extended the margin of production in a good way. Once the suburbs extended to the limit of practical distance, the price of land resumed its rapid rise, with wages and capital eaten up by rent.

Whoever is correct, and perhaps they both are to some extent, one cannot argue with the facts.

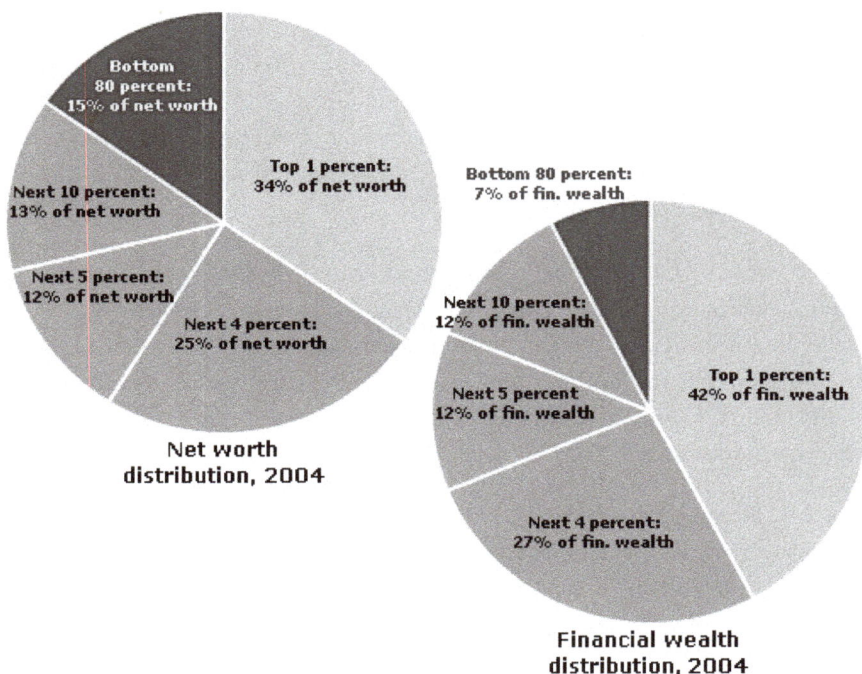

Net worth
distribution, 2004

Financial wealth
distribution, 2004

In this diagram by Domhoff[FTN10.12], for the year 2004, the bottom 80% had 7% of the wealth. In this next diagram by Domhoff, for the year 2010[FTN10.13], the situation gets considerably worse. In 2010, the bottom 80% has only 5% of the wealth, a reduction of 29%! This is a result of feeding trillions to the banks to avert financial Armageddon.

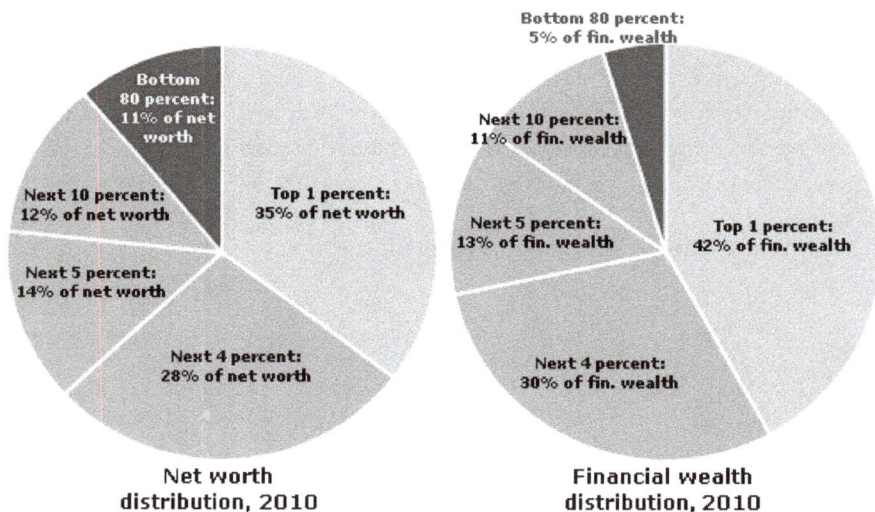

Net worth
distribution, 2010

Financial wealth
distribution, 2010

If one takes the poor, the middle class and the upper middle class, or 90% of our nation, combined, they owned 19% of the wealth in 2004 and 16% of the wealth in 2010.

In an AFFEERCE economy, the dynamics of the collection and distribution of ground rent cause about 33% of the return on capital to be distributed through universal distribution. At the very least, the lower 50% will have a return on 15% of the wealth, and the lower 90% a return on 30% to 50% of the wealth. If the upper 10% has 50% of the wealth, the lower 10% still has a return on 3% of the wealth, a ratio of only 16/1.

Will this increase in wealth equality adversely affect productivity? Absolutely not! We have seen how collection and distribution of the rents, cellular democracy and free enterprise, work together to bring huge increases in productivity. Those productivity boosters are listed below. Any one of them could significantly increase the wealth of the nation. Taken together, we cannot even imagine the explosion of new wealth they will bring to the world!

The Amazing List

Required Reading

1. New businesses will form in formerly poor neighborhoods to profit from the distributions.
2. The distributions will financially enable workers to fill lower wage positions.
3. The collection of ground rents forces optimal land productivity through trebling and fear of trebling.
4. The collection of ground rents encourages homesteading, increased mobility, and the rise of towns.
5. The collection of ground rents eliminates land speculation, reigning in the margin and increasing wages.
6. Deregulation will cause an explosion of new business.
7. Deregulation will increase profits for existing business.
8. Elimination of the minimum wage will allow many businesses to form that could not otherwise.
9. Elimination of the minimum wage will make existing businesses more efficient.
10. Elimination of the corporate income tax will allow more money for investment in tools, machinery, research and development.
11. Elimination of the corporate income tax will cause hundreds of billions of foreign corporate profits to be repatriated back to the United States.
12. Corporations can avoid or significantly reduce liability with a VOS (violation of standards document).
13. Collusion will allow for an increase in competition.
14. Colluders and monopolies can no longer shutdown businesses with the force of law.
15. Monopolies can legally exploit the economies of scale for greater productivity and more money for research and development.
16. No government bailouts or government support of any business.
17. Consumption taxation of spending accounts provides an incentive to save.
18. Advance ground rent payments and future-baby funds provide a massive pool of savings
19. The ground rents and consumption tax are far less of a burden than today's taxes. Ground rent is a purchase of location value and not a tax at all.
20. There will be no additional taxes in any dominion, unless earmarked for specific projects, based on a flat percentage, and approved by super plurality of citizens in the dominion.
21. Alternative families create wealth through the economies of scale and division of labor.
22. Alternative families provide good support for budding entrepreneurs and increase competition.
23. The education distribution will increase skill and eliminate grade inflation.
24. VIP eliminates identity theft, lost credit cards, cost of money creation, and credit card fees.
25. The online land system increases real property liquidity.
26. Government has incentive to reduce crime.
27. The food and housing distributions will end poverty and greatly reduce the cost of crime. Urban mobility at night will be increased.
28. Reduction of day care centers and nursing homes for the elderly, as families become much larger and self-sufficient.
29. The intellectual property distribution will allow all content to be free
30. The intellectual property distribution will explode software productivity with inter-organizational libraries

31. The intellectual property distribution allows the entire population to benefit from innovation at once, and at the lowest possible cost. The wealth created from a dollar spent on intellectual property might be 6 to 10 times greater than today. Intellectual property will significantly reduce the cost of medical care. It could save us over $1 trillion annually!

32. The intellectual property distribution transfers profits from location value to innovation.

33. Citizen investors provide unprecedented capital to small business.

34. Investments by citizen investors can only be for capital goods, not services.

35. Citizen investors will seek out and suggest investment opportunities in the community.

36. Government is motivated to reduce liability and liability is limited.

37. Government has incentive to dispose of unused buildings, increase efficiency and streamline bureaucracy.

38. Cellular democracy and the approval of earmarked, sunset taxes by a 2/3 plurality of the dominion will eliminate corruption in politics.

39. Cellular democracy will eliminate wasteful campaign spending.

40. The cellular aristocracy will save taxpayers money, increase demand for land, and simultaneously provide entertainment. Savings could be as high as $100 billion!

41. Open borders and the ability to purchase citizenship will create a "brain surge" in the early years.

42. Deregulation of the medical industry drastically reduces costs through the use of rebates.

43. Teachers, police, and other professions have built in performance incentives (*See Chapter 11 – Education Distribution.*)

Part III – Speculations

Part I, Funding Freedom through the Collection and Distribution of the Ground Rents, is the financial basis of AFFEERCE, while Part II, A Free Society, is the political basis. The constitutional amendment package leading to capitulation will be crafted from the salient points.

In this part, I'll speculate on what the specific distributions might look like, and on how highly unorthodox alternative families might prosper under AFFEERCE. Finally I'll look at a few ideas of the AFFEERCE Enlightenment, which are more my personal views than anything fundamental to the politics or economics.

While the Chapter 11 on Universal Distribution is not meant to be definitive, it should serve as a good starting point for affeercianado discussions going forward. Beginning in Chapter 11, I will no longer follow the format of summarizing a section, or indicating it is required reading.

Chapter 11 – Universal Distribution

When it shall be said in any country in the world my poor are happy; neither ignorance nor distress is to be found among them; my jails are empty of prisoners, my streets of beggars; the aged are not in want; the taxes are not oppressive; the rational world is my friend, because I am a friend of its happiness: When these things can be said, there may that country boast its Constitution and its Government – Thomas Paine

The amount and nature of the distributions in this section are speculative. The only requirement of distribution theory is that the amount of personal distributions (basic income) be greater than or equal to the amount of public distributions (head taxes) and that some portion be used for intellectual property. That said, I believe the nature and amount of the distributions discussed below will turn out to be a reasonably good approximation of the future reality.

> **Four out of five U.S. adults struggle with joblessness, near-poverty or reliance on welfare for at least parts of their lives, a sign of deteriorating economic security and an elusive American dream.** [FTN11.01]

The water fountain in the park gives free water to anyone who wants it. Even foreign nationals can partake in the beneficence of the taxpayer. It is free to the homeless. It is free to the jogger. It is free to the executive on his way to the golf course.

Water is a necessity. Without it, there could be no life. But I've never heard it said that if water was free, people would lose their incentive to work, their incentive to get ahead, their drive. That free water would turn our population into a bunch of lazy parasites.

Perhaps the bottled water people would like to start a campaign that free water will turn us all into lazy parasites. But it would be hard to convince many people of its validity. Take a runner who is hot and exhausted. When they hit the water fountain and get that free water, there is often new incentive, a second wind. On the other hand, one can drink so much they are bloated and useless. Those who oppose entitlements could argue that between the water being free and greed being part of human nature, bloating, and even stomach ruptures, would be a constant problem. But, of course, they aren't. Nor are there any sane people arguing that they are.

But move from one necessity, water, to another necessity, food, and all the foolish arguments against free water are no less foolish when used against free food. We still hear, "With free food, people would lose their incentive to work, their incentive to get ahead, their drive."

There's free food in the army. Has that turned our soldiers into a bunch of lazy parasites? Children get free food for the first eighteen years of their lives. Is that the problem with kids today? Parents spoil their kids with smart phones, autos, designer clothes, international travel, and so forth. But how can they do so with nutritious food?

Like the runner who gets a new burst of energy with that swig of free water, three nutritious meals renew everyone's drive to fulfill their dreams; dreams that are further nurtured in their nightly dreams inside a warm and safe shelter.

Want is a precious gift. Without want, there would be little incentive to live. We should be grateful so many things in life come only to the hard worker. Luxuries must be earned. Nevertheless, the playing field must be level. Nutritious meals, safe shelter, quality health care, and unlimited continuing education are everyone's right in an AFFEERCE economy. By the same token, each of us has a right to know that these are available to all our fellow citizens. It makes rational business decisions much easier.

Class Warfare

Try this thought experiment. Consider the free water fountain. Suppose a government edict came down that henceforth only the poor would be able to use the fountain. If you earn over $10,000 a year or have over $3,000 in assets, you are expected to buy bottled water. An entire bureaucracy is established to verify income levels and issue cards. A cop is stationed at the fountain to check IDs.

The water fountain becomes a source of controversy. There is anger and resentment from those who are no longer entitled to the water. Some might say, "How dare they use our tax dollars so those people can drink water when we can't?" Amongst the not quite so poor, there would be incentive to lie about income and hide assets. Of course this scenario is ridiculous. But there are important points.

1. With the entitlement available to everyone (universal distribution) the costs are far less. There are no police stationed at every water fountain to check ID's.
2. With universal distribution nobody is concerned about the existence of the entitlement, or who gets it and who doesn't. The entitlement goes unnoticed.
3. Once the entitlement is restricted to the poor, costs increase. Class-conflict results. The rules encourage dishonesty. Rage and resentment at the water fountain become likely.

Water is certainly no less a necessity than food or shelter. Unfortunately, save the lowly water fountain, all of our entitlements today are handled in the worst possible way; bureaucracy, high costs, rules that encourage dishonesty, rules that punish families for staying together, rules that discourage savings and employment. And these rules really do discourage work, by making it very difficult to get into the programs like Medicaid or Section 8 housing. Once a person has made it through the hurdles, there is the very real fear that should they get a job and lose it, they could never again get back into the program. Qualifications that are ever changing and ever tightening, only add to the fear. Entitlements today continue the cycle of poverty. If one choses to get a job and break free of the entitlements, they lose more than benefits. There is the cost of transportation, the cost of a new wardrobe, the cost of ignored household chores, and the cost of child care. It rarely pays to move from welfare to work.

Other than Medicare and water fountains, there are no real entitlements in the United States today. I mean entitlements that are universal; entitlements that benefit everyone regardless of income, assets, and family size. The rest, Medicaid, Link, Section 8, and aid to mothers with dependent children, are just weapons of class warfare. Even Social Security functions more like a government sponsored annuity.

Benefits of Universal Distribution

1. No resentment, racism, or classism because all Americans receive the same benefit.
2. No disincentive to work because benefits are not lost when employed.
3. No incentive to be dishonest as assets and income do not disqualify.
4. No bureaucracy to administer because all are eligible.
5. Eliminate the disincentive to form a family, live with others or share resources found in the current rules and regulations.
6. Incentive to join together into large families to take advantage of the economies of scale.
7. Large families increase productivity through division of labor, provide a "village" for raising children and caring for the sick and elderly, and increase the chance of a successful family business.
8. Allows those whose skills are replaced by technology to pursue their own dreams without fear.
9. Allows those whose skills are replaced by technology to learn new technologies without cost.
10. Levels the playing field.
11. Provides for a mobile workforce.

12. Provides a safety net through which none can fall.
13. Hunger and homelessness are eliminated.
14. Allows for a free market economy without harm.

In AFFEERCE, distributions are everyone's basic income. The unemployed, the artist, the student and the billionaire all work off the same level playing field; a field of dreams that is within everyone's reach.

Tranches

Distributions are subdivided into tranches. There can be up to eight tranches (or 10 tranches internationally), seven for the levels of federation, and one for the individual. For most distributions, the majority, if not all of the allocation, is directed at a single tranche. The food, housing and cash distributions are all directed at level 0, the individual. The national defense distribution is directed at level 7, but there could be a tranche at level 5 for national guards, and even a tranche at level 1 or level 2 for local militias.

In Table 9.2 (Chapter 9), the proposed tranches for the government distribution are shown. Table 9.3, shows a possible set of tranches for the law enforcement distribution. Allocations and tranches of distributions will be established at capitulation, and modifications are recommended by a panel of the judiciary and must be ratified by a 2/3 plurality of nationwide voters. Net increases must be ratified by a 5/6 plurality nationwide, thus encouraging a withering away of the allocations.

There is nothing to stop a 2/3 super plurality of a dominion from changing the usage of allocated public funds. For example, some funds for police might be re-allocated to flood control.

Non-transferability of Distributions

Personal distributions are not transferable outside of the family. They cannot be used to satisfy debts of any kind, except at the point of sale. They can be spent only by the person, or that person's family, to which they were given. The rules for using distributions in commerce vary from distribution to distribution. In no case can a personal distribution be used to purchase something for which it was not intended, save the cash distribution that can be spent anywhere.

A merchant, who can accept the distribution, can also accept payment of a specific portion, such as a meal, or one night in a motel. The distribution is treated like a debit account which is replenished each month.

Although distribution funds can accumulate, no purchases can be made with future distribution funds. No punishment, by the family or by the state, can deny the food and housing distribution, although those distributions can be administered by a third party with VOS certification if judicially ordered or voluntarily surrendered for a stay in the hospital or rehab.

Beyond the food, housing, and cash distributions, all distributions are dispensed to those who provide services for the entitled individual. These distributions are not transferable outside the dominion. For instance monthly funds for fire protection are directly tied to individuals in the district. If a citizen in the district dies or leaves, the money for firefighters in the district drops, and if a child is born, or a new person moves to the district, the money for those firefighters increases.

Rebates

Rules regarding rebates vary from distribution to distribution. Food and housing distributions are rebated at 50% spending account cash (consumption tax free). However, families with children under 14 might have special conditions on food rebates. Medical distribution rebates (see, *Chapter 11 – Medical Distribution* below) are rebated at 50% corporate account cash from the chosen provider (purchases with the cash must pay consumption tax, if any). In the same manner as capital expenditures, there is no consumption tax on distribution spending at any level of dominion. E.g. police uniforms, fire trucks, government buildings.

Rogue States and Distributions

Rogue States and other dominions with an alternative currency receive distributions for each citizen in a special account at the Treasury. This account can be spent on imports, and can serve as backing for an internal currency if that is desired. Internal distributions at a minimum must include nutritious meals, medical care, and warm and safe shelter for children under 14. Knowingly violating the right to life of children or the right to leave of adults could lead to military intervention. Rogue states receive 100% rebates on all distributions, but must pay consumption tax on all imports.

The Food Distribution - $220

Government report shows 15% of Americans had trouble putting food on the table -- a record high. The one-year jump is all the more significant, given the number of hungry Americans had never been higher than 11.9% since these surveys began.

Of the near-15% of the nation that couldn't secure enough food last year, the USDA said one-third of them had "very low food security," meaning they reduced the amount that they ate or disrupted their eating patterns during the year. That group made up 5.7% of all U.S. households, which was also a record high. [FTN11.02]

In 2011, according to the Agriculture Department, nearly one in four young children (23.6 percent) lived in a family that had difficulty affording sufficient food at some point during the year[FTN11.32]

The United States has been called "The Breadbasket of the World." Such abundance makes it especially shameful so many are having trouble getting enough to eat. And the numbers would be above 20% without the food stamp program, disincentives to work and incentives for dishonesty notwithstanding[FTN11.04].

Here are the SNAP (Supplemental Nutrition Assistance Program) entitlements for the year 2009. The actual calculations are rather involved. Two people living separately, each earning $800 per month, (assume $400 per month rent) are each entitled to $95.45 per month in food distribution. If they form a family, as you can see below, they are entitled to nothing. Suppose one of them stops working, then they are each entitled to $131.22 per month for food [FTN11.03]. Imagine the damage done to the character and wealth of the nation by this penalty on family and work.

Determine whether your income meets the gross income limit. In 2009, this limit was $1,174 per month for one person. Add $405 for each household member up to eight people. Add $406 per household member over eight people.

In 2009, the maximum monthly allotment was $200 for one person, $367 for two, $526 for three, $668 for four, $793 for five, $952 for six $1,052 for seven and $1,202 for eight. Add $150 for every household member over eight people. [FTN11.03]

With universal distribution, everyone would simply get $220. Because nutritious food is so important, an amount that is up to $70/person/month higher than the federal SNAP program should insure abundance. Large families will feast and even be able to score a small cash rebate.

The scope of the food distribution is determined by the VSG and ratifying legislation. The most liberal standard, and one likely to apply where all family members are adults, is that anything intended to be orally consumed, with the explicit exception of alcohol, tobacco, pharmaceuticals, and other intoxicants, can be purchased with the food distribution. Prepared foods, food packaged as a complete meal, and all dining out fare would be limited to the per meal allowance.

Breakfast	$1.75
Lunch	$2.55
Dinner	$3.03

The total comes to $7.33. It is based on a 30 day month. $7.33 * 30 = $220. This would be a problem for a month with 31 days only if the following were all true

A) You never prepared your own food.
B) You spent the maximum on every prepared meal.
C) Your cash distribution was exhausted.
D) You had no funds of your own.

This might be a typical first grocery bill of the month. It is assumed this is the early days of AFFEERCE and there is an 11% consumption tax(8% base + 3% local projects) on non-entitled purchases.

Item	Distribution	VIP$	11% CT	Debit PCA
Sack of flour - $4.00	4.00			
Cinnamon - $1.50	1.50			
24 pack Lite Beer - $11.25		11.25	1.24	12.49
1 Rotisserie Chicken ($6.99 [2 meals])	6.06 (2 dinners)	.93	.10	1.03
1 Cooked Pot Pie ($1.60 [1 meal])	1.60 (1 breakfast)			
2 Beef Filets	9.80			
TOTAL $36.84	$22.96	$12.18	$1.34	$13.52
Food distribution remaining: $197.04 28 dinners, 30 lunches, 29 breakfasts				

The totals at the bottom tell us that this is the first time during the month the food distribution was used. The month begins on a person's birthday to prevent everyone's distribution from running out at the same time. Because of the shortened month of February, March 1st will be an especially good day for grocery stores.

Other than the prepared foods and alcohol, everything is simply debited from the food distribution. Notice that the distribution purchases are not subject to the consumption tax. Food distribution funds cannot be used for alcoholic beverages. The beer is paid for completely with VIP$. The alcohol costs $11.25, so $12.49 was debited from the personal corporate account, $1.24 went to the citizens, and the other $11.25 went to the merchant. This assumes no excise tax.

The prepared foods are treated as though they were meals. The rotisserie chicken has been declared by a VSG (Voluntary Standards Group) somewhere to be worth 2 meals. If you don't like the VSG meal allocation, you can:

214

1) Push legislation that eliminates prepared food meal allocation.
2) Pass certification and send in your resume to join the offending VSG and lobby for your ideas.
3) Buy a chicken and cook it yourself

The 2 allocated meals are taken from the lowest available meals that maximize use of the distribution. With dinner having an allowance of $3.03 per meal, two dinners, or the full $6.06 of food distribution money will be spent on the rotisserie chicken. That is still 93 cents short of the $6.99 price of the chicken, so $1.03 must be taken from the personal corporate account, with 10 cents going to the citizens and 93 cents going to the merchant.

The pot pie, prepared food worth 1 meal, is paid for completely with a breakfast, even though pot pies are not usually eaten for breakfast. Better to save the lunch allocation for a more expensive item.

The food distribution can be used for dining out. I've seen 2 hot dogs, fries and a medium beverage for $2.80, so a dinner meal allocation could be used. Inevitably, many restaurants in an AFFEERCE economy will carry $1.75, $2.55 and $3.03 specials of the day. Overages must be paid with VIP$.

The food distribution is not valid for tips. Tips, like any transfer of money for labor, are not taxable. The money goes directly from your personal corporate account to the personal corporate account of the waiter or corporate account of the staff if tips are divided. Should the waiter spend that money, as opposed to saving or investing it, she will pay consumption tax at that time.

Children have a right to nutritious meals. Even in a free society, some vestiges of a nanny state remain. For families with children less than 14 years of age, VSG standards might require several months food reserve before the excess can be converted into cash rebates.

Since the food distribution is non-taxable, the rebate goes to a spending account and not a corporate account. However, the rebate for food and housing is only 50% of the distribution, saving the citizens money.

The family shopper is authorized to spend the food distributions for the entire family. Individuals also retain control of their own account. Grocery shopping will deplete the accounts equally or as directed by a family specific spending strategy. The family is typically a level-0 district. At the discretion of the family, the VIP can enforce division of the food distribution into two tranches: one for the individual and one for the family.

The monthly food distribution is sufficiently large so even a single person can eat comfortably. However, accidents, power failures, insects, and natural disasters, could destroy a significant portion of the monthly supplies leaving a person or family of adults without food before the month is over. The first step in preventing this is to build up several months' worth of food distribution reserves. Families with children under 14 can build reserves to any number of months. The second is to accept charity.

Churches, charities, and community centers, even today, love to host meals for the community. That will be truer in an AFFEERCE society where these institutions can receive up to $3.03 per person if they have a VIP reader. The VIP reader can be set to silent mode, so no one will be turned away or embarrassed, if their food distribution for the month has run out. One would expect these charitable meals to be more generous than they are today.

Large families, especially those with family members who love to cook, can eat sumptuously on the food distribution. A family of 8 has $1,760 of food distributions every month. A large turkey, ham or roast beef, every night of the month, could be had for $800 with plenty left over for sandwiches the next day. Mounds of spaghetti with meatballs, and a family salad could be prepared for $12. Chicken pot pie for the whole family: $10, a breakfast of bacon, eggs, toast, pancakes and orange juice for under $10. Cereal with milk and a cup of coffee: $6.

The family of 8, who spend an average of $10 for breakfast, $15 for lunch, and $25 for dinner, can feast with many leftovers, all for a cost of $1,500 a month. That would still leave $260 unspent which would convert to a $130 spending account cash rebate. That $130 could be used to buy $130 worth of goods, tax free, such as beverages not covered by the distribution like beer or wine, or for anything else money can buy. Rebates increase the citizens' dividend for everyone, by saving 50% of the distribution cost.

A beer-drinking family of 8 might very well want to consider their own home brewery. The food distribution can be used for hops and yeast, as these are raw ingredients.

For families of 6 or more, there would be no way to exhaust the food distribution. There are only so many pies, and cakes, and cookies, pulled pork sandwiches and briskets, that one can eat. And home-made protein-energy smoothies, ones that everyone will crave after getting on the bathroom scale, will cost even less.

The family of 8 could eat nutritious, filling meals for $25 a day, or $750 a month, leaving an excess of $1,010 or $505 of spendable cash. That's a night of dinner, theater, and drinks afterward for all. Of course, a family of 8, where nobody is bringing in income, would have more pressing uses for that $505.

The Housing Distribution - $370

There were about 643,000 sheltered and unsheltered homeless persons nationwide in January 2009. Almost two-thirds stayed in an emergency shelter or transitional housing program and the other third were living on the street, in an abandoned building, or another place not meant for human habitation. About 1.56 million people, or about 0.5% of the U.S. population, used an emergency shelter or a transitional housing program between October 1, 2008 and September 30, 2009. [FTN11.05]

At $370 per month, the housing distribution will not only obliterate homelessness, but will be the main impetus for people to form large alternative families. This cultural change will tend to end loneliness, nursing homes for the elderly, and many mental disorders symptomatic of our times.

The distribution first pays the ground rent or apartment rent, then the mortgage, and then utilities. If there is any remaining, it can be used for repairs, renovations, or saved for a down payment or security deposit.

According to Wikipedia [FTN11.05], these are the primary causes of homelessness. I examine each one and show how AFFEERCE, not just the housing distribution, addresses each problem.

Cause of Homelessness Today	AFFEERCE Solution
The deinstitutionalization movement from the 1950s onwards in state mental health systems, to shift towards 'community-based' treatment of the mentally ill, as opposed to long-term commitment in institutions.	Voluntary commitment in rehab centers is a right. This is paid for by the standard distributions, the medical distribution, and the disability distribution. Although mental illness and substance abuse are not crimes, they often lead to criminal behavior. A judge will sentence an offender whose crime seems to be a consequence of a mental illness or some sort of addiction, to rehab. Involuntary commitment is paid for with the same distributions, although added security costs are paid out of the government distribution.

Redevelopment and gentrification activities instituted by cities across the country through which low income neighborhoods are declared blighted and demolished to make way for projects that generate higher property taxes and other revenue, create a shortage of housing affordable to low-income working families, the elderly poor, and the disabled.	Cities do not institute redevelopment and gentrification. Property owners do. These owners will demolish their own buildings when competition makes the property un-rentable, or treblers will come in and do the same. Because of the housing distribution, money will never be an issue for renters. Addicts who are welcome nowhere else but rat-infested hovels, are welcome in rehab, or if they insist on remaining addicts and can't find any substandard housing for $370, are welcome in the isolation centers where they will be supplied with unlimited heroin or methamphetamine
The failure of urban housing projects to provide safe, secure, and affordable housing to the poor	The concept of a state housing project will not exist. The $370 per person per month housing distribution ends any such need.
The economic crises and "stagflation" of the 1970s, which caused high unemployment. Unlike European countries, US unemployment insurance does not allow unemployed insurance recipients to obtain job training/education while receiving benefits except under very limited situations.	Unemployment is not an issue in housing affordability. Every person receives $370 per month in housing distribution. Being unemployed, is a perfect opportunity for job training and education, which is both free and unlimited.
The failure of the U.S. Department of Veterans Affairs to provide effective mental health care and meaningful job training for many homeless veterans, particularly those of the Vietnam War.	Foreign wars require a 2/3 vote of the population and are financed privately or through the discretionary tax. Veterans who are injured or suffer from mental health issues are entitled, as is everyone, to quality medical care, rehab, and unlimited education and job training.
Deprived of normal childhoods, nearly half of foster children in the United States become homeless when they are released from foster care at age 18.	There is no such thing as a foster family. When you enter a family, you are part of that family, whether you were born into the family, or unioned into the family. While every person is free to leave a family at the age of 14, many will never leave, seeking to bring their spouses, sexual partners, dear friends, and those who share the same enterprising, intellectual, spiritual or cultural pursuits, into the family.
Natural disasters that destroy homes: hurricanes, floods, earthquakes, etc. Places of employment are often destroyed too, causing unemployment and transience.	While nothing can stop the temporary homelessness caused by severe natural disasters, the unity of the nation will finance well-known private rescue agencies through the discretionary tax. These agencies and a mobilized national defense will be coordinated by a tiny Federal Emergency Management Agency (FEMA). People in a declared natural disaster can void their leases and refill their distribution accounts prorated to the end of their distribution month. Most families will view natural disasters as an opportunity for recruiting new members into their household in a society where People = Wealth.
People who have served time in prison, have abused drugs and alcohol, or have a history of mental illness find it difficult to impossible to find employment for years at a time because of the use of computer background checks by potential employers.	Employment is not required for housing, or rehab. Because of the lack of a minimum wage, there is full employment. You will always be given a chance to prove yourself.
According to the Institute of Housing in 2005, the U.S. Government has focused 42% more on foreign countries rather than homeless Americans including veterans.	Foreign aid is only possible through private donations or the discretionary tax.

People who are hiding in order to evade law enforcement.	With a cashless, VIP society, you would have to forego all distributions, and avoid all purchases outside the black market, to avoid detection. AFFEERCE penitentiaries are geared for rehabilitation. It is a great opportunity to improve your education and get nutritious meals in a safe shelter. It is nothing like the prison hells that exist today. You lose your liberty for the duration of the sentence, but not your right to life.
Women and children who flee domestic violence.	Every family is entitled to a social worker, who monitors for domestic and child abuse. Large alternative families make abuse unlikely. The right to leave is assured by the distributions. If housing is paid for from the housing distribution, it will be the abuser expelled from the family by judicial order, not the woman and children. If the abuser subsidizes the housing costs, or the house is in his name, not the family name, the rest of the family will be welcomed into new housing leaving the abuser alone.
Teenagers who flee or are thrown out by parents who disapprove of their child's sexual orientation. A 2010 study by the Center for American Progress shows that a disproportionately high number of homeless youth (between 20–40%) identify as LGBTQ.	Children = Wealth, and many families would welcome LGBTQ youth. Parents will rarely throw out precious youth and their distributions. Rather the young person will chose to leave an unwelcoming household at the age of 14. A judge can grant majority status (legal age) as early as age 12, or more likely oversee the transfer of a child under the age of 14 to a new family. However, discrimination against LGBT people will tend to cease, as they will be recognized as the most important innovators of new relationship types in the AFFEERCE alternative family. Strict gender roles are a serious impediment to the division of labor within the family, which is an impediment to family wealth. LGBT diversity in the family breaks down those roles and increases the likelihood of success in family ventures.
Overly complex building codes make it difficult for most people to build. Traditional huts, cars, and tents are illegal, classified as substandard and may be removed by government, even though the occupant may own the land. Land owner cannot live on the land cheaply, and so sells the land and becomes homeless.	You can build any structure on your own land unless explicitly prohibited by a paid covenant on the land. However, children under the age of 14 might be prohibited from living there and nobody has immunity from community protest. With $370 a month, there is little reason to live in a car or tent when you could live in a camper trailer. An owner who is the sole occupant of his own building need not pay any attention to standards at all, although a VOS is required if others live in the building.
Foreclosures of homes	No bank will make a loan to the marginally employed if the mortgage payments are not covered by the housing distribution with enough housing distribution left over for insurance and basic utilities. However, there is no way to insure against loss of family, so foreclosures will happen. Loans will be restructured to new family size. If you lose your home to foreclosure, there will be no shortage of places to rent. Once you leave the foreclosed home, the bank has no more claims to your housing distribution.
Evictions from apartments	Evictions will be more likely due to rules violations than funding problems. Whatever the violation, there will be apartments that satisfy needs, although if your problem is being a slob, don't expect to rent apartments that are clean, neat and up to standard.

Lack of support from friends or family	If you have family and friends they will likely want you to join their family and add to the family wealth. If you have problems that prevent this, there are plenty of options for help. If you are too eccentric for your friends, try hooking up with a different set of friends. Consider a mobile housing lifestyle.

Leasing

Lease terms and all payments are handled through the VIP. All transactions are permanently stored.

Upon expiration of the lease, if the tenant refuses to vacate, they are subject to immediate eviction. Because contracts and monies paid are handled through the VIP, there is no need to get a court order to verify non-compliance with the contract. The tenant will be removed by the police the same day non-compliance occurs. The only point of contention is how much, if any, of the security deposit is to be returned. Because homelessness is virtually impossible in AFFEERCE, landlords are able to receive equal protection of their right to property. The housing distribution will remove all unfair tenant biases that exist today.

In the less expensive areas, studios, with all utilities included, can be found today for $370 per month. Entrepreneurs, however, will likely take advantage of this rent-assured single person housing market and construct new, efficient, studios with utilities included, in most cities. The size of the studios would be a function of the ground rent and construction costs. Single persons could choose to rent larger apartments in older buildings, perhaps by paying their own utilities, or providing some service.

One obstacle to quality housing for a destitute single person is the security deposit. This will not be common since family charters will likely provide a small severance package whether the separation was voluntary or involuntary. While a single person is prey for large families anxious to recruit them, many will prefer to be alone. Those who do, and lack minimal funds for a security deposit, can amass those funds in substandard housing where no security deposit or application fee is required, or in halfway houses in exchange for some restrictions on liberty. Leases in either case are unenforceable contracts and can be broken since a domicile not up to code, and restrictions on liberty, are violations of the right to life.

It will be illegal for children under the age of 14 to live in substandard housing. However, there will be many families willing to take temporary custody of children whose families need time to get back on their feet. This can be arranged through the social worker, as a free service, without having to go to family court. In an AFFEERCE society, destitution will likely be the consequence of an untreated addiction. Absent such addiction, unemployed families can supply wholesome environments for their children on the distributions and readily available charity.

Nightly single rooms for $12.33 (1/30 of the housing distribution) will probably be available only if you bring your own linen, share a bath, and are willing to forego eating facilities. Traveling with a companion will increase options considerably. Hopefully entrepreneurs will tackle the difficult area of distribution-only nightly accommodations with innovative ideas to facilitate a mobile workforce.

The housing distribution will bring people together into large alternative families. This is not so much by design, but the serendipitous result of good policy. A family of two has a distribution of $740. A family of three has a distribution of $1,110.

The housing distribution has a broad range of application. It can be used to pay for utilities, such as gas, electric, water, phone, internet, and cable. For homeowners, the first draw is for ground rent, the second for mortgage. For renters, the first draw is rent to the landlord. If you own your home, the distribution can also be used for repairs and major or minor renovations, exterior buildings and areas such as swimming pools, greenhouses, driveways, landscaping and gardens. If your main home is a trailer, RV, camper or boat, the distribution can be used for fuel, repair, and docking or campsite fees.

The housing distribution can be saved indefinitely for security deposits, down payments, renovations and repairs, or rebated for 50% spending account cash.

The Housing Distribution and Home Ownership

A traditional family with 2 adults and 2 children would have a housing distribution of $1,480 per month. In most areas of the country, this would pay for a newer two bedroom, and all the utilities including summer AC. An alternative family with 4 adults and 4 children would have a housing distribution of $2,960 per month. This would easily pay for a luxury 6-bedroom home in the suburbs, with backyard pool, all the utilities and, savings or a small cash rebate.

Suppose a group of 30 like-minded spirits decide to form a monastic family. The monthly housing distribution totals an astounding $11,100. Such a monastery could have 50 small private rooms (20 for guests), a communal dining area, a chapel, and still leave the monks with a cash rebate from the housing distribution alone of at least $1,000 per month for missionary/charitable work.

A couple could save up for a luxury RV. Once purchased, they could travel the nation. The $740 per month housing distribution pays for gasoline, repairs and campsites. The $440 per month food distribution will keep them well-fed. To dine-out in expensive restaurants and meet new people at the same time, they can earn extra money with VIP-safe hitchhiker pickups (See *Chapter 11 – Transportation and Sanitation Distribution*).

The AFFEERCE economy is designed for no inflation. This is very different from an inflationary economy where assets are purchased as an inflation hedge. For homes, there is also depreciation. Although depreciation schedules will vary, a home after 30 years of no repairs or renovation will be worthless, particularly if demolition is required.

When a bank loan is made for a mortgage, they should assume a decline of 3% of the original home value, every year. With a small down payment, the principal paid the first year must be at least 3% to counter the loss in home value. At a 3% interest rate, the term of the mortgage will be around 24 years. In an AFFEERCE economy, 3-3-3 loans will protect the bank. That is 3% down, 3% interest and 3% initial principal, which equates to a 24 year mortgage. If the total family housing distribution is sufficient, banks will jump at the chance to make these loans. To determine qualification, the bank must look at expected utility costs and the availability of funds for repair, and renovation.

Ground rent will always be the first draw on the housing distribution, mortgage payments the second. Once the monthly distribution has been exhausted, additional loan payments, utilities, and repairs must be paid for with ordinary taxable income.

In the following examples, a 1 million dollar home sits on a 1 acre estate in the country. The cost of ground rent, mortgage and utilities is $101,000 per year. For a family of 4, the distribution would pay: $17,760.

Ground Rent	Mortgage	Utilities	Saved for Repairs
$17,760 + $2,240 = $20,000	$71,000	$10,000	

The bank would require a household income of $250,000 to make the loan.

Now look at the same home for a family of 18: Here the distribution would pay: $79,920.

Ground Rent	Mortgage	Utilities	Saved for Repairs
$20,000	$59,920+$11,080	$10,000	

The bank would require a household income of $63,000 to make the loan.

Finally we show the same estate housing 2 couples, each with 12 children. (Assume the top floor has 14 dormitory style bedrooms for the kids.) The distribution would pay: $124,320.

Ground Rent	Mortgage	Utilities	Saved for Repairs
$20,000	$71,000	$10,000	$23,320

A bank could make this loan without any additional household income beyond the distributions. The family would not get in trouble with the bank unless family size fell below 21 members.

Not only can these two families live on this 1 acre estate for free, but they have an extra $23,320 for repairs, cable, internet, etc. or family shrinkage. By the way, the annual food distribution for this alternative family of 28 is $73,920. The family chef can prepare a daily feast.

Suppose an occasionally employed family of 4 adults wanted to purchase a $120,000 home on a 1/10th of an acre lot. The lot has a ground rent of $20,000 per acre or $166 per month for their portion. After paying a $3,600 down payment, the monthly P&I (Principal and Interest) on the house would be $567, the electric would be $200, heat would average $300 per month, telephone, water, internet, and insurance would be another $115 per month. Thus the monthly cost of the home would be $1,432. However, our family of 4 receives $1,480 in housing distribution, leaving $48 a month for repairs, and renovations. This is a safe loan for the bank and is financed at 3% for 24 years.

Ground Rent	Mortgage	Utilities	Saved for Repairs
$2,000	$6,804	$7,380	$1576

Enforceable building codes require a 2/3 plurality of the dominion, or can be done with paid covenants that yield large nuisance fees for violations. However, there are standards for every project set by a VSG (voluntary standards group) and specified in the VOS (violation of standards document) of the company doing the construction. The bank can require all major renovations be VOS standard until the mortgage is paid off. Handy family members should take the available free courses, and become VOS certified before beginning home renovations, or obtain an insurance policy for potential damage. The bank can demand an extra payment of principal equal to the damage done by a non VOS standard renovation, including restructuring the loan for faster payment of principal.

The bank also has a great deal of protection should the family break apart. In the above family of 4 adults, if two adults went their own way, leaving two behind, the housing distribution would drop to $740 per month. The bank would take the $6,804 for the mortgage leaving only $76 for utilities, after ground rent, forcing one of the following actions:

1. One of the remaining adults can get a job.
2. They can recruit a new family member.
3. They can allow the ground rent to drop.
4. They can sell the house quickly before the utilities are cut off and walk away with some cash.
5. They both can walk and leave the house to the bank.

The bank can also convert the loan to interest only for a short period of time, such as 4 months, if all parties expect a solution in that time frame. The bank is paid first in the event of a treble, so bankers will not object to floating rents.

If only one person remains in the house, the housing distribution will be only $370. The bank will take the remaining $204 after ground rent, causing all utilities to be cut off. The bank will probably foreclose, although they might give the sole resident a few days to quickly recruit new housemates, quickly sell the house, or leave the house to the bank. However, the courtesy will not be extended if the bank expects property damage. Intentional property damage of a house with a mortgage is a criminal offense and a civil tort.

Foreclosure and eviction will require a judicial hearing and 1 weeks' notice to vacate, before forcible removal of the occupant. The bank has the right to all profits from foreclosed or abandoned property, not just profits equal to their losses. (With a 50% reserve ratio, banking is no longer a high profit business. This is an added loan protection for smaller banks.)

The Cash Distribution - $35

Every person receives $35 a month tax-free spending cash, to spend however they wish. The funds are deposited in their personal spending account. VIP debit transactions will exhaust the personal spending account, before debiting the personal corporate account and applying the consumption tax. Personal spending or corporate accounts are not accessible to other family members (except see children below), although funds can be freely transferred between personal accounts of family members. The $35 cash is easily exhausted on clothing, sundry items, meal overages, furniture, kitchen supplies....

The $35 cash distribution is also an educational tool that teaches children the value of saving, the value of signature, the value of chores, and the value of diplomacy. Prior to age 4, the cash distribution for each child is placed in a family spending account, accessible to all family members as specified in the family charter (discussed later in *Chapter 12 – Families*). Once the child reaches the age of 4, the $35 is placed in the child's personal spending account. However, to debit from this personal account requires the VIP signature of both the child and a family member specified as a guardian in the charter. Access to some of this money could be made contingent on chores. The child learns how to decide between nice clothing for school vs. toys, etc. The process will encourage dialogue and maturity. At the age of 14, the balance of the personal spending account becomes the sole property of the young adult.

Significantly, the cash distribution will also function as the universal deductible. There are many services that are part of the distributions that one should not use too frequently, both for one's own good as well as that of the nation. This would include visits to the emergency room; patient initiated medical diagnostics; patent and copyright applications, and bringing matters to court. Under debate will be whether the universal deductible can be used for such things as ordinary doctor appointments or community center annual passes, as both of these should be encouraged behaviors. In any given month universal deductible services are used, the $35 universal deductible will be debited from the following month's cash distribution. This is the only case where a future distribution will be used to pay current bills. Once the deductible has been satisfied, all subsequent visits to any of these facilities would be free for a period of 30 days. The proceeds of the deductible are divided equally between all claimants for the period.

The Education Distribution - $50

With what the federal government spent on its various and sundry student aid initiatives last year, it could have covered the tuition bill of every student at every public college in the country. Doing so might have required cutting off financial aid at Yale, Amherst, the University of Phoenix, and every other private university. [FTN11.06]

Claudia Goldin and Lawrence Katz demonstrated from the period 1890-2005 in the United States, the smaller the number of people who graduated college, the greater the wage gap between those who graduated and those who did not. Thus graduating from college increases the wealth of the nation beyond one's own remuneration[FTN10.19]. In a sense, this distribution is both public and private.

The goal of the education distribution is to create a society based on the acquisition and sharing of knowledge. It rewards both the formal and informal educational experience; private tutors, the homeschool, on the job training, and on-campus learning. Part of the remuneration does not come from the $50 distribution, but from a 4% consumption tax, paid by the student and routed to the teachers and schools who made this consumer a success.

In AFFEERCE, we get away from the idea that education is packed into the youthful years and then forgotten. Prior to the age of majority (14 is proposed), education and play will be more integrated. This is a natural result of home schooling in commune, kibbutz, and other innovative large families. Because of the tendency toward family enterprise, primary education might also be integrated with work. At the age of 14, young adults will chart their own course in life. There is no reason to cram secondary and university education into the next 8 years.

The education distribution is distributed differently than most other distributions in that every person is given equal access to education, but not equal funds. Distribution is based on the time spent in school or directed study. As Goldin and Katz showed, this time benefits society as a whole.

Today there are three major obstacles towards continuing an education.

1. The high price of a continuing education.
2. The burden of caring for children.
3. The need to work full time to support yourself and your family.

AFFEERCE eliminates all three. Education is free. There are likely plenty of loving parent figures in large alternative families, and children entering the world receive the full distributions. Finally, every person is entitled to nutritious meals, warm and safe shelter, and quality medical care in addition to free and unlimited education. Life after 14 years of age can be any combination of work, hobby, art, sport, education, and adventure according to personal preference.

The fluid and organic nature of free and unlimited education in an AFFEERCE society is not only a strong point, but a necessity for the future. Any society that cannot afford to provide a dynamic educational experience for all its citizens in both the new technologies and old philosophies will simply perish from this earth.

The U.S. has been transformed from a manufacturing-based economy to an economy based on knowledge, and the importance of a college education today can be compared to that of a high school education forty years ago. FTN11.07

Most Americans cannot afford a college education. Only a few of those who take the path of student loans make a profit on the deal. In fact, only 150 out of 3500 U.S. universities are profitable ventures for the majority of their students.[FTN11.08]

Taylor-made curricula which combine a liberal education with highly specific vocational needs are almost non-existent, yet that is the kind of continuing education required to be a successful entrepreneur, professional, or technician. Today, the high cost of education discourages flexibility and experimentation. For the lower middle class, at best there is community college and tuition at those schools is also rising rapidly.

The education distribution is designed around a society based on learning. It combines base pay, merit pay, and the very radical achievement annuities mentioned earlier. Such an amazing annuity, paid from a 4% consumption tax, is only possible with VIP technology.

Chancelleries

Most public university land will be under jurisdictional covenant. Jurisdictional covenants on land associated with educational and medical institutions can be designated as chancelleries.

Chancelleries are mixed-use home/institution buildings, not unlike the palaces of the cellular aristocracy. The improvements are owned by the institution. A chancellery treble can be matched by the current chancellor. All of the ground rent goes to the institution, rather than the national distribution package.

A university chancellor receives a luxury home and great social prestige in exchange for a large annual rent payment to the university, and the agreement to pay utilities, maintenance, and landscaping on the mixed use building. The details of the agreement are specified by the school's board of trustees.

Chancellors host graduations, faculty and alumni receptions, and visiting dignitaries. The chancellor might host delegates traveling to other universities. Although the chancellor has no say in the operation of the university, academic or otherwise, they should be well versed in the issues, as they might be called upon to serve as the public face of the university. To attract a high-paying chancellor, a university might consider a lavish chancellor's box at the stadium. Seizing a chancellery will probably be the least expensive way to enter the aristocracy.

Consider a high-rise university with 200 laboratories, classrooms, lecture halls and 400 small offices topped with a 3-story luxury penthouse with ballroom for the chancellor's family. The chancellor pays $100,000/year in ground rent and $4 million/year in utilities and maintenance, greatly reducing school expenses. The chancellery can be trebled, pending board approval, with a rent of $300,000/year or higher.

A large university can establish vice-chancelleries for different colleges, each with their own mixed use building.

Revenue from chancelleries is not included in the following discussion on the educational distribution. The numbers work without chancelleries, so their inclusion can only improve the bottom line. However, the business plan found in *Volume II – The Plan* makes extensive use of chancelleries.

While the details will be hammered out by educational scholars over the next 60 years, the plan outlined below fits within budget and is a good starting point for discussions.

Teachers

The salary of teachers K-12, whether public, private or home-schooled, comes from one or more of the following income sources.

1. A .35 per student per hour education distribution
2. A maximum .35 per student per hour subject-difficulty distribution

3. A .70 per hour (0-$1.40) merit distribution
4. A lifetime annuity from the student's 2% teacher achievement annuity
5. A stipend from the school or extra charges for private instruction
6. An optional portion of the 2% discretionary tax

The base pay for K-12 is .35 per student-hour. If 20 students are in the class, the base pay of the teacher is $7 per hour.

A hypothetical subject-difficulty distribution is apportioned as follows: K 0, 1st .02, 2nd .05, 3rd .08, 4th .11, 5th .14, 6th .17, 7th .20, 8th .23, 9th .26, 10th .29, 11th .32, 12th .35 (Phys. Ed, Art, Band, Choir, Shop, Librarian, Drama, Debate .35)

A 4th grade teacher with 20 students would receive a base pay of $9.20 per hour. This would be the total pay of a substitute 4th grade teacher. However, regular teachers would also receive merit pay.

Students once a month will take random grade appropriate tests in random subjects or occasionally specific tests for specific students. All tests will be used to compute teacher merit; however only the top 25% of the tests students take individually will appear on the student's transcript. Testing is important in AFFEERCE for merit, and skills certification. Although test questions are created by the VSG's, tests are uniformly administered by the Department of Education.

Teachers will receive from 0% to 200% of their subject-difficulty-enhanced base in merit pay.

A 6th grade teacher whose students' test scores place his merit performance at the 45 percentile would earn $2,613.60 per month with 20 students. The best 6th grade teacher with 20 students would make $4,114.80 per month.

To estimate the cost of a K-12 education in terms of teacher's salaries, assume the average 100% merit distribution, 6 hours of teaching per day, 22 days of teaching per month, 10 months per year. Here is a sampling of monthly cost per student per grade.

K – 92.40 per school month
1 – 97.68 per school month
3 – 113.52 per school month
6 – 137.28 per school month
9 – 161.04 per school month
12 – 184.80 per school month

The average education distribution for teacher salaries per person for grades K-12 is $114 per month, or $17,784 total for teacher's salaries from kindergarten through the end of high school.

Schools

In addition to teachers, there are schools, utilities, janitorial staff, administrators, desks, chairs, textbooks, lab equipment, gyms, an auditorium, landscaping, and so on.

Since the school is in use all year, the school distribution is set at a fixed $20 per month. For K-12, the total cost of the school distribution will be $3,120. This money is distinct from the school's 2% achievement annuity which continues for the lifetime of the school and the student. Because private schools have access to the same funds as public schools, tuition at private schools will be much lower than it is today, all other things being equal.

The total of both the educational and school distribution for grades K-12 is $20,900.

The University

Courses at the university pay .35 per student hour when the class is taught by a graduate student, and .80 per student-hour when the class is taught by a professor. Merit pay, as it does for primary and secondary teachers, goes from 0% to 200%.

Suppose a professor gives three hour-long lectures a week, each with 250 students. Based on merit, the lowest paid professor would receive $2,400 a month while the highest ranking professor would receive $7,200 a month for these 3 lecture hours.

The 250 students might be divided into groups of 25 for 2 hour long recitations (classes taught by grad students) or labs a week, under the direction of graduate students. Grad students would earn $70 per month to $210 a month depending on merit for the two hour long recitations. This might seem low, but the graduate students are receiving their education free of charge, living in graduate dorms courtesy of the housing distribution, and eating well-balanced dormitory food via the food distribution. Leading recitation is considered part of a graduate student's education.

Graduate student instructors as well as professors are entitled to the teacher achievement annuity from their student's income for the rest of their lives.

Public university administration and staff might be partially paid from the government distribution and will often be beneficiaries of the capital expense distribution. There is an additional $40 per month per student enrolled at the school. In addition, universities receive a generous portion of the 2% school achievement annuity, along with income from chancelleries. Private universities are free to charge additional tuition and fees.

The amount of a full year's university distribution for both education and the school itself is $1680 at $140 per month.

Notice that $140 per month is the maximum ever paid for education (outside of the 4 high school years). If we assume rather generously that on average, people will spend 1/3 of their lives in school the education distribution is fully satisfied with $50 per person per month.

Which Level of the Dominion Pays for Education?

Education is paid at the highest level of dominion and merit pay is determined by test questions devised by VSGs at the Bureau of Standards. However, historically, lower levels of federation have felt strongly about setting educational standards. It will be quite common to have VSGs at level-4 or level-5 to either approve or override standards set at higher levels. Although non-standard education is permitted with VOS sign-off, VSG certification of schools will be required to receive funds from the education distribution. It is likely the high level VSGs will maintain a liberal policy regarding homeschools, additional curriculum, training for a trade and tutor certification, reducing the need for lower level dominions to foot the expense of these VSGs.

Online Education

The price we pay for unlimited free education is small compared to food and housing distributions, but still quite large when the consumption tax annuities are added in. However, competition from online education could bring about another revolution in educational pricing. This revolution could bring down both the $50 distribution as well as the 4% consumption tax annuities.

With online education, students can learn from the best professors in the nation. Combine online education with graduate student recitation or even the virtual reality graduate student recitation, and the cost of education drops. Continual testing will winnow out unpopular courses and courses with little merit. Teachers at all grade levels will find that they can supplement their teaching with online and recorded lessons.

Online and multi-media courses on the same subject compete against each other, so most of the successful ones will come from leading universities, and well-known trade schools.

It remains to be seen whether recitation in a virtual reality classroom with a graduate student instructor, in conjunction with online lectures from a noted professor, can replace the university experience. The answer will be found in comparative test scores. The university experience also plays an important cultural role in many lives. The debate won't be settled until we have more information.

Online/multi-media courses pay .05 per hour, with merit potential up to .15 per hour. The student must complete ¾ of the course for the lecturer to receive payment and be registered for the teacher achievement annuity. Merit is determined by comparison with similarly educated students who did not take the course. Online courses must include their merit ratings in the VOS.

When online education is used in the classroom, the distribution is the same. However, all students in the classroom will be registered as taking the course, and they will all provide an annuity to the online lecturer from their 2% teacher achievement annuity for the duration of their lives. This will encourage use of online education in the classroom. The teacher's salary is not affected.

The owners of online classroom instruction also qualify for the intellectual property distribution.

Trade Schools

Trade schools are excellent business opportunities for businesses and mutual organizations engaged in a particular trade. Not only do these mutual organizations collect income as schools, but they have access to the cream of the crop for their own partnerships. Trade societies can also establish schools to bring in revenue and continue traditions of the trade.

Trade schools pay at the rate of .35 per student-hour, with merit pay bringing the maximum distribution to $1.05 per student hour. The Department of Education incorporates test questions from the VSG for that particular trade in determining merit. Like colleges and universities, there is also a $40 per month school distribution.

Instructors in trade schools receive extremely large annuities from the 2% teacher achievement annuity, if the student becomes employed in that trade. This is due to relevance weighting (relevance of curriculum to job – discussed below). Trade schools receive the same relevance weighting for their cut of the 2% school achievement annuity.

Tutors and Home Instruction

All schools, professors and instructors have a VOS indicating their qualifications. The school itself has a VOS stating that all of their instructors are up to standard, and if there are violations of the standards, they are explicitly listed, such as "Our computer security instructor did not complete his undergraduate degree, but has hacked into eight of the Fortune 400 companies."

Tutors and home school teachers must have a certified VOS. The Department of Education will administer tests to show basic competency. People in a free society have a right to choose their teachers, even if those teachers trained in an unorthodox way, or who use unorthodox techniques, or emphasize unorthodox theories. However, core competency in the subject area is required if distribution funds will be used.

One-on-one tutors receive .80 cents distribution per student-hour in academic subjects taught through the graduate level or in trades recognized by a VSG. Tutors receive no merit pay though they are entitled to a portion of the 2% teacher achievement annuity, based on relevance. Tutors are free to charge extra for their services, and schools can sponsor tutors.

Home school teachers are paid the same rate as the corresponding primary school teachers and are judged according to the same merit standards. Home schools receive the $20 school distribution, only when school is in session. Home school teachers, however, participate completely in the 2% teacher achievement annuity.

Textbooks, Papers, and other Assigned reading

Assigned electronic books are treated like online courses. There might be an e-book stipend of 1 cent for every 4000 words. To qualify, at least 2/3 of the book, article or paper must be assigned reading in the class, or in successive classes. This distribution will go to the authors of these books, papers, and articles. The e-book stipend is also good for a discount on the hard copy, if desired. In some cases, textbook publishers might provide the hard copy free in exchange for the e-book stipend, the author and publisher annuities, as well as the intellectual property distribution.

Grades

Grades in today's society have become weapons that aggressive students and parents use against teachers. Tactics include lawsuits, verbal threats, and using influence with the school board. Grade inflation – the decade's long trend where "average" merits an increasingly higher grade than C – results. Grade inflation hurts achievers by failing to differentiate them from non-achievers. Business is hurt, making it more difficult to find the best candidate for a position. In fact, it has a double impact on business because the skills in extorting grades and the skills in managing the job interview are similar, and the grades serve to encourage the cockiness of the applicant. As a result, productivity and overall wages are impacted. Grade inflation is a consequence of the "right to a job," gone in AFFEERCE.

> In 1890 Harvard's average GPA (grade point average) was 2.27. In 1950, its average GPA was 2.55. By 2004, its GPA, as a result of dramatic rises in the 1960s and gradual rises since, had risen to 3.48 [FTN11.09]

In an AFFEERCE society, grades are important. They are used by business in making hiring decisions. The average, nationwide, will be 2.0. Monthly testing is an indication of where the student is vis-à-vis other students in the class and other students in the nation. After ignoring the extremes, test rankings and grades should correlate. Large deviations will affect the merit rankings of the teacher.

AFFEERCE grades will more accurately reflect the subject skills of the student, but unlike today a bad grade is not a career killer. Education in an AFFEERCE society is free and unlimited. A course can be repeated over and over, with the same or different instructors until the material is mastered and the desired grade achieved. Older marks will be removed from the transcript and grade point average.

The 2% + 2% Achievement Annuity

4% of the consumption tax paid by AFFEERCE citizens goes to reward the teachers and schools that made them what they are. That is 2% for those who taught them and 2% for the schools they attended. The calculations are done automatically by VIP-integrated computer systems. The taxpayer need not do any calculations, although there is access if the taxpayer wishes to verify recipients.

The 2% teacher achievement annuity is allocated as described below. The 2% school achievement annuity is allocated in a similar way.

First, a computer program generates a list of the living teachers, instructors, professors, and tutors that ever instructed the taxpayer. The list will be much longer than found in the examples below. In the column after each name is the number of hours taught. The column after that contains the following code: 1 – elementary school, 2 – secondary school, 3 – colleges and trade schools, 5 – private tutors and one-on-one instruction. In the next column is the subject matter taught. Next column, the program will access data prepared by the VSG (voluntary standards group) of the taxpayer's trade, and enter the ranking 0-10 specified for the subject matter in the VSG table. The ranking of 0 is rarely used, because it denies that teacher any annuity. Multiply the hours times the code times the VSG rank which is the weighted product.

Assume our taxpayer is a chemist.

Instructor	Hours	Code	Subject Taught	VSG Rank	Weighted Product
Joe Smith	960	1	4th grade general	5	4800
Mary Brown	36	3	Organic chemistry	10	1080
Sam Tutor	6	5	Physical chemistry	10	300
TOTAL					6180

Let the tax to be divvied up be $100. Take 90% (the remaining 10% is discussed below) or $90 and multiply by the weighted product, then divide by the weighted product total. If our taxpayer is a chemist, Joe Smith gets $69.90, Mary Brown gets $15.73 and Sam Tutor gets $4.37.

If the same taxpayer is a commercial artist, weightings will be different.

Instructor	Hours	Code	Subject Taught	VSG Rank	Weighted Product
Joe Smith	960	1	4th grade general	5	4800
Mary Brown	36	3	Organic chemistry	1	108
Sam Tutor	6	5	Physical chemistry	1	30
TOTAL					4938

In that case, Joe Smith gets $87.49, Mary Brown gets $1.96 and Sam Tutor gets 55 cents. Notice that the specialized chemistry instruction has far less relevance than a year of primary school.

Of the remaining 10%, half pays the authors of reading material. In a similar manner to classes, career choice affects the weighting. For this $100 of taxes, $5 would be divvied up for each book, article, or paper read in association with a completed course, including online courses.

The final 5% of the teacher achievement annuity goes to pay for online course instructors. As with teachers, this allocation uses a code: 1- elementary school level, 2-secondary school level, 3-university or trade school level.

VSG rank serves an important role in promoting fast economic growth. If a new technology is developed that few people understand, the initial VSG rank for relevant courses will be 10, regardless of the enrollee's occupation. High achievement annuities provide an incentive for schools to teach this technology as quickly as possible. Private instructors and tutors will rush in. Information about this technology will be shared quickly.

The 2% School Achievement Annuity

The 2% school achievement annuity is allocated as follows:

Elementary School(s)	15% Rounded to months attended
Secondary School(s)	20% Rounded to months attended
University and Trade Schools	45% By hours, VSG ranked courses
Textbook, article publishers	10% By words, VSG ranked
Multimedia, online education producers	10% By hours, code, VSG ranked

The university and trade school, textbook and online education categories use the same VSG rankings as their counterparts in the 2% teacher achievement annuity. This school achievement annuity only goes to schools, publishers, and producers that are still in business.

Achievement Annuity Distribution in the Early Days of AFFEERCE

For teachers and schools that predate capitulation and electronic record keeping, hypothetical average students could be used as surrogates. This would only be used for established schools and teachers with sufficient tenure, such that their students have entered the workforce. These "average students" should "spend" on the low side, so the actual achievement annuities are not a disappointment. Sixteen years after capitulation, no new "average students" would be assigned.

The Testing/Certification Distribution - $2

Those who take advantage of free unlimited education should feel obligated to spend two hours a month taking tests. Although not mandatory, the top 25% of test results appear on the student's transcript, and no shows are zero scores in this regard. The tests are used primarily to determine the merit of teachers in teaching skills and proper assignment of student grades. The results have a direct impact on their pay. Merit rankings must also appear on the teacher's VOS.

The test questions will be prepared by voluntary standards groups that represent trades and professions, academic pursuits, and schools, made up of dues-paying members from trade groups, corporations and schools, and paid consumer advocates. The VSG for a particular profession, or sub-profession for diverse fields, will set positive curriculum standards and generate a large set of test questions to show proficiency in the field. Test questions will be generated for each course in which the student is enrolled. Software will generate individualized tests, selecting questions at random based on the VOS standard for teachers of the subject. The questions reflect what the VSG feels students should know at various stages of their education. Different questions will likely reflect different philosophies within these groups.

Lower level VSGs can overwrite the test questions or certification requirements generated by higher level VSGs, although these can only be used for allocation of merit pay within the dominion.

Test administrators are low-paid personnel from the Department of Education, stationed at schools and independent testing centers, who monitor students.

The VSG not only uses the test scores of the students to determine the merit of the teachers, but they can set the deviation from the median in determining merit. The distribution of merit goes from 0% to 200%. The VSG will use a normal distribution and a standard deviation to convert percentile into merit. If all instructors in the field were equally qualified, they might all have a merit rating of 100%.

The teachers are graded from the top 50% of test results. If more than 50% of a class fails to take the monthly test, the teacher is hurt by a score of zero. Students taking multiple classes, potentially hurt all their teachers if they fail to take the test. Students, too, are also hurt. The top 25% of all tests, whether taken or not, will appear on a student's public transcript for the benefit of employers. Good results push bad results off the transcript. There is also a benefit of $2, each time a test is taken. When there is only one week remaining to take the test, there will be a VIP reminder.

The testing/certificate distribution is also used to administer certification for all of the professions and trades regulated by a VSG, as well as the VSG appointment of consumer advocates. Although bar exams and medical school diplomas will likely still be given, they have no force of law. Only through VSG designed tests can one be certified in a profession. Failure to pass certification must be specified on the VOS (violation of standards document) for an individual to remain engaged in that particular profession or trade. If a certification test is failed, it can be repeated again every three months. Some VSG's might require recertification on a yearly basis. The VSG will also provide a suggested curriculum.

For certification testing, $3 goes for computer time, test administration, and scoring. Certification testing requires payment of the $35 universal deductible, which is a major source of income for the Department of Education.

For merit testing, one dollar goes for administration and scoring of online results and $2 is deposited in the student's personal spending account. This is a small incentive for people with time on their hands to be enrolled in a class. It is assumed that less than half the population will be either taking courses requiring monthly testing or attempting to be certified, so the actual cost of this distribution is $2 per month.

Non-Universal/Disability Distribution - $97

There is a maximum $300 non-universal distribution, also called the disability distribution. Because a non-universal distribution is needed, the rules surrounding its distribution must be strict. If loopholes or unintended obstacles are discovered, they must be resolved by legislation. The essence of the rules is simplicity in order to reduce chances of corruption and favoritism. Here are some of those rules:

The first rule restores some degree of universality. The age related distributions are:

Age	Distribution	Comment
60	$50 per month	
65	$100 per month	
70	$150 or $175 per month	Extra $25 if never incarcerated
75	$200 or $225 per month	Extra $25 if never incarcerated
80	$300 per month	In all cases

The second rule is that anyone who would likely die without a caregiver is entitled by judicial order to the $300 disability distribution. The money will go to the caregiver who must be part of the same family or co-resident, or the caregivers who oversee a larger residence.

The third rule is that for anyone voluntarily or involuntarily confined to a hospital, penitentiary, mental health facility, or rehabilitation facility, the $300 is disbursed to the facility during confinement.

The fourth rule pays out a monthly annuity to any facility previously confining the individual that encourages wellness, non-recidivism, and staying clean and sober. For this rule, there are two categories of confinement. There is confinement in a hospital or mental health facility for non-substance abuse problems, and there is confinement in a penitentiary, substance abuse facility, or disciplinary facility. The payouts are a $25 wellness/hospital annuity and a $25 non-recidivism annuity. While a person is confined to an institution, the institution receives the $300 monthly distribution. Once released, the facility will continue to receive either the $25 per month wellness annuity for hospitals or the $25 non-recidivism annuity for penal or addiction-related facilities. These payments will continue until the person is hospitalized again, or is once again voluntarily or involuntarily confined to a penitentiary or addiction-related facility. The annuity will then go to the next institution.

In the case of the non-recidivism annuity, it is unlikely judges will sentence a repeat offender to the same institution twice, so the institution will do everything it can to prevent recidivism and the loss of its annuity. The wellness annuity will encourage inexpensive or free inpatient facilities, and motivate these facilities to encourage their patients to lead long and healthy lives.

We will assume that on average, by age 20, most everyone will have spent some time in a hospital. This contributes $22.50 to the actual cost of the distribution. Going on the extremely conservative assumption that at any given time, 10% of the population will be confined to an institution or in home nursing care, another $30 is added to the actual cost. If we assume 10% of the population will go to rehab or be sentenced to the penitentiary at one time in their lives, $2.50 is added to the cost of the distribution. If we assume the average person dies at age 80, the actual cost of the $50/month distribution at age 60 will be $12.50, at age 65 it will be $9.37, at age 70 it will be $6.25, at age 75 it will be $3.12, and at age 80, it will be .62. So the total actual cost per person per month of the non-universal disability distribution is $87. I've added $10, for a total of $97, as a safety cushion.

Social Security and government pension contributions will cease after capitulation. Those who paid into the system will receive 70% of their benefit in addition to the distributions.

The Medical Distribution - $120

> Among workers ages 40 through 50, nearly half fear the financial consequences of a critical illness-compared with just 29 percent who rate dying as their biggest concern, according to a new study. [FTN11.10]
>
> Of the 285 survey respondents who had suffered a critical illness, two-thirds had to take special measures to cover related costs. A total of 28 percent tapped their retirement savings and other funds earmarked for future needs, 28 percent dipped into emergency funds and 21 percent borrowed money from family or friends. Twelve percent declared bankruptcy and 11 percent either sold their homes or had them foreclosed upon. [FTN11.10]

> According to the World Bank, life expectancy in the United States ranked fortieth overall, just below Cuba. Infant mortality and maternal mortality is little better than in some developing countries; for infant mortality the U.S. is worse than Cuba, Belarus, and Malaysia[FTN10.23].

A medical distribution as low as $120/month will work when we apply the following remedies, many of them a natural part of the AFFEERCE solution: deregulation, rebates, self-insurance, the intellectual property distribution, other distributions, and VOS limited liability. To see how this is true, we can begin with today's outrageous costs and work down.

The average premium for full health coverage for people under 65 was $5,615 in 2010[FTN11.11]. For seniors and the disabled on Medicare, about 48 million, $560 billion was spent in 2010 which covered only half of all expenses[FTN11.12]. All told the average full medical coverage for seniors and the disabled is almost $21,000 per year. If seniors are 1/5 of the population the average per person full medical coverage is $8,692 per year.

Why is this so expensive? The health care profession is a monopoly actively protected by the force of law of the United States government. If you dare to compete, that is, set up a practice without a license, you will likely be sentenced to prison. You could lose all of your assets in civil court. The same is true for the pharmaceutical industry. The criminal penalties for selling drugs without a license are even worse than the criminal penalties for practicing medicine. The underworld created by this government protection of monopoly costs billions of dollars to the taxpayer in law enforcement and is the leading cause of death among African-American youth. As the only source of income for unskilled youth shut-out of a job, it has led to a huge prison industry.

A second government enforced monopoly responsible for high medical costs is the archaic way that intellectual property is handled. Patents allow drug companies and makers of innovative medical devices to charge exorbitant monopoly prices that both limit profits for innovators and bankrupt the nation.

Most hospitals have an itemized chargemaster list for everything the hospital dispenses, which serves to bankrupt those too poor to afford health insurance. If you have insurance, the insurance companies will negotiate this down and Medicare negotiates this down even further. Medicare is a fantastic entitlement program that despite the protests coming from those claiming to support free markets, is doing far better at containing costs than private health insurance. [FTN11.13]

> **Insurers with the most leverage, because they have the most customers to offer a hospital that needs patients, will try to negotiate prices 30% to 50% above the Medicare rates, rather than discounts off the sky-high chargemaster rates.** [FTN11.14]

Adjusting the $5,615 down by 1/3 to account for Medicare prices, gives an annual cost of $3742.96. Unfortunately, the $21,000 annual medical cost for seniors does not drop since that is already Medicare pricing. This brings the average annual cost per person down to $7194.36 if 20% of the insured are senior citizens. That is $599 per month which is 5 times the $120 allocated for the medical distribution.

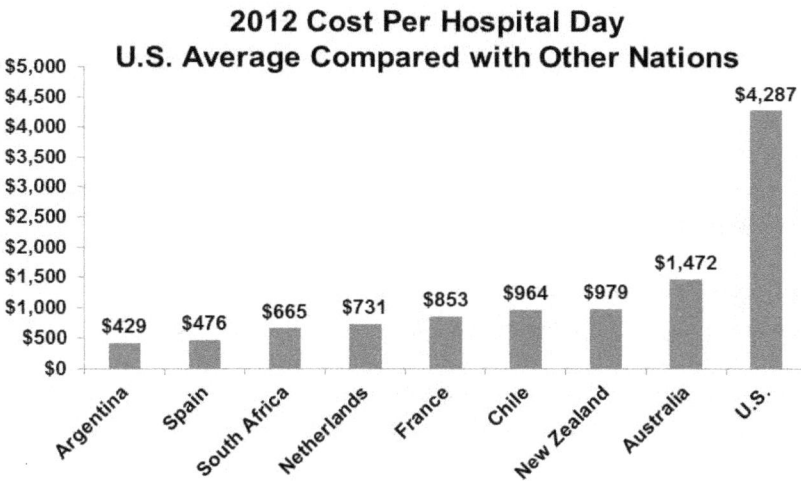

2012 Cost Per Hospital Day
U.S. Average Compared with Other Nations

Argentina $429, Spain $476, South Africa $665, Netherlands $731, France $853, Chile $964, New Zealand $979, Australia $1,472, U.S. $4,287

Seniors spend an average of 5.6 days in the hospital per stay versus 4.3 for non-seniors[FTN11.16]. Seniors over 65 have 4.5 times as many inpatient days as those under 65[FTN11.17]. Thus senior hospital costs are 5.9 times that of the general population. Since $3,742 x 5.9 is approximately $21,000, it is reasonable to assume days in the hospital are the main contributor to health care costs for all ages. One day in U.S. hospital cost in 2012 an average of $4,287 which is twice the cost in Australia, the next highest country[FTN11.15].

The $4,287 does not include prescribed medication or tests beyond those administered by aides, such as temperature and blood pressure. The actual cost to the hospital for an inpatient day is $1,630, which does not include profit[FTN11.18]. Even without profit, the costs are higher than the rest of the world.

The AFFEERCE Medical Plan

This is the current state of things, or at least how things were back in 2012. Costs today, are no doubt much higher. So how can we reduce these costs to $120/month?

From the HMO concept, we begin with hospital affiliation. All doctors, including specialists must be affiliated with hospitals, although a specialist can be affiliated with more than one hospital, and surgeons who are leaders in their field can be independent. A citizen chooses a local hospital based on its reputation, convenience, services offered over the basic plan, and the affiliated doctors. Location monopoly will always be a factor in hospital selection, but various features of the plan mitigate this problem.

A tranche of 83% of each citizen's medical distribution goes to this hospital as an insurance premium. A hospital can charge optional additional premiums for private rooms, private nurses, exotic treatments, very expensive treatments for the aged and anything else excluded from basic coverage. Visits to doctors and specialists affiliated with this hospital are covered under the plan. They are paid from the hospital's insurance arm. As you will see below, this is not a protected monopoly. Collusion between the insurance arm and the treatment arm of a hospital is impossible.

The remaining 17% of the distribution goes to a federal payer at level-7. This covers a portion of all diagnostic costs, certain costs for illness and injury away from the local hospital, deregulation costs, local hospital bankruptcy, and some CDC and NIH costs.

The dilemma of Sun Yat-Sen is used to prevent collusion between the insurance arm and treatment arm of a hospital. The treatment arm has a fixed rate for every procedure or service. This is the rate it charges its insurance arm. However, if the patient affiliated with this hospital can receive the same treatment or service elsewhere for less, the insurance arm will pay for that service elsewhere and rebate 50% of the difference to the patient. Both the patient and the insurance arm profit from competition.

By the same token, patients can choose independent surgeons or special facilities provided they pay the difference over the HMO charge or have a private policy that does so. The HMO insurance arm can charge a 5% service charge for treatment elsewhere. This would be covered automatically for rebates that exceed 10%.

Although this has radical implications for treatment costs, the most dramatic cost savings come from what we have shown above to be the most costly part of medical care: a night in the hospital.

Those supplying accommodation services need only treble land on the hospital campus adjacent to the hospital. Weatherproof passageways will provide easy access. Although a hospital could fight this by matching trebles and restricting access, none will. Those that accept independent vendors on a hospital campus, will be hyper-competitive with those that do not. How hyper-competitive? Remember that the cost of a night in the hospital was over $4,000 in 2012. We will see that allowing independent accommodations on the hospital campus will reduce this to $200/night instantly and possibly as low as $100/night. You read that correctly. A night in the hospital will cost $100-$200/night!

Consider a high-rise on a hospital campus with a passageway to the hospital itself. The land for such a high rise can be easily seized or purchased. For optimal efficiency, assume a medical collective owns or rents one 6,000 sq. ft. floor of the high rise. Leaving out children, assume 8 skilled nurses and paramedics are members of the collective, along with 8 spouses who cook, clean and can help with patient care.

The family brings in $5,920 in housing distribution which is insufficient for the $20,000 monthly rental. The $3,520 monthly food distribution is overly abundant. Suppose the family lives in 4000 sq. ft. and 2000 sq. ft. is used for 10 patient rooms and a nurses' station.

This family will gladly charge $200 a day for inpatient care, 1/8 the current U.S. cost of an inpatient day, half of the cost in Argentina, and even less than India. How could this possibly work?

The first things to look at are the other distributions which contribute to funding. For 10 patients, these are the monthly receivables. (The largest receivable of all is not even being shown in this table. More on that later.)

Distribution	Amount (10 patients)	Comment
Housing	$3,700	Direct transfer, pre-pay, private insurance, or waived
Food	$2,200	Direct transfer always
Disability	$3,000	$300 non universal
Inpatient care	$60,000	$200 per day
Total	$68,900	

Now look at the monthly expenses:

Expense	Amount (10 patients)	Comment
Rent	$14,080	Makes $20,000 with family housing distribution
Food	0	Patients provided by family food distribution alone
Equipment depreciation	$6,000	Assumes $300,000 over 4 years. Including beds, linen, monitors, EKG's, gurneys, uniforms, and ambulance.
Supplies	$1,000	Bandages, catheters, pain killers, antiseptic, etc.
Utilities	$3,000	Heat, air, electric, phone, cable, internet
Liability insurance	$1,000	$100 per patient per month
Salaries	$43,820	$5,477 average salary per couple
Total	$68,900	

In a world where food, housing, medical care and education are free and in a world without income taxes, $5,477 per couple per month is a very nice salary. It is almost all discretionary. There are no student loans to pay off because the nurses received their education free. And remember that half of each couple is unskilled.

With a staff ratio of 16:10, patients will be well cared for. Because the high-rise is connected to the hospital, doctors can make their rounds, and patients can be taken for tests and surgeries. With patient care collectives on other floors of the high-rise, families can easily transfer long-term patients to other facilities in the building for vacation time. Specialization is likely, and can increase profits.

It is clear that providing $200/day is sufficient for inpatient care. But, is it necessary. A big source of wealth for this medical collective has yet to be revealed. Principally, this is the wellness annuity.

When the patient is released from the hospital, the hospital (or medical collective) continues to receive $25 per month from the disability distribution for the remainder of the patient's life or until they are hospitalized at another facility. Since the average hospital stay is 5 days, and I will hazard a guess that that is no more than 5 days every 5 years, on average, this medical collective would treat, on average, 60 inpatients a month, yielding an average annuity of $1,500 a month for 5 years. Assuming this collective takes one month of vacation per year, after 5 years, the annuities would max out at $82,500 a year! This all goes to the bottom line, adding $1,146 of monthly income for each couple.

Because the housing distribution adds only $616/month to couple salaries, competition will likely cause the housing distribution to be waived. Can we go further and provide inpatient care for as little as $100/day? If the hospital's self-insurance arm is paying $200/day, then if the medical collective is able to charge only $100/day, the patient will receive a $50/day rebate from the insurance arm. This daily stipend can go a long way to help pay bills while the patient is hospitalized. It beats "the duck" any day.

Unfortunately at $100/day, the monthly income per couple drops to $2,833 including maximum wellness annuities and excluding the housing distribution. Discretionary, or not, this is nothing to write home about.

However, there are other sources of income for the medical collective that can restore income to the previous level. One of these is specialization. The collective can specialize in a particular condition and offer specialized diagnostic tests and procedures at low prices. Also remember, the nurses are already on site. Administration of medication, and taking blood is paid in addition to standard inpatient care (although at rates much lower than today).

This is a hospital campus and patients are searching for the best prices to maximize their rebates. That very search opens the door for even larger profits. The medical collective can act as advocates for their patients in locating the best testing and treatment options, on or off campus. If the patient decides on an off campus solution, the medical collective will provide transportation. This advocacy and transport is done in exchange for 20% of the rebate.

Malpractice Liability

> ...the real cost associated with medical malpractice litigation. It's not as much about the verdict or the settlements (or considerable malpractice premiums) that hospitals and doctors pay as it is about what they do to avoid being sued. The most practical malpractice reform proposals...would allow doctors to use what is called a safe-harbor defense. Under safe-harbor, a defendant doctor or hospital could argue that the care provided was within the bounds of what peers have established as reasonable under the circumstances. [FTN11.14]

As Stephan Brill points out above, it is the extra tests ordered by doctors to protect themselves from liability that contributes most to the high cost of malpractice liability. In an AFFEERCE economy, there is no liability if you follow the standards set by the VSG. In fact, you can violate those standards without liability as long as it is clearly stated in the VOS and the patient signs off on those violations.

There are also significant caps on liability. This means that only lawyers interested in justice will take on liability cases as opposed to lawyers looking for the multi-million dollar payoffs. Because of the distributions, both lawyers who are interested in justice and their injured clients will never starve no matter how lengthy the litigation.

> Liability costs from premiums due to extra tests will be reduced by as much as 90%.

Intellectual Property

The intellectual property distribution, discussed in Chapter 3, will qualitatively reduce the cost of patent drugs, prosthesis, implants, medical testing equipment, genetic therapy, and surgical supplies. For instance, of the $376 billion spent on prescription drugs in the United States each year, a study from the Center on Economic and Policy Research showed that $326 of that was spent on intellectual property [FTN12.06]. Successful drug companies will make their profits on volume and worldwide distribution, and the elimination of free promotions. Shockingly, for drug companies, the bloated marketing budget is twice that of R&D! [FTN12.07]

Medical School

To justify their high salaries, doctors need to get top grades in college. They then must spend another four years in medical school, and more time as an intern. This costs a fortune and preserves the monopoly.

In an AFFEERCE economy, nobody needs to pay for education. Because of the high salary commanded by doctors, competing medical schools will open up and the supply of VOS-certified doctors will rise to meet the demand and bring down costs.

More importantly, AFFEERCE is all about deregulation. Specialists who do not spend four years in medical school, but rather learn only about a very specific procedure, can pass certification or specify deviations from the standards on their VOS, along with the risks, and be protected from liability.

But who would go to these less qualified professionals when free quality medical care is available to all? The lifeblood of free markets, in an entitlement environment, is the rebate. 50% of the money saved by the patient on less expensive treatments is rebated to the patient by the self-insurance arm of the HMO.

Diagnosis and Prognosis

Diagnosis and prognosis plays a critical role in medical costing. To have an accurate measure of how well hospitals are performing in this regard, the federal payer will pay half the costs of diagnosis and publish the per-patient expenditures by each hospital. Because the diagnostician plays such a critical role in determining the value of the distribution for a particular illness or injury, this field is regulated to the extent that the federal payer will only pay for diagnosis by an AMA VSG-certified medical professional. All diagnoses must be checked by a licensed diagnostician against diagnostic software. If the program agrees with the doctor, the diagnosis is confirmed. If not, a second VSG-certified medical professional will be called upon to make an independent diagnosis. If the two licensed medical professionals agree, the diagnosis is confirmed. If the two medical professionals disagree, a third professional must be consulted.

Partial diagnosis occurs when the output of the diagnosis is one or more tests. Tests should be prescribed in the proper order to maximize information and minimize costs.

Absent competitive pressures, diagnosis will cost more in an AFFEERCE economy than it does today. Once the diagnosis is rendered, or earlier in the case of scheduled diagnostic testing, the benefits of deregulation will pay off.

If the illness or injuries are not acute, the patient or their advocate is free to shop around for the best rates on VOS-certified CT scans, MRI's, EEG's, EKG's, expensive lab work, etc. and collect the 50% rebate from the hospital price for the differential.

Once testing is complete, there is a final diagnosis and a prognosis that includes the course of treatment and the estimated cost of that treatment, a cost paid by the hospital's insurance arm. Once again, failure to give accurate estimates will be reflected on the VOS. The course of treatment could be a referral to a specialist for diagnosis, in which case the process repeats.

HMO hospitals will have a set cost for all treatments covered by the national basic policy. If a hospital is unable or unwilling to provide certain treatments, it must have a contract with a neighboring hospital for that treatment, and provide transit to and from that hospital.

Sickness Away from Home

For patients that get sick or injured away from their chosen hospital, the chosen hospital will pay the lesser of their own charges or the providing hospitals charges for tests, procedures, surgeries, etc. The federal payer will make up the difference to the providing hospital if the HMO hospital charges less than the providing hospital for services.

This expands the dilemma of Sun Yat-Sen. If a hospital's charge to its self-insurance arm is too small, they will receive little remuneration for providing services to a patient with a different HMO hospital (they can turn away no one). If they charge too much, patients will shop around for better deals and the hospitals insurance arm must pay for the outside services and the rebate.

Effects of Self-Insurance and the Medical Rebate

Self-insurance and the medical rebate will drive down prices and ultimately the cost of the distribution. To see how far, take a look at these cost comparisons from Steven Brill's groundbreaking article in Time Magazine. [FTN11.14]

	CT Scan (Head)	Appendectomy	Coronary Bypass
U.S.	$510	$13,003	$67,583
France	$141	$ 3,164	$16,140
India	$ 43	$ 254	$ 4,525

This chart and everything discussed above, including the over 90% drop in the cost of inpatient care, suggests the medical distribution could be under $40/month. Can we rely on this? It sounds too good to be true and maybe it is. But the point here is that a $120/month medical distribution is a conservative estimate. $100/month pays an insurance premium at the patient's local hospital of choice. The other $20/month goes to the national payer.

Test Results and the VIP

Test results along with the patient's entire medical record, are saved in the VIP and associated with the patient for life. A certified diagnostician can access the VIP medical history of an unconscious or otherwise disabled patient with only the patient's iris or palm.

Radical Medical Deregulation

Suppose you consider yourself an artist self-trained at the non-surgical setting of broken bones, even though you never went to medical school. Your VOS lists the lack of medical school, but includes one year of training courses. It warns the patient that the cast will have to stay on for two months or more, and the possible limitations to mobility that surgery might have prevented. The VOS lists the number of procedures performed and the number of complaints received.

The adult patient is x-rayed at the hospital with a simple leg fracture, and a certified diagnostician determines that $18,000 of surgery is prescribed. The diagnosis is backed by a second opinion. This is covered by the medical distribution. However, the patient is not an athlete, works at a desk job, and isn't worried about the unlikely outcome of a small limp. So the patient comes to you, the bone is set, and the cast applied for $400. Thus $17,600 is saved and the patient receives a rebate of $8,800.

While this works well where every simple fracture has become a surgery in waiting, what are the implications for more deadly diseases? What are the full implications of deregulation?

Joe read *The Idiot's Guide to Brain Surgery*, and *Brain Surgery for Dummies*. He does his surgery in the basement, but uses plenty of disinfectant. After listing the numerous standards that Joe violates at his Brain Surgery Shack, his VOS shows that of his twelve patients so far, three had their tumors removed with no side effects and a complete return to health. Three more had minor but tolerable side effects, and the remaining six either died or were left in a permanent vegetative state.

Joe charges $3,000 for removal of a tumor that is partially visible on the brain's surface. This includes 8 days of recovery with Joe's family caring for your needs (The nursing VOS also indicates several standards violations.) An analysis of the MRI by the two certified diagnosticians and diagnostic software indicates a surgery and recovery that would be paid at $93,000. If the patient decides to have his tumor removed by Joe, $90,000 will be saved in healthcare bills, and the patient or his heirs, will receive $45,000 in a rebate.

To see if this is acceptable, examine the natural rights of man. Firstly, the right to life implies a right to terminate one's own life. A patient has a right to suicide, and by extension, a right to have Joe perform the surgery.

What about the vegetative outcome? In that case, a patient's housing distribution will pay for a bed in a ward, and their food distribution will pay for IV and administration. Medical and disability distributions will pay for physical therapy and nursing.

Only a nurse's aide is needed to manage a comatose patient. The food, housing, disability distributions, and the $100 medical distribution sent directly to the nursing center would suffice to attract competition. A comatose patient needs very little space. If Joe's Brain Surgery Shack left a patient in a vegetative state, there would be an extra cost of $300/month for the disability distribution, but the taxpayer would save on the education distribution and likely gain tremendous actuarial savings.

There is a conflict of rights if Joe leaves the patient conscious and aware, but with a serious disability. Although it is difficult to say whether such a disability would have occurred in a hospital with expert brain surgeons, it is likely that in many cases, it would not. Because the patient chose to risk Joe's handiwork and collect the $45,000 for himself and his family, what kind of liability does the hospital or distribution fund have for this patient's disability? In other words, suppose there was a medical procedure to fix this disability, which cost $100,000. Why should the taxpayer, or the insurer, have to pay for this procedure because our patient chose to patronize Joe's Brain Surgery Shack?

There is both a partial solution and a justification for this. The partial solution demands that a risk of disabling complications be associated with the procedure. The diagnosticians would be held accountable on their VOS for failure to properly assess risk, that is, risks on average way too high, or way too low. To encourage the cost-saving procedures, the risk would be doubled and that portion of the rebate would be guaranteed the patient. For instance, a 15% risk would guarantee 30% of the rebate. A 50% risk or higher would guarantee 100% of the rebate. This portion of the rebate is transferred to the patient immediately after surgery. In the next two years, if a disabling complication arose that led to an expense beyond the disability distribution, the money would be taken first from the escrowed rebate. Any rebate remaining in the escrow account after two years, would revert to the patient. In the case of Joe's patient who required $100,000 worth of surgery, no rebate would remain and the insurer or taxpayer would still be out over $50,000. However, to promote medical deregulation, the federal payer will pick up the tab.

There is a justification for this. In a free society, we do not monitor the sports activities, eating behaviors, smoking, and recreational drug use of the citizenry. There is nothing morally superior about extreme skiing or extreme climbing for the thrill, than there is about extreme medicine for the rebate. If anything, the latter drives down medical costs, and increases the wealth of the nation.

Realistically, there will not be a Joe's Brain Surgery Shack. Low cost options will include foreign doctors who are not VOS-certified by the AMA VSG, specialists who followed alternative educational paths, and a few medical school dropouts working on the cheap. All that a free society demands is full disclosure, including a patient-signed VOS. However, doctors need to understand that fraud is a very serious offense in a free society.

Another issue raised by rebates, is that people might purposely injure themselves to collect the rebate. First of all, this is illegal. If it can be proven in a court of law that the injury was both intentional and done with the purpose of defrauding the insurance, that is a crime punishable by incarceration or a fine that well exceeds the rebate. Furthermore, the more an accident is made to look accidental, the more likely unexpected, and possibly permanently disabling or fatal injuries will occur. For those desperate for money, truly free markets open up far more lucrative ways of collecting, including being a human guinea pig for dangerous pharmaceuticals, selling a kidney or lung, or the oldest profession, prostitution. With food, housing, medical care and education covered in the basic distribution, desperation for money will be found only in those with addictions or obsessions.

Uncovered Medical Procedures

New highly expensive life-saving technologies are always being developed. In the beginning the cost of these technologies can be prohibitive. Until the price becomes affordable, the basic plan will not require coverage for these innovations, although individual hospitals can promote themselves by promising coverage. In general, as the price of the technology drops, first young people will be covered, and only as the price drops further will coverage extend to older people. Those over 80 will almost never be covered for expensive procedures unless successful results are fairly certain and their health is otherwise very good.

People are free to buy supplemental policies covering new technology, independent surgeons, special facilities, and expensive technologies for those over 80. These policies should be considered unnecessary. Basic coverage is intended to be comprehensive and of high quality.

Mental Health

Psychiatrists are inordinately expensive because they have a government enforced monopoly on dispensing drugs. With self-medication completely legal in AFFEERCE, most people will be perfectly content to discuss their problems and minor neuroses with their social worker. Social workers should be trained to recognize when a client needs psychiatric treatment. (See, *Social Worker Distribution*, below) With decreased demand, psychiatric care should be on par with other health care.

Serious mental illness is not a crime, but when crimes are committed by the mentally ill, they will be sentenced to mental health facilities. Psychiatrists might recommend voluntary commitment to a mental health facility. Self-commitment is also allowed without psychiatric recommendation. However, for all instances of confinement, the patient must be assigned a VOS-certified psychiatrist.

Furthermore, when a patient voluntarily commits themselves to a mental health facility, they must sign away their liberty for a specified period of time. Only the psychiatrist can restore liberty before the time period has expired. The same applies to voluntary commitment for drug and alcohol addictions. Voluntary commitment almost always requires transfer of the housing distribution or payment of $370 a month. It is also possible that charities will pick up the cost of private rooms.

The full $300 disability distribution applies for both voluntary and involuntary commitment. Involuntary loss of liberty will bring in extra funding for jailing and guards from the government distribution.

Reproduction and Gestation

Because reproductive control is essential for keeping the AFFEERCE economy in balance, contraceptives and contraceptive medical procedures are always free. There is never a copay. This includes removal of bodily devices and their reinsertion as often as the patient desires. Safe contraception is so important to AFFEERCE that there is no rebate. There is no copay for condoms, birth-control or morning-after pills. There is free abortion on demand in the first trimester without copay. Abortion is available in the second and third trimester, but preliminary counseling and $35 universal deductible is required.

Doctors can specify on their VOS those procedures they will not perform due to moral or religious beliefs; for example, abortion or assisted suicide.

Hypochondria

Hypochondriacs are responsible for 10-20% of the U.S. health cost because of all the tests they ask for. Every year the U.S. has to take 150 billion dollars out of the medical system just for having to repeatedly test the patients. This disorder is continually draining money from the medical system on tests for hypochondriacs which could be spent on other more helpful medical treatments...[FTN11.19]

With hypochondriacs costing 10%-20% of the healthcare budget, potential savings are significant. Innovative solutions will appeal to hypochondriacs by catering to their symptoms to get results, at the same time provide a valuable check on hospital diagnostics.

These solutions might be called hypochondriac hotels and will be associated with medical schools. The "hotels" will provide two kinds of services: diagnostic and treatment.

Patients, with two confirming diagnoses of no physical problem who are still convinced that something is wrong, can check into a hypochondriac hotel, by surrendering their food and housing distributions, or paying the equivalent in VIP$. By doing so, they agree to be tested for up to 10 hours a day, with 60% of the tests prescribed by the institution and 40% self-prescribed. Patients sign a VOS allowing the hospital to perform tests with a certain low level of radiation per week. The VOS states the risks. Any self-prescribed tests involving radiation are in addition to the hospitals tests. All tests will be conducted by medical students or technician students, usually in small groups with professional supervision. Some psychological testing/treatment will likely be mandatory.

A stint in the hotel is for one month at a time. For that month, it is like a penitentiary, where non-recidivism annuities go into effect. The patient cannot leave, although they have every amenity, quality food, telephone privileges and visitors. At the end of the month, the patient can sign on for an additional month. In fact, patients can spend their entire lifetime, from the age 14 on, in the hypochondriac hotel.

Here is why the hotel is of immense subjective value to the hypochondriac. In the first six months after diagnosis by the original physicians, if testing reveals that both confirming diagnoses were incorrect, and a new diagnosis is confirmed by an outside source, given the additional test results, the hotel will receive $1,500 from the federal payer. The patient will also receive $1,500. The two original doctors will be docked for their incorrect diagnosis, and they will be required to post this failure on their VOS. Anecdotally, based on my limited experience with hypochondriacs, no outcome would give them more pleasure than to be vindicated and to have the original doctors who failed to diagnose their problem docked and forced to admit this failure on their VOS.

In a double win, the hypochondriac hotel concept gives medical schools a ready supply of volunteers to train doctors and technicians in the administration and interpretation of tests, in addition to serving as a valuable check on the diagnosis process.

These "hotels" can serve as centers for treatment innovation as well as diagnostics. Some patients will want to define their own treatments, including the use of faith in healing. This does not include paid trials by pharmaceutical and medical technology companies, which can be done in any inpatient facility. It does include those treatments in which the physician must violate the Hippocratic Oath due to omission, or commission. However, violations of commission must be neither fatal, nor cause permanent debilitating damage. That is, the physician will honor a patients request not to amputate a diseased limb, but will not honor a patients request to amputate a healthy one.

In a free society, this is a way for the patient to prescribe their own treatment, having signed the appropriate VOS. It is quite different than the right of a patient to shop around and find the best value for an indicated treatment, since the distribution will not pay for a non-indicated treatment.

The sponsoring medical school wins by providing medical students with cases that can grow more acute with time, demonstrate psychology in patient interviews, raise ethical questions, as well as show the efficacy of patient directed treatment.

Nursing Home, Long Term, and Hospice Care

Once upon a time in the days of extended families, when Children=Wealth was more true than it is today, old people died in their own home, surrounded by loving family. In today's sometimes frightening society, old people, usually alone, are packaged off to nursing homes, which often provide little care, strip older people of all their wealth and dignity, and gouge the taxpayers once all of a patient's lifetime accumulated wealth has been exhausted. When I worked in a nursing home in the 1970s, the number one request from patients, ahead of food, water, and being changed, was, "Please kill me."

The nurse's aides, cooks and janitors who provide all the care services for the elderly are paid minimum wage. Yet nursing home care averages $81,000 per year[FTN11.20]. This is not much more than the expected $200/day paid from the hospital's insurance arm for inpatient care. Even so, it is not profitable for inpatient facilities to house long term/terminal patients due to the absence of annuities. Nor would it be ethical to extend these annuities after death, as this is an incentive for foul play. But affordability is not really the issue. Warehousing of the elderly, is.

The answer lies in the AFFEERCE alternative family, where People=Wealth. Beginning at age 60, a disability stipend kicks in and when a person reaches 80, the full monthly $300 disability distribution is given, even if the elder person is completely able. This is a powerful incentive to care for parents in the home. An 80 year old family member brings $975 ($220 (f) + $370 (h) + $300(d) + $35 (c)) into the household every month. Bringing elderly neighbors into the family increases the efficiency of elder care.

That is the goal; to incorporate elder care into the dynamics of a large family. By also caring for the friends of an elderly parent, the operation becomes more efficient. It does not pay as well as a medical collective, but it is also a labor of love. Not all of the elderly will be lucky enough to be cared for in their home, or the home of a neighbor. However, small operations can go beyond family and neighbors and still maintain a homelike environment by restricting the number of residents to under ten, like the medical collective. This family business can provide reasonable wages. The business plan can also include long term care of accident victims and the developmentally disabled.

There is a unique bonus where the nursing or home care facility gets a portion of "the patient's estate" after the patient is deceased. It is not actually the patient's estate, but rather a pool of all the estates of all the patients who died in the same year and ever spent time in a qualified nursing facility. For each three months the patient spends in a qualified nursing home facility, the facility receives 1% of the average estate in the bonus pool. For instance, if a patient spent 18 months in a nursing facility before they died, the patient's estate would be charged 6% and the facility would receive 6% of the average estate in the bonus pool. Facilities must accept all patients without income qualification to qualify for this bonus.

With a 1% loss to the estate for 3 months of nursing care, it will take 25 years of nursing care to deplete an estate. For individuals with estates valued at less than two million dollars, it is a far better bet to opt for bonus-qualified nursing care than a non-qualified facility.

Caregivers should also choose the bonus pool when caring for a developmentally disabled child. The child will likely live many years, leaving the caregiver a large percentage of the bonus pool. Large spiritual families who provide long-term care can use this money to further their charitable work.

There is another good reason to choose bonus-qualified home nursing care. Private facilities know the patient's worth and have a financial incentive to either terminate or unnecessarily prolong life. However strictly the law is enforced, it is difficult to eliminate the incentive for foul play.

Large contributions to the bonus pool can come from unexpected sources. Suppose, early in life, an accident victim spends 6 months in a nursing facility. Once again healthy, they go on to become a billionaire. Years later when the billionaire passes away, 2% of their estate goes into the bonus pool together with a portion of the estates of all nursing home patients who died that year. Twenty million dollars from the billionaire's estate goes into the pool. If there are 10,000 patient-percentage units in the pool then each nursing facility receives $2,000 from this billionaire alone for each former patient-percentage unit. It might be good policy to smooth the top two extreme legacies into the next year, so that in any year no estate contributes more to the pool than the third highest estate.

If the average estate is $200,000, then the home nursing care facility receives $8,000/year/resident in estate revenue. With $975/month in other distributions, the home care facility receives a total of $19,700/year/resident. With room and board costs of less than $4,000/year, over $15,000/year/resident is available for wages. Although the pay is very low, in conjunction with the distributions a large alternative family can live quite well doing this labor of love.

The social worker will insure that the elderly person is receiving adequate care wherever they reside. If the elderly or disabled person wishes to move into another nursing environment, they will be free to do so. If the social worker determines that the elderly person is not able to make a decision, and appears to be suffering from neglect, the social worker can recommend movement into a different nursing care facility and will petition a judge, if the family refuses.

The Social Worker Distribution - $10

Few things scream Big Brother louder than a social worker assigned to every family. This distribution will be debated over the 60 years, and many will be tempted to eliminate it. That would be unfortunate. The social worker:

1.   Is the first line of defense against child abuse, child abandonment, child endangerment, domestic abuse, domestic battery, and elder abuse.
2.   Provides counseling for day to day mental health issues, and arranges for the seriously mentally ill to get the care they need.
3.   Provides union, marriage, divorce, and family counseling.
4.   Negotiates minor disputes, relieving law enforcement and the courts of that responsibility.
5.   Helps people who do not understand their way around the new society, navigate through the distributions and sort through the options.
6.   Brings people with complimentary needs together into permanent or temporary families, communes, collectives, and mutual organizations, so they might best enjoy the benefits of AFFEERCE.

Social workers are expected to serve 30 families. A family can, at any time, request a new social worker. To understand social worker motivation and compensation is to understand the theory of alternative families in an AFFEERCE society. A large alternative family, such as a kibbutz, is ideally a miniature well-functioning society. There will naturally be the "cops" who prevent child-abuse, domestic abuse and elder abuse. There will be natural counselors who can offer advice to other family members. With a wide diversity of skills, mutual support in the family will eliminate the need for a social worker altogether. This leads to the ironic situation where the social worker will be paid exceptionally well to oversee a large commune, and yet have little responsibility, save interfacing with a few liaisons within the family who do the actual work. Even if the social worker agrees to share income, this can still be a dream job.

For this reason it is the goal of every social worker to build large functional families. That is the way to help people help themselves. Social workers new to the job are given a case load of 30 single person families. With a social worker distribution of $120 per person per year, the beginning social worker will earn $3,600 per year, a rather paltry salary of little more than $1 an hour. The social worker distribution will be administered at cellular level-2.

Some people prefer to remain loners, but most want to be part of a group where there is synergy. The social worker, by introducing people with complimentary aspirations, and through counseling, will facilitate the building of large, healthy families. Healthy families will tend to grow, both through the addition of children as well as new adults.

The growth of the social worker's income is governed by the total number of people in all 30 families. As families grow, the social worker's income grows. If families break apart or older children leave the nest, temporarily or permanently, the social worker's income shrinks.

The social worker is tied to a level-2 district. Smaller families and singles tend to be more mobile, and that tendency will be even greater in an AFFEERCE economy. If a family of 3 moves away, the social worker has an open spot for a new family of 3, if one is available. If a family of 12 dismisses a social worker, there is an open spot for a new family of 12, but such large families are geographically stable and hard to come by. The social worker might have to accept a family of 5 or less, instead.

The social worker has every incentive to help remove an abuser. AFFEERCE guarantees that nobody will be tied to their abuser by economic necessity. People will leave, rather than be abused. A healthy family is a growing family and a growing family will be lucrative for the social worker.

Assume an experienced social worker's 30 families are divided as such: 7 singles, 7 childless couples, 10 couples with 2 children each, one family of 8 adults and 6 children, one family of 24 adults, one family of 31 adults and 5 children, one family of 64 adults and 64 children, one family with 82 adults, and one family with 117 adults and 16 children. The social worker has a total of 478 clients. That means an income of $57,360 per year. Perhaps $10,000 is rebated to the three large families for internal social work, leaving a net income of $47,360. Additionally, the social worker might be frequently recognized in the discretionary tax for the lifesaving help they can give.

Big families will often be recruiting to grow the family business. The social worker will recognize how this family works well together and perhaps encourage one of the singles or childless couples to union (merge) with this larger family. The union will raise the social worker's income, by creating a new opening for a family of the same size.

Fire Protection Distribution - $5

Because of the on-call nature of the job, including sleeping arrangements, local fire-fighting organizations might organize themselves as large families or collectives to maximize resources and profit. This discussion on the fire-fighting distribution assumes a fire-fighting family, although arbitrary arrangements are possible.

An urban fire-fighting family might have 25,000 people to protect in houses, mid-rises and high-rises. Equipment might consist of 2 engines, 1 ladder, 2 ambulances, and a command vehicle. Personnel might include a battalion chief,

10 trained general purpose fire-fighters, 4 more specializing in rescue, and 4 more with specialties in safety, special operations, tactical support and communications. The cost of all vehicles and equipment is about $2 million with a life expectancy of 15 years [FTN11.30]. Depreciation is about $12,000 per month. Twenty percent of all local fire distribution goes to regional command.

A typical fire family might include 2 shifts of 18 field personnel, plus 6 station support personnel. That is 42 family members, excluding children. With a $5 per month fire distribution, total revenue is $125,000 per month with a $25,000 tranche going to regional support. An additional $12,000 goes to equipment and vehicles depreciation, leaving $88,000 for salaries, or an average of over $2,000 per month, all of it discretionary.

Fire stations need to be near the most expensive part of downtown. However, a jurisdictional covenant restricts treblers to other fire fighters. A 5-story building on 1/10 of an acre would spaciously accommodate family and equipment. Even if the neighborhood ground rent were 1 million per acre, the jurisdictional covenant would likely provide treble safety of this 1/10 acre property at far less than the normal $8,400 a month. However, even in the unlikely event there is no covenant, the housing distribution for just the workers, excluding any other family members is $15,540 per month which should easily pay the ground rent, the mortgage, and utilities on a high tech fire station, common eating hall, and spacious bedrooms, baths and workshops for all. When one shift is on vacation, the other shift is on 24/7.

Because of the nature of fire-fighting work, fire-fighters can engage in other money-making pursuits in the home between fires, such as commercial art, tutoring, authoring, computer programming, arts and crafts, knitwear, and any other task that can be interrupted for a fire or emergency.

Fire fighters perform building, sprinkler, and fire-system inspections for fees that add significantly to the $2,000 per month base salary, although such fees must be approved by a 2/3 plurality of the fire-fighting district. Fire-fighters will also receive actual and punitive damages from convicted arsonists.

In addition to responding to district local fires, fire-fighters respond to 2 and higher alarm fires in neighboring districts. Regional command responds to 3 alarm fires and higher[FTN11.31]. Urban regional command has choppers, ladders, satellite communications centers, and other specialty equipment. They might oversee 10 fire-fighting collectives or more, with revenue of at least $250,000 a month, $50,000 of which goes to depreciation on the high tech equipment. There are 40 highly trained personnel, including the fire chief and assistant chief. At least 30 are on duty at any one time. All are trained in tactical fire-fighting and special operations. They earn an average of $5000 per month in addition to distributions. When the regional command is called to a fire, all local fire-fighting families must obey their direction. Otherwise authority falls on the battalion chief whose district contains the fire.

This example was for a level-4 city with a population of 250,000. The city had 10 district fire-fighting collectives serving 25,000 people each (districts composed of 1 or 2 level-3 cells), and a regional command center. This powerful fire safety net was all done on a $5 per month fire distribution. Larger cities can have even greater efficiencies with a 2nd layer of regional command.

Rural level-2 communities with 5,000 citizens will choose to do things differently. With a total of $25,000 per month revenue, there could be $12,000 depreciation on equipment, two pumper engines and two tankers and an ambulance. Two shifts of six fire-fighters each could work on a farm within 200 yards of the engine house or a road access point. In the event of a rare two-alarm fire, both shifts might be called to the scene. Fires would be rare and the firefighter income would bring in over $1000 a month.

Rural level-1 communities with 2,000 citizens could allocate an additional $5 from the transportation distribution for fire protection. With a total of $20,000 per month revenue and $12,000 depreciation on equipment, the 12 fire fighters/farmers would receive about $600 a month for their fire-fighting duties however rare those fires might be.

Level-1 communities with 1000 citizens could allocate an additional $10 from the transportation distribution for fire protection, assuming a ratio of less than 1 vehicle per person (See *Transportation Distribution* below). From the $15,000, $12,000 would go to equipment depreciation and each fire-fighter/farmer would receive $250 per month, although fires would most likely happen only once or twice per year.

Isolated level-0 large family compounds of say 50 members, with no outside fire protection, could use the $250 per month fire distribution to finance one or more pumps, hoses and other equipment. These will be hooked up to their large water tower and several family members might take courses on fighting fires.

Law Enforcement and Prosecution Distribution - $30

Law enforcement is currently a growing expense. In Chicago, based on today's cost, the distribution would need to be about $60 per person. In *Chapter 9 – How AFFEERCE Eliminates Crime*, arguments are presented to show how crime will drop by about 90%. This will give police time to pursue cases that they would otherwise ignore.

The law enforcement distribution will be kept high at $30. This will cover five tranches at levels 1, 3, 4, 5, and 7 as proposed in table 9.4. In most cases, the vast majority of funds will go to the local police at level-3, receiving $24 per person per month. Assume, like today, there will be one officer for every 250 citizens. From this distribution the officer will receive $10 per month or $2,500 per month on average. $3 per month will go for prosecution. The other $11 per person-month will be used for police cars, choppers, other vehicles, equipment, guns and ammunition, and maintenance of police stations. Police officers also share in fines paid in lieu of penitentiary time. This can be considerable. All government servants should remember that the distributions for food, shelter, medical and education, are worth over $14,000 in pre-tax money. If you include this in income calculations, AFFEERCE police officers will be higher paid than today's officers, with far less danger. Over time, crime is predicted to drop considerably. Even with a drop in the distribution, police work can become more efficient and officer salaries increased.

The largest law enforcement agency in the country will be the Bureau of Standards, enforcing VOS (violation of standards document) fraud in conjunction with the VSGs (voluntary standards groups). Because of the large fines involved, and a dues paying membership, this agency should get by on little if any distribution money. The largest portion of the federal law enforcement distribution will go to the FBI.

Judiciary and Public Defense Distribution - $9

This distribution was discussed in *Chapter 9 – Judiciary and Public Defense*. Jurists are selected from law school nominations, and are the highest paid public officials.

This distribution also pays for the public defender, and oversight of police and prosecutors, including investigations into misconduct and special prosecution.

There is about 1 judge for every 6,600 people[FTN11.21]. The judge will be the highest paid public servant, earning $18,000 per month on average. They will administer large fines that can make police officers, prosecutors and victims rich. There must be no temptation for corruption. They must decide on competing penitentiaries for sentencing based on needs and personality of the accused. The decision must be based on the best interest of the accused and society, again with no temptation for corruption.

The judge also has assistants. There are court reporters and bailiffs. Courthouses must be maintained. Each judge will have an average of six public defenders, paid $2,000 per month.

Transportation and Sanitation - $35

Streets and sanitation in Chicago has an annual budget of $304,000,000[FTN11.22]. Divided by the 3 million residents of Chicago, that is 10 dollars per resident a month. Using this as an estimate, it is proposed that sanitation receives $5 per resident per month distribution and is responsible for three different drainage systems.

The first is freshwater drainage. Sanitation can earn additional money through cellular enterprise by selling fresh water to the water utility. This is done with water reclamation; water reclaimed from runoff of rain, collected through drains at the side of the road. In some areas, reclamation is even possible from the second drainage system, grey-water drainage, where the grey-water from bathtub, shower, and sink, is reclaimed. There is also black-water drainage from toilets. Each of these three separate drainage systems requires different treatment.

All roads have an easement for utilities, such as drainage systems, fresh water, agricultural water, electricity, natural gas, oil, telephone, fiber optics and cable. This easement uses a fortified tunnel several feet below the surface, large enough to hold a sufficient number of tubes and pipes for competing utilities, and a person, accessible through manholes every block. A connecting tunnel, under street, parkway, and sidewalk should end at each property, or where future building is expected.

All new roads, whether public or private, must be built with this utility tunnel. The easement also protects the road from being torn up by the utilities. For use of space within the tunnel, the utility must pay a small rent to the owner of the road, based on diameter of the pipe or tube.

Roads receive the bulk of their revenue from the transportation distribution in conjunction with the auto pass. The transportation distribution is $30 per person per month.

The universal automobile pass is actually a tax. However, it is an innovation that could end up saving drivers' money rather than costing them money, and certainly will be beneficial for cities as well as provide incentive for privatization of the automobile infrastructure, such as roads, bridges, tunnels and parking. It will also stop auto theft cold. Owners of infrastructure use revenue from the pass to pay for the ground rent on roads and parking, maintenance, and even profit.

Although there is no prohibition against public and private owners of infrastructure from charging extra for parking, or charging road or bridge tolls, revenue from the auto pass is completely automated, and requires a single electronic reader at entry points to the infrastructure.

Every month, the entire transportation distribution of the vehicle owner, $30, is placed on the pass. Fifty percent of the transportation distribution of all other family members is placed on the pass. If there are four family members and one vehicle, a total of $75 will be placed on the pass each month, the required amount for a standard automobile. However, if there are 2 autos in the household, they will each have $45 automatically placed on the passes. In order to use the vehicles, $30 must be added to each pass. A single person with an automobile would need to add $45 to the pass each month.

A laser readable VIN (vehicle identification number) is placed on the front and rear license plates and on the hood of the car. The VIN is associated with a funded auto account. At most intersections, and entrances to parking lots, garages, bridges, and tunnels, the VIN is read. If the VIN cannot be read, pictures are taken of the auto, and law enforcement is notified.

The money is divided each month based on time spent in each road segment. The owner of the road, bridge, parking lot, garage, whether government or private, receives the funds. Distribution is generally equal. Bridges might count triple, due to special maintenance costs.

The bulk of the money will go to the garage or street where the car is parked at night, and the garage or street where the car is parked during the workday. This will represent a huge savings for most drivers. Garages in apartments will tend to be free, garages downtown will cost much less, people who install a reader will be happy to let you park in their garage for free. Except for congested downtowns, metered parking on most streets will be a thing of the past. Large malls will better be able to afford the ground rent on their parking lots or profit from building efficient multi-level parking.

Private corporations will have every incentive to treble away infrastructure and maintain it.

The ground rent on roads will only be slightly correlated with surrounding rent, and more a function of road usage. Privatizing a road through trebling does not eliminate the travel or utility easements, nor does it eliminate the need for plowing and maintenance. The city or county can profitably supply plowing, salting, and other maintenance services to private roads.

The remainder of the transportation distribution goes to fund free urban mass transit, or subsidize suburban metro rail. The resultant increase in worker and consumer mobility pays off in productivity gains and reduced carbon emissions pay off in general well-being.

A rail pass (for railroad cars) and the trebling of rails is worthy of future study but is not covered in this discussion.

Like roads, rails can be cellular enterprises or privately owned. Taking public transportation, even free public transportation, requires VIP identification to use. The transportation distribution, ex autos, is divided between the owners of the various transits riders take, based on the time spent on each.

While more expensive forms of transportation will charge fares over and above the amount of money they expect to receive from the transportation distribution, it will still mean cost savings for the traveler. Rural citizens might direct part of the transportation distribution to additional fire protection and fuel.

It is expected that this distribution will allow for free urban rail mass transit. The Chicago Transit Authority has operating expenses of $451 million for trains, tracks, and stations. Elimination of fare machines, fare cards, and all station personnel, would easily reduce expenses to 300 million for current ridership[FTN11.24]. Because track and track maintenance is relatively independent of ridership, doubling the ridership would bring the expense up to no more than $500 million.

Currently there are about 400,000 regular commuters with another 100,000 occasional commuters[FTN11.23]. Doubling ridership, a likely outcome of free transit, the elimination of homelessness, and greatly reduced crime, would bring the total riders to 1 million. This, in a city of 3 million, is a rather conservative estimate for free mass transit. If the entire transportation distribution for each rider, $360 each year, went to the CTA, that would only produce $360 million.

However, there are about a million citizens who are not primary owners of the family vehicle, and pay only 50% of their distribution toward an automobile pass. The other half goes directly to fund mass transit. That would be another $150 million reaching the required expense of $500 million. This is cutting it very close but tourists who purchase a city pass should make up the difference. And of course, with the distributions providing a base wage, nominal wages will likely drop.

Rural districts can use the large revenues from the small number of private roads to pay for gasoline and vehicle repair. With each adult a primary vehicle owner and children helping to fund the passes, most of the $75 auto pass will come from distributions. This $75 will be primarily distributed back to the vehicle owner parking on a private road on the owner's property. A small amount will go to the owner of the main road to town, and the main street in town.

With free rapid transit, low wage workers have access to a large part of the city. How can we open up the rest of the city cheaply to low wage workers? How can we create an efficient nationwide transportation system, such that people could safely travel hundreds of miles between cities for a few dollars? The answer is by allowing jitney cabs to compete on the roads.

What is a Jitney cab? In AFFEERCE, it is an ordinary automobile, truck, or SUV, equipped with a VIP reader. The rider and the driver engage in a VIP transaction where the rider agrees to share gasoline costs, pay a fixed amount, or pay an amount per mile for the ride. It is very safe because the identity of the driver and the rider along with the transaction are recorded by the VIP. Those who drive jitney cabs for a living, as opposed to ordinary people seeking companionship and expense sharing on the road, will follow an advertised route, like a bus today, picking up and dropping off people along the way. The beginning of the jitney revolution is happening today with companies like Uber and Lyft.

Depending on the route, the jitney cab is allowed to go a certain number of blocks out of the way. In a major city, that might be up to 2 blocks. Routes can be a single street, two streets at right angles, a large square, or a set of landmarks. Many routes will include rapid transit stations at their start and end. Routes are designed so that anyplace in the city is accessible via a 2 mile jitney cab ride to a free rapid transit station and a 2 mile jitney cab ride from a free rapid transit station. Thus a person can be guaranteed that if they are willing to walk up to 4 blocks, and are willing to take a potentially long transit ride, they can travel anywhere in the city for $1, assuming a 25 cent per mile cost. A person can travel from any point in the city to any other point for free if they are willing to walk up to 4 miles and 4 blocks, in the worst case.

Inter-city jitneys might leave from a single downtown location. Mileage can be negotiated if the jitney does not fill up for a long haul. Any automobile can be a jitney by installing a VIP reader. Any person can be a professional jitney driver by passing the jitney certification exam, and installing a car-top jitney console which includes GPS position transmitter to nearest dispatch tower, route info and number, vacancy number, route rate and off route rate.

Jitney is a good way to pay for the commute, conserve gasoline, reduce the carbon footprint, save on road trips to other cities, and safely meet new people. You are a registered jitney driver and they are VIP identified as soon as they enter the cab.

As you drive to your destination, your location, route, vacancy number, and rates are all being sent to a central computer. Independent dispatchers are competing to find customers for you because they collect a dispatch fee from the customer when the customer boards your cab. Alternatively, a customer can flag you down on the correct side of the street, and they pay no dispatch fee. Customers will pay the dispatch fee if they wish to be picked up at their front door to avoid inclement

Figure 11.2 - Electronic jacket for hailing a jitney cab to Peoria indicating rider willing to pay 5 cents per mile

weather, avoid waiting outside in the dark, if they have a disability, or if they have packages. The jitney driver will charge for an extra person or even more for packages that won't fit on the person's lap. Space is money.

A typical dispatch fee might be 50 cents. A typical off route pickup might also be 50 cents. A typical per mile charge might be 25 cents and a typical off route drop-off might be 50 cents. Monopoly dispatchers at airports, for instance, inform customers of the dispatch cost. Funds are automatically routed from the VIP in the jitney. Thus all of the fees collected by the driver go to the driver. There is no middle man.

A full jitney will bring in as much or more revenue than one of today's taxicabs. And today's cab drivers have to make do without food, housing, and medical distributions for themselves and their family. AFFEERCE jitney drivers need not worry about crime or getting shafted out of fares. At 25 cents per mile, demand for cabs will keep vacancies low.

Intellectual Property - $92

The intellectual property distribution is $92/person/month, larger than the distribution for national defense, and a reason the national defense and medical distributions can be so low. It is $320 billion annually for a population of 290 million. The money is used to reward inventors, artists, architects, authors, chefs, musicians, programmers, producers, engineers, and others who create intellectual property that can be shared.

The intellectual property distribution is fundamental to distribution theory and discussed in *Chapter 3 – Distribution of the Ground Rents*.

National Defense - $75

The 2009 U.S. military budget accounts for approximately 40% of global arms spending. The 2012 budget is 6–7 times larger than the $106 billion military budget of China, and is more than the next twenty largest military spenders combined. The United States and its close allies are responsible for two-thirds to three-quarters of the world's military spending (of which, in turn, the U.S. is responsible for the majority) [FTN11.25]

The military budget of the United States in 2012 was about $921 billion dollars including defense spending outside the DOD, and not counting the interest on the debt incurred from past wars or $243 per person per month. This is greater than the AFFEERCE food distribution which allows all Americans to eat nutritious meals. It could easily provide unlimited free education for all citizens. Some consider our military budget to be nothing less than theft.

Some cuts will follow naturally in an AFFEERCE economy. The current $921 billion dollar budget includes the cost of foreign wars, foreign bases as well as the food, housing, medical, and educational needs of the soldiers.

The military currently has 1,430,000 active personnel. Each of them will receive a $4,440 housing distribution and a $2,640 food distribution per year. That shaves only $12 billion off the military budget[FTN11.26].

Closing all foreign bases or supporting those bases through private donation or the discretionary tax saves an additional $250 billion. In an AFFEERCE economy, quality medical benefits will be available to all U.S. citizens, so there is no more need for the Veterans Administration, allowing another $70 billion to be cut. The FBI counter-terrorism is funded from the law enforcement distribution, saving another $2.9 billion, although by withdrawing from all foreign conflicts, we will have far fewer enemies. Homeland security is $47 billion. However, this is redundant. The entire purpose of the AFFEERCE military is homeland security. The VIP will make it very difficult for terrorists to operate within our borders. Family housing is only $3 billion, but it is covered by the housing distribution. The cost to the military to "sell" arms to foreign nations is $5 billion. Education in the military costs $14 billion, but this cost could be reduced by $10 billion through the education distribution, school and teacher achievement annuities[FTN11.26].

Military Savings	
Housing and food distributions	$12 billion
Overseas contingency operations	$88 billion
Closing all foreign bases	$250 billion
Veteran's Affairs	$70 billion
FBI counter-terrorism	$3 billion
Homeland Security	$47 billion
Family housing	$3 billion
"Selling" arms to foreign nations	$5 billion
Educational savings	$10 billion
Total	**$488 billion**

These cost savings do not even address increasing competition for procurement, operations and maintenance cost savings, delaying projects that involve weaponry for foreign soil, the use of the government distribution to supplement Pentagon salaries, and the wealth that could be created through large military families. Based on the above savings, the national defense budget becomes $433 billion or an distribution of $114 per person. However, this is still a military 4 times the size of China, the 2nd biggest military. If the U.S. military remained the strongest in the world, at over twice the size of the Chinese military, it could still be supported at $75 per person per month.

Even more significantly, the U.S. military pays huge amounts for intellectual property. With the new intellectual property distribution, prices will be cut in half, at least, so the move from $114 to $75 per month is not a reduction at all. But we can go farther. For extra income, and a rebate to the population of the expensive military distribution, the military could act as a level-7 cellular enterprise.

The military is constrained in what ventures it can undertake. In an AFFEERCE society, foreign adventures require a majority vote of the U.S. population if sanctioned by the United Nations and a super plurality if they are not sanctioned by the UN. However, sales of small arms and weapons at a profit might just require majority support for that nation or rebel group. Sale of weapons of mass destruction is illegal.

All funding for foreign adventures must come from domestic or foreign private donations or from the 2% discretionary tax. If representatives at level-7 support the war, they will make it a large portion of the default level-7 discretionary allocation.

Adventures include peacekeeping, airlifts, natural disasters, military bases, wars of liberation, protection of assets abroad, naval blockades, small mercenary units, and retaliation beyond 2 weeks of an attack on US soil. However, if the attack was sufficient to take down the infrastructure that allows the population to vote, retaliation can continue until such time as the infrastructure is reconstituted.

The gathering of defense intelligence abroad is considered part of national defense and covered under the general distribution. Any clandestine activities must be paid out of the national defense distribution. It will be illegal to fund clandestine activities from any other distribution. The use of weapons of mass destruction; nuclear, chemical, or biological; is illegal. Possession of nuclear weapons is allowed only as a deterrent.

The participation of the military in domestic natural disasters is covered under the military distribution and is not a for-profit undertaking. However, the military has many options for domestic wealth creation, in addition to the sale of arms and other weapons. These follow naturally from a free market. Simply put, the military can use its vast resources to compete with its own suppliers.

Suppose, in addition to 1.5 million fighting personnel, a number that assumes the private financing of all foreign bases, another 1.5 million personnel were used to create the uniforms, guns, ammo, build the tanks, aircraft, ships, missiles, special ops gear from raw commodities. If these 1.5 million workers produced $200 billion in military equipment annually, and received an average salary of $30,000, the profit plus savings on military equipment could eliminate half of the $75/month military distribution.

Capital Expenses, Depreciation, and Ground Rent - $20

These funds are distributed to levels 3, 4, 5, 6, and 7. They can spent by the governing councils at their discretion on construction projects, buildings, parks, furniture, vehicles, and equipment, or saved for capital replacement. Infrastructure built with these funds are not eligible for local land capture reimbursement. These funds are not used for interstate highways and bridges, national labs, or the VIP and other online software, as these are handled by a separate distribution.

It is hoped that these funds can be augmented by the cellular aristocracy. The governing council can propose joint funding with an aristocrat, however, all buildings are property of the dominion and the aristocrat only receives 150% ODV compensation on privately funded portions of the government building when trebled.

Table 11.2 Capital Expense Distribution	Tranche	Average Population	Monthly Revenue @$20/population
Level – 3	50%	15,400	$154,000
Level – 4	10%	169,400	$338,800
Level – 5	10%	1,863,400	$3,726,800
Level – 6	10%	20,497,400	$40,994,800
Level – 7	20%	225,471,400	$901,885,600

National Infrastructure, VIP and Online Land System - $10

Currently, the federal government spends about $36 billion annually on highways and bridges[FTN11.27]. Because maintenance will be easily supported by the universal auto pass for roads and bridges in common use, no additional funding is needed. Considering that much of the infrastructure can be operated for profit, a reduction of the total infrastructure costs to $15 billion will be more than adequate.

The National Oceanic and Atmospheric Administration (NOAA), and various national laboratories will receive a combined total of 25% of this distribution, about $9 billion. They will receive the majority of funding from partnerships with industry.

The remainder of this distribution, about $14 billion, will go to support the VIP network, although considerable national defense resources will go toward defending and supporting the VIP.

The VIP must not only store the identity of every person, and allow them to vote, but store a record of every transaction and contract between people. Every movement of money in the economy is documented. It must integrate seamlessly with the online land system in order to record all improvements to land. It must be online 24/7 with no failures possible. Data must be stored redundantly in multiple locations throughout the country, secured by national defense forces as well as nature itself, such as the interior of a mountain. State of the art security protects transactions. Transactions can go through the internet, cellular, and satellite communication. All VIP readers must be able to work on battery power. All VIP storage facilities will have backup power generation.

VIP readers must be purchased by merchants and families. These include GPS devices, as well as voice, iris, and palm detectors. They can be sold as computer peripherals or stand alone with keyboard and screens. Every VIP reader is registered. Only certain accounts are authorized to receive funds on any given VIP reader. VIP transactions have no associated charge, although a merchant will need to have unlimited internet, satellite or cellular connectivity. For more details see, *Chapter 1 – The VIP.*

Because the VIP is so important, it is reasonable to allocate $14 billion a year for its construction and maintenance, in addition to national defense allocations and government distribution allocations through the Treasury Department. The insignificant cost of maintaining the online land database is also covered by this distribution.

The total infrastructure allocation is $38 billion or $10 per person-month.

Monthly Distribution Total

Table 11.2 Assumed Monthly Distributions in U.S. Dollars	
Food	220
Housing	370
Cash	35
Education	50
Testing	2
Medical	120
Non Universal (disability, age, incarceration)	97
Social Worker	10
Fire Protection	5
Law Enforcement	30
Judiciary and Public Defense	9
Transportation and sanitation	35
Infrastructure and VIP	10
Government	20
Building Capital/Depreciation/Rents	20
Intellectual Property Royalties	92
National Defense	75
TOTAL MONTHLY DISTRIBUTION	**1,200**

The total monthly distribution per AFFEERCE citizen is $1,200 or $351 billion dollars for all citizens in the year 2002. The yearly distribution for the entire 2002 nation is $4.18 trillion dollars. This assumes a population of 290 million.

The ground rent is initialized to pay $4 trillion of this. There is also an 8% consumption tax that includes 2% earmarked for the distributions until the baby tax reserve fund is built up.

Total B2C commerce in 2013 was projected to be 8.6 trillion based on $75 of spending per day. We assume conservatively that despite the distributions, spending will not change. [FTN11.28]

Based on this spending level, 2% of the consumption tax earmarked for the distribution package yields $172 billion which is needed to complete funding until the baby tax reserve fund is built. There will be an expected 5 million births a year, yielding $250 billion for the baby tax reserve fund.

How do AFFEERCE expenditures in 2002 dollars stack up to current government expenditures?

Revenue Source	Revenue in Trillions
Ground rent	$4.00
2% CT on $8.6 trillion spending	.17
Baby tax	.25
Total	**$4.42**

The total spending of federal, state, and local governments for 2013 was 6.3 trillion dollars. [FTN11.29] The deflation following the housing crash kept the dollars fairly constant. Even allowing $300 billion for inflation:

Total annual AFFEERCE expenditures are over $1.5 trillion less than current government expenditures!

Saving $1.5 trillion and at the same time ending hunger, homelessness and providing quality medical care and unlimited free education for all is the AFFEERCE revolution!

Chapter 12 –Families, Collectives, and Mutual Organizations

The homemaker has the ultimate career. All other careers exist for one purpose only - and that is to support the ultimate career. – *C.S. Lewis*

Due to economies of scale that follow from the distributions, people will tend to organize themselves into large families. The distributions at both the family and higher levels will similarly lead families to organize themselves into communities and mutual organizations of every type. The distributions not only create an economic safety net, but at the same time provide a catalyst for society's bottom-up evolution which in turn forms a far stronger social safety net.

Love, friendship, sexual attraction, common interests, collectivist needs, the desire to raise children, and economic efficiency will be reasons to join a family or community. Large families and collectives through economies of scale and division of labor naturally form new enterprises and provide the means to raise many children. They function as a miniature economy, and in the case of families, do not pay any consumption tax on the value added by other family members for products produced in the family business.

Each family can have its own rules, roles, and rituals. The same rules, roles, and rituals in a community require class III legislation with the trebling option. Adults always have exit rights – the right to leave any family or community – although in the case of families, judicial restructuring might be required if children are directly affected.

The smallest family is of size one: the individual. A family of one enjoys as many privileges as a family of many. Under the law, all families have the same rights. However, there are enumerable opportunities available to the large family due to the economies of scale, and division of labor. The wealth effect from adding people to a family will create some social pressure for singles and even couples to join a larger family. Families will vigorously pursue potential members, especially those who fill needed roles.

In the language of the cellular democracy, a family is typically a level-0 district composed of one or more level-0 cells (individuals). However, very large families (> 100) can be level-1 districts, and extremely large families (> 1400) can be level-2 districts. Mutual organizations that combine living and working space can possibly operate efficiently as high as level-3, and tribes at level-2 can one day become empires at level-5 or higher through success of the culture, economy, and form of government.

Physical Family Requirements

It is in the interest of AFFEERCE that family members are not strangers to one another. The roles played by family and community are different enough that one would expect strangers at the community level but not in the family. Community is a democracy unless overridden by a 5/6 plurality, family need not be. The presence of strangers in the family would blur the distinction.

Because family members temporarily surrender some natural rights in exchange for membership, well-defined physical boundaries of the family authority is both psychologically and physically important.

Entrance to the family compound must be through a locked door, or guarded gate. Guests must ring a bell, have pre-approved VIP access, be given a key, or call at the gate. It is not a family compound if anyone can walk in freely.

Secondly, there must be one common kitchen and dining area for the entire family. The family charter can allow people to eat wherever they wish. Snacks and breakfast might be taken in the rooms or entertainment centers, but the common kitchen and dining area will encourage communal dining.

Note that a standard apartment building or condo does not have a common dining area, therefore does not qualify as a family domicile (the apartments do, just not the building as a whole). However, both a dormitory and mansion make excellent housing for large families. Condos and apartment buildings can be converted into large family housing by adding the common kitchen and dining area. AFFEERCE large-family considerations might radically alter the architecture of new construction.

Family Law

The family is the smallest unit of government. It can be a tyranny, a theocracy, a monarchy, an oligarchy, a meritocracy, a democracy, a matriarchy, anarchy, or consensus body. Although the community can arbitrarily modify the administration of local cellular government, this requires class III legislation with the treble option. The family is the only unit of society where rules conflicting with the natural rights of its members can be imposed absent a 5/6 plurality. These rules cannot violate the right to life of children or the exit rights of adults.

Families are defined by a charter. Because each family is a culture in and of itself, prospective members, before joining a family should study the family charter on sexuality, dowry, tithing, religion, traditions, ritual, business, rules, regulations and governance. The family charter is the contract that the family makes with its members. It is both constitution and body of legislation. The default family charter (for families that don't bother with a charter) is based on the principle of maximum personal freedom and is approved by the citizens at large. The VOS associated with a particular family charter must specify serious deviations from the standard charter in a bolder type.

A family could require that certain adult members be employed, at a certain income, and control the amount of that income going into the family corporate account. A family can impose any set of sexual requirements and sexual restrictions on its adult members. A family can forbid (or require) the use of any or all intoxicants, and even forbid the consumption of certain types of food. A family can contradict the freedom of speech, forbidding certain words to be used, or certain topics to be discussed. A family can restrict the associations of its members and restrict the property that can be owned. A family can require its members partake in certain rituals and worship.

Family membership for an adult is voluntary and adherence to the rules of the family charter is also voluntary. While expulsion is the only remedy for violation of those rules, renegotiation of the charter is often in the best interests of all parties. Thus the family charter is dynamic.

The family charter vis-à-vis specially protected individuals, that is, children under the age of 14, the elderly, and the feeble-minded is subject to court, social worker and community scrutiny. The judicial system includes a family court, much as it does today, to insure that the right to life of children is not infringed upon. The law insures that children receive nutritious meals as required, warm and safe shelter, access to education and quality healthcare.

By default, the family charter will be a fluid document that can be modified by a super-majority of family members 14 and older. Clauses relating to a specific family member must also be approved by that family member. Of course, on any point the family charter can differ with the default charter. That is, modification of the document might require a consensus or a simple majority. Modification might require a simple majority plus approval by the matriarch, the patriarch, the elite counsel, or "the king."

The charter defines roles, if any, and responsibilities of each family member, or if responsibilities are shared, how they are shared. It also defines the procedure for admitting new family members.

The default family charter has no financial obligations save insuring judicious use of the distributions when children under 14 years of age are family members. Social workers will help connect families who have no income beyond the distributions with charities for clothing and furniture.

Divorce from a family requires only a simple VIP transaction unless the person is a primary caregiver of a child under the age of 14, or family assets are contested. A judge will always grant divorce. However, if there are children under the age of 14, the judge could require additional financial obligations, or even break the family apart. Because of the distributions, child support payments will be rare. An exception would be when mortgage/housing costs or rent obligations exceed the housing distribution and the divorcing party is the source of that income. In small families, where the children have only one caretaker, and the caretaker wishes a divorce, the judge can keep the children with the caretaker, be satisfied with a new caretaking arrangement, or have the social worker find a family who will take the children in as members of their family. Due in part to the financial benefits that accrue from taking in more children, many loving families will volunteer to take them in. In addition to young children, a judge might also give a divorce more scrutiny if there are disabled or elderly family members involved.

Age of Majority

In today's world, childhood is extended well past the age of puberty. Some children remain dependent on their parents into their twenties or even thirties. However, for 99% of mankind's time on this earth, children were considered adults in their early teens. Bar Mitzvah, confirmation, and other coming-of age ceremonies were closely tied to puberty.

In an AFFEERCE society, the age of majority will be 14. Furthermore, a child as young as age 12, of exceptional maturity, will be able to petition a judge in family court to be granted majority status. In a free society, it is important that freedom be obtained at the earliest possible age. With this comes maturity and responsibility. Education, free and unlimited, is a lifelong endeavor. Cramming that education into the latter half of the teenage years is not always the best course for one's life.

Reaching the age of majority does not imply that the new adult will leave the family. In fact, it might be common to remain in the same family from birth until death. Quality loving families will tend to grow with quality loving people. Dysfunctional families will tend to break apart, with their members going to diverse families, or remaining as single-person families. Because raising the funds to have a child will be a collaborative effort for the many families, dysfunctional families will tend to have fewer children than loving families. Also, loving families will be more content with each other's company and have more money for children that would otherwise go for the frequent escapes (gambling, alcohol, vacations, etc.) that dysfunctional families require.

As young adults experiment with sexuality, coupling, sacred bonds, ritual, and secret societies, many will feel the need to form families, based on "new" mores, "new" forms of sexual expression, "new" work ethics, and so on. The distributions make this easy. Reproductive control discourages young people from having unwanted children and saves them from the burden of parenthood. The free market gives these new families the best chance of success. If such families break down, the young adults might return to their original family, older and wiser. They might bring a partner, or return to their partner's family, or start a smaller family with one or two members from their experimental family. In a free society, family options are unlimited.

Child Abuse

The right to life includes the right to be free from abuse, be that sexual, verbal, physical, religious, or educational. The question remains, "Who decides what constitutes abuse, whether a family is 'at risk,' for such abuse, and whether one form of abuse is worse than another?"

The chief difficulty is that many of the answers are a function of the ever-changing culture; and a diverse society has many sub-cultures, each with their own set of answers.

In Ancient Greece, one of the highest compliments you could pay a young man was to fondle his testicles. It was a way of saying you admired his cojones. Young men whose testicles were not fondled were the ones traumatized [FTN12.08]. In our own culture, victims of child molesters are told repeatedly that an unspeakable act of horror has been perpetrated on them. They are told this by their peers, their parents, their teachers, their counselors, their spiritual guides, the press, the police, and the courts. It is hardly a wonder that many are traumatized.

I do not believe that because two different acts are objectively identical, society should ignore the cultural baggage surrounding those acts. Cultures develop for a reason. That said; cultures are dynamic. And it is only when a disparaged act involves children, the elderly, the feeble-minded, and people with certain other disabilities should cultural and legal issues intersect. The VSG's set standards and those who cannot or are deemed unable to set their own standards are constrained to live within the VSG standards. We can imagine that at least for the foreseeable future, if not forever, adult sexual expression with prepubescent children will remain a crime.

What about educational abuse? Home schooling will play an important role in AFFEERCE. It is not only a way to spread ideas to one's children and one's neighbor's children, but also bring income to the family, and tap into achievement annuities down the road.

Merit pay probably matters little to parent teachers with a religious or cultural agenda. For these teachers, it is most important to stress dearly-held ideas that often run counter to the general consensus.

Thus, creationism and the biblical version of various sciences might receive more attention in a home school than evolution and those various sciences would receive in a community school. Teaching that global warming does not exist would likely receive more attention in a home school than teaching global warming does exist in a community school. There is no doubt that conspiracy theories, UFO's, ghosts and the paranormal, would receive far more attention in home schools that promoted them, than any view of those topics in community schools.

Critics of these home school curriculums call this educational abuse of children. Firstly, they claim that the subject matter has been disproven by science, rational investigations, and the like. Secondly, they claim that an inordinate amount of time is spent on these subjects at the expense of other less controversial ones.

First of all, scientific proofs are nothing more than taking the empirical evidence and fitting it into a theoretical framework, and fitting that theoretical framework into a philosophical framework. Currently the predominant philosophy of science is scientific materialism: the notion that the entire universe is reducible to forces on objects that follow the physical laws. This is debated in *Volume III – The Philosophy*. The important point is that none of us have a monopoly on the truth.

In a free society, truth is determined by the marketplace. If you believe in creationism, you probably won't be hired on a fossil dig. If you believe in multiple conspiracy theories, you probably won't be elected to public office. If you believe the earth is flat, you probably won't be hired as a surveyor.

The distribution for unlimited education means you can always learn the consensus opinion at a university. Your early exposure to a different point of view might even lead to new insights that evolve into a new consensus. Merit and achievement incentives help keep home school teachers on track with the standard curriculum, but apart from a few exceptional cases, there is no such thing as educational abuse.

Physical and verbal abuse, often in the guise of discipline, certainly exists. The question remains: what constitutes physical abuse, what constitutes verbal abuse, what is good discipline, and who decides?

The first line of defense against child abuse is the AFFEERCE family. Families will tend to be large and diverse. All adults in the family share a responsibility for the child. Very possibly, the child was funded by the family as a whole. Those who stay at home and are committed to raising children will tend to be the ones responsible for raising them. In a large family, that will often include both paternal and maternal figures who will feel very protective of the children and act as a buffer from less sensitive family members; those who come home from work tired and obsessed with the problems of the day, or those who abuse alcohol or drugs. A family member who engages in child abuse is likely to be quickly expelled. Large families protect children by their very nature.

Social workers will have incentives to build large families. Because large families take care of themselves, this both reduces work and increases pay. In small families, abuse is more likely to go unchallenged given no internal support structure. The social worker will tend to scrutinize these families more assiduously. Families with abusers do not grow into thriving collectives.

Roles

Some families will eschew roles, perhaps as a response to the very narrow roles that today's society tends to impose. In a free society, families can organize themselves however they wish. However, I would speculate that a successful family, one that can grow quite large and thusly bring great love and great wealth to its members, is one where roles are defined.

Consider the staff at the Montbush family: nannies, drivers, gardeners, cooks, maintenance, cleaning personnel, butlers, and waiters. Assuming the entire staff resides in the mansion, the distributions are paid to the Montbush's as transactions. Profits from these transactions cannot be used for personal use by the family without paying the consumption tax which includes additional revenue raised by a super plurality.

It was here that Jed Montbush's legendary cheapness finally paid off. He outraged the heirs and unioned the help into the family. The family charter was amended to maintain the same household hierarchy. A small legacy was awarded to get the staff to go along; a few new privileges and added security had them all anxious to get on board. The staff's housing distributions could now be spent on estate upkeep without paying consumption taxes. Just as the younger Montbush's were beginning to accept the new arrangement, they were horrified to find families, "at the bottom of the hill," organizing themselves in the same manner – just for the fun of being an upper crust family with all that distribution wealth. "They mock us," said young Hamish Montbush.

Those who eschew such exotic roles might still organize the family along traditional family roles such as breadwinner, homemaker, and so on. Inherent in roles are hierarchies, however, these hierarchies will tend to be voluntary. Unless it was specified in the charter, no one can be given financial or labor obligations they do not agree to. People gravitate to the roles that give them the greatest pleasure, or interfere least with their passions. As technology continues to advance to where fewer, more highly skilled workers are needed in the workplace, service to the family may become even more common as a career path. Playing the roles of a nineteenth century upper class British family might be fun, especially for previously poor families in the first few generations of AFFEERCE, however it is the family business that will create an infinite diversity of family service roles.

The innumerable possibilities for AFFEERCE families are even greater when family and community are combined into new social structures. You might not approve of your neighbor's family choice, but in a free society, life, liberty, and the pursuit of happiness are everything. Natural experimentation will lead us toward ever more rewarding family structures.

Final Thoughts

Throughout history, family structure has undergone many changes. But in AFFEERCE we embrace them all, and countless new ones as well. It is here that we take the qualitative leap from conformity to creativity. The relationships we choose to have with the ones we love are as diverse as the number of living organisms. We might even imagine that the same emotions that drove single cells into multi-cellular organisms years ago, will draw us tomorrow into families and collectives that create wealth and happiness as efficiently as a living creature uses energy.

The AFFEERCE family will be the integration of fantasy and reality, work and play, love and friendship. The role we assume or strive to attain is our destiny. It is the role that will bring us peace on Earth.

Home, Sweet, Home

Loneliness, isolation, poverty, and homelessness become forgotten relics of a distant past, as new families embrace all who choose to enter their bosom. Each of us is valuable and carrying our share of God or Nature's gift to the world, the land, minerals, forests, and streams, collected as ground rent and distributed to each of us as nutritious meals, warm and safe shelter, quality medical care, unlimited free education, police and fire protection, a government to protect our rights, streets, sanitation, and a national defense.

Check-out an eclectic group of possible alternative families on the website.

Chapter 13 – Enlightenment

The word of God is the creation we behold and it is in this word, which no human invention can counterfeit or alter, that God speaks universally to man. --Thomas Paine[FTN12.49]

Free Will and Moral Responsibility

Without free will, there can be no moral responsibility. And without moral responsibility, there can be no just society. Both religious and secular tyrants thrive on the notion that there is no real freedom; God almighty or the impersonal forces on particles having left them fated by destiny to lead.

Whatever one's take on these ideas, the highest principle must always remain that freedom of religion and freedom of science are foundations of liberty.

AFFEERCE and Enlightenment

That which we produce with our own labor belongs to us alone. That which God or Nature provides belongs to each of us and all of us. This is the bedrock moral principle on which AFFEERCE is built. Paraphrasing Henry George, it succeeds through one short statement in affirming both free enterprise and the collection and distribution of ground rents. It succeeds in obliterating the differences between right and left, individualism and collectivism, socialism and capitalism. It is the economic output of the grand synthesis between objectivism and subjectivism.

As for government, it is easy to fall into a trap believing that the purpose of government is the distribution of the ground rents. But that would be a serious error. For it is through the distribution of ground rents that we create a government to protect our natural rights.

Like all creatures on Earth, we are entitled to nutritious meals and warm and safe shelter. But as human beings, we are also entitled to education, medical care, sanitation, a judiciary, police and fire protection, and a government to protect our natural rights. Having conquered all predators, the balance of nature for the human species is now in our hands.

Nor must the wisdom of our forefathers be lost. As it was said in the first enlightenment: **Every person has the right to life, liberty, personal property, and the pursuit of happiness**

The Future of AFFEERCE Enlightenment

AFFEERCE ushers in a new epoch. We can only speculate on any changes AFFEERCE might promote in human behavior.

We know that fear and greed, today, play an important role in economic decision making. Both are motivated by the fear of losing everything. The safety net through which none can fall will end that fear. But there is also the adrenalin rush that accompanies risky financial decisions. Will that be channeled into trebling, business competition, or family gaming? Will people instead seek the high of a warm embrace?

What of the tragedy of the commons? Will the new AFFEERCE individual be more likely to play the roles espoused by Elinor Ostrom, or fall into the roles predicted by Garrett Hardin. The legal system and business environment are built on honesty and trust. The consequence of mistakes are generally less severe. This is conducive for an ethical system that favors the commons.

The distributions give every individual a monetary value. Will this translate into value as a human being? It is natural to value others as human beings. But fear of those who would financially prey upon us causes the building of fences and walls to isolate us from others. That fear should evaporate when everyone brings something to the table. Children and people in general will be seen as valuable. This too, will end loneliness.

Trebler wars have all the adrenalin of violent war and none of the injury. When the desire for war, and a confluence of negative emotions can all be channeled into dominion trebling, where all parties, including society as a whole, come out winners, it certainly could be called our greatest achievement ever!

AFFEERCE is the synthesis of objectivism and subjectivism in politics and economics. Will the same synthesis in science and philosophy show us that this is a universe blessed with meaning and purpose? Will postmodernism finally come to an end as new truths are discovered in Nature?

Only time can answer these questions.

In this volume, I have shared a vision. I hope you too see its elegance and beauty. If I have presented my case well, you are also sharing that vision.

In Conclusion

Our time on Earth might be rapidly coming to an end. We have reason to fear the demons of nuclear war, destruction of the environment, a breakdown in government, deconstruction of all our institutions, dehumanization, incarceration, polarization, and hatred toward the groups we deem most responsible for this tragic state of affairs.

If only we can plant the seed of AFFEERCE and nurture the embryo as it comes to life. This is the mission of *AFFEERCE Volume II – The Plan*. It is based on viral community theory and the law of rent, much as The Vision is based on collection, distribution, balance, and cellular democracy theories. It is a business plan to take us from where we are now to the AFFEERCE vision within the span of 60 years. Most of us reading these words will not live to see that glorious day. It is a legacy for our children and our children's children and all those who come after.

But we can plant the seed and by reigniting hope, save the world until that gestation is complete and a new nation is born.

I hope you have learned much in *AFFEERCE Volume I – The Vision*. But if you learned one thing only, let it be this:

That which we produce with our own hands belongs to us alone. That which God or Nature provides belongs to each of us and all of us. You have learned that the collection and distribution of ground rents at the highest possible level provides a harmonious economic basis for world peace, prosperity and freedom.

Know too, that a cellular democracy is the perfect framework for a minimum government that protects our natural rights, including the right to form a different kind of political or economic system and maintain a culture of our choosing. This is called the panarchy. In that way, the complete freedom and direct democracy of AFFEERCE provide a home for those who want neither freedom nor democracy.

AFFEERCE is a new face on the old values, an end to hunger and poverty, desperation and loneliness, an explosion of both freedom and responsibility, of technology and humanity, a journey to reach our full potential. AFFEERCE will be embraced by the left and the right and everyone in between, once those first green shoots appear above our embryo, whose name shall be Prosperity.

There was a list at the end of Chapter 10 with over 40 multipliers of productivity. Several of these will increase the wealth of the nation two or three times. Taken together, the increase is both unfathomable and epochal.

I have spent many years unearthing these secrets, incorporating the wisdom of both friend and foe. I stand on the shoulders of giants, the angry, the joyful and the suffering. AFFEERCE is our last chance to save our species from self-destruction. But I believe there is still hope.

Even if you have lost all personal hope, I implore you to read *Volume II – The Plan*. When you see how we can create this world, perhaps you will become a believer. Perhaps you will become an affeercianado.

AFFEERCIANADOS – Proclaim Freedom Everywhere!

Appendix I - The Fundamental Relations

These are the AFFEERCE postulates. All of them take the form of relations. For the most part, they are based on simple logic and common sense. These relations knit together free enterprise, universal distribution, and the balance of the RCs. Some of the fundamental relations are more fundamental than others. Relations 1 and 5 (in the diagram below) are critical. Without them, AFFEERCE would have no theoretical basis.

Nevertheless, a free population must never be slave to theory. The relationships between free enterprise, universal distribution, and the balance of the RCs should remain works in progress.

The diagram on the following page shows the fundamental relations. All twelve of the fundamental relations are shown below and briefly described.

Since these relations were created, many new relations were developed that define AFFEERCE. While the relations remain true, they are incomplete and expansion to encompass collection, distribution and cellular democracy theory would be a good exercise.

The Fundamental Relations

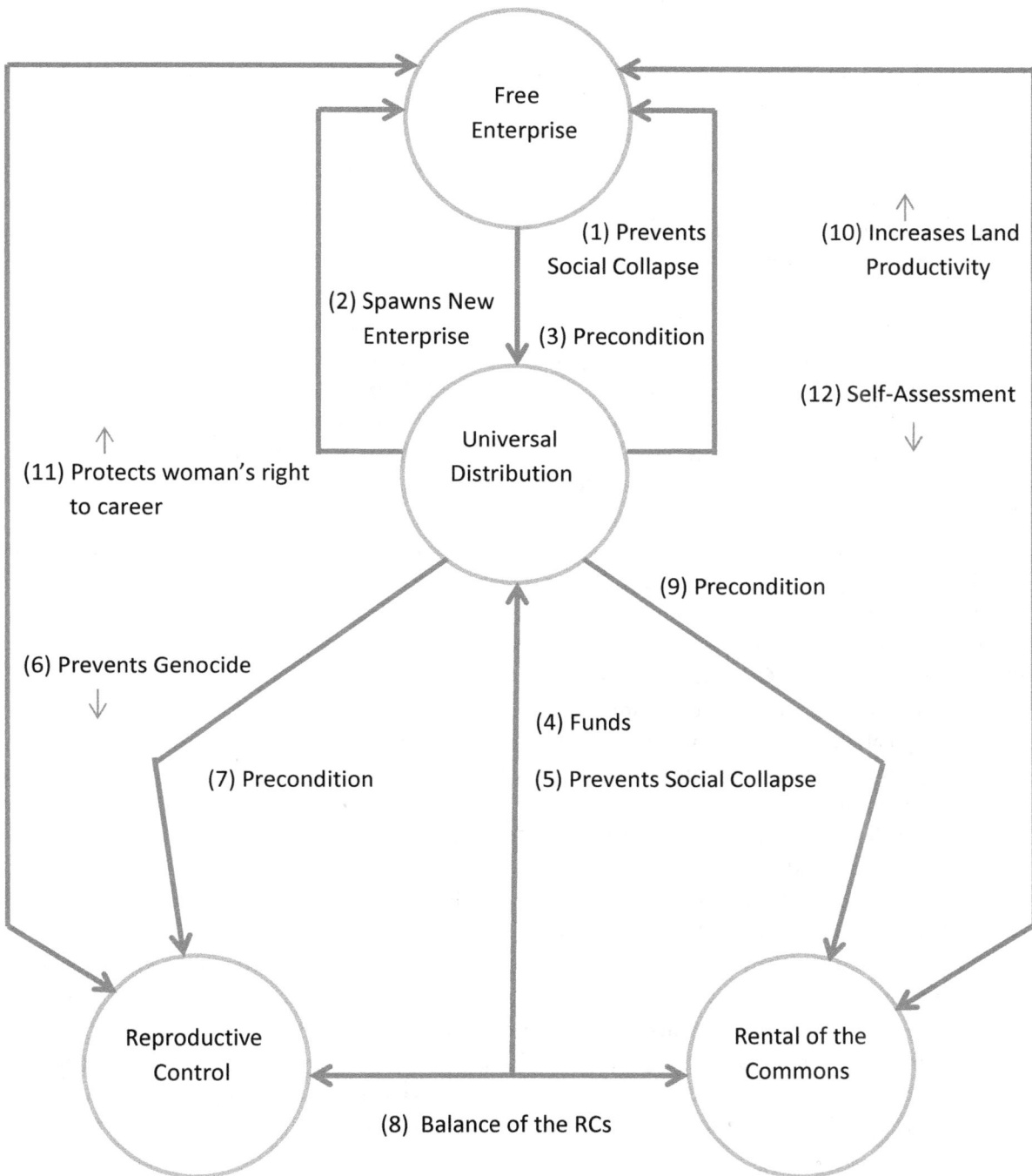

Free
Enterprise

(1) Prevents
Social Collapse

(10) Increases Land
Productivity

(2) Spawns New
Enterprise

(3) Precondition

(12) Self-Assessment

Universal
Distribution

(11) Protects woman's right
to career

(9) Precondition

(6) Prevents Genocide

(4) Funds

(7) Precondition

(5) Prevents Social Collapse

Reproductive
Control

Rental of the
Commons

(8) Balance of the RCs

(1) Prevents Social Collapse – Without entitlements, free markets show no mercy. Massive dislocations can occur as unproductive companies are punished. Workers bargain in desperation. Conditions lead to theft, sabotage and revolution. However, entitlements allow the free market to function without causing harm.

(2) Spawns New Enterprise – Distributions spawns new business in formerly poor and lower-middle class neighborhoods. Domestic workers are financially able to fill low paying jobs.

(3) Precondition – Deregulation drives down the cost of the distributions, healthcare costs in particular. The free market is needed to generate sufficient productivity to support the distributions through the balance of the RCs.

(4) Funds – The balance of the RCs funds the distribution package.

(5) Prevents Social Collapse – Universal distribution means children add to the wealth of a household. For those households with little wealth, children might be the only way to obtain more. The balance of the RCs insures that the productivity of the nation grows faster than or equal to population growth. Otherwise, should automation push marginal productivity below subsistence, barbarism would result.

(6) Prevents Genocide – By using market forces and projected future population needs to set the baby tax, and by allowing equal access for all to pay the tax, control of reproduction is taken away from politicians and bureaucrats, who might base decisions of who could reproduce on a whim, ethnic loyalties, personal and popular prejudices.

(7) Precondition – Entitlement is a precondition for any kind of reproductive control. Without entitlement, children provide the poor with many of the same necessities as in pre-modern times or the third-world today, such as income, social security, and safety. Likewise, without entitlement, a parent cannot always afford to stay home and provide care for the child. Entitlement is the engine that allows for both an orderly increase and decrease in population.

(8) The Balance of the RCs – Just as government has replaced the balance of nature for humans, the balance of the RC's replaces government in the same way. Balances the baby tax and ground rent, so that population growth does not exceed growth in productivity. Restores cropland to free market pricing, and maintains an optimal balance between cropland and commercial/residential land. Allows humanity to flourish without predators.

(9) Precondition – Universal distribution is a precondition for ground rent. Otherwise the poor could be driven off their land.

(10) Increases Land Productivity – The ground rent punishes inefficiency in land use and places the land in the hands of those who would use it most productively.

(11) Protects Woman's Right to a Career – The wealth generated by a new person in the household can put undue pressure on a woman to create babies and to forego a career. The baby tax can be raised sufficiently high to protect women's rights. However, this is independent of the balance of the RCs and could lead to an underpopulation problem, which can be mitigated by decreasing the citizenship tax.

(12) Self-Assessment – The free market allows all land rights owners to raise their ground rent to a level that maximizes profits and minimizes the probability of land seizure.

These are the twelve fundamental relations that unite the pillars of AFFEERCE. Notice the symmetry in the graph. It is a finely-tuned instrument. Neither free enterprise, universal distribution, nor the balance of the RCs (neither reproductive control nor rental of the commons) can be removed without causing mortal failure of the model.

When the pillars have an interesting relationship with another concept that is important to AFFEERCE, these are called secondary relationships. The natural tendency toward large alternative families is one such concept and the natural tendency toward spiritual enlightenment is another. These are predicted outcomes of free agents in a free society. There is no mechanism to enforce these tendencies, nor funding to enable them. The predictions could fail because they fail, for instance, to grasp human nature.

The secondary relationships form the basis for many predictions in this book.

Jeff Graubart

The Family Relations

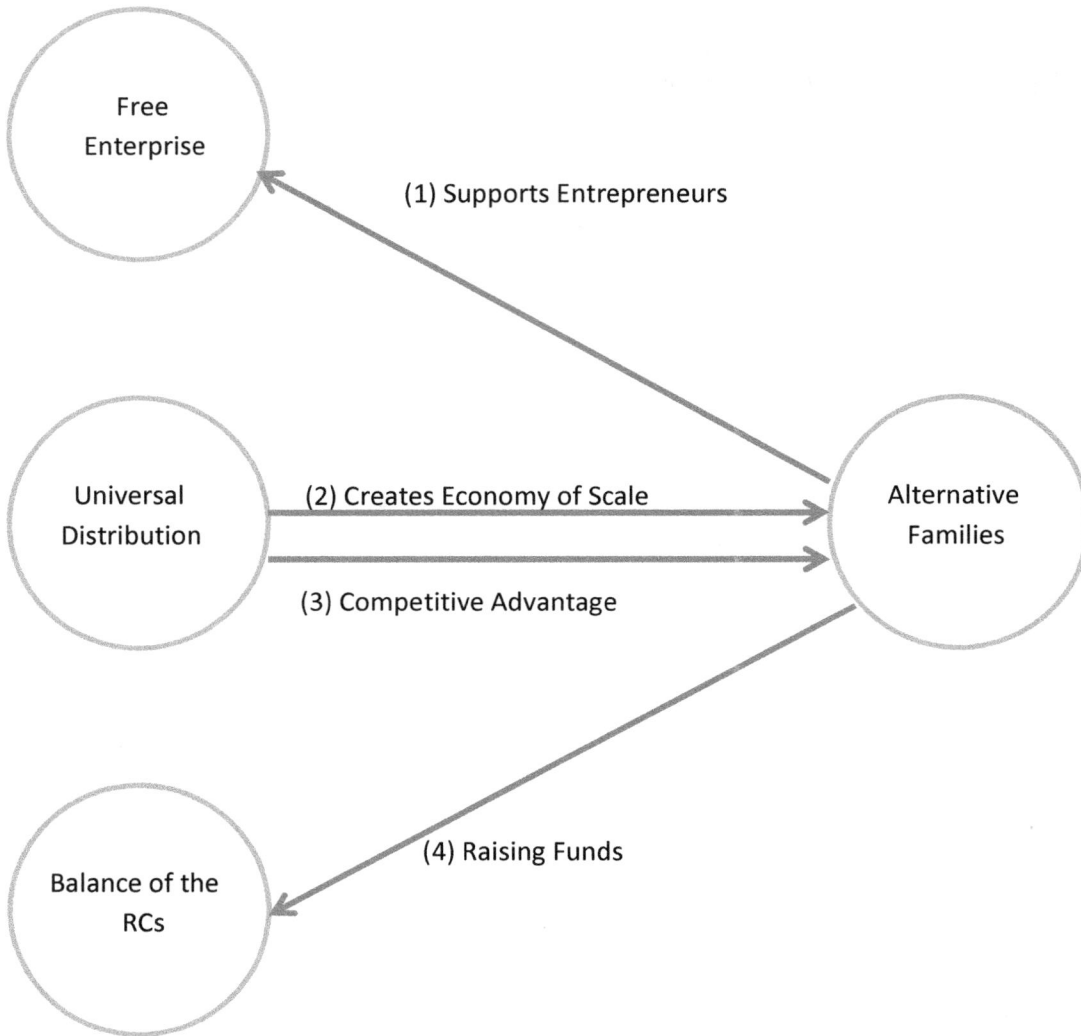

(1) Supports Entrepreneurs – Large families allow some members to take on risk and provide a greater division of labor for startups.

(2) Creates Economy of Scale – Each additional family member allows a more efficient use for the total housing, food and sundry distributions, thereby creating wealth.

(3) Competitive Advantage – Universal distribution enables family business to compete with big business by making low wages practical.

(4) Raising Funds – Large families can pool their resources to fund children, even if individual incomes are small.

268

The Enlightenment Relations

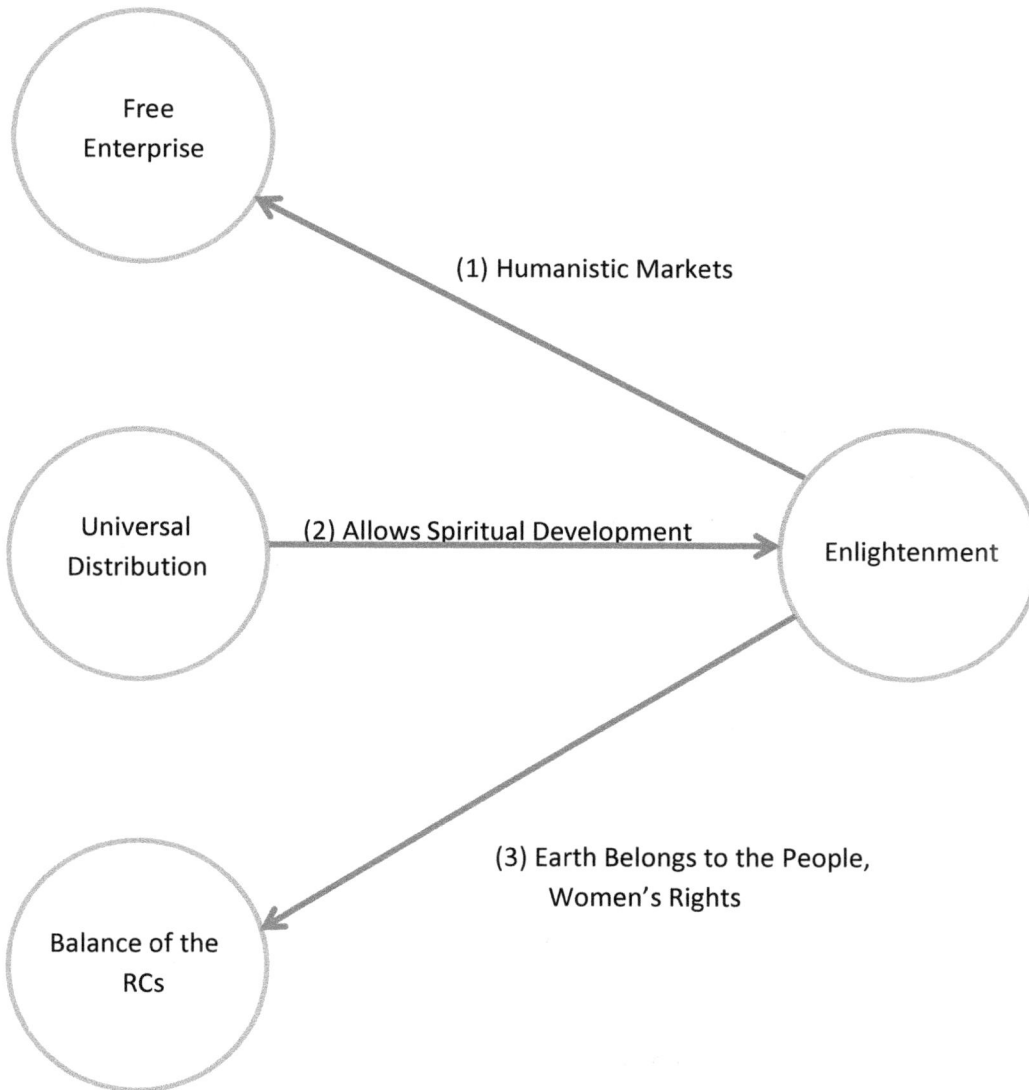

Free Enterprise

(1) Humanistic Markets

Universal Distribution

(2) Allows Spiritual Development

Enlightenment

(3) Earth Belongs to the People, Women's Rights

Balance of the RCs

(1) Humanistic Markets – The greatest wealth is a loving family and children, not fetishized commodities that lose value in a deflationary economy. Honesty and concern for the customer is good business and good for the soul. Without trust, markets do not function.

(2) Allows Spiritual Development – Universal distribution allows as much time as needed for people to engage in prayer, meditation, art, education, and spiritual growth.

(3) The balance of Nature. The Earth belongs to all of its inhabitants and the ground rent insures a fair rental for use of the land. Woman must not be viewed as baby creating wealth machines. Population growth must not exceed growth in productivity.

The Cellular Democracy Relations

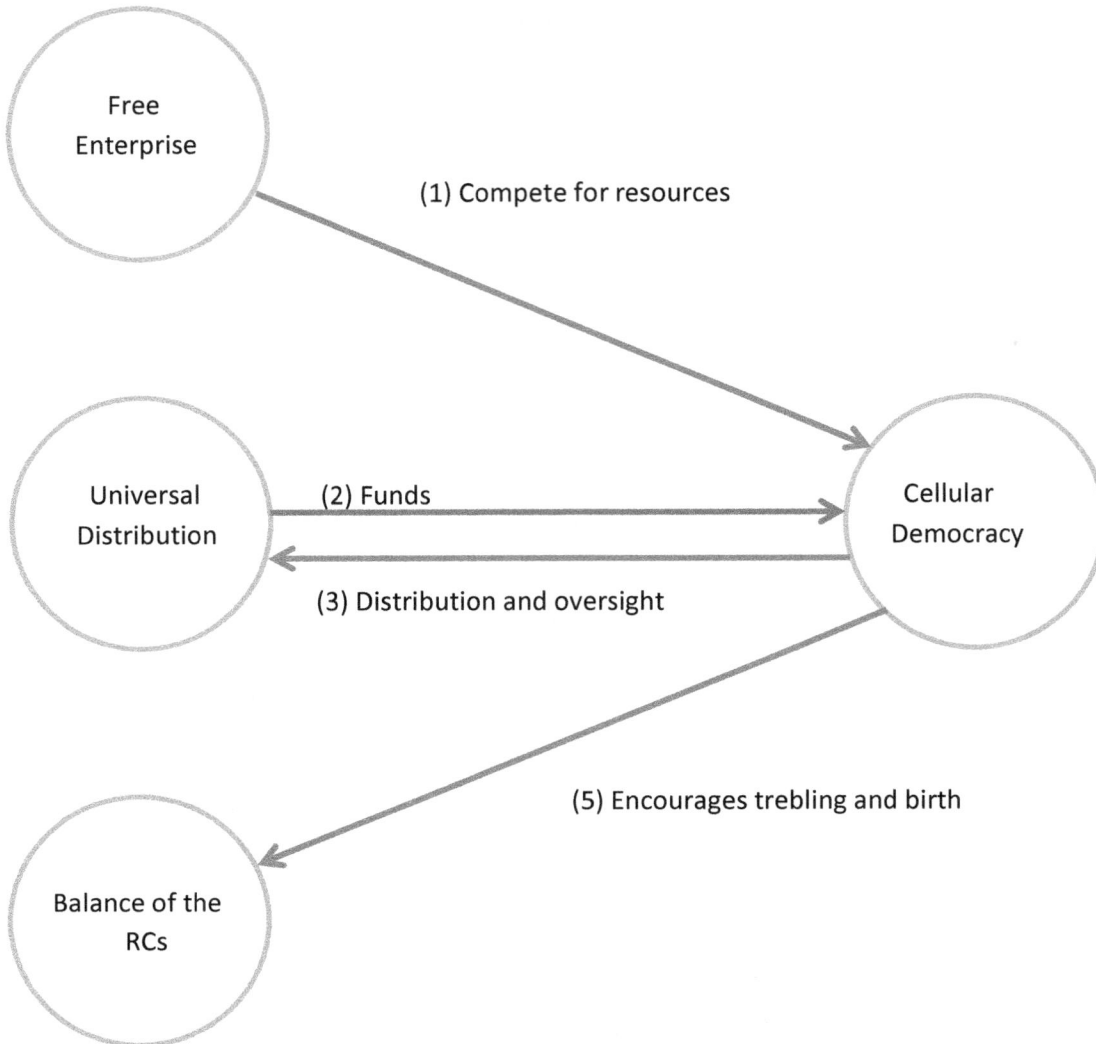

(1) Compete for resources

(2) Funds

(3) Distribution and oversight

(5) Encourages trebling and birth

Free Enterprise

Universal Distribution

Cellular Democracy

Balance of the RCs

(1) Compete for resources – The government distribution forces government employees to compete for limited funds.
(2) Funds – The distributions include a government distribution to fund the cellular democracy.
(3) Distribution and oversight – The cellular democracy identifies tranches for distribution. These functions are administered by the cellular democracy at the level of distribution.
(4) Encourages trebling and birth – Dominion trebling and aristocratic intentions facilitate the rise and fall of towns. Population increases increase political power.

Appendix II – Anatomy of AFFEERCE Mercantilism

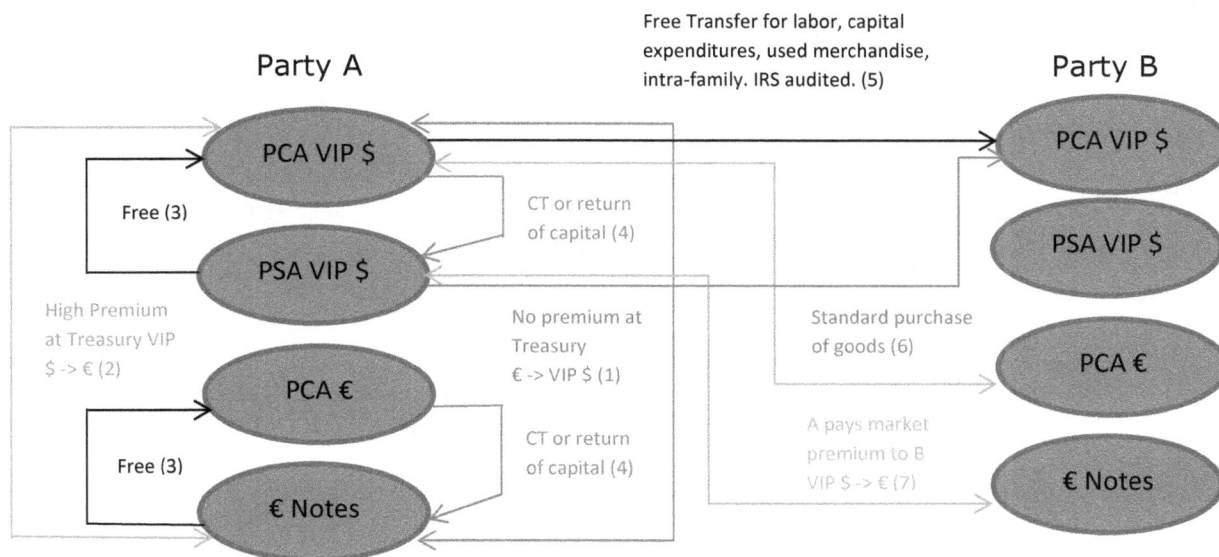

Figure 6.2

Single arrows are transfers. Double arrows are fund exchanges. Any foreign currency, including the U.S. dollar can substitute for the Euro. The following transactions are shown:

1. Blue: Treasury sells VIP $ for foreign currency at no premium to exchange rate.
2. Green: Treasury sells foreign currency for VIP $ at high premium to exchange rate – rare.
3. Black: Free transfers of spending account or physical notes to corporate account for either VIP $ or foreign currency.
4. Red: Transfer from corporate account to spending account or physical notes of either VIP $ or foreign currency requires payment of consumption tax in excess of return of capital for free transfers.
5. Black: Free transfer between VIP $ corporate accounts for payment of labor, capital expenditures, already taxed goods, and intra-family transfers. These transfers are IRS audited.
6. Purple: Transfer from Party A spending account to Party B corporate account for standard purchase of goods from Party B.
7. Orange: Corporate VIP $ purchases foreign currency in a corporate account for speculation and saving. Spending VIP $ purchases foreign currency in a spending account or as physical notes. Party A also pays Party B the market premium to the exchange rate.

Footnotes

Introduction

FTN.3 http://www.cooperative-individualism.org/georgism_01.htm

FTN.4 Monroe, Adam (2015), Opening Statement of the Georgist Party of America

FTN.6 http://en.wikipedia.org/wiki/Law_of_rent

Chapter 1 – What is AFFEERCE?

FTN1.01 H&R Block at Home Tax Software

FTN1.02 Hawking, Stephen, The Grand Design

Chapter 2 – Collection of the Rents

FTN2.01 Lubowski, et al. (2006) Economic Information Bulletin No. (EIB-14) 54 pp, United States Department of Agriculture, Economic Research Service, http://ers.usda.gov/publications/eib-economic-information-bulletin/eib14.aspx

FTN2.02 http://wiki.answers.com/Q/How_many_acres_of_Indian_Reservation_land_in_the_US

FTN2.03 http://taxfoundation.org/article/oil-company-profits-and-tax-collections-does-us-need-new-windfall-profits-tax

FTN2.04 http://www.irs.gov/pub/irs-utl/mining_industry_overview_november_2006.pdf

FTN2.06 http://articles.chicagotribune.com/2011-06-18/business/ct-biz-0619-mag-mile-20110618_1_retail-space-rent-burberry

FTN2.07 http://www.loopnet.com/Illinois/Chicago_Retail-Space-For-Lease/3/

FTN2.08 http://evstudio.com/price-per-square-foot-construction-cost-for-multi-story-office-buildings/

FTN2.10 http://www.nytimes.com/2014/04/05/business/economy/corporate-profits-grow-ever-larger-as-slice-of-economy-as-wages-slide.html

FTN2.13 http://www.tax-rates.org/taxtables/corporate-income-tax-by-state

FTN2.14 http://taxfoundation.org/article/summary-latest-federal-income-tax-data

FTN2.15 http://www.zillow.com/homes/for_rent/Gold--Coast-Chicago-IL/house,condo,apartment,duplex,townhouse_type

FTN2.17 http://en.wikipedia.org/wiki/Citizen%27s_dividend

FTN2.18 http://en.wikipedia.org/wiki/Georgism

FTN2.19 Paine, Thomas, (1791) The Rights of Man

FTN2.20 http://en.wikipedia.org/wiki/Law_of_Rent

FTN2.21 http://en.wikipedia.org/wiki/Land_value_tax

FTN2.23 http://en.wikipedia.org/wiki/Thomas_Spence

FTN2.25 http://en.wikipedia.org/wiki/Pigovian_tax

FTN2.26 http://www.labourland.org/in_the_news/articles/sun_yat_sen.php

FTN2.28 http://en.wikipedia.org/wiki/Progress_and_Poverty

FTN2.29 http://www.profitableplantsdigest.com/10-most-profitable-specialty-crops-to-grow/

FTN2.30 http://www.farmdocdaily.illinois.edu/2011/05/profitability_and_farm_size_on.html

FTN2.31 http://www.noble.org/Ag/Economics/ProfitInWheat/

FTN2.32 http://www.answers.com/Q/For_every_dollar_you_spend_for_produce_at_the_supermarket_what_percentage_goes_to_the_farmer_who_grew_the_product

FTN2.33 http://en.wikipedia.org/wiki/Spectrum_auction

FTN2.34 D. Paul, The Politics of the Property Tax 27 (1975)

FTN2.35 D. Netzer, Economics of the Property Tax (1966);

FTN2.36 S. Levmore, Self-Assessed Valuation Systems for Tort and Other Law, University of Chicago Law   School (1982)

FTN2.37 M. Gaffney, Adequacy of Land as a Tax Base (1969), The Assessment of Land Value (1970), Donald M. Holland, University of Wisconsin Press

Chapter 4– Reproductive Freedom and Control

FTN4.01 http://en.wikipedia.org/wiki/Anthropocene

FTN4.02 Charter of the United Nations, Article 2(4)

FTN4.03 http://www.ehow.com/info_8437261_concerns-depletion-natural-resources.html

FTN4.04 http://www.census.gov/prod/2010pubs/p20-563.pdf

FTN4.05 http://www.scilogs.eu/en/blog/biology-of-religion/2010-06-03/religions-and-fertility-in-the-us-gss-data

FTN4.06 http://www.overpopulation.org/religion.html

FTN4.07 http://www.garretthardinsociety.org/articles/art_tragedy_of_the_commons.html

FTN4.08 Regulating Reproduction, BLANK p2

FTN4.09 Regulating Reproduction, BLANK p3

FTN4.10 Regulating Reproduction, BLANK p4

FTN4.11 Reproductive Rights and Wrongs, Hartmann, P8

FTN4.12 What are we doing with our lives?, Sept. 8, 2014, Time Magazine

FTN4.13 http://nces.ed.gov/FastFacts/display.asp?id=76

FTN4.14 Reproductive Rights and Wrongs, Hartmann, P9

FTN4.15 Regulating Reproduction, BLANK p17

FTN4.16 Regulating Reproduction, BLANK p19

FTN4.17 8 Reproductive Rights and Wrongs, Hartmann, P55

FTN4.18 http://www.livescience.com/7088-history-human-sex.html
FTN4.19 Reproductive Rights and Wrongs, Hartmann, P6
FTN4.20 http://www.sarahwoodbury.com/life-expectancy-in-the-middle-ages/
FTN4.21 http://www.dailykos.com/story/2012/05/15/1092027/-Thanks-a-Union-36-Ways-Unions-Have-Improved-Your-Life#
FTN4.22 http://en.m.wikipedia.org/wiki/Head_tax
FTN4.23 http://en.wikipedia.org/wiki/Tithe
FTN4.24 http://en.wikipedia.org/wiki/Conscription_in_the_United_States
FTN4.25 https://www.childwelfare.gov/pubs/factsheets/whatiscan.pdf
FTN4.26 http://healthyyounow.com/home/2013/10/how-to-talk-with-your-child-about-inappropiate-touching/#.VGN5mc90x9A
FTN4.27 http://www.nea.org/home/15941.htm
FTN4.30 http://www.kundansrivastava.com/child-beggars/
FTN4.31 http://www.ncbi.nlm.nih.gov/pubmed/10852365
FTN4.32 http://www.thedailybeast.com/articles/2013/08/30/the-myth-of-welfare-and-drug-use.html
FTN4.33 http://finance.yahoo.com/news/study--poor-children-have-smaller-brains-than-wealthy-peers-204438119.html
FTN4.34 George, Henry (xxx) Progress and Poverty, P 139-140
FTN4.35 http://www.theguardian.com/society/2012/feb/18/britain-learn-denmark-childcare-model
FTN4.36 http://www.indexmundi.com/g/r.aspx?v=31
FTN4.37 https://en.wikipedia.org/wiki/Elinor_Ostrom
FTN4.38 http://www.iflscience.com/health-and-medicine/sperm-blocking-implant-could-be-latest-male-contraceptive
FTN4.39 https://en.wikipedia.org/wiki/Total_fertility_rate

Chapter 8 – The Natural Rights of Mankind

FTN8.09 http://www.miwatch.org/2011/02/_ronald_reagan_and_mental.html
FTN8.10 http://en.wikipedia.org/wiki/Morality
FTN8.11 http://en.wikipedia.org/wiki/Generation_Y
FTN8.12 http://www.adamsmith.org/sites/default/files/images/uploads/publications/millennial-generation.pdf
FTN8.13 http://en.wikipedia.org/wiki/Labour_theory_of_property
FTN8.14 http://en.wikipedia.org/wiki/Geoism

Chapter 9 – Government, Law, and Justice

FTN9.02 http://en.wikipedia.org/wiki/Prison%E2%80%93industrial_complex
FTN9.03 http://www.bjs.gov/index.cfm?ty=tp&tid=17
FTN9.04 http://www.drugpolicy.org/sites/default/files/One_Million_Police_Hours_0.pdf
FTN9.05 http://www.time.com/time/world/article/0,8599,1887488,00.html
FTN9.06 http://crimevictimsmediareport.com/?p=1640
FTN9.07 http://economics.fundamentalfinance.com/povertycrime.php
FTN9.08 http://sa18.state.fl.us/page/about-repeat-offenders.html
FTN9.09 http://www.unodc.org/pdf/crime/eighthsurvey/8sv.pdf
FTN9.10 http://www.easternstate.org/home
FTN9.11 https://en.wikipedia.org/wiki/Dunbar%27s_number
FTN9.12 https://en.wikipedia.org/wiki/Panarchism

Chapter 10 – Economic Principles

FTN10.02 - Karl Marx, Capital, Volume 1
FTN10.03 - http://en.wikipedia.org/wiki/Productivity
FTN10.04 Adapted from old Buddhist parable
FTN10.05 http://richleebruce.com/economics/3rd-world.html
FTN10.06 http://www.nhi.org/online/issues/135/reagan.html
FTN10.07 http://blog.ctnews.com/kantrowitz/2012/02/22/cuts-to-public-housing-and-section-8-in-president-obamas-proposed-budget/
FTN10.08 http://www.laprogressive.com/african-american-teen-unemployment/
FTN10.09 http://ezinearticles.com/?The-Effects-Of-Balance-Of-Trade-Surplus-And-Deficit-On-A-Countrys-Economy&id=7452746
FTN10.10 http://en.wikipedia.org/wiki/American_National_Standards_Institute
FTN10.11 http://www.tigersoft.com/Tiger-Blogs/Jan-24-2008/index.htm
FTN10.12 http://www.doctorhousingbubble.com/the-gospel-of-economic-prosperity-lessons-from-the-great-depression-part-xviii-pretend-and-spend-and-success-will-come/
FTN10.19 Piketty, Thomas, Capital in the Twenty First Century, 2014
FTN10.22 http://www.law360.com/articles/350734/small-bookstore-group-rips-doj-s-e-book-antitrust-deal
FTN10.23 Stiglitz, Joseph, The Price of Inequality, 2013
FTN10.24 https://en.wikipedia.org/wiki/Fractional-reserve_banking
FTN10.25 https://en.wikipedia.org/wiki/Inflation

Chapter 11 – Distribution

FTN11.01 http://usnews.nbcnews.com/_news/2013/07/28/19738595-ap-4-in-5-americans-live-in-danger-of-falling-into-poverty-joblessness?lite
FTN11.02 http://money.cnn.com/2009/11/16/news/economy/food_insecurity/index.htm
FTN11.03 http://www.ehow.com/how_6668733_calculate-food-stamp-allottment.html
FTN11.04 http://cnsnews.com/blog/joe-schoffstall/record-number-households-food-stamps-1-out-every-5
FTN11.05 http://en.wikipedia.org/wiki/Homelessness_in_the_United_States
FTN11.06 http://www.theatlantic.com/business/archive/2013/03/how-washington-could-make-college-tuition-free-without-spending-a-penny-more-on-education/273801/
FTN11.07 http://www.collegeview.com/articles/article/importance-of-college-education
FTN11.08 http://investmentwatchblog.com/96-of-colleges-not-worth-it-ex-official/
FTN11.09 http://en.wikipedia.org/wiki/Grade_inflation
FTN11.10 http://finance.yahoo.com/news/more-feared-death-long-term-151540946.html
FTN11.11 http://www.ncsl.org/research/health/health-insurance-premiums.aspx
FTN11.12 http://en.wikipedia.org/wiki/Medicare_(United_States)
FTN11.13 http://krugman.blogs.nytimes.com/2011/06/12/medicare-versus-private-insurance-the-data/
FTN11.14 Time Magazine, Steven Brill Article.
FTN11.15 http://www.psmag.com/big_one/one-day-in-a-u-s-hospital-costs-an-average-of-4287-more-than-twice-the-cost-in-australia-the-country-with-the-next-highest-rate-marchapril-2014/
FTN11.16 http://www.cdc.gov/mmwr/preview/mmwrhtml/mm5517a7.htm
FTN11.17 http://apprisehealthinsights.com/public-reports/state-comparison/inpatient-days-per-1000-population-age-adjusted-2/
FTN11.18 http://www.beckershospitalreview.com/lists/average-cost-per-inpatient-day-across-50-states-in-2010.html
FTN11.19 http://voices.yahoo.com/hypochondria-serious-problem-our-country-3507279.html
FTN11.20 http://www.ehow.com/about_5602262_average-cost-nursing-home.html
FTN11.21 http://www.judicialreform.in/forums/showthread.php?tid=325
FTN11.22 http://newsblogs.chicagotribune.com/clout_st/2008/10/aldermen-gripe.html
FTN11.23 http://www.transitchicago.com/assets/1/ridership_reports/2011-Annual.pdf
FTN11.24 http://www.transitchicago.com/assets/1/finance_budget/2013_Budget_Book_Final_20121120.pdf
FTN11.25 http://uslaboragainstwar.org/article.php?id=25700
FTN11.26 http://en.wikipedia.org/wiki/Military_budget_of_the_United_States
FTN11.27 http://www.cbo.gov/sites/default/files/cbofiles/ftpdocs/120$/doc12043/01-19-highwayspending_brief.pdf
FTN11.28 http://ycharts.com/indicators/consumer_spending
FTN11.29 http://www.usgovernmentspending.com/
FTN11.30 http://en.wikipedia.org/wiki/Fire_engine
FTN11.31 http://en.wikipedia.org/wiki/Multiple-alarm_fire
FTN11.32 Reich, Robert (2012) Beyond Outrage
FTN11.33 George, Henry, (xxx) Protection or Free Trade, P 138.

Chapter 12– Family
FTN12.01 http://en.wikipedia.org/wiki/Legal_drinking_age
FTN12.02 http://www.worldlifeexpectancy.com/cause-of-death/alcohol/by-country/
FTN12.03 http://www.safehorizon.org/page/10-signs-of-child-abuse-58.html
FTN12.04 http://en.wikipedia.org/wiki/Kibbutz
FTN12.05 Gavron, Daniel. The Kibbutz: Awakening from Utopia Rowman & Littlefield, Lanham, 2000, p. 45
FTN12.06 http://www.cepr.net/documents/mismarketing-drugs-2015-04.pdf
FTN12.07 http://journals.plos.org/plosmedicine/article?id=10.1371/journal.pmed.0050001

FTN12.08 The Birds, Aristophanes, Translation by William Arrowsmith, New York, 1970, Mentor Books, P 28

Chapter 13 – Enlightenment
FTN13.01 The Future, Al Gore

Index

2

2002 Land Survey, 14, 35, 60, 122, 186, 253, 254

A

Abortion, 14, 98, 107, 108, 109, 110, 116, 240, 241
Abusers, 169, 174, 218, 244, 258
Accuracy of information, 182
Achievement annuities, 87, 97, 113, 114, 117, 199, 224, 225, 226, 227, 228, 229, 230, 250, 258
Addicted, 107, 112
Addiction, 87, 93, 167, 168, 171, 216, 219, 232
Addictions, 197, 231, 240
Adoption, 92, 106, 107, 127
AFFEERCE, 9, 10, 11, 12, 13, 14, 15, 16
    Business plan, 1, 9, 19, 224
    downtown, 248
    embryonic nation, 1, 9, 10, 29, 117, 134, 141, 200, 201
    fundamental relations, 105, 264, 265, 266
    medical plan, 234
        federal payer, 234, 237, 239, 241
        hospital affiliation, 234
        insurance
            exclusions, 234, 240
        insurance arm, 234, 235, 237, 238, 242
        treatment arm, 234
    Phase-II, 71
    Phase-III, 141
    pillars, 266
    spreading, 201
    territory, 71
    Treasury, 19, 21, 38, 39, 42, 47, 53, 60, 85, 107, 111, 121, 123, 124, 125, 126, 127, 128, 129, 132, 133, 191, 192, 194, 200, 203, 253, 271
Affeercianado, 209, 263
    Guild, 21
African-American, 99, 195, 233
    middle class, 165
Age of majority, 111, 128, 140, 143,

176, 178, 199, 217, 218, 219, 222, 223, 256, 257
Alcohol, 86, 87, 93, 112, 168, 214, 216, 217, 240, 257, 259
All of us. *See* Land: belongs to all
Ambassadors, 71, 160, 161, 162
Ancient Greece, 258
ANSI, 176, 182
Anthropocene epoch, 121
Apartment buildings, 60, 61, 218, 219, 248, 256
Apocryphal racist narrative, 99, 112
Apple iPhone, 191
Arbitration, 180
Architectures, 256
Aristocracy
    cellular, 5, 9, 10, 18, 36, 71, 154, 157, 160, 161, 162, 163, 208, 224, 252
        chancellor, 163
        more than one per district, 161
        title, 160, 161, 162
            baron, 69, 154, 160, 161, 162
            gender variant, 154, 161
Armies, 90, 91, 92, 93, 111, 112, 210
Arrest, 21, 150, 166, 169, 172, 173, 180, 233
Artificial rights, 137, 139
Artists, 11, 13, 73, 74, 77, 78, 116, 127, 197, 212, 229, 250
Arts, 135, 168, 187, 188, 223, 245, 269
Asset seizure, 145, 170, 171, 183
Authors, 73, 77
Automation, 3, 4, 11, 94, 95, 105, 266

B

Bailouts, 195, 207
    auto, 195
    Wall Street, 195, 205
Balance of payments, 200, 201
Balance of the RCs, 12, 85, 89, 105, 121, 133, 201, 264, 266
Balance of trade, 200, 201
Balance theory, 121, 133
Ballot, 149, 172, 181, 184
Banishment. *See* Dominion: banishment
Bankruptcy, 87, 202, 232, 233
Banks, 19, 22, 40, 103, 127, 191, 198, 203, 204, 206, 218, 220, 221, 222

Barbarism, 32, 79, 82, 83, 95, 105, 111, 112, 167, 195, 196, 198, 266
Barter, 199, 200
Basic income, 86, *See* Distributions: personal
Battery backup, 21
Be fruitful and multiply, 91, 92, 93
Biblical law, 91
Big Brother, 20, 243
Biological parents, 110
Biometrics, 19, 21, 74
    currency, 36
    identity, 19, 21, 22, 74
Blank, Robert, 101, 106, 107, 110
Bonds, 192, 199, 201, 204
Booksellers, 190
Boycott, 13, 166, 181
Bribery, 184, 201
Bridges, 116, 247, 248, 252
Brill, Stephan, 236, 238
Bubble-up economics, 194, 195
Buffet, Warren, 185
Bureau of Standards, 176, 177, 182, 246
Bureau of Testing, 225, 227
Bureaucracy
    government, 18, 22, 37, 86, 103, 106, 157, 175, 176, 208, 211
    land assessment, 28, 33, 40
    reproductive control, 106, 266
Business
    bad practices, 14, 175, 191
    big, 268
    expansion, 202
    failure, 180, 196, 204
    good practices, 13, 68, 166, 269
    hires inspection agency, 178
    home, 188, 190
    new, 116, 192, 195, 207, 266
    opportunities, 227
    protection from liability, 180
    protest against, 13, 180, 191
    success, 187, 190, 191, 207
    takeover, 48, 69
        worksheet, 45, 49, 50, 51, 61, 62
    uses student grade point average, 228
    VOS, 176, 178
        example, 179

C

Capital, 2, 26, 45, 104, 128, 183, 193,
195, 200, 201, 205, 271
availability, 20, 82, 186, 187, 191,
192, 193, 208
building, 15, 252
concentration, 194, 205, 206
expatriated, 183
expenditure, 76
expenditures, 18, 187, 193, 199, 213,
252, 271
foreign, 201
foreign, 201
gains, 17, 199
goods, 77, 81, 123, 193, 201, 208
Picketty's work, 205
replacement, 252
return on, 74, 97, 131, 189, 201,
205, 206, 271
social, 198
under management, 192, 193
wage, 193, 204
Capitalism, 87
Capitulation, 10, 43, 60, 66, 71, 141
Caregivers, 11, 202, 231
Cashless, 19, 169, 203, 218
Catastrophic failure, 186, 196
Catering, 241
Catholic Church, 109
Cellular
aristocracy
palaces, 46, 153, 160, 161, 162,
163, 224
Certification, 173, 215, 225, 231, 237,
238, 239, 249
Chancellery, 163, 224
Chancellery trebling, 36, 69, 72, 224
Chancellor, 163, 224
Chancery court, 39, 40, 43, 47, 70, 72,
88, 172
Chaos, 24, 79, 88, 132, 134
Chargemaster, 233
Charities, 92, 107, 108, 111, 115, 116,
182, 215, 219, 220, 240, 243, 256
Cheating, 88, 198
Child abuse, 93, 94, 129, 166, 174, 218,
243, 244, 257, 258, 259
Child care, 97, 211
Child pornography, 168
Child support payments, 257
Childbearing
form of aggression, 99, 100, 101

Childbirth, 108, 137
fine, 108
form of aggression, 94
form of aggression, 137
Children
=poverty, 94, 95, 96, 121
=wealth, 12, 17, 90, 91, 94, 96, 102,
106, 111, 121, 140, 218, 219, 242
adopting, 106, 110
affordable, 110, 127, 179, 268
age of maturity, 257
burden, 93, 94, 98, 99, 137, 223, 257
effect on judicial family restructuring,
255, 256, 257
entitlement cash as learning tool, 222
foster, 217
privilege of property, 140
raising, 97, 110, 211, 259
reasons to have, 90, 91, 92, 94, 95
reasons to not have, 91, 92, 93, 94
restricted ownership, 256
right to be intoxicated, 139
rights, 12, 14, 86, 87, 99, 107, 140,
143, 144, 166
severely disabled, 107
social security, 105, 266
standards enforced, 174, 176, 184,
215, 218, 219, 256, 258
unfunded, 102, 107
unwanted, 257
valuable, 134, 138, 266, 269
China, 60, 250
Choke, 116, 123, 124, 125, 126, 127,
133
Citizen, 201
Citizen investors, 20, 44, 48, 49, 123,
127, 157, 165, 181, 187, 191, 192,
193, 194, 204, 208
Citizens
AFFEERCE, 128
born before birth tax, 15
U.S., 71
Citizens dividend, 16, 79, 88, 96, 98,
125, 126, 127, 146, 158, 162, 216
Citizenship, 129, 150, 168, 208
Citizenship tax, 266
City pass, 198
Civil disobedience, 116, 166, 180, 181,
191
Civil rights, 13, 165, 166
Civil servants, 157
Civil tort, 107, 222, 233
Class warfare, 101, 138, 211

Clothing, 93, 94, 210, 222, 256
Coercive force, 11, 99, 103, 104, 106,
111
Collection theory. *See* Ground rent:
collection
Collective
rights, 14, 87, 99
Collectivism, 34, 133
Colleges, 96, 223, 224, 227, 229, 236
Collusion, 13, 32, 187, 190, 191, 207
contract, 190
land price, 29, 31, 32, 131
medical insurance, 234
spectrum auction, 54
standards, 174
Colonialism, 201
Commodity, 184, 185, 190
Commodity fetishism, 112, 184, 185,
269
Communal dining, 168, 220, 255, 256
Communes, 11, 12, 52, 223, 244
Communism, 198
Community, i, 4, 11, 14, 15, 23, 24, 67,
78, 79, 84, 111, 115, 139, 140, 149,
151, 159, 164, 166, 180, 181, 191,
255, 256, 259
borders, 47
bottom-up, 164
centers, 215, 222
collects rent, 32, 79, 115
creates land value, 35, 78
forming, 164
infrastructure, 80
local land capture, 84
sanction, 180
standards, 13, 165
top-down, 164
Compensation, 36, 37, 43, 48, 60, 68,
92, 156, 157, 170, 171, 243
Competition, 67, 177, 187, 217, 226,
251
collusion, 190, 207
deregulation, 238, 239
family business, 187, 190, 196, 207
jobs, 197
monopoly, 190
profit, 53
thwarted, 51, 190, 195
Competitors, 48, 190, 191
Computers, 19, 20, 116, 129, 175, 217,
227, 229, 249, 253
Consciousness, 93, 94, 164, 239

Conservatives, 195, 205

Consideration (in law), 14, 116, 181, 182

Constitution, 143, 256

Constitutional amendment package, 9, 98, 119, 141

Consumer advocates, 177, 230, 231

Consumer senators, 176, 177

Consumers, 13, 35, 52, 53, 174, 175, 176, 177, 182, 186, 190, 248

Content
free. *See* Intellectual property: content: free

Contraception, 14, 92, 93, 94, 96, 98, 108, 109, 116, 240

Contract, 92, 115, 116, 121, 144, 176, 179, 181, 183, 185, 198, 200, 219, 252, 256
enforceable, 116, 136, 182, 185, 190, 219
not enforceable, 31, 115, 144, 150, 180, 182, 183

Contradictions, 137, 138, 139, 174, 175, 196
of capitalism, 196

Copay, 240, 241

Copyright. *See* Intellectual property: copyright

Corporate account, 18, 116, 196, 199, 201, 202, 204, 256, 271

Corporations, 18, 21, 22, 66, 115, 116, 176, 199, 200, 227, 230, 248, 251

Corruption, 20, 22, 106, 139, 141, 172, 173, 174, 175, 191, 201, 208, 231, 246
land assessment, 28, 31, 32, 33, 40

Couples, 12, 13, 103, 129, 188, 220, 221, 235, 244, 255

Covenants, 45, 46, 47, 66, 71
jurisdictional, 46, 132, 161, 224, 245
patterns, 47, 71
purchased, 45, 46, 47, 66, 115

Crack cocaine, 100, 101, 107

Creationism, 258

Crime, 99, 100, 101, 116, 136, 166, 167, 168, 169, 170, 171, 207, 216, 240, 258

Crime reduced, 167, 169, 170, 172, 198, 207, 246, 248, 250

Criminal behavior, 198, 216

Criminal offense, 99, 180, 222, 233, 239

Culture wars, 194

Cultures, 11, 43, 69, 88, 144, 147, 151, 164, 167, 183, 188, 194, 256, 257, 258

Currency
alternative, 21, 117, 118, 119, 150, 199, 200
backed by land, 85, 133, 136, 203
domain, 85
foreign, 199, 200, 201, 271
inflationary, 133
monetizing, 126
scrip, 193
virtual, 19

Curriculum, 227, 230, 231, 258

Customers, 139, 178, 181, 249, 269

D

Darwin, Charles, 103

Day care centers, 207

de Puydt, Paul, 148

Death, 90, 103, 156, 174, 179, 202, 233, 238, 240, 242, 243, 257

Death penalty, 145

Debtor's prison, 202

Debts, 87, 202, 212

Deceased, 171, 202, 242

Deconstruction, 93

Default (on payment), 21, 87, 198, 200, 202, 204

Deflation, 56, 204, 220

Deflationary, 269

Democracy, 139, 255, 256
cellular, 10, 18, 19, 20, 46, 54, 69, 141, 142, 143, 146, 148, 152, 153, 154, 155, 157, 158, 160, 161, 162, 164, 172, 173, 201, 208, 255, 270
breakout, 153
child, 152, 154
daughter cell, 153
distribution, 153
district, 152, 154, 156, 158
council, 21, 140, 141, 142, 143, 145, 146, 149, 152, 153, 154, 155, 157, 159, 160, 161, 162, 164, 173, 177, 252
aristocratic hosting, 162
hire chief executive, 160
level-1, 142, 154
level-2, 142, 143
level-7, 144, 145, 157, 159,

162, 163, 172, 178
military cellular
enterprise, 251
support war, 251
meetings, 156
disbursement, 152
dominion, 152
enterprise, 152, 158
executive, 152
geographic, 152
governing, 152
population, 152
dominion, 152
encirclement capture, 153
level 0 is individual, 154
Level N, 152, 154
mitosis, 153
national cell populations, 154
orphan cell, 72, 148, 149, 153, 156, 164
orphaned cell, 153
parent, 152, 154
population, 152
representative, 154, 155, 156
representatives, 156, 157, 159
sibling, 152
switching allegiance, 153
direct, 5, 10, 141, 142, 143, 146, 149, 163, 164
representative, 10

Democrats, 195, 205

Denial of service, 181

Denmark, 89

Depreciation, 193, 245
effects of, 62

Depreciation schedules, 45, 72, 200, 220

Depression, 195, 196, 205

Deregulation, 172, 179, 180, 185, 207, 208, 232, 237, 238, 266

Derivatives, 204

Detroit, 195, 196

Diagnosticians, 237, 238, 239

Disability, 21, 92, 98, 231, 239, 249, 258

Disabled, 92, 107, 184, 185, 217, 232, 238, 242, 243, 256, 257, 258

Discretionary income, 14, 112, 128, 197, 202

Discrimination, 98, 106, 107, 165, 166, 181, 202, 218

Disease, 11, 69, 89, 112, 121

Dishonesty, 13, 14, 102, 171, 172, 198,

211
Dislocations, 19, 266
Distribution
  education, 86
  food, 82
  government, 155, 156, 157, 158,
    160, 164, 167, 202, 212, 216,
    225, 226, 240, 251, 253, 270
    tranche, 155, 156, 157
  housing, 86
  intellectual property, 40, 74, 77, 78,
    83, 190, 207, 208, 250, 251
    lowers costs, 83, 132
  law enforcement, 159
  local, 78, 79
    problem, 78, 79, 80
  package, 39, 52, 53, 54, 59, 60, 84,
    88, 114, 121, 122, 123, 124, 125,
    126, 128, 131, 133, 156, 163,
    224, 254, 266
    add funds, 126
    interest, 123
  personal, 122
  universal, 106
  tranche, 15, 83, 142, 148, 152, 159,
    160, 164, 212, 215, 245, 246,
    252, 270
    medical plan, 234
  universal, 10, 11, 13, 14, 15, 16, 18,
    20, 40, 83, 86, 89, 95, 96, 105,
    111, 126, 129, 141, 147, 156,
    157, 159, 165, 187, 193, 206,
    209, 210, 211, 214, 210–54, 264
    benefits, 211
    enlightenment, 269
    enticement, 9
    exempt from judgements, 156
    families, 188, 268
    freedom, 180, 181, 185
    fundamental, 12, 13, 19, 264, 266
    funding, 12, 14, 37, 60, 121
    prison reform, 169
    productivity, 197, 207
    protectionism, 195, 200
    reproduction, 101, 105, 106, 112
    right to leave, 144, 147
    tames free enterprise, 137, 139,
      183, 184, 196, 204
Distribution domain, 78, 79, 80, 81, 84,
  85, 132
Distribution of wealth, 206
Distribution theory. *See* Ground rent:

distribution
Distributions
  allocated, 86, 87, 88, 215
  cash, 88, 171, 212, 222
    all cash, 87
  disability, 167, 202, 216, 231, 232,
    235, 239, 240, 242
  education, 88, 97, 207, 223, 224,
    225, 226, 237, 258
  fire protection, 88, 212, 244, 245,
    246, 248
  food, 21, 35, 53, 87, 128, 188, 207,
    212, 213–16, 220, 226, 239, *See*
    also Right to nutritious meals
  housing, 16, 17, 19, 20, 39, 52, 61,
    63, 64, 65, 66, 83, 87, 128, 163,
    167, 169, 179, 201, 202, 207,
    212, 216, 217, 218, 219, 220,
    221, 222, 216–22, 226, 234, 235,
    236, 239, 240, 241, 245, 250,
    257, 259
  infrastructure and VIP, 252, 253
  judiciary, 173, 246
  law enforcement, 15, 88, 246
  medical, 88, 97, 109, 157, 168, 185,
    202, 216, 232, 238, 239, 240, 242
  move with the person, 83, 132, 156,
    160, 212
  national defense, 15, 69, 217, 250,
    251, 252, 253
  personal, 11, 13, 82, 83, 86, 88, 122,
    132, 133, 148, 180, 202, 210, 212
    bias, 83, 84
  public, 11, 13, 122, 210
  rebate, 20, 213, 214, 215, 216, 239,
    244
    housing, 87, 220
    medical, 107, 109, 172, 179, 208,
      213, 232, 234, 235, 236, 237,
      238, 239, 240
  social worker, 243, 244
  testing, 230, 231
  transportation and sanitation, 97,
    181, 189, 246, 247, 248, 249
Diversity, 43, 69, 138, 140, 144, 164,
  166, 218, 244, 257, 259
Dividend accounts, 125, 126, 127, 128,
  133
Division of labor, 186, 187, 188, 189,
  196, 207, 211, 218, 255, 268
Divorce, 243, 257
Doctors, 175, 235, 236, 237, 239, 241
Dollarnado, 200

Domestic violence, 139, 144, 167, 169,
  218, 243, 244
Domhoff, G. William, 206
Dominion, 45, 46, 54, 69, 79, 114, 138,
  146, 147, 148, 149, 150, 152, 153,
  154, 156, 157, 160, 161, 162, 163,
  164, 173, 177, 207, 208, 212, 213,
  221, 252
  banishment, 150
  seven levels, 54, 72, 115, 161
Dominion trebling, 36, 45, 46, 47, 69,
  72, 132, 148, 153, 160, 162, 164,
  166, 202, 262, 270
Donations, 116, 182, 217, 251
Dormitories, 128, 221, 226, 256
Double jeopardy, 172
Drug abuse, 140, 167, 240
Drug addicts, 94, 108, 111, 168, 169,
  175, 217
Drug use, 136, 239

E

Each of us, 4, 11, 13, 14, 15, 73, 80, 81,
  82, 83, 86, 132
Earth's bounty, 11, 12, 66, 69, 87, 121,
  138, 141
Easements, 46, 66, 67, 68, 247, 248
EBITDA, 49, 51, 63
Economic growth, 91, 96, 191, 229
Economists, 91, 174
Economy of scale, 10, 87, 96, 169, 186,
  187, 188, 189, 190, 196, 207, 211,
  255, 268, 270
Education, 88, 93, 97, 101, 104, 129,
  134, 167, 185, 187, 217, 222–32,
  254, 257
  as pastime, 269
  college, 97
  continuing, 165
  costs, 95, 105
  pastime, 187, 223
  sex education, 98
Educational abuse, 258
Egg fusion, 202
Elder care, 188, 242, 243
Elderly, 90, 91, 207, 210, 211, 216, 217,
  232, 233, 240, 242, 243, 256, 257,
  258
  abuse, 243, 244
Elections, 181
Electorate, 21, 111, 127, 140, 172, 180
Elements of a bill, 144

extent, 145, 146, 147, 150

prohibition, 144, 145, 146, 147

punishment, 145, 146, 147, 150, 164, 173

Emergency room, 88, 222

Emigration, 150, 201

Emotions, 69, 99, 184, 185

Employers, 13, 165, 183, 217, 231

Encrypted, 21, 182

Enlightenment, 11, 12, 14, 16, 36, 88, 91, 94, 95, 105, 108, 126, 170, 198, 209, 269

Enterprise, 36, 179, 183, 187, 196, 223

Entrepreneurs, 11, 18, 36, 37, 47, 68, 69, 139, 165, 178, 180, 192, 207, 219, 224, 268

Environment, 13, 97, 102, 115, 174, 175, 248

Escape, 102, 168

Estate, 43, 66, 70, 185, 202, 203, 220, 221, 242, 243

bonus pool, 242, 243

Ethics, 171, 257

Eugenics, 106

Evictions, 218, 219, 222

Evolution, 69, 91, 103, 111, 121, 258

Exchange rate, 271

Expensive life-saving technology, 240

Extortion, 100, 139, 141, 183, 190, 191, 228

Extradite, 150

F

Falderal, 11, 69, 161

Families, 37, 88, 90, 96, 97, 98, 101, 102, 219

alternative, 12, 13, 20, 97, 111, 138, 172, 218, 221, 243, 244

aristocratic title, 160

built on fantasy, 134

children, 106, 202, 203, 223

economy of scale, 188, 207, 216, 220, 221, 242, 268

end domestic violence, 139, 218

fire fighting, 244, 245, 246

gender, 218

LGBT contribution, 93

logical consequence of AFFEERCE, 266

registered, 161

reproduction, 110, 111, 112

biological, 161

business, 96, 181, 187, 190, 196, 198, 207, 211, 223, 244, 255, 256, 259, 268

counseling, 243, 244

dowries, 256

dysfunctional, 257

expulsion, 192, 256, 257

intra-family transfers, 88, 271

large, 11, 164, 173, 188, 219, 223, 244

afford children, 202, 268

built around fantasy, 11

capture community entitlement, 188

division of labor, 96, 188, 189, 211, 268

economy of scale, 87, 169, 187, 188, 189, 211, 214, 215, 216, 219, 268

end loneliness, 170

increase productivity, 18, 187, 211, 244, 268

increase wealth, 13, 15

village to raise children, 97, 211

rituals, 11, 255, 256, 257

roles, 93, 110, 218, 255, 256, 259

severance, 219

shopper, 20, 21, 87, 188, 215

single person, 12, 87, 106, 188, 244, 255

spiritual, 220, 243

unioning into, 168, 243, 244

Family charter, 98, 139, 176, 222, 255, 256, 259

default, 256

Family court, 88, 172, 173, 219, 256, 257

Farm subsidies, 35, 52, 87, 128

Farmers, 35, 52, 53, 66, 87, 102, 246

Farms, 52, 53, 128, 129, 245

FBI, 159, 174, 246, 250, 251

Fear, 69, 87, 93, 101, 138, 180, 184, 185, 186, 187, 204, 207, 211, 232

FEMA, 217

Feminists, 96, 97

Fertility, 90, 92, 105, 107

Fertility rate, 12, 14, 89, 90, 105, 123, 133

Feudalism, 32, 69, 81, 82, 83, 92, 196

Financial instruments, 16, 90, 111, 136, 191, 200, 204

Fines, 103, 108, 145, 156, 157, 170,

171, 173, 183, 246

Fire stations, 245

Fire-fighters, 245, 246

Fix prices, 190

Food stamps, 93, 213, 214

Foreclosure, 168, 218, 222, 232

Foreign aid, 217

Foreign corporations, 200

Foreign investment, 186

Foreign investor, 201

Foreign trade, 200

Foreign workers, 20, 128

Forgery, 182

Framework

government, 141, 145

legal, 141

Fraud, 116, 141, 149, 156, 170, 171, 174, 180, 182, 185, 191, 202, 239, 240, 246

Free enterprise, 5, 9, 11, 12, 13, 18, 34, 88, 158, 183, 184, 264, 266

Free markets, 14, 19, 69, 137, 175, 183, 185, 190, 198, 200, 266

agriculture, 35, 52, 53, 266

benefits, 18, 195, 251, 257

cause no harm, 19, 69, 266

deregulation, 179

radical, 240

entitlement, 137, 196, 237, 266

harmful dislocations, 196

land, 35

not free today, 99, 195

Free will, 14, 261

Freedom, 11, 96, 104, 106, 111, 183, 184, 261, 262, 263

maximum personal, 13, 87, 151, 256

of assembly, 21

of association, 166, 167, 180

of community, 151

of religion, 21, 261

of speech, 21, 140, 256

of the commons, 102, 103

of youth, 257

to breed, 103, 104, 107

to refuse service, 166

to travel, 20, 166

Friedan, Betty, 93

Friends, 101, 166, 167, 175, 200, 217, 219, 232

Full disclosure, 176, 180, 182, 239

Full employment, 195, 197, 217

Future baby account, 107, 110, 116,

127, 186, 196, 202, 207
exercised, 107, 127, 128
fully funded, 110, 127, 128
heritable, 127

G

Gaffney, Mason, 28
Gags played on the customer, 175
Gambling, 86, 87, 112, 167, 184, 257
Game rooms, 168
Game theory, 101
Gay liberation, 93
Gender, 218
Genetics, 106, 108, 110, 121, 202
Gentrification, 217
George, Henry, 2, 3, 4, 5, 6, 7, 8, 11, 12, 23, 24, 25, 27, 31, 34, 41, 60, 73, 74, 89, 104, 113, 124, 132, 135, 136, 141, 158, 197
Georgism, 5, 9, 16, 29, 79
Global warming, 102, 258
God, 4, 11, 26, 73, 80, 86, 91, 92, 99, 100, 132, 261
Gold, 21, 52, 199, 200
Government, 141, 208, 210, 213, 217
  bloated, 18, 175
  borrowing, 186, 194, 204
  buildings, 156, 157, 208
  debt, 88, 92, 157, 200, 250
  hands off business, 13, 207
  maintains balance of nature, 11, 266
  maintains power of privileged, 11
  protectionism, 233
  spying, 20
GPS location, 249, 253
Grade inflation, 207, 228
Grades, 225, 226, 228, 230, 236
Graduate students, 226, 227
Green cities, 11
Grocery stores, 21, 215
Ground rent, 16, 17, 36, 107, 126, 128, 191, 207, 248, 266, 269
  advance payment, 38, 41, 42, 43, 44, 52, 67, 68, 70, 105, 107, 122, 132, 133, 191
    compensation, 60, 67
    refund, 36, 38, 43, 44, 48, 50, 60, 67, 68, 70
  collection, 9, 12, 18, 24, 33, 34, 39, 61, 63, 74, 81, 89, 114, 121, 131, 133, 134, 141, 145, 148, 201, 206, 207, 209

distribution, 12, 18, 24, 34, 53, 73, 74, 78, 79, 82, 83, 86, 89, 104, 105, 122, 125, 132, 133, 141, 209, 210, 250
  fair, 40, 41, 190
  floating, 66, 72
  freeze, 60, 70
  initial, 46, 52, 53, 70, 71, 132
  minimum, 40, 42, 46, 48, 52, 53, 60, 62, 66, 82, 161
  multiplier, 37, 38, 39, 46, 53, 60, 128
    rate of fall, 39, 42, 44, 47, 49, 53, 60, 121, 123, 124, 127, 133
      10%, 127
    second derivative, 124
  not a tax, 81, 132
  productivity, 36, 52, 207, 266
  raising, 41, 50, 53, 63, 70, 80, 84, 124, 131, 160, 162
  safe and efficient, 60
  surcharge, 47, 52, 53, 66, 71, 128
  treble safe, 41, 46, 50, 52, 55, 56, 124, 159, 245
Ground rents
  collection, 117
  initial, 60, 61, 66
Guardian, 222
Gun control, 137, 138
Gymnasium, 96, 168

H

Halfway houses, 168, 219
Hamptons, 14, 17, 18
Hardin, Garrett, 32, 80, 102, 104, 105, 106
Hartmann, Betsy, 97, 105, 108
Healthcare, 17, 69, 93, 94, 99, 100, 134, 157, 185, 186, 232, 233, 239, 241, 254, 256, 266
Hegel, Georg, 104
Help word, 21
Heterosexual, 107
High frequency trading, 204
Higher education, 17, 95, 223, 224
Home care, 211, 232, 242
Home schooling, 164, 188, 223, 227, 228, 258
Homelessness, 17, 69, 86, 87, 133, 137, 180, 184, 210, 212, 216, 217, 218, 219, 254
Homophobia, 165, 166
Honesty, 13, 172, 198, 202, 269

Hong Kong, 60
Hospitals, 16, 100, 107, 127, 231, 232, 233, 234, 235, 236, 238, 239, 240, 241
Hostile takeover. *See* Business: takeover
Human guinea pig, 179, 240
Humanity, 34, 88, 95, 100, 101, 108, 111, 121, 262
  biological machines, 14
  every child is valuable, 95, 112, 134
  every person is valuable, 88
  random accident, 14
Hunger, 17, 86, 87, 100, 101, 133, 136, 137, 180, 184, 212, 213, 236, 254, 262
Hypochondriac hotels, 241
Hypochondriacs, 241

I

Idiotocracy, 111
Immigrant, 128, 129
  illegal, 128
Immigration, 128
Imprisonment, 21, 100, 108, 116, 171
In vitro gestation, 111, 112
Incarceration, 93, 138, 166, 169, 170, 240
Incentive, 21, 37, 91, 115, 138, 157, 166, 167, 168, 171, 173, 186, 194, 207, 208, 210, 211, 229, 231, 242, 243, 244, 247, 248
Incursion, 145, 146, 147
Indigent, 11, 16, 87, 93, 94, 95, 99, 110, 147, 171, 194, 196, 197, 206, 210, 211, 217, 224, 233, 266
  AFFEERCE
    large families, 202
    no longer poor, 18, 171, 194, 195, 207, 219, 249, 259, 266
    nursing bonus, 202
    get poorer, 205
Individualism, 6, 34, 133
Industrial revolution, 91
Inequality, 198
Infant mortality, 106
  rate, 232
Inflation, 13, 203, 205, 220
  one-time land, 60, 68, 70
Information overload, 175
Infrastructure, 47, 127, 146, 247, 248, 251, 252, 253
  department, 158

local, 80, 81, 84, 127

Inheritance, 35, 71, 90, 91, 92, 93, 127, 147, 202

Injustice, 173

Innocent, 116, 171, 172

Innovation, 69, 91, 94, 186, 187, 189, 241, 247

profit from, 74

Innovators, 11, 13, 67, 73, 74, 77, 78, 127, 136, 186, 187, 188, 190, 204, 218, 219, 223, 233, 250

Inpatient facilities, 232, 233, 235, 238, 241, 242

Inspection agencies, 176, 178, 179, 180, 182

Instructors, 226, 227, 228, 229, 230

Insurance companies, 233, 240

Insurance policy, 88, 128, 192, 221

Insurrection, 137, 180, 196

Integrated solution, 1, 74, 80, 85, 134

Intellectual property, 13, 15, 40, 48, 73, 74, 75, 76, 77, 83, 122, 125, 127, 133, 136, 187, 189, 190, 199, 207, 208, 227, 228, 232, 233, 236, 250, 251, 253

content

free, 77, 78, 132, 187, 207

copyrights, 73, 75, 77, 190, 222

distribution tranches, 77, 78

monopoly, 73

patents, 13, 73, 74, 75, 76, 77, 78, 189, 190, 222, 233, 236

algebra, 75, 76

drug, 73, 77, 78, 233, 236

profit from, 190

Intelligence, 93, 94, 251

Interest rate, 30, 31, 42, 87, 123, 186, 187, 204, 220

Internal affairs, 157

Internships, 197

Intestate, 202

Investment, 53, 91, 186, 194

abroad, 201

birth tax, 97, 112

citizen investors, 191

drives productivity, 186

in research and development, 191

real estate, 45

savings, 204

taxes, 207

trickle down, 194

Investors, 192, 201

Involuntary confinement, 170

Involuntary servitude, 150, 151, 183

IRS, 71, 271

Isolation centers, 108, 167, 168, 169, 217

J

Jitney cabs, 249

dispatch, 158

dispatch fee, 249, 250

Job interview, 228

Joe's Brain Surgery Shack, 179, 238, 239

Judges, 38, 45, 168, 170, 171, 172, 173, 174, 181, 185, 216, 218, 232, 243, 246, 247, 257

Judiciary, 19, 144, 145, 157, 167, 171, 172, 173, 184, 212, 218, 222, 231, 246, 255, 256

independent, 148, 156, 164, 172

special prosecution, 171, 173, 246

Justice, 28, 141, 150, 171, 236

K

Key-less, 19

Kibbutzim, 11, 52, 223, 243

King, Martin Luther, 98, 135, 166

Kings, 20, 90, 100, 256

L

Labor, 26, 104, 105, 106, 168, 186, 194, 200

cost, 57, 71, 72

imputed, 37, 45

family obligation, 259

fruits of, 87, 99

land ownership, 136

market, 91, 105, 196

pool, 90, 91, 93

relations, 180, 181

tax free, 200, 215, 271

theory of property, 136

unions, 180, 197, 199

Land, i, 17, 23, 90, 102, 136, 172, 207

assessment, 28, 29, 32, 33, 40, 41, 85, 131

auction, 43, 60, 67, 68, 71, 72

badlands, 3, 14, 35, 68, 87, 189

belongs to all, 4, 11, 14, 15, 73, 80, 81, 82, 86, 132

borderlands, 46, 153, 164

collective ownership, 34, 121, 180, 183

commercial/residential, 35, 59, 60, 266

common ownership, 11

conquest, 34, 47, 69, 90

converting cropland, 52, 53, 128

cropland, 35, 37, 52, 53, 59, 66, 68, 87, 128, 266

imbalance, 128

exclusive use, 9, 11, 14, 32, 34, 42, 74, 75

improvements, 3, 24, 25, 29, 36, 37, 38, 39, 40, 41, 43, 44, 45, 47, 48, 51, 53, 55, 58, 63, 68, 69, 71, 72, 78, 83, 84, 85, 87, 131, 132, 136, 149, 183, 200, 252

not taxed, 24

minerals. *See* Minerals

no market for, 28, 32, 131

objectively worthless, 14, 26, 66, 69, 131

online system, 36, 37, 38, 40, 45, 66, 71, 72, 149, 200, 207, 252

alerts, 43, 72

application, 71

database, 36, 37, 72, 253

owners of exclusive rights, 34, 35, 37, 38, 39, 40, 43, 45, 47, 52, 60, 66, 67, 68, 71, 136, 162, 164, 183, 217, 218

history, 71

price, 28, 29, 30, 31, 32, 33, 72, 131, 205

rangeland, 35, 53, 59, 66, 68

Seized by force, 14, 34, 131

seizure, 33, 34, 36, 40, 45, 58, 131, 132, 183, 234, 266

self-assessment, 33, 34, 39, 40, 41, 43, 48, 60, 73, 85, 123, 131, 265, 266

severing, 66

speculation, 1, 4, 5, 25, 29, 30, 31, 32, 33, 35, 40, 68, 207

surrender, 60, 66, 67, 68, 71, 72

timberland, 14, 35, 37, 45, 53, 59, 115

transfer, 43, 71, 183

value, 3, 4, 7, 16, 24, 25, 81, 84, 85, 133

subjective, 32, 131

arbitrarily high value, 26

tends to zero, 26, 32, 131
Land assessment
    corruption. *See* Corruption: land assessment
Land value
    comparable sales, 29, 31, 131
    objective scores, 28, 29, 131
Landlords, 17, 87, 168, 202, 219
Law enforcement, 13, 88, 168–72, 173, 194, 208, 218, 219, 233, 243, 247, 257
    BOS, 176, 246
    cost, 100, 246
    federal, 250
    misconduct, 157, 173
Law of objective criteria, 32, 33, 34, 131
Law of rent, 1, 2, 5, 9, 12, 25, 26, 62
Law of subjective criteria, 32, 33, 34, 131
Law schools, 172, 173, 246
Laws, 14, 104, 141, 151, 191
    child labor, 91, 94
    constitutional protection, 20, 21, 88, 98, 127, 140, 141, 143, 144, 145, 146, 147, 148, 150, 157, 160, 164, 174, 181
    in AFFEERCE, 146, 172
    of the state and federal governments, 91, 94
    passed by electorate, 146, 147
    passed by the electorate, 21, 147
    physical in nature, 258, 261
    tyrannical, 157
Lawsuits, 171, 228
Lawyers, 13, 59, 171, 172, 173, 198, 236
Leaflet, 13, 166, 180, 191
Leasing, 52, 54, 55, 219
Lectures, 226, 227
Left-wing, 196, 201
Legislation
    class I, 140, 145, 146, 149, 150, 155
    class II, 117, 140, 141, 145, 146, 147, 149, 150, 158, 164, 166, 177
    Class II, 118
    class III, 117, 140, 141, 145, 146, 147, 148, 149, 150, 151, 153, 157, 164, 174, 255
        with treble option, 72, 144, 146, 147, 148, 149, 256
    Class III, 119
        with treble option, 119
Legislators cannot raise revenue, 19, 21,

198
Level playing field, 11
Levels of federation, 146, 172, 173
LGBT, 106, 166, 181, 218
Liability, 107, 157, 171, 172, 174, 176, 178, 179, 180, 183, 207, 208, 236, 237, 239
    limited, 157, 208
Liberals, 88, 103, 106, 195
Libertarians, 29, 195
Liberty, 100, 140, 168, 171, 240, 259, 261
    loss of, 108, 150, 156, 167, 218, 240
    restrictions on, 169, 219, 240, 241
Library of Congress, 75, 76, 144, 177
Lien against improvements, 39, 40, 43
Life expectancy, 232, 245
Limited liability, 236
Limited resources, 69, 93, 94, 96, 107, 112
Living wage, 197
Loans, 198, 202, 203, 204, 218, 220, 221, 222
    student, 223
Lobbying, 175
Lobbyists, 177
Local cash, 21
Local distribution. *See* Distribution: local
Local land capture, 84, 85, 125, 127, 133, 146, 203, 252
Location value, 11, 12, 16, 19, 24, 26, 27, 28, 29, 30, 31, 32, 33, 40, 41, 42, 43, 44, 48, 49, 50, 51, 55, 56, 58, 59, 61, 62, 63, 64, 65, 68, 74, 75, 78, 79, 81, 84, 85, 112, 124, 125, 126, 127, 131, 133, 189, 190, 208
    intellectual property symmetry, 74
    profit from, 74, 189, 190
    profits from, 131, 189
Locke, John, 136
Logical consistency, 1, 10
Loneliness, 87, 91, 92, 93, 133, 138, 170, 216, 262

M

Malicious prosecution, 156, 157, 171, 172, 173
Malthusian, 89, 104, 106
Management, 53, 58, 181
Manning, Bradley, 20
Margin of production, 2, 25, 26, 29, 48,

81, 82, 83, 205
Marginal productivity, 197, 198, 266
Marijuana, 168, 169
Marriage, 98, 243
Marx, Karl, 184, 185, 205
Materialism, 138
Meal allowance, 214
Means of reproduction, 90
Medicaid, 211
Medical campus, 234, 235
Medical diagnosis, 88, 237, 238, 241
Medical diagnostics, 222, 236, 237, 239, 241
Medical insurance, 16, 17, 92, 96, 128, 129, 233
Medical malpractice, 236
Medical prognosis, 237
Medical schools, 231, 236, 237, 238, 239, 241
Medical students, 241, 242
Medicare, 16, 17, 18, 194, 211, 232, 233
Medication, 233, 240
Medicine, 110, 179, 233, 239
Meltdown, 123, 124, 126, 127, 133
Mental health, 108, 138, 170, 171, 202, 216, 217, 231, 240, 243
    facility, 170, 171, 217, 231, 240
        voluntary commitment, 168, 216, 231, 232, 240
Mental illness, 138, 171, 216, 217, 240, 243
Mercantilism, 200, 201
Merchants, 13, 22, 212, 214, 215, 253
Merit pay, 230, 258
Microprocessor, 93
Microsoft Windows, 191
Middle-class, 16, 17, 18, 95, 99, 100, 165, 195, 203, 206, 266
    destruction, 99, 196
Migrant workers, 128, 129
Military bases, 116, 250, 251, 252
Military service, 150
Military spending, 18, 250
Millionaires, 18, 96, 171
Minerals, 14, 28, 50, 52, 115, 159, 201
Minimum wage, 2, 13, 18, 128, 137, 183, 187, 195, 196, 197, 207, 217, 242
Mining, 45, 50, 52, 59
Mobile workforce, 19, 92, 211, 219, 248, 249

Monastery, 220

Monopoly, 13, 22, 29, 68, 73, 158, 183, 190, 191, 232, 233, 236, 240, 250, 258

   intellectual property, 74, 75, 189

   location value, 29, 40, 68, 74, 131, 234

   regulated, 158

Moral code, 99, 138

Moral hazard, 32, 82, 203

Moral responsibility, 107, 261

Morality, 172, 198

Mortgage, 19, 40, 71, 87, 168, 218, 219, 220, 221, 222, 245, 257

Most efficient user, 27, 29, 33, 40, 41, 42, 48, 50, 57, 58, 59, 131, 132

Murder, 101, 141, 167

Musicians, 77

Mutual organizations, 5, 67, 76, 82, 83, 123, 127, 134, 164, 187, 189, 192, 193, 196, 234, 235, 236, 242, 243, 255

   business plans, 168, 187, 191, 192, 193, 242

N

Nader, Ralph, 176

Nanny state, 86, 215

National income, 204

Natural disasters, 128, 215, 217, 251

Natural laws, 1, 10, 19, 31, 41, 73, 74, 80, 81, 83, 85, 86, 105, 124, 126

   distribution, 73, 132

   production, 73, 132

Natural resources, 3, 11, 50, 52, 54, 55, 127, 136, 175, 200, 201

Natural rights. *See* Rights: natural rights

Natural selection, 91, 96, 102, 103

Nature, 4, 11, 13, 24, 34, 51, 73, 80, 86, 102, 104, 121, 132, 136, 137

   balance of, 11, 12, 35, 121, 133, 261, 266, 269

   human, 1, 12, 13, 101, 139, 210, 267

   truths, 14, 34

Necessities, 93, 94, 104, 106, 129, 135, 197, 202, 210, 211, 223, 244, 266

Net rent, 44, 54, 55

Nightly accommodations, 19, 20, 219

Non-recidivism annuity, 167, 168, 231, 232

Norplant, 108

Not guilty by reason of insanity, 171

Nurse's aides, 239, 242

Nurses, 234, 242

Nursing, 202, 207, 216, 232, 239, 242, 243

Nursing homes, 202, 207, 216, 242, 243

O

Obama, Barack, 194

Objective, 196, 198

Objective depreciated value, 36, 37, 39, 41, 42, 43, 44, 45, 48, 50, 51, 54, 55, 58, 65, 71, 78, 124, 131, 144, 149, 183, 252

Objective value, 37, 38, 40, 48, 184, 186

Objectivism, 14, 198

Objectivists, 133, 136, 174, 195, 198

Obligation

   to hire, 139, 165, 196

   to live, 139, 143, 144

   to pay for your child, 95, 137

   to pay taxes on your land, 136, 183

Offers of employment, 176

Office buildings, 54, 55, 60, 61

Oil, 50, 51, 52, 59, 70, 247

Older workers, 183, 197

On the job training, 183, 187

Online education, 187, 226, 227, 228, 229, 230

Open borders, 128, 208

Opportunity, 10, 20, 36, 60, 88, 97, 106, 133, 169, 170, 179, 180, 191, 192, 196, 217, 218, 227, 255

Organized crime, 198

OSHA, 179

Ostrom, Elinor, 32, 80, 105

P

Pain, 184, 185, 235

Paine, Thomas, i, 23, 135, 210

Panarchy, 9, 134, 141, 147, 148, 151, 160, 164

Pansexuality, 13

Parking, 67, 68, 103, 247, 248, 249

Parks, 46

Passwords, 19

Paternity

   multiple, 91, 110, 202

Patient, 183, 222, 234, 235, 236, 237, 238, 239, 240, 241, 242, 243

PCA. *See* Personal corporate account

Pedophiles, 175, 258

Penitentiary, 88, 108, 138, 145, 150, 156, 166, 167, 168, 169, 170, 171, 172, 173, 182, 183, 202, 218, 231, 232, 241, 246

People=wealth, 12, 17, 242

Personal corporate account, 21, 37, 115, 179, 199, 200, 202, 214, 215, 222, 238, 239

Personal spending account, 18, 21, 115, 179, 201, 202, 214, 216, 222, 231

Personal wealth, 102, 184, 186, 187, 188

Pharmaceuticals, 108, 214, 233, 240

   early trials, 179, 241

Philosophy, 34, 96, 121, 136

   AFFEERCE

      Volume III, 14, 258, 261

   free markets, 183

   Henry George, 25

   meaning and purpose, 198

   of justice, 171

   of science, 258

   on regulation, 176

Physical therapy, 239

Picket, 13, 166, 180, 191

Pigou, Arthur, 115

Piketty, Thomas, 183, 197

Plea bargaining, 171

Plot size, 45

Poland, 90

Police misconduct, 156, 157, 173, 246

Police officers, 116, 157, 170, 171, 173, 246

Police protection, 81, 82, 86, 155

Political contributions, 175

Political correctness, 11

Politicians, 139, 167, 181, 182, 198, 199, 203, 205, 266

Pollution, 13, 102, 115, 146, 175

Polygamy, 91, 111, 112

Poor. *See* Indigent

Population

   birth rates, 89, 106

   density, 30, 31, 48, 50, 81, 82, 132, 158, 160

   urban, 48

   exceeds productivity, 11, 266, 269

   growth, 36, 89, 94, 96, 101, 102, 106, 266, 269

   overcrowding, 11

   overpopulation, 89, 94, 96, 104, 133

   underpopulation, 89, 133

Population growth, 111

Postmodernism, 34, 93, 94, 110, 121

Poverty, 11, 17, 95, 100, 101, 135, 138, 157, 169, 194, 207, 210, 211, 262
  cycle of, 82, 94

Predators, 11, 104, 112, 121, 261, 266
  child, 167, 168

Pregnancy, 90, 107, 108, 109, 111

Pre-modern times, 90, 94, 95, 266

Prepared foods, 214, 215

President of the United States, 99, 154, 160, 163

Principalities, 11

Prisoner's dilemma, 101, 102

Prisons, 100, 101, 102, 150, 166, 167, 170, 217, 218, 233
  as industry, 166, 233
  reform, 101, 167, 169

Private key, 182

Private schools, 97, 225, 226, 228

Privilege of parenting, 140

Privilege to drive, 139

Product, 13, 174, 176, 186, 190, 203, 229

Product id, 76, 199

Productivity, 14, 18, 25, 60, 196, 201, 228
  AFFEERCE incentives, 37, 138, 248
  agriculture, 53, 128
  entitlements, 196
  free enterprise, 18, 186, 207, 266
  large families, 18, 211
  national wealth, 18
  of nation, 28, 30, 31, 91, 105, 111, 158, 203, 205, 266
  population, 269
  taxes, 183

Professors, 192, 226, 227, 229

Profit, 25, 90, 190, 191, 192, 199, 207, 266

Progeny, 90, 258

Propaganda, 182

Property, 43, 45, 47, 52, 66, 67, 71, 72, 100, 247, 249
  abandoned, 222
  appraisals, 37, 38, 45, 71, 72
  attributes, 72
  boundary, 36, 45, 71, 255
  contiguous, 37, 45
  liquidity, 207
  maintaining, 37, 41, 63, 65, 132, 161, 162, 163, 248
  personal, 37, 40, 45, 183, 200, 201,

202
  private, 34, 68, 183

Prosecutors, 13, 88, 116, 156, 157, 170, 171, 172, 173, 198, 246

Prosperity, 12, 69, 111

Prostitution, 94, 151, 167, 169, 240

Protectionism, 195, 200

Proteins, 216

PSA. *See* Personal spending account

Psychiatrists, 240

Puberty, 90, 96, 111, 257

Public accommodations, 175

Public defenders, 157, 173, 246, 247

Public key, 182

Publishers, 228, 230

Punitive damages, 170, 171, 245

Purchase paths, 76, 199

Pursuit of happiness, 100, 165, 179, 259, 261

R

Race, i, 23, 98, 101, 103, 111, 138, 165

Racism, 99, 112, 164, 165, 166, 181, 197, 211

Radical medical deregulation, 238

Radio spectrum, 14, 54

Rand, Ayn, 135

Random violence, 138

Rape, 141, 171

Rapid transit, 194, 198, 248, 249

Rational, 102, 174, 210, 258

Reagan, Ronald, 194, 205

Real estate, 55, 60, 71, 199, 204

Real wages, 2, 25, 63, 64, 65, 156
  effect on land market, 63, 64, 65

Reasonable use of land, 45

Rebate. *See* Distributions rebate

Recidivism, 138, 167, 169, 231, 232, 241

Recitation, 226, 227

Recreational drugs, 108, 112, 259

Redistribution of wealth, 202

Regulation, 23, 35, 166, 174, 175, 176, 179, 180, 183, 184, 186, 196, 211, 218, 256

Rehabilitation, 167, 168, 169, 170, 171, 172, 216, 217, 218, 219, 231, 232

Religion, 11, 92, 111, 256

Renovations, 220, 221

Rent
  apartment, 17, 19, 24, 61, 86, 87, 168, 169, 179, 213, 218, 219, 257

net rent, 42, 55, 56, 57, 58, 59, 61, 62, 63, 64, 65, 68, 234, 247
  of commons, i, 23, 26
  Pigovian, 175

Rental of the commons, 11, 12, 14, 15, 33, 36, 51, 121, 131, 133, 183, 266

Reproduction, 90, 91, 101, 110
  ceasing, 94
  maturity, 101, 103, 104
  rights, 96, 97, 106, 110

Reproductive
  control, 12, 14, 89, 95, 97, 105, 106, 111, 121, 240, 257, 266
  freedom, 89, 93, 106, 108

Reproductive
  control, 89

Reproductive control, 11

Republicans, 195, 205

Requests for funds, 116, 171, 176, 181, 182
  consideration, 116

Research and development, 191, 207

Reserve ratio, 203, 204, 222

Retail, 21, 54, 55, 57, 200

Return on investment, 112

Revolution, 19, 69, 110, 195, 205, 226, 254, 266

Ricardo, David, 2, 12, 26

Right
  to a free and unlimited education, 197
  to a job, 13, 137, 139, 180, 187, 228
  to a judiciary, 173
  to a national defense, 10
  to a safe workplace, 97, 139, 179, 180
  to basic medical care, 10, 98, 99, 137, 167, 183, 217, 223
    penitentiary, 150, 167, 169
  to be intoxicated, 139
  to bear children, 96, 98, 99, 101, 107, 110, 128, 137
  to business without government interference, 183
  to deny service, 13
  to die, 139
  to education, 11
  to entitlement, 136
  to fire protection, 88
  to full disclosure, 97
  to insurrection, 137, 166
  to leave, 83, 97, 139, 140, 141, 144, 145, 147, 148, 149, 150, 151,

164, 166, 168, 169, 173, 174,
201, 218, 244, 255, 256
exceptions, 150
to life, 136–40, 143, 144, 147, 166,
174, 175, 179, 180, 197, 202,
218, 219, 239, 261
children, 86, 99, 100, 140, 143,
256, 257
of children, 141, 148, 164
to medical care, 11
to nutritious meals, 10, 11, 86, 93,
99, 101, 129, 137, 167, 183, 210,
215, 218, 223, 250, 256
penitentiary, 150, 167, 169
to property, 99, 100, 136–40, 144,
166, 174, 179, 180, 183, 195,
202, 219, 256, 261
to refuse service, 165, 166
to sacrifice freedom, 141
to sacrifice ones natural rights, 151
to security, 138
to self-defense, 136, 137, 138
to steal food, 136
to the fruits of one's labor, 11, 73,
87, 99, 132, 183, 188
to unlimited free education, 10, 99,
101, 137, 167, 183, 186, 217,
223, 226, 250, 256
penitentiary, 150
to warm and safe shelter, 10, 11, 99,
137, 167, 183, 210, 223, 256
penitentiary, 150
to work in a smoke-free environment,
139
to work in an unsafe workplace, 179,
180
Rights
natural rights, 5, 11, 21, 99, 100,
108, 136, 137, 138, 139, 140,
141, 142, 143, 146, 151, 155,
156, 165, 166, 180, 183, 190,
195, 196, 239, 261
conflicts, 21, 137, 139, 140, 142,
146, 174, 183, 191, 197, 256
restrictions on, 255
violations, 108, 147, 149, 180,
183, 195, 219
Right-wing, 99
Risk free rate of return, 42, 49, 58
Risk of disabling complication, 239
Risk-taking, 86
Roads, 67, 68, 140, 196, 247, 248, 249,

252
private, 67
Robots, 3, 77, 94
Rogue state, 119, 148, 149, 150, 151,
153, 164, 173, 174
Rothbard, Murray, 29
Royal family, 160, 161, 163
Rural, 69, 70, 159, 189, 245, 246
districts, 248, 249
residential, 52, 53, 66
RV, 87, 220

S

Sabotage, 19, 180, 266
Sadomasochism, 151
Safety net, 9, 33, 86, 196, 212, 245, 255
San Francisco, 2, 3
Sanger, Margaret, 96
Satisfy desires with least exertion, 31, 41,
124
Savings, 112, 186, 196, 204
baby fund, 112, 127, 186, 207
cost, 52, 66, 239, 241, 248, 251
discouraged for poor, 211
encouraged by deflation, 204
rate, 204
retirement, 91, 232
tax free, 16, 204
Schools, 46, 97, 128, 187, 194, 225,
227, 228, 229, 230, 241, 258
Science, 14, 102, 110, 111, 258, 261
Scientific materialism, 258
Scientists, 11, 14
Scrip. *See* Currency: scrip
Section 8 housing, 211
Security, 21, 94, 97, 137, 201, 210, 213
homeland, 250
penitentiary, 156, 167, 168, 216
social, 90, 91, 92
software, 181, 227, 252
Security deposit, 219, 220
Self-assessment. *See* Land: self-
assessment
Self-interest, 174, 175
Selling organs, 136, 240
Severability of land, 66, 67
Sexism, 165, 166
Sexual orientation, 12, 218
Sexuality, 11, 12, 13, 90, 91, 92, 93, 94,
110, 140, 144, 167, 175, 256, 257
Sharia law, 151
Shopping, 87, 188, 215

Singapore, 60
Single payer, 233, 240
Sixty years to capitulation, 1, 9, 10, 15,
19, 37, 117, 141, 224, 243
Skills, 100, 187, 197, 211, 225, 228,
230, 244
Slavery, 151, 183
Small business, 183, 187, 194, 196
Smokers
rights, 138, 139
Snowden, Edward, 20
Social constructivism, 117
Social satisfaction, 175
Social Security, 11, 14, 16, 17, 18, 64,
91, 106, 194, 211, 232
Social workers, 100, 116, 129, 150, 167,
168, 169, 173, 218, 219, 240, 243,
244, 256, 257, 259
Soviet Union, 198
Spending account, 199, 200, 201, 207,
271
Spiritual growth, 91, 92, 266, 269
Spiritual rebirth, 168, 172
Spooner, Lysander, 136
Sports, 223
Standard of living, 96, 111, 201
Standards, 13, 68, 157, 166, 174, 175,
176, 178, 180, 182, 183, 191, 218,
221, 227, 230, 236, 237, 258
Sterilization, 97, 107, 108
Stiglitz, Joseph, 198
Stocks, 192, 199, 204
Strike, 13, 180, 191
Students, 88, 172, 181, 183, 191, 192,
197, 212, 223, 224, 225, 226, 227,
228, 230, 231, 241
Subcultures, 164, 166, 219, 257
Subjective, 138, 184, 186, 198, 241
Subjectivity, 14
Substandard housing, 87, 99, 217, 218,
219
Suicide, 136, 139, 144, 179, 239
assisted, 241
Sun Yat-Sen, 12, 23, 33, 34, 134
dilemma of, 60, 70, 234, 238
Sundries, 222
Super plurality, 21, 46, 54, 114, 115,
116, 138, 140, 142, 144, 146, 147,
148, 160, 161, 166, 173, 177, 183,
191, 207, 208, 212, 217, 221, 251,
256, 259
Super-duper plurality, 140, 256

Supreme Court, 28, 98, 147
Surrogate mothers, 110, 202
Survival, 101, 129
Synergy, 244
Synthesis, 34, 82, 133, 136
Synthesis of objectivism and
    subjectivism, 34, 82, 133, 136

T

Taiwan, 60
Tariffs, 200
Taxation, 100, 137, 201
Taxes
    baby tax, 11, 12, 14, 15, 16, 89, 95,
        96, 97, 98, 105, 106, 107, 111,
        114, 118, 119, 121, 123, 126,
        127, 129, 133, 137, 166, 191,
        253, 254
        as an investment, 97
        defends from in-vitro-gestation,
            111
        funding entitlements, 121
        new state coercive power, 111
        prevents genocide, 106, 266
        too low, 106, 111
        tool of the Treasury, 266
    citizenship, 129
    consumption tax, 15, 16, 17, 18, 21,
        76, 81, 87, 96, 113, 114, 115,
        116, 117, 127, 133, 146, 199,
        200, 201, 207, 213, 214, 215,
        222, 226, 228, 253, 254, 255,
        259, 271
        feeds distribution package, 126
    destroy productivity, 11
    discretionary
        default allocation, 115
    discretionary tax, 46, 87, 107, 113,
        114, 115, 116, 117, 128, 157,
        171, 182, 199, 217, 225, 244,
        250, 251
        cycles, 115
    excise tax, 67, 115, 118
    head tax, 81, 82, 83, 84, 86, 92, 122,
        132, 133, 210
    income tax, 11, 16, 17, 66, 70, 207,
        235
    Income tax
        corporate, 13, 18, 56, 183, 199,
            207
    land value, 12, 29, 32, 33
    Pigovian, 115, 118, 119

progressive, 81, 87, 113
property tax, 16, 17, 21, 24, 59, 60,
    61, 66, 68, 71, 136, 194, 217
social constructivism, 117
Taxpayers, 16, 94, 99, 100, 101, 169,
    182, 195, 210, 229, 233, 239, 242,
    266
Teachers, 101, 128, 146, 175, 183, 192,
    208, 224, 225, 226, 227, 228, 229,
    230, 231, 258
    merit pay, 225, 226, 227, 228
    Merit pay, 224–28
Technology, 93, 195, 262
    expensive medical, 240
    new, 94, 197, 211, 229
    replaces labor, 3, 4, 11, 91, 94, 95,
        211, 259
    reproductive, 98, 107
        vasectomy with on/off switch,
            109
    training, 223, 229
Teenage, 218, 257
    rebellion, 93, 94
Tenants, 56, 179, 219
Terrorism, 250
Testing, 172, 225, 227, 228, 230, 231,
    237, 241
Tests, 179, 225, 227, 228, 230, 231,
    233, 235, 236, 237, 241
Textbooks, 225, 228, 230
Thatcher, Margaret, 205
The 1%, 198, 206
Theft, 19, 20, 99, 100, 136, 137, 141,
    167, 169, 170, 183, 207, 247, 250,
    266
Theory of value
    AFFEERCE, 184, 185
    Georgist, 27, 34
    labor, 26, 184
    objective, 26, 113, 181, 184, 185
    subjective, 26, 174, 184, 185
Third world nation, 105, 106, 194, 201
Tips, 215
Tithing, 92, 256
Tobacco, 168, 214
Too big to fail, 195, 196
Totalitarianism, 32
Tourists, 20, 128, 198, 248
Trade schools, 88, 227, 229, 230
Tragedy of the commons, 12, 32, 80,
    101, 102, 104, 105, 106, 112, 127
Transgenic sperm, 110

Transportation, 47, 169, 181, 189, 211,
    246, 247, 248, 249
Treble point, 42, 48, 49, 50, 51, 56, 58
Trebler
    mortgage, 44, 45
    wars, 12, 48, 52, 66, 69, 121, 134,
        141, 151
Treblers, 36, 37, 38, 39, 40, 41, 42, 43,
    44, 46, 48, 49, 50, 51, 52, 54, 55, 56,
    58, 59, 60, 61, 62, 63, 64, 65, 66, 67,
    81, 124, 127, 132, 153, 158, 183,
    200, 245
    of spectrum, 54
Trebling, 36–47, 122, 128, 193, 207,
    217, 248
    dominion. *See* Dominion trebling
Trebling and bank loans, 44
Trickle-down economics, 194, 195, 200
Trust, 198, 269
Tuition, 223, 225, 226, 228
Tutors, 167, 228, 229
Tyranny, 16, 20, 111, 139, 184, 261

U

U.S. Capitol, 163
UN sanctioned wars, 116, 251
Unemployment, 87, 91, 93, 94, 100,
    195, 197, 210, 217
United Nations, 115, 116, 143, 251
United Nations Declaration of Human
    Rights, 98
United States, 54, 106, 129, 150, 213
    AFFEERCE, 195, 207
    apocryphal racist narrative, 99, 101
    land, 35, 36, 52
    Land
        online system mapping, 71
    national defense, 250
    serious problems today, 167, 170,
        183, 197, 198, 202, 211, 217,
        223, 232
    Supreme Court, 147
    Treasury, 54
Universal auto pass, 67, 68, 198, 247,
    249, 252
Universal deductible, 88, 109, 222, 241
Universe, 258
    has purpose, 14, 138
Universities, 88, 181, 223, 226, 227,
    229, 230, 258
Unlisted violation, 178
Unorthodox theories, 228

Unpaid labor, 74, 187, 189
  profit from, 189
  profits from, 131
Urban, 25, 28, 35, 43, 48, 159, 166, 194, 207, 217, 244, 245, 248
Utilities, 20, 45, 66, 67, 188, 219, 220, 247
Utopia, 20, 96

V

Vacancies, 59, 132, 172, 173, 249
Values, 135, 185, 262
Vasectomy, 14, 108, 109
Veterans Administration, 250
Veto, 46, 47, 145, 147, 148, 149, 170
  down, 147, 148, 151
  up, 147, 148
Victims, 69, 70, 88, 99, 101, 115, 116, 139, 144, 157, 167, 169, 170, 171, 173, 243, 246, 258
Violation of standards, 13, 166, 175, 176, 178, 179, 180, 219
VIP, 19, 20, 21, 22, 36, 37, 45, 115, 138, 169, 182, 199, 200, 204, 207, 218, 219, 222, 224, 229, 238, 249, 250, 252, 253, 255, 257
  account, 128
  account number, 115
  application, 21, 198
  disabled, 150
  dollar, 39, 118, 119, 193, 200, 201, 203, 214, 271
  dollars, 19
  enforced, 160, 187, 192, 215
  identity, 19, 22, 71, 72, 77, 149, 198, 248, 249, 252
  locates fugitive, 168, 169
  medical history, 231, 238
  reader, 19, 22, 72, 176, 249, 253
  readers, 116, 215
  reminder, 38
  safe, 220
  signature, 19, 72, 75, 180, 222
  voting, 19, 149
    infrastructure, 158
Viral city, 29, 134, 201
Virtual reality, 227
Voluntary taxation, 39
Volunteer standards group, 13, 176, 177, 174–81, 258
  academic, 228

  banking, 204
  building codes, 221
  community standards, 166
  food entitlement, 214, 215
  food service, 181
  fraud, 246
  functions, 177
  intellectual property tranches, 77
  media, 182
  medical certification, 237, 239
  medical standards, 236
  penitentiaries, 167
  testing, 230, 231
  testing, 225, 227
  trade rank, 229, 230
  trade ranking, 229
VOS, 166, 175, 176, 178, 179, 182, 200, 204, 227, 238, 239, 242
  building codes, 221
  certified, 172
  child services, 176
  contract with the public, 181
  curriculum, 230
  danger, 179, 241
  denial of service, 181
    on moral grounds, 241
  failure to pass certification, 231, 237, 238
  failures to do job accurately, 173, 237, 239, 241, 247
  family charter, 256
  fraudulent, 156, 246
  merit, 227, 230
  must sign, 178, 179, 180, 236, 240
  penitentiary, 167
  reduces liability, 172, 176, 178, 207, 218
  workplace safety, 180
VOS certification, 176, 178, 180, 182, 204, 212, 221, 227, 231, 237, 239, 240
VR. *See* Virtual reality

W

Wall Street, 198
Wallet-free, 19, 22
War on drugs, 138, 169, 170
Warren, Elizabeth, 176
Wars, 11, 12, 112, 116, 141, 205, 217, 250
  for land, 69, 89

  the end of war, 121
Washington D.C., 198
Water fountain, 184, 210, 211
Wealth of the nation, 18, 36, 184, 186, 188, 194, 195, 196, 198, 199, 223, 239
Wealthy, 16, 147, 188, 202
  get richer, 205
Welfare, 99, 101, 103, 106, 141, 205, 210, 211
Wellness annuity, 231, 232
Withering away of the allocations, 88, 126
Women
  as baby-creating wealth machines, 90, 95, 96, 100, 111, 266, 269
  rights, 12, 14, 90, 92, 96, 147, 166, 266
Women's liberation, 93
Workers, 92, 165, 179, 180, 183, 184, 197
  AFFEERCE, 197, 249
    can take low pay, 195, 200, 207, 266
    outnumbered by entrepreneurs, 180
  as owners, 187, 196
  need for skilled workers, 94, 95, 259
  organizing, 13, 180
  sick or injured, 90, 92
  unskilled, 196, 197, 233
Workers control of the means of production, 196
Working class, 196
World wars, 205
Wrongful life, 107
WWII, 91, 205

Y

Yellowstone Park, 46
Youth, 87, 93, 140, 195, 218, 223, 233, 240, 257

Z

Zero population growth, 39, 121, 123, 126, 129, 131, 133
Zero-sum, 39, 42, 60
Zoning, 35